The TLINGIT *of* SITKA

The TLINGIT
of SITKA

The Photography of
ELBRIDGE W. MERRILL

SERGEI KAN

Sealaska Heritage Institute
in association with the
University of Washington Press • Seattle

The Tlingit in Sitka was made possible in part by a grant from the Sealaska Heritage Institute.

The research this book is based on was supported by the Claire Garber Goodman Fund of the Department of Anthropology, Dartmouth College.

Design by Kate Huber-Parker
Composed in 12.5/17pt Change, typeface designed by Mateusz Machalski

29 28 27 26 25   5 4 3 2 1

Printed and bound in the United States of America

UNIVERSITY OF WASHINGTON PRESS

uwapress.uw.edu

LIBRARY OF CONGRESS CATALOGING-IN-PUBLICATION DATA

Names: Kan, Sergei, author. | Merrill, Elbridge W., 1870–1929, photographer.
Title: The Tlingit in Sitka : the photography of Elbridge W. Merrill / Sergei Kan.
Other titles: Photography of Elbridge W. Merrill
Description: Seattle : Sealaska Heritage Institute, in association with the University
    of Washington Press, [2025] | Includes bibliographical references and index.
Identifiers: LCCN 2024023395 | ISBN 9780295753478 (cloth) | ISBN 9780295753485 (ebook)
Subjects: LCSH: Tlingit Indians—Alaska—Sitka—Pictorial works. | Sitka (Alaska)—
    History—20th century—Pictorial works. | Merrill, Elbridge W., 1870–1929.
Classification: LCC F914.S6 K36 2025 | DDC 979.8004/9727—dc23/eng/20240523
LC record available at https://lccn.loc.gov/2024023395

∞ This paper meets the requirements of ANSI/NISO Z39.48-1992 (Permanence of Paper).

I like to think that my pictures go out into the world taking the healing spirit of my country to those who need it, to those who understand it.

—ELBRIDGE WARREN MERRILL

Contents

Foreword

Rosita K̲aaháni Worl

WE, THE INDIGENOUS PEOPLE of Southeast Alaska, are forever indebted to Elbridge W. Merrill for his photographic documentation of Tlingit life as the Tlingit people were transitioning into Western society and lifestyles in the early 1900s. Merrill's great respect for the Tlingit is evident in his photographs. That he was held in equal regard by the Tlingit is apparent from the fact that they allowed him to photograph their ceremonial and private lives—a privilege that even today is granted to only a few individuals. They also commissioned him to take photographs of them and to document their sacred moments, such as funerals.

With his photographs of hunting and fishing camps, Merrill shows us that the Tlingit remained deeply attached to the land in the early 1900s. Drawing their livelihood from the resources of the land and sea, they are depicted drying herring eggs, smoking fish, and tanning skins. The integration of traditional Tlingit lifestyles with Euro-American culture is evidenced by the canoes in front of Western-style houses. Tlingit participation in the cash economy is also evidenced by craftspeople selling their weavings and carvings to tourists.

Merrill's documentation of sacred cultural practices and traditional harvesting activities is significant because during this time, Western institutions, including the church, the US military, the territorial government, and boarding schools were part of a campaign to suppress traditional customs and practices. Conversely, his photographs of groups of young men in military uniforms and young women in school uniforms reflect the shift toward a Western lifestyle. These photos are concrete evidence of the implementation of assimilationist policies.

What is not evident is that during the period Merrill was photographing, Sitka was a segregated community. Sharon Bohn Gmelch, in her 2008 book *The Tlingit Encounter with Photography*, gives us insight into the discrimination and segregation that existed during Merrill's time in Sitka. Non-Natives lived in the center of town, while some Tlingit lived in the area known as the Village, and others lived in the cottages near the Sitka Industrial and Training School grounds. However, to Merrill's credit, he does not romanticize or exoticize the Tlingit, as did other famous photographers of Indian tribes.

Merrill's photographs reflect the simultaneous participation of the Tlingit in their traditional lifestyles and in Western society. Merrill photographed the reality of Tlingit life. Tlingit people today will be grateful to have the opportunity to see and study the

Merrill photographs. They will search them for the likenesses of their ancestors and study the traditional regalia and crest designs of the different clans. Elbridge W. Merrill has brought the history of the Tlingit of Sitka into the twenty-first century.

Acknowledgments

OVER THE YEARS a number of individuals and institutions have helped in my work on this project. To begin with, I am forever grateful to my Tlingit friends and consultants, who helped identify many of the Tlingit people in Merrill's photographs. Among them I must single out Harold Jacobs (G̲ooch Shaayí, Kaawóotk G̲uwakaan), cultural resource coordinator, Native Lands and Resources Department of the Central Council of the Tlingit and Haida Indian Tribes of Alaska, whose superb knowledge of Tlingit history and culture enabled him to offer tremendous help to me throughout this entire project.

A special thank you goes to Devlin Anderstrom for his assistance with identifying the people of Yakutat. I am also grateful to Herman Davis (L'eiwtu.éesh) of the L'uknax̲.ádi clan and the late Andrew Gamble Jr. (Anaxóots) of the Kaagwaantaan clan for reviewing and commenting on some of the Merrill photographs, as well as for their kind permission to reproduce his images of the sacred *at.óow* belonging to their respective clans and depicted in funeral scenes involving their clan ancestors. Willis Osbakken generously shared several of his own photographs with me and identified several members of the Creole community photographed by Merrill.

The staff of the Sitka National Historical Park, which owns and curates most of the Merrill photographs, and especially Sue Thorsen, Kelsey Lutz, Tracy Laqua, and Mary Miller, have helped me a great deal as well. The staff of the Alaska State Library and Archives, especially Sandra Johnston and Connie Hamann, as well as Nicole Fiorino of the Sitka Historical Society, also deserve my thanks. I am also grateful to Richard B. Trask of the Danvers Historical Society for providing information on Merrill's early photography. Chuck Smythe, the director of the Department of History and Culture of the Sealaska Heritage Institute, offered helpful comments and criticism of the final draft of this work. The helpful staff members of the Sealaska Heritage Institute Archives and Collections Department also deserve thanks.

I thank the Sealaska Heritage Institute for its generous subvention for the publication of this book. Additional financial support, which made this project a reality, came from my home institution, Dartmouth College, and more specifically from the associate dean of the faculty for the social sciences and the Claire Garber Goodman Fund for Anthropological Research, Department of Anthropology.

Words of gratitude should also be sent to the very helpful staff of the University of Washington Press, who encouraged my work on this book and labored diligently on the manuscript. They are

Larin R. McLaughlin, Justine Sargent, Joeth Zucco, Erika Bŭky, and Mindy B. Hill.

Last but not least, the work of Sharon Bohn Gmelch, who preceded me in her research on the Merrill photographs, has been a very useful source of information for this book.

The TLINGIT *of* SITKA

Introduction

THE FATHER OF PICTURES

WHO WAS ELBRIDGE W. MERRILL, what brought him to the town of Sitka, Alaska, where he spent the second half of his life, and why did the Tlingit people of that community call him "the father of pictures"?

Merrill was born on June 23, 1870, in West Newbury, Massachusetts, and christened Elbridge Samuel Merrill.[1] His parents were Samuel F. Merrill (1844–73) and Mary E. Pillsbury (1846–1932), descendants of English settlers who had come to the New World in the seventeenth century. Merrill's early life was difficult. Before his third birthday, his father died, and his mother had to move with her three children (Adelaide, Elbridge, and Samuel) into her brother's home in Danvers, just north of Boston. A year later Elbridge's mother married Leander S. Falls (1840–80), a local milk collector, but her new husband and her son Samuel died within a year. Mary and her two surviving children returned to live with her brother, a successful businessman. Sometime after 1885, when Adelaide married Albert Merrill (a shipping clerk), Elbridge and his mother moved into their home. By 1890 Albert had become a successful horse dealer and professional horse-racing judge who officiated at many important races throughout the Northeast.

Elbridge's name first appeared in the Danvers city directory with his occupation listed as "necktie cutter." His mother also earned money making ties. By 1890, Elbridge had begun experimenting with photography. His earliest known photographs include a portrait of his sister and brother-in-law and depictions of his uncle's business (the Harvey Pillsbury Carriage Exchange) and Danvers's Fourth of July parade (see Zollo et al. 1989: 154–68). Around his twenty-first birthday, Merrill changed his middle name from Samuel to Warren, perhaps because of the deaths of his father and younger brother, both named Samuel. By 1895, the *Danvers Directory* reported that he was employed in Boston as an "artist" and a "photo printer." His income, however, apparently remained modest, since in 1896 he owed the town of Danvers only $2 in taxes.

While some of Merrill's early photographs appear conventional, a few prefigure the beautiful professional work of his Sitka years. Especially charming is a photograph titled *The Girl Reading*, dated circa 1894 (Zollo et al. 1989: 4). The last record of Merrill's photographs taken in New England shows Company K of the Danvers volunteer militia on parade down Maple Street.

In 1898 Merrill, like many other Americans, learned about the gold rush in the Klondike region of Canada's Yukon Territory. Merrill, who was still living with his sister's family, must have been attracted by the opportunity to improve his financial situation and the chance to take pictures of the natural beauty, diehard sourdoughs, and Indigenous inhabitants of Alaska and Canada.

According to several oral traditions in Sitka, Merrill arrived there in September 1898 aboard the small steamer *Gertrude*, built in Bellingham, Washington, and purchased by him and his business partners a month earlier. *Gertrude* sputtered into Sitka Sound and met its end on the Sitka beach, where it eventually rotted away (see Gmelch 2008: 112, fig. 65).

Once in Sitka, Merrill decided to stay rather than proceed to the Klondike region. He had brought several cameras with him to Alaska. His note on a photograph showing Tlingit "potlatch dancers in the winter," with a copyright date of 1899, suggests that this was the year he began taking pictures in the area. His portrait of the Danish immigrant Charles C. Georgeson, who lived in Sitka for a while, bears a stamp on the reverse side that identifies Merrill as based in Boston. This photo suggests that Merrill had not yet decided to settle in Alaska for good (Charles C. Georgeson, Sitka Historical Society, Elbridge W. Merrill, 1899). A photograph from ca. 1910, depicting the house of Annahootz, a prominent leader of the Sitka Kaagwaantaan clan, also bears the inscription "Merrill Boston" at the lower left (fig. 1).

It appears that Merrill left Sitka for a while, perhaps to explore other areas of Alaska or to wind up his affairs in Boston. In his entry in Sitka's Millmore Hotel guest register on January 31, 1900, his place of residence is given as Boston. Yet sometime in late 1899 or early 1900 he settled in Sitka permanently, leaving only once in thirty years to testify in a court case in nearby Juneau.

In December 22, 1900, an advertisement in the *Alaskan*, a local paper, read "E. W. Merrill, photographist, has a quantity of first-class negatives from which he can supply orders for views of Sitka and vicinity." His first studio was located in the old trading-post

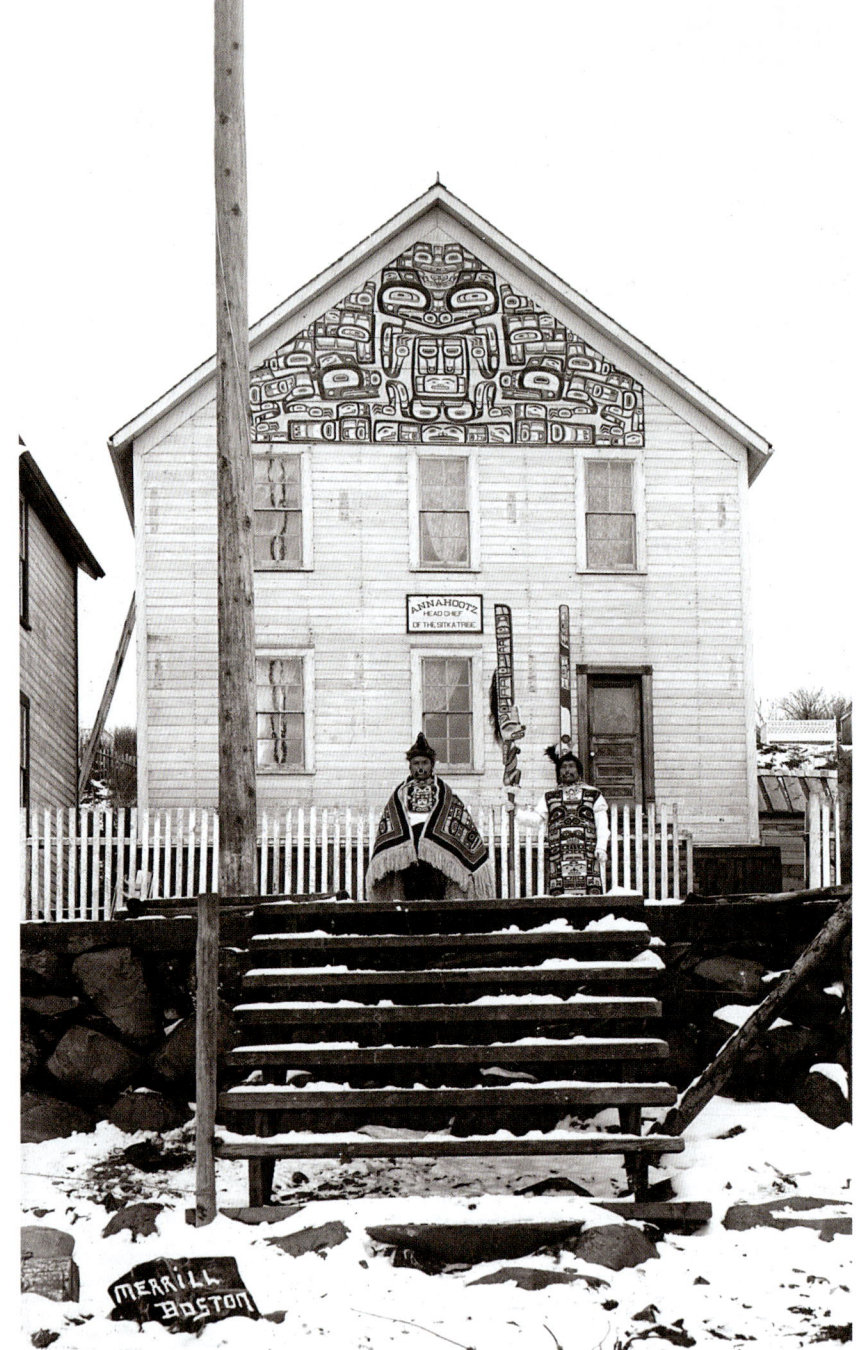

FIGURE 1. Elbridge W. Merrill. Two men dressed in ceremonial clothing in front of the house of Annahootz (James Jackson), one of the leaders of the Sitka Kaagwaantaan clan, ca. 1910. This house was known as Multiplying Wolf House. The plaque on the house states that Annahootz is "the head chief of the Sitka tribe." This claim was first made during the Russian era by an earlier Annahootz, head of the same house. The Russians recognized this friendly "chief," and so did the Americans. However, the Sheet'ká Ḵwáan never had a single chief. Courtesy of the Sitka Historical Society, Sitka, Alaska. PH1737B.

log building on Lincoln Street, Sitka's main street, dating back to the Russian era (see fig. 2).

The early years in Sitka must have been hard for Merrill. He is remembered as working as a clerk in a local store one Christmas (Chambers 1977: 139). However, in early 1905 he moved to a bigger studio in the Tilson Building, also located on Lincoln Street. There he displayed and sold not only his photographs but also Tlingit artifacts and curios. From that time until his death, advertisements for "E. W. Merrill Photography" and "E. W. Merrill, Dealer in Alaskan Curios and Photographs" appeared regularly in local newspapers and magazines (see fig. 3).

FIGURE 2. Elbridge W. Merrill. The Russian trading post on Lincoln Street in downtown Sitka, 1900. Merrill's studio and shop sign are visible on the left of the building. His dog, Rover, is in the foreground. Courtesy of the National Park Service, Sitka National Historical Park, 25627.

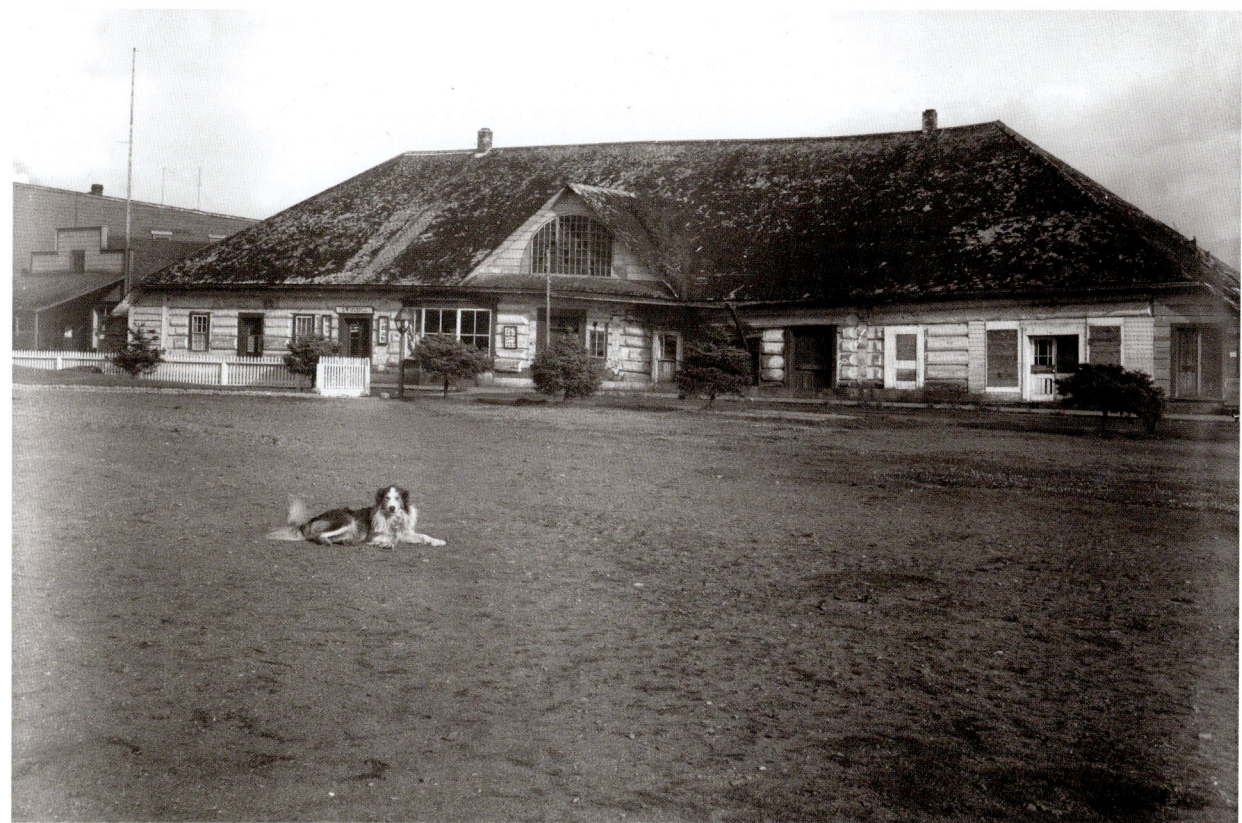

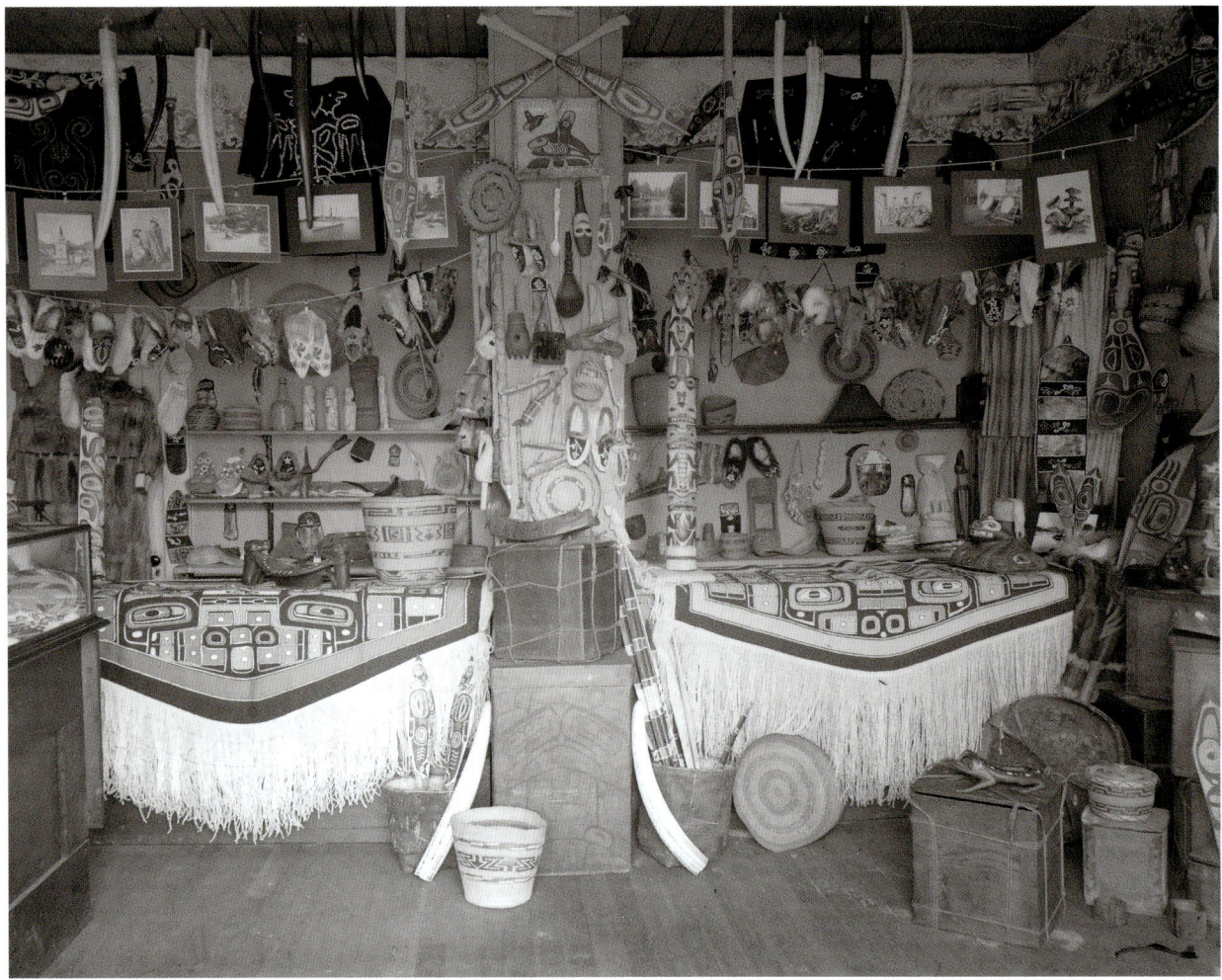

FIGURE 3. Elbridge W. Merrill. Merrill's studio and curio shop in Elizabeth Barron's store in Sitka, 1920. The photographs and paintings hanging from a line give some idea of the kinds of works that were offered for sale. Courtesy of the National Park Service, Sitka National Historical Park, 03897.

Judging by the number of portraits and other photographs he took of Sitka's community members, it appears that Merrill was able to establish a good rapport with a variety of townspeople, including the Tlingit, the Russian Creoles, and white Americans, and ranging from working-class folk to the town's wealthiest families. Doris Ulrich Grundy, who came to Sitka with her family in 1918 at the age of one and lived there until 1935, remembered him as a very tall and handsome man with grey eyes and long, flowing black hair who walked through the town with "an aristocratic straight-back manner" and a long black rain cape over his shoulders (see fig. 4). Often Merrill was accompanied by his collie dog, Rover, who appeared in several of his photographs.

According to Buchanan, the son of Sitka's Presbyterian minister from 1916 to 1924, "He was a fascinating person to listen to because he had a beautiful soft voice with a Bostonian accent. . . . His choice of language was beautiful" (Gmelch 1985: 161). According to his friend James Condit, Merrill "was familiar with the best literature of the day, reveled in poetry and lived in [the] atmosphere of his thinking" (James Condit, *Alaska Weekly*, November 22, 1929). Because of this he was often called upon to entertain prominent visitors to Sitka (Gmelch 1985: 161).

Although called "a proud loner" by Doris Grundy and others, Merrill always stopped to talk to local children and sometimes shared treats with them. At Christmas he visited the DeArmond home to give each child a small handmade gift, such as a wooden bird or a whistle (Gmelch 1995: 161). In Grundy's words, Merrill "was an articulate person and an artist in every sense of the word. He was a person, a presence. He was somebody special. He was highly respected by the native and the non-Native Community" (recorded interview with Doris Ulrich Grundy, Sitka Historical Society, 1991). Leslie Yaw, who moved to Sitka in 1923, reminisced that Merrill "had none of the racial prejudice" that many Sitka whites still harbored at that time (Kan 1979–2021).

Yet Merrill was definitely seen as solitary and mysterious. A number of people who remembered him and referred to him respectfully as "Mr. Merrill" commented on his not having many friends in town. When he first arrived, he shared a small house on

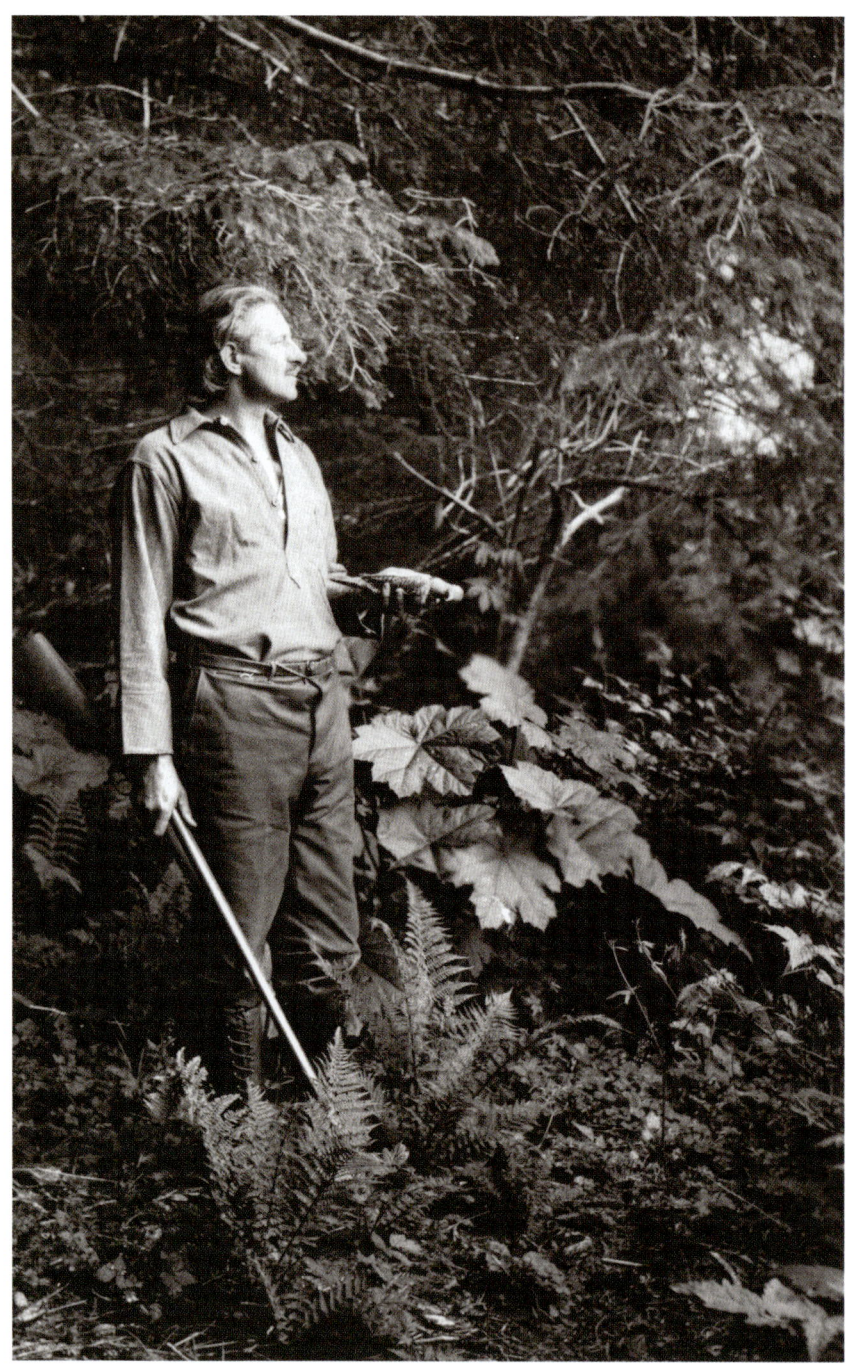

FIGURE 4. Unidentified photographer. Elbridge Warren Merrill, ca. 1910–20. Alaska State Library P57-237.

Etolin Street in the non-Native section of town with two bachelors, Henry Woodruff and Robert DeArmond Sr. Woodruff and Merrill became close friends and later shared another house, but DeArmond Sr., according to his son, felt he never really knew Merrill (interview with Robert R. N. DeArmond, 2007). Still, Merrill pitched on a Sitka baseball team during his early years in town and took part in some community organizations and events: for example, he served on the town's Independence and Memorial Day committees and on the Election Board (Gmelch 1985: 161). He also joined the Arctic Brotherhood, an all-white fraternal organization, which owned one of the best libraries in the region, but there is no record that he was active in it.

Although Merrill never married, he was emotionally connected to two Euro-American women in Sitka. One of them was Julia Haley (ca. 1880–1943), the attractive daughter of a local miner and a lifelong town resident (fig. 5). She clerked in Merrill's shop between 1905 and 1910 and, as Sharon Gmelch observes, "a candid shot of Julia fishing suggests a certain intimacy" (2008: 123). The town expected them to get married, but they never did. In 1911 Julia opened her own curio store.

Merrill was also close to Elizabeth Barron (fig. 6), whose husband, George (1863–1916), was a fellow member of the Arctic Brotherhood. After George's death, Merrill remained a close friend of Elizabeth (1871–1933) and her daughter, Frances (1909–60), who called him "Unckie Merrill." Merrill took many pictures of Elizabeth and of Frances over the years (see Gmelch 2008: 121; ASL-P57-235; SITK 2509; SITK 25509).[2]

Some people in Sitka believed that Frances was actually Merrill's daughter, but Neill Anderson, a close friend of Elizabeth and Frances, disagreed (Gmelch 2008: 123). While Merrill remained a

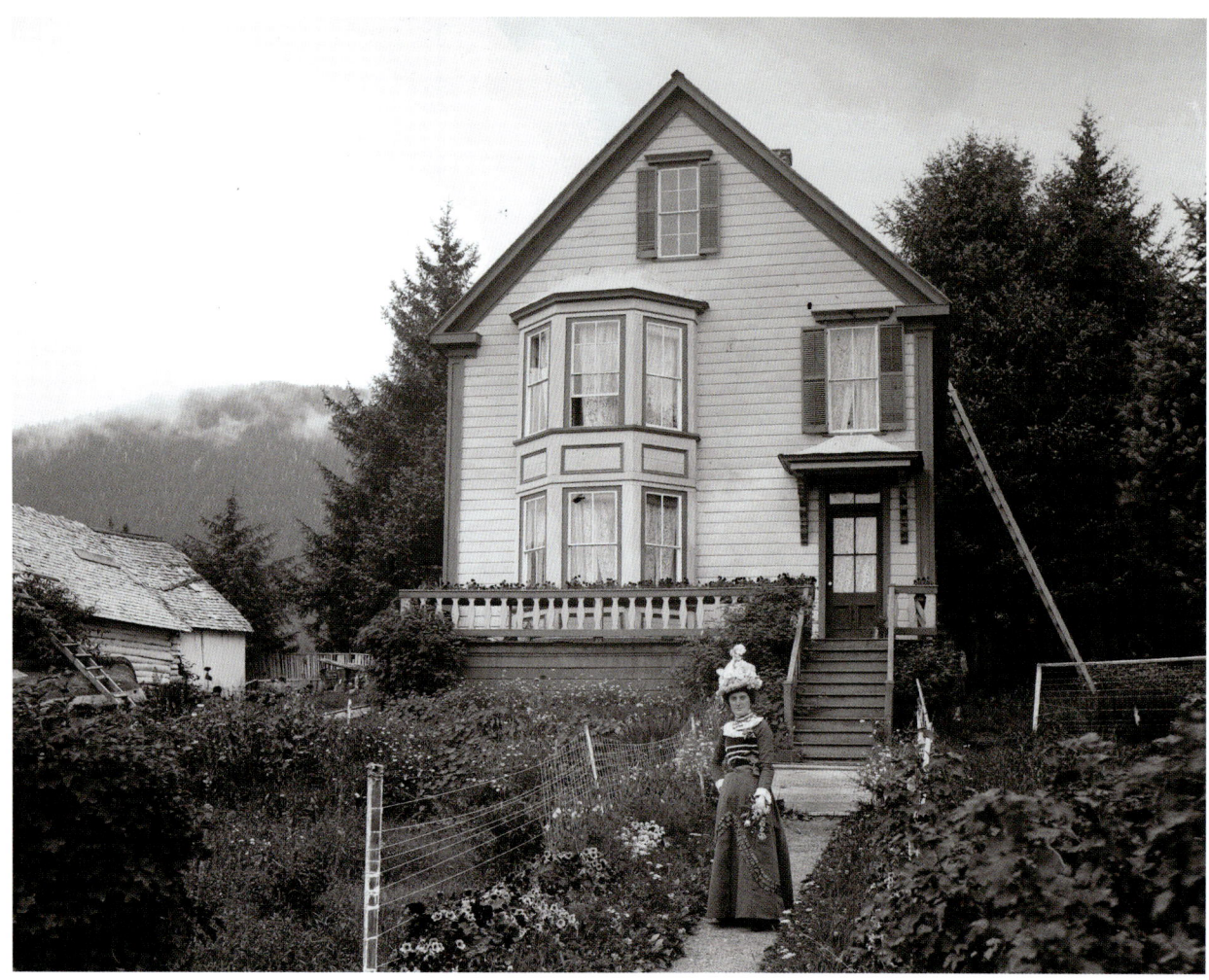

FIGURE 5. Elbridge W. Merrill. Julia Haley, Merrill's store clerk, in front of her house, Sitka, ca. 1910. Courtesy of the National Park Service, Sitka National Historical Park, 25580.

bachelor and lived alone, he eventually moved his shop into Elizabeth's general store, and she and Frances became his adoptive family.

Another good friend of Merrill, James Condit, reminisced in an obituary, published in the *Alaska Weekly* on November 29, 1929, "His courtesy was founded upon a respect for others and a sympathy which over-leaped artificial boundary lines and gave him understanding. No one conversed with him for any length of time without being stimulated to better and higher thinking."

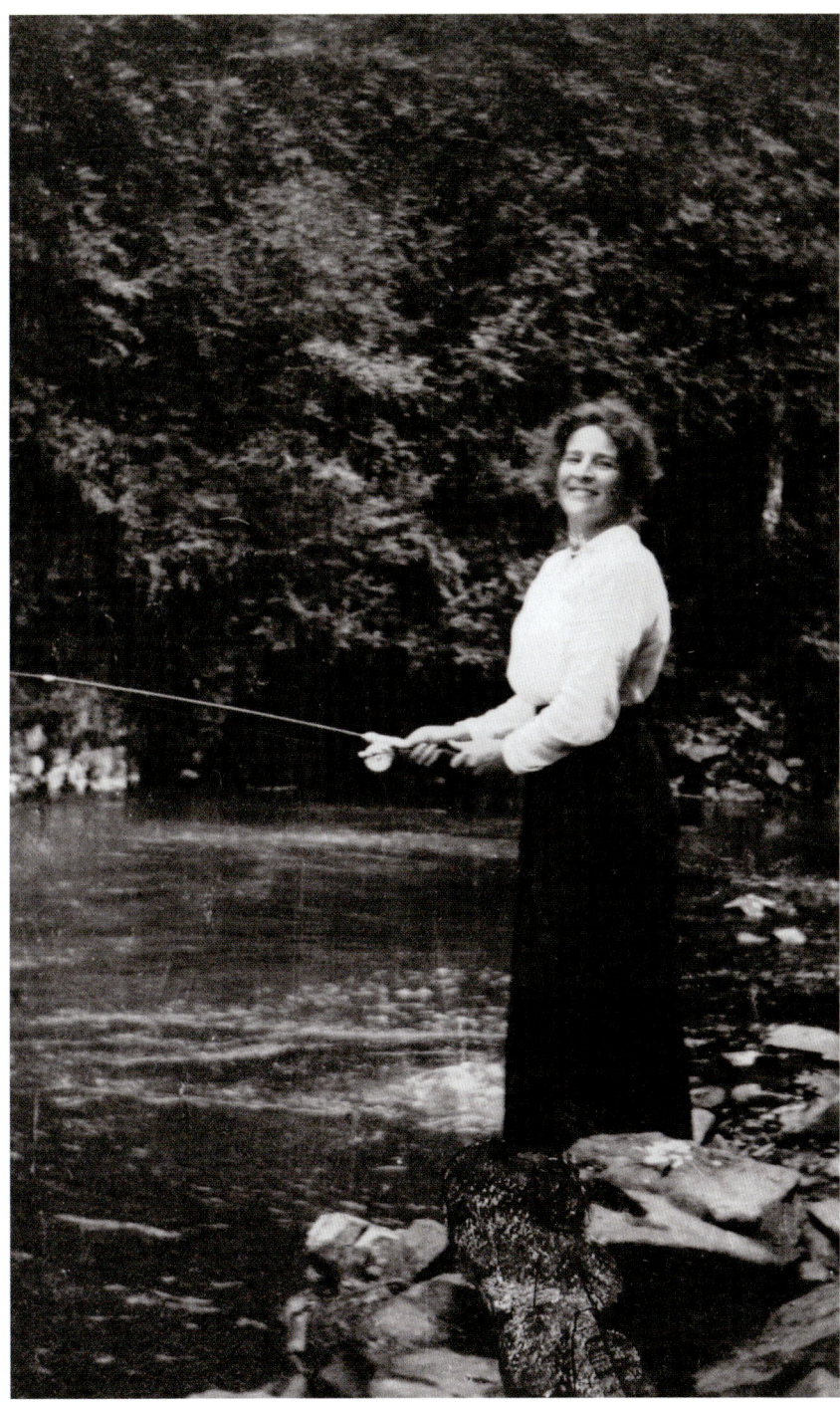

FIGURE 6. Elbridge W. Merrill, Elizabeth Barron fishing, Sitka, ca. 1908. Alaska State Historical Library P57-228.

Merrill considered himself an artist (his business card presented him as an "Art Photographer"), and many of the people who knew him concurred. He was also a painstaking nature photographer. As Robert DeArmond wrote, "In his photography, he had infinite patience and would wait for days to get exactly the right cloud formation on a mountain, or the water reflections exactly as he wanted them" (DeArmond to Daniel R. Kuehn, January 27, 1973, SNHP Archive). He was also technically skilled at taking and printing photographs. According to Gmelch (1995: 163), who obtained this information in 1986–87 from Rod Slemmons, the associate curator for photography at the Seattle Art Museum, Merrill used sharp lenses and small apertures. He used gelatin dry plates that were easy to develop and could be processed long after exposure, provided that they were properly stored. He printed his images as either contact prints or enlargements. Merrill also used some cartridge roll film, primarily for the personal snapshots.

At the time of his death in 1929 Merrill owned six large-format cameras. According to Gmelch (2008: 128), his 8 × 10-inch camera had a convertible lens that gave him three focal lengths. The appraised value of his six cameras at the time of his death was $250. Unfortunately, the appraisal does not describe the cameras, and the only one remaining today is an Eastman Kodak Bullet #2 (1896 model). Other possessions listed in the appraisal included an enlarging camera, 1,500 8 × 10-inch glass negatives, about seven hundred framed and unframed prints, eight hundred postcards, and miscellaneous photographic equipment. Their total value in 2007 purchasing power was about $20,000 (Gmelch 2008: 129–30).

Merrill's biggest passions, and the main subjects of his photography, were Sitka's Indigenous people and their arts, along with the town's spectacular natural setting. He decorated his home with the works of Tlingit craftspeople as well as his own photographs (fig. 7).

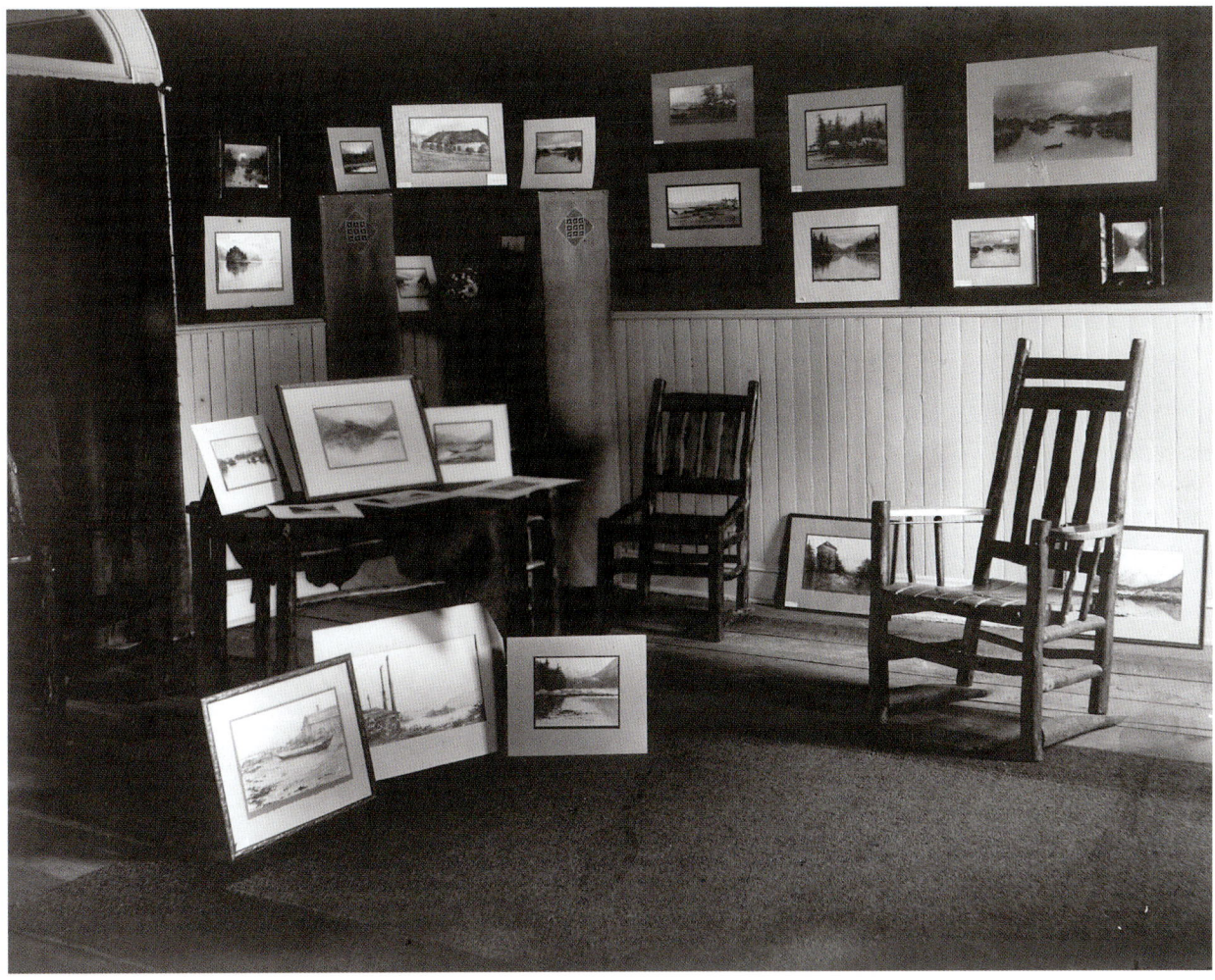

FIGURE 7. Elbridge W. Merrill. A room in Merrill's home with his photographs displayed, date unknown. Courtesy of the National Park Service, Sitka National Historical Park, 03942.

Merrill found nature to be a source of spiritual healing and wisdom. His favorite activity was watching the sunset over Sitka's Mount Edgecumbe. In fact, some of his acquaintances considered him a pantheist who sensed the presence of God or a higher power in the mountains and forests (see Gmelch 2008: 117–18). Here is how he explained these emotions to Barrett Willoughby, an Alaska novelist:

On the mountain-tops there is a great silence that fills one with wonder—and reverence. It seems a holy place. Often as I have climbed, I have felt exhilarated by the joy of motion and the rarefied air and satisfied just with the strength of myself. I'd throw off my pack to camp for the night and start to shout and sing. Then I'd stop—startled. It was as if the sound of my voice had trespassed on the silence of the gods—as if I were intruding. But after this passed, I'd begin to feel big and strong and alone up there with the Source of all Power. At such times man knows there is something within him that is immortal. (Willoughby 1930: 223)

Merrill often spent days away from Sitka hiking, taking photographs, painting landscapes, watching birds, and collecting specimens for taxidermy (another hobby of his). In 1912 and 1913 he accompanied the visiting ornithologist George Willett on birding expeditions into the mountains, where he helped collect several valuable specimens. He also shared his notes on the local birds with Willett (1914: 71).

Eventually he built himself a cabin near Sitka on the slope of Mount Verstovia, which he named Hideaway. From there he often went hunting and fishing, relying heavily on these activities for subsistence, as his Tlingit neighbors did. Sometime later he built another cabin called Ferndale. Located in Jamestown Bay, this simple two-room cabin was hidden behind ferns and bushes and could be reached from town only on foot or by boat. When Willoughby visited him one summer in the mid-1920s, she found a house cluttered with photographic equipment and decorated simply with "a few pictures of hunting dogs, a cluster of cedar cones, a rack of guns[,] . . . a long, old-fashioned telescope" on the walls, and a bowl of flowers on the table (Willoughby 1930, cited in Gmelch 2008: 119–21).

While Merrill made a modest living from making portraits of Sitkans and selling his photographs and Tlingit curios, he was an indifferent businessman. Local people sometimes had to wait for months to get photographs they had ordered. In 1908 he accepted a commission to take photographs for a special report on the Sitka National Monument, but he took a long time to complete the task (A. G. Shoup to W. A. Langille, November 22, 1908; E. W. Merrill File, SNHP Archive). If Merrill did not like a customer, he would not sell them photos or curios and would ask them to leave his shop (Merrill obituary, *Daily Alaska Empire*, October 28, 1929). Money did not seem to interest him as long as he had enough to eat and to pursue his passions and hobbies. As he put it to Willoughby: "Many travelers have asked me why I linger in this little Northern village. They tell me I might go down to the States and make far more money. But why should I leave a place I love when I am contended and happy and have enough money for all my needs? Can a man be more than happy? Alaska has given me perfect health, strength beyond that of an average man, and an abiding saneness. It has sharpened all my senses, until now I am totally unfitted to endure the smoke and stench of cities" (Willoughby 1930: 223–24).

Merrill's images of wild Alaska nature were popular with visitors and appeared in a variety of magazines, including publications by the Sitka Industrial and Training School, the *Alaska-Yukon Magazine*, and such books as Dazie M. Stromstadt-Brown's *Sitka, the Beautiful* (1906), Robert E. Coontz's *From Mississippi to the Sea* (1930), Barrett Willoughby's *Sitka, Portal to Romance* (1930), and several others. He also contributed fine photographs of birds to *Condor* magazine. Some of his best images were made into postcards and sold to visitors in his own store as well by other local merchants. Occasionally these postcards were colored to enhance the image. Local people also liked buying Merrill's beautiful nature prints to decorate their homes (figs. 8 and 9).

Still, some of Merrill's best-known and most interesting and impressive photographs are those of the local people, and especially the Tlingit, for whom he had a special place in his heart. He not only collected a variety of objects made by Tlingit craftspeople and artists but also learned to sing and appreciate a number of Tlingit songs (Willoughby 1930: 211–12). He was familiar with Tlingit customs and beliefs and might have had at least an elementary command of

FIGURE 8. Elbridge W. Merrill. Two Tlingit women in a canoe, date unknown. Hand-colored image. Alaska State Historical Library P57-253.

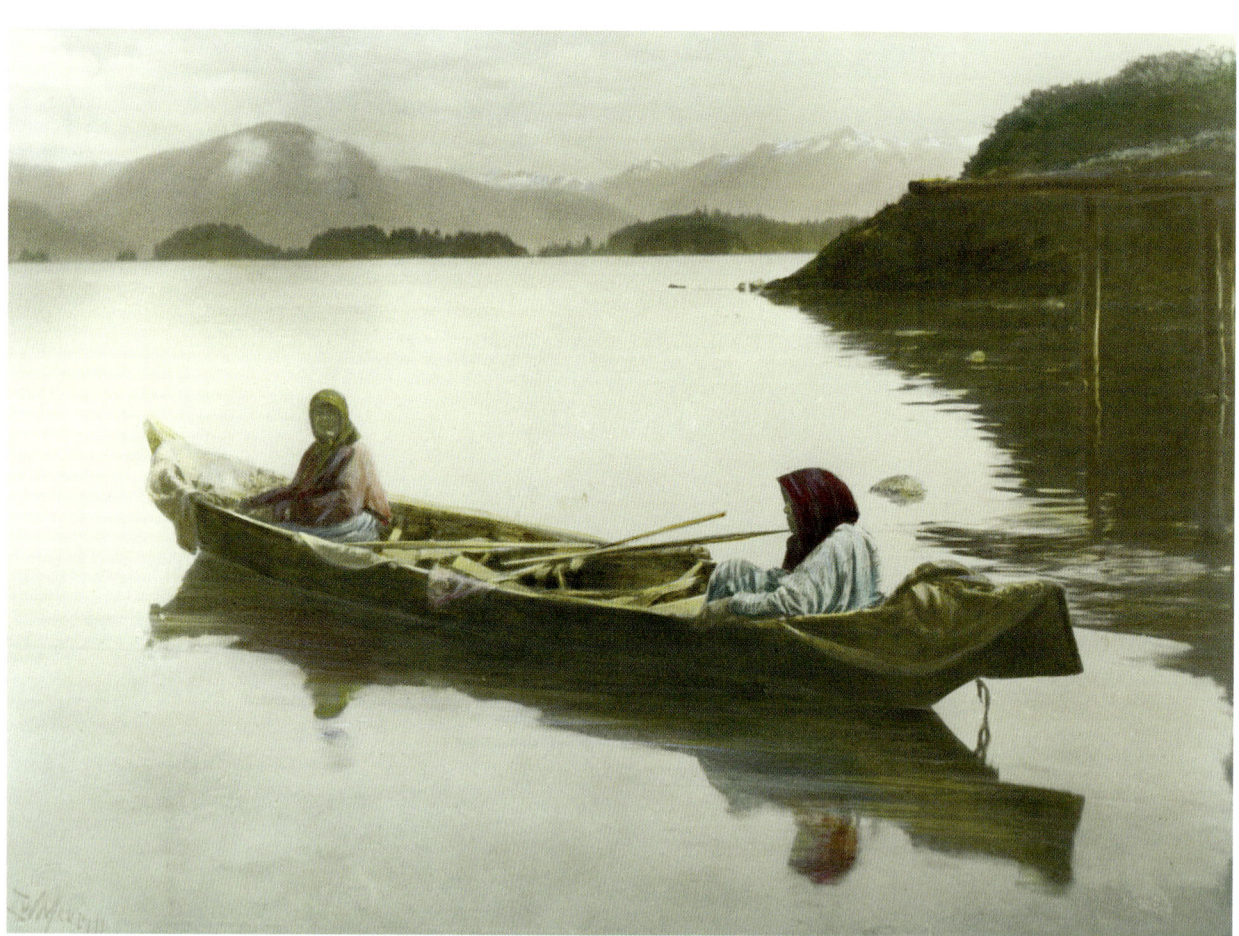

16

the Tlingit language. He hunted regularly with at least one Tlingit man, whose son he helped with photography (Willoughby 1930: 219–20; Kan 1979–2021).[3] The Tlingit gave him the name Father of Pictures—a typical example of teknonymy, by which a person's name indicates mastery of some activity. According to Gmelch (1995: 164), he had another Tlingit name, but we do not know what it was or what it meant. Several elderly Tlingit men and women attended his funeral (obituary, *Alaska Weekly*, November 22, 1929).

Merrill's interest in Indigenous culture went beyond collecting and photographing. In 1906 he organized the restoration work on the Haida totem poles that were returned to Sitka following their display at the Louisiana Purchase Exposition in St. Louis in 1904 and the Lewis and Clark Exposition in Portland, Oregon, in 1905. The day the ship arrived with the poles, Merrill went with Governor John G. Brady and his sons on a walk along the Indian River to discuss the best location for placing the poles in the scenic area that in 1910 became the Sitka National Historical Park (Hugh Brady to Marilyn Knapp, May 30, 1980, E. W. Merrill File, SNHP Archive). Afterward he worked with a dozen Tlingit craftsmen to repair and paint them. In 1913 Merrill repainted all of the poles by himself (Hugh Brady to Raymond Geerdes, July 21, 1967, SNHP). As he told Willoughby, "Each totem is a record in wood of a different legend or a different family history. That is why it took me so many weeks to select the sites for them. I tried to preserve the spirit of the old order, which is passing. The white man had educated the Thlinget of to-day to be scornful of the totem art of his forefathers. Soon, I fear, these will be the only specimens left in Alaska" (Willoughby 1925: 41).

For years Merrill acted as the unofficial caretaker of the Sitka National Historical Park (with a nominal salary of $12 a year) and advocated making the park into a national monument. In 1922 Arno Cammemer, the acting head of the National Park Service, wrote to James G. Steese, the Juneau-based president of the Alaska Road Commission, asking him to appoint Merrill as the official custodian of the Sitka National Monument (Cammemer to Steese, October 2, 1922, E. W. Merrill File, SNHP Archive). However, Steese suggested appointing a local man, Peter Triershield, instead. Triershield had already done some repair work on the grounds of the monument and was described by Steese as a "substantial citizen of Sitka and a master carpenter." Here is how Steese characterized Merrill:

> I am well acquainted with Mr. E. W. Merrill of Sitka and his activities. Mr. Merrill is an expert photographer and taxidermist and has painted some really remarkable landscapes. There is quite a demand for his pictures and if he would pay attention to business, he could make a good income. He is particularly interested in the totems in the Sitka Monument and has several times painted them, presumably at his own expense or at the expense of whoever furnished the paint. Unfortunately, Mr. Merrill has all the temperamental disabilities of an artist; inattention to regular and steady business being an outstanding characteristic. Were it not for his unreliability in this respect he would be an ideal for the monument. (Steese to Cammemer, October 12, 1922; SNHP Archive).

Merrill obviously knew that tourists, as well as some of the local non-Native residents, were intrigued by the images of the town's Indigenous inhabitants dressed in their traditional regalia. This was a time when romanticized images of Native Americans were in great demand, even as their political power and land base were being diminished by the United States government and its non-Native citizens. Yet it is hard to believe that Merrill took so many pictures of the Tlingit solely because there was a market for them.

Many of his early portraits of Indigenous Sitkans were made at the request of the subjects themselves and ended up in their homes rather than for sale (see fig. 9). Those portraits, some of which depicted the subjects in traditional attire and others in festive or fashionable Euro-American clothing, were far from romantic or staged. Some were commissioned portraits taken inside Merrill's studio. Others were taken outdoors, but again, these tend not to present their subjects as romantic or "primitive" Indians. The portraits clearly speak of the photographer's good rapport with his subjects.

Merrill's photographs thus contrast strongly with the romanticized images of Native Americans created by the famous Edward Curtis (see Gidley 2003). According to Gmelch, Merrill "adopted a straight style characterized by sharp focus, detail, and broad tonal

FIGURE 9. Elbridge W. Merrill. 1904 Sitka potlatch (ḵu.éex'). Hand-colored image. Author's personal collection. Original photograph courtesy of the National Park Service, Sitka National Historical Park, 03768.

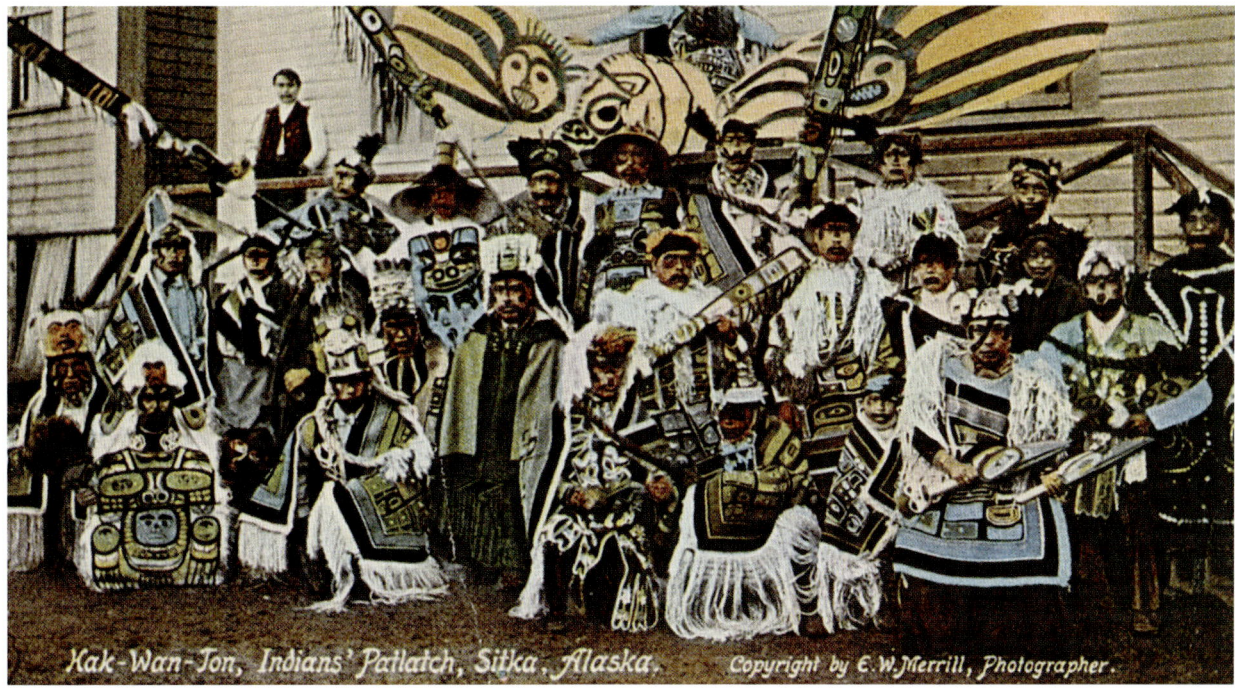

Kak-Wan-Ton, Indians' Patlatch, Sitka, Alaska.   Copyright by E. W. Merrill, Photographer.

range, and minimal, if any, manipulation of the photographic process." According to David Ogawa, whom Gmelch interviewed in 2007, Merrill's work is reminiscent of the German photographer August Sander's modernist documentary style; he may have also been influenced by French realist photography (Gmelch 2008: 131).

Merrill's work also differed significantly from that of the two well-known and prolific commercial photographers William H. Case (1868–1920) and Horace H. Draper (1855–1913), who began their work in southeastern Alaska in 1898 in Skagway. When their partnership dissolved in 1907, Case opened his own photography studio and moved it to Juneau, where it existed until his death in 1920. Draper remained with the original business in Skagway, which operated under the name Draper and Co. until 1913. While some of the photographs by Case and Draper depict the Tlingit and their life in a realistic manner, others are clearly staged: see, for example, the photograph of a Tlingit woman weaving (ASL-P39-0062) or that of a young Tlingit woman wearing a bearskin and labeled "Hootz-Du-Gu girl" (fig. 10), which depicts a strange mix of Tlingit and Eskimo artifacts.

These photographers also produced obviously staged and exoticized images of Tlingit shamans (see, for example, a picture by Case and Draper. ASL-P39-0782), one of whom they described as a "witch doctor." They did not hesitate to use a non-Native man to impersonate a Tlingit shaman in a staged curing ceremony (fig. 11).

Among the Case and Draper photographs are several disturbing seminude photographs of Tlingit women, clearly intended for white gold miners and other lonely frontiersmen. The two photographers also occasionally used such derogatory words as *clootch* ("wife, woman") to label their images, something Merrill never did.[4] Photographs of Tlingit shamans, portrayed as the epitome of Native wildness and

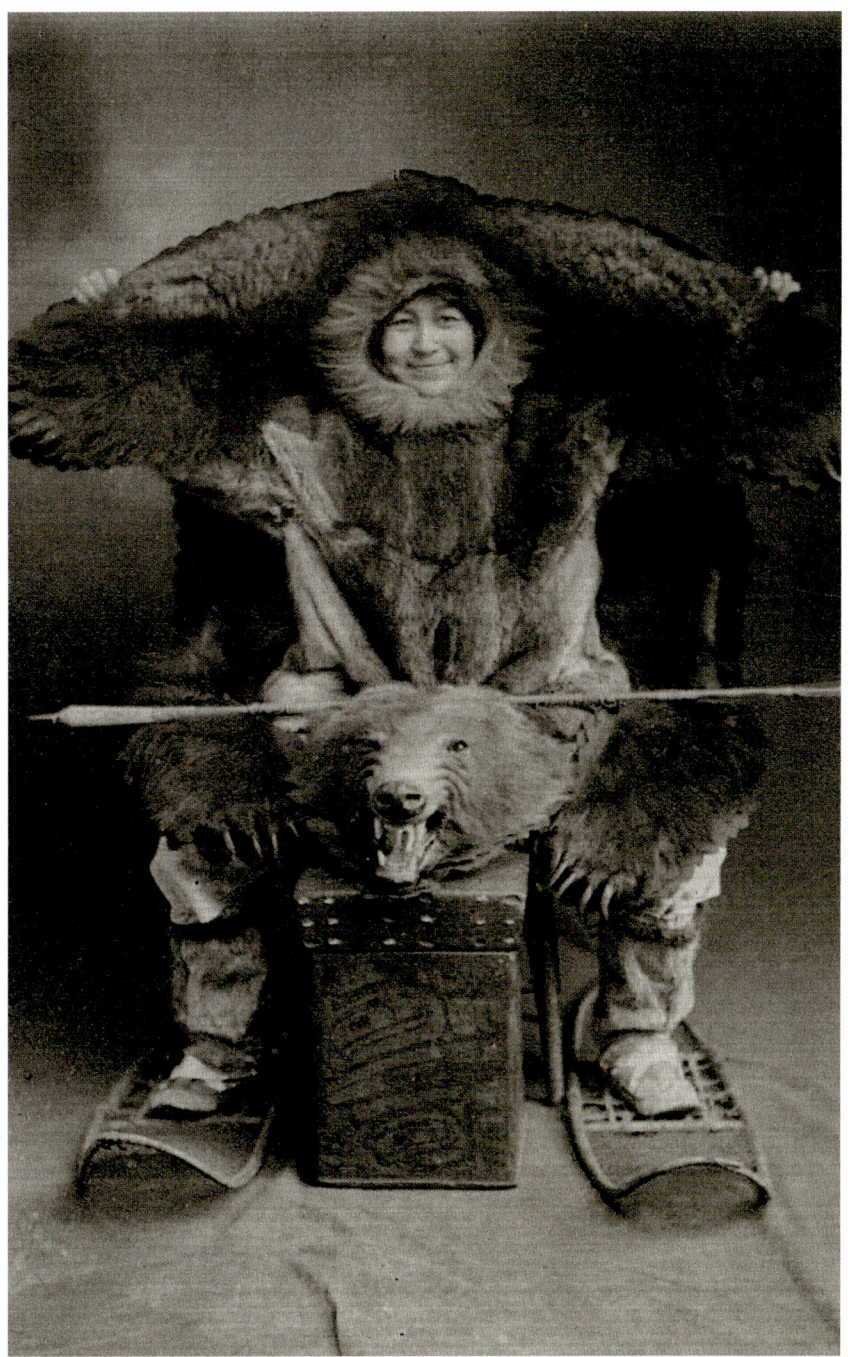

FIGURE 10. William H. Case and Horace H. Draper. A Tlingit woman wearing a bearskin and snowshoes, sitting on top of a decorated Tlingit wooden box. Juneau, 1907–20. The photograph is labeled "Hootz-Du-Gu girl." Alaska State Historical Library P226-042.

FIGURE 11. William H. Case and Horace H. Draper. Staged studio photograph of a non-Native man impersonating a shaman during a curing ceremony, Juneau, 1907–20. The inscription reads "Native shaman drives away devil spirits." Alaska State Historical Library P39-0428.

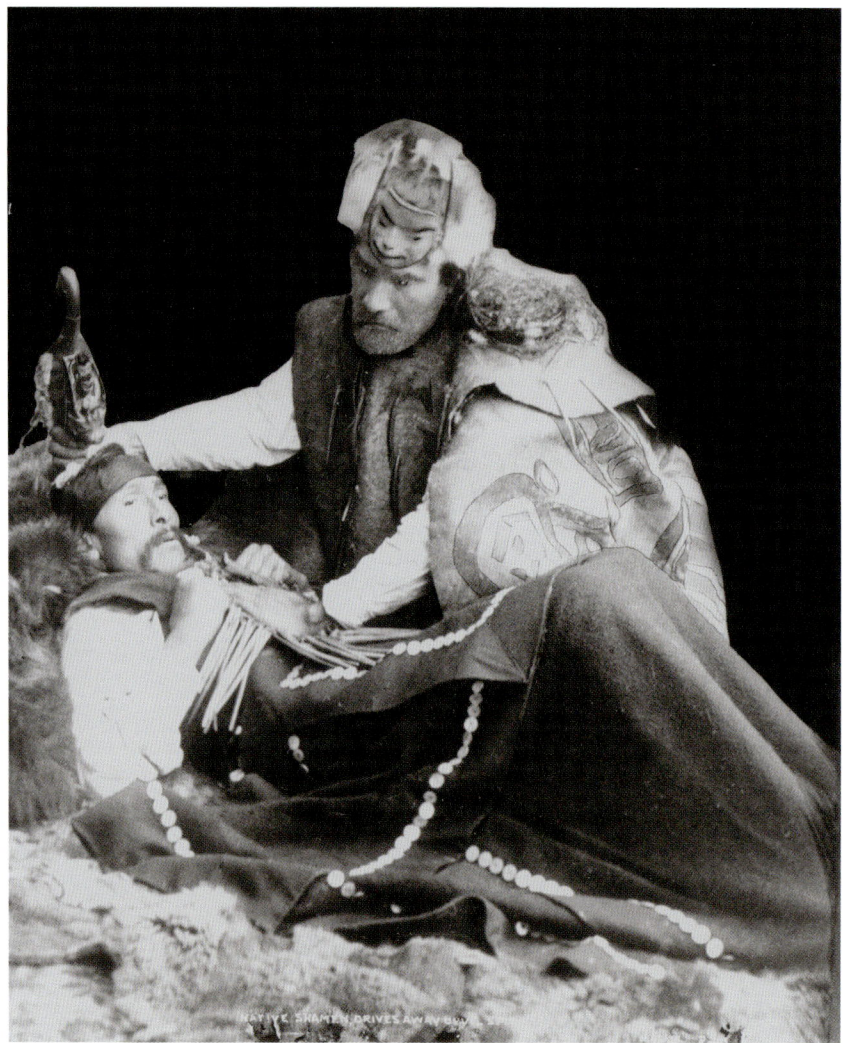

exotic character, were apparently popular with non-Natives. Even the talented Lloyd V. Winter (1866–1945) and Edwin P. Pond (1872–1943), who operated a curio shop and a photography studio in Juneau between 1893 and 1945, and whose work tended to be realistic rather than exoticized (though lacking Merrill's artistic touch), did not shy away from producing several staged photos of Native medicine men holding rattles and other accoutrements.

Merrill's photographs of the Tlingit tend to be closer in their style to those created by the young amateur photographer Vincent Soboleff (1882–1950) (Kan 2013b). A son of a Russian Orthodox priest stationed in an isolated Tlingit village, Soboleff developed a close rapport with many of its Indigenous inhabitants and was able to photograph them with his Kodak camera. While his images lack the artistic quality of Merrill's, they share a realistic and nonexoticized style of portraying the Tlingit (fig. 12).

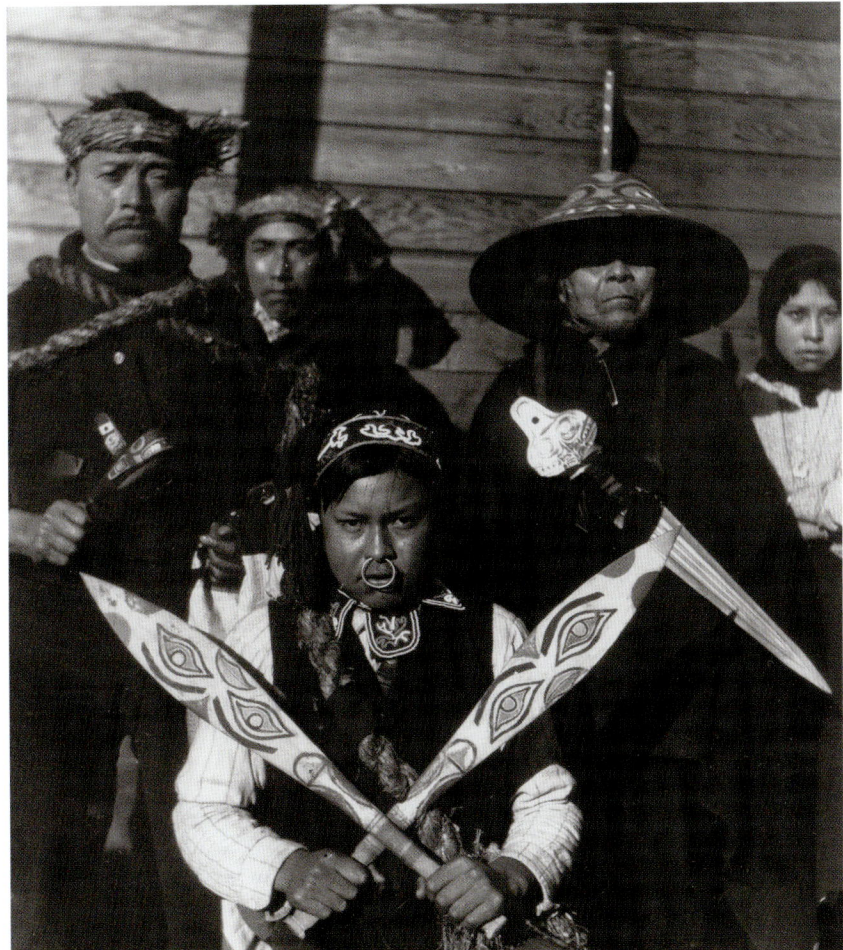

FIGURE 12. Vincent Soboleff. Three Tlingit men, a Tlingit boy, and a Tlingit girl in front of an unidentified lineage house, Angoon, ca. 1890. Three of the subjects are wearing and displaying traditional regalia and ceremonial objects decorated with their lineage or clan crests. The inscription on the plate identifies the image as "paddle boy in Indian costume" (see Kan 2013b: 76–77). Alaska State Historical Library P1-022.

Particularly expressive of the trust between Merrill and the Tlingit people he photographed are the images of funeral scenes, showing the deceased surrounded by his or her kin and sacred regalia. Only a non-Native person enjoying a great deal of trust would have been allowed to take them. Merrill's living Tlingit subjects clearly wanted to be photographed and appreciated the way he portrayed them. Participants in the 1904 Kaagwaantaan *ku.éex'* (potlatch) proudly posed for him wearing their most sacred and precious lineage- and clan-owned regalia (*at.óow*).[5] In Tlingit and other Indigenous Northwest Coast cultures, formal public or ritual display of crest objects belonging to one's own kinship group to a group of witnesses from other kinship groups was the best way of confirming the group's ownership of these sacred ancestral objects (Dauenhauer 1995; Kan 2016). Wearing or holding such objects also confirmed a person's membership in that group and hence their right to display and speak about the objects. Such public legitimation of individual and group claims became particularly important in an era when, due to depopulation and other consequences of Euro-American colonization, disputes between kinship groups over the ownership of traditional objects became common. Since such photographs could be used as evidence of prior possession of such sacred objects, the Tlingit and their coastal neighbors seized on photography to advance their own cultural and historically specific goals. The Indigenous people portrayed by Merrill appear proud and dignified, projecting an image that they considered culturally appropriate.

While most of Merrill's images of the Tlingit people are either portraits or depictions of ceremonies, he also took a number of pictures of Native men and women at work: fishing, processing animal skins, carving, weaving, and even fixing Sitka's roads. His informal images of Tlingit children at play reflect the children's own sense of self as well as the photographer's well-known affection for children.

Many of Merrill's photographs of the Tlingit were taken on the campus of the Sitka Industrial and Training School, established in Sitka as a Presbyterian-affiliated boarding school for Alaska Native children in 1878 and renamed the Sheldon Jackson School in 1910. These images represent a very different aspect of the lives of southeastern Alaska's Indigenous people. His young subjects are portrayed in school uniforms and other attire imposed on them by the missionary educators. Yet they are not presented as victims: their own agency comes through, especially in such images as that of the school's first graduating high school class in 1921 (fig. 13). These group portraits

FIGURE 13. Elbridge W. Merrill. Sheldon Jackson School (formerly the Sitka Industrial and Training School) graduating class of 1921. For identification of persons portrayed, see the caption to plate 98. Courtesy of the National Park Service, Sitka National Historical Park, 03751.

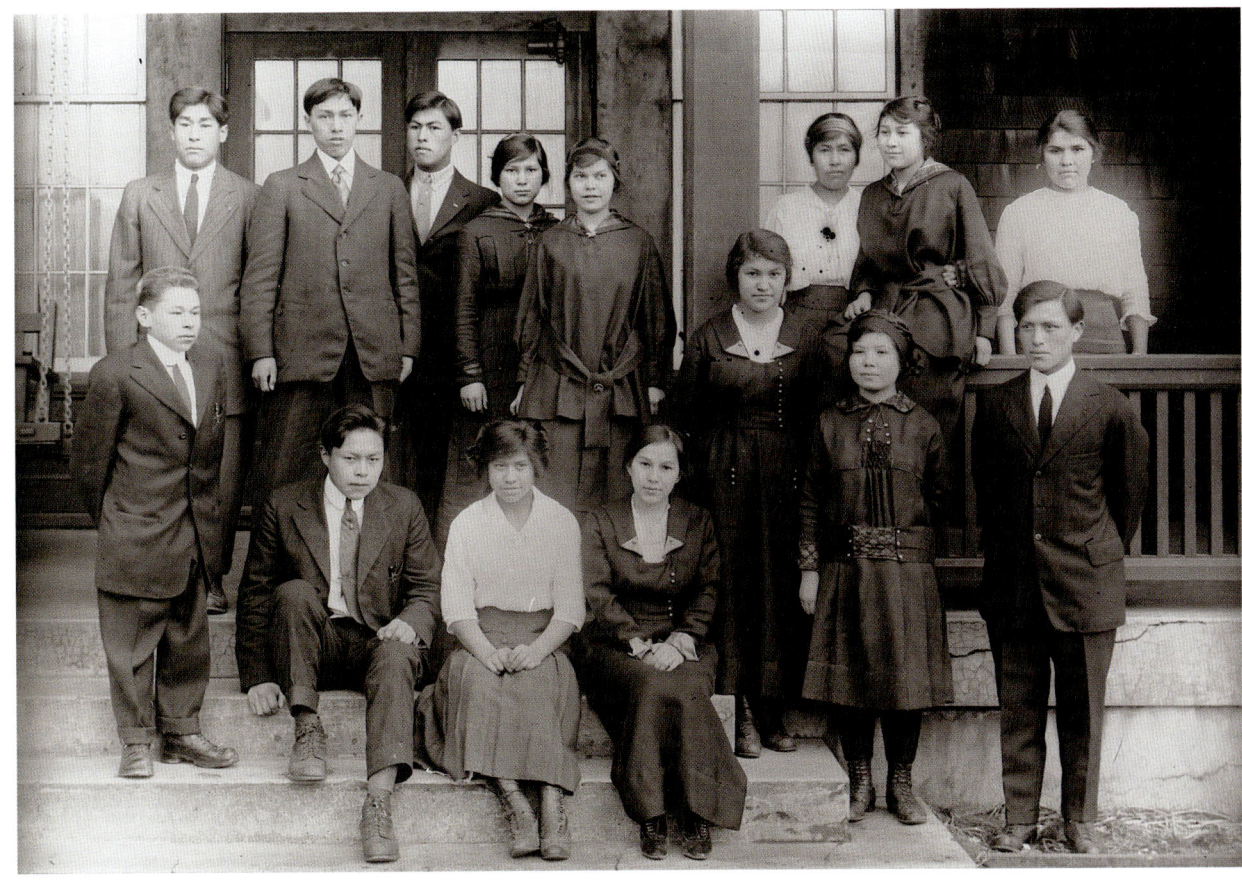

tend to convey the same impression of their subjects' dignity and self-control as Merrill's studio portraits of Tlingit people and his pictures of the 1904 potlatch participants. While some of these school pictures were likely commissioned by the institution, their large number and variety suggest that Merrill was determined to document the changes taking place in the Native community.

Merrill was also fond of photographing Tlingit art objects, and he clearly knew their value. He corresponded with George T. Emmons, a well-known collector of Northwest Coast art, and willed a portion of his own collection to him. The remainder ended up in the Alaska State Museum, whose first director, the Reverend Andrew Kashevaroff, Merrill knew well (Steve Henrikson, personal communication; Kan June 20, 2023). Peter Corey, who headed Sitka's Sheldon Jackson Museum from the 1970s to the 1990s, told me that Merrill had a very good eye for high-quality spruce-root baskets (fig. 14), suggesting that he had a fine rapport with the women who made them and had paid a fair price for these objects (Corey, personal communication; Kan May 1, 1980). Moreover, he clearly knew a good deal about the cultural meaning and ceremonial use of the artifacts he collected.

As Sitka's number one resident photographer, Merrill also took a number of pictures of its "Russian" community (actually Tlingit-Russian Creoles).[6] These included portraits of individual Russian Orthodox clergymen (from deacons to bishops) as well as lay members of the community. Group portraits of members of the St. Michael's Cathedral parish, taken by Merrill between the late 1890s and the 1920s (likely at the parishioners' request), offer a valuable historical record of the life of a religious community that consisted of both Creoles and numerous Tlingit who joined the Russian Orthodox Church in the late nineteenth and early twentieth centuries. Along with making formal group portraits, he photographed Orthodox religious processions and funerals, the

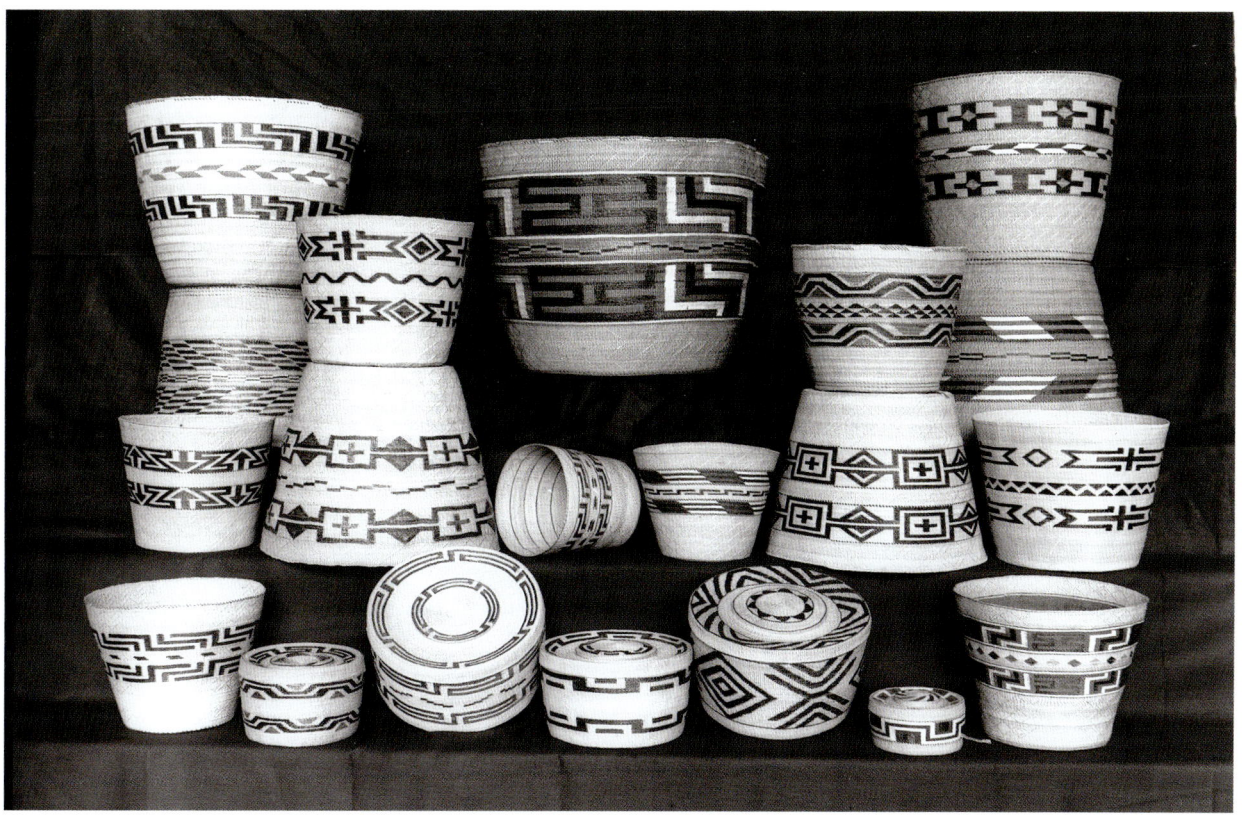

FIGURE 14. Elbridge W. Merrill, Tlingit spruce-root baskets, Sitka, date unknown. Courtesy of the National Park Service, Sitka National Historical Park, 03848.

blessing of the Native fishing fleet in the spring, and other ritual activities. Several of his group portraits depict Creole and Tlingit church societies (brotherhoods) and the residents of the Orthodox boarding school and seminary located in the building known as Bishop's House. There are also a few informal portrayals of these ethnically mixed inhabitants of the town.

Finally, Merrill was known for his masterful portraits of Sitka's Euro-American population. These range from formal portraits of the town's upper- and middle-class inhabitants (including the governor of Alaska) to those of ordinary folk at work and at play. Some of his subjects are depicted inside or in front of their middle-class homes, conveying their pride in their property and their status in the community. Several Euro-American women and girls are portrayed in their gardens, surrounded by flowers, as if to underscore their femininity and a setting appropriate for women of their race and class. And yet Merrill seems to have been equally interested in portraying Euro-American fishermen, construction workers, hunters, and even patients recovering in the local hospital. A local working-class mother is lovingly depicted with her many children (SITK 25552), and a group of teenage Campfire Girls are shown relaxing in front of a cabin in the woods (SITK 25483). Merrill was also drawn to photographing town holidays and special events, from the Fourth of July parades (ASL-P57-235) to the schoolchildren's Maypole dancing (SITK 25485). No other Alaska community's history and multiethnic population is documented in such detail as Sitka's, and we have Elbridge Warren Merrill to thank for this.

SITKA IN THE FIRST DECADES OF THE TWENTIETH CENTURY

The town of Sitka has an interesting history. Originally settled by the Tlingit people of the Kiks.ádi clan, it had a row of large winter log houses belonging to several clans (fig. 15). Tlingit society was divided into two halves, or moieties, referred to as Ravens and Eagles (the latter sometimes also called Wolves). Moieties were further subdivided into clans, and clans into lineages, the latter usually identified with a particular winter house. Like other Tlingit people, the Sitka Tlingit lived in their winter houses from late fall through spring, when they departed to their camps to pursue various subsistence activities, such as hunting and fishing. All the kinship groups of Tlingit society were matrilineal, with marriage allowed only between members of opposite moieties. Thus members of the Kiks.ádi clan, who belonged to the Raven moiety, intermarried

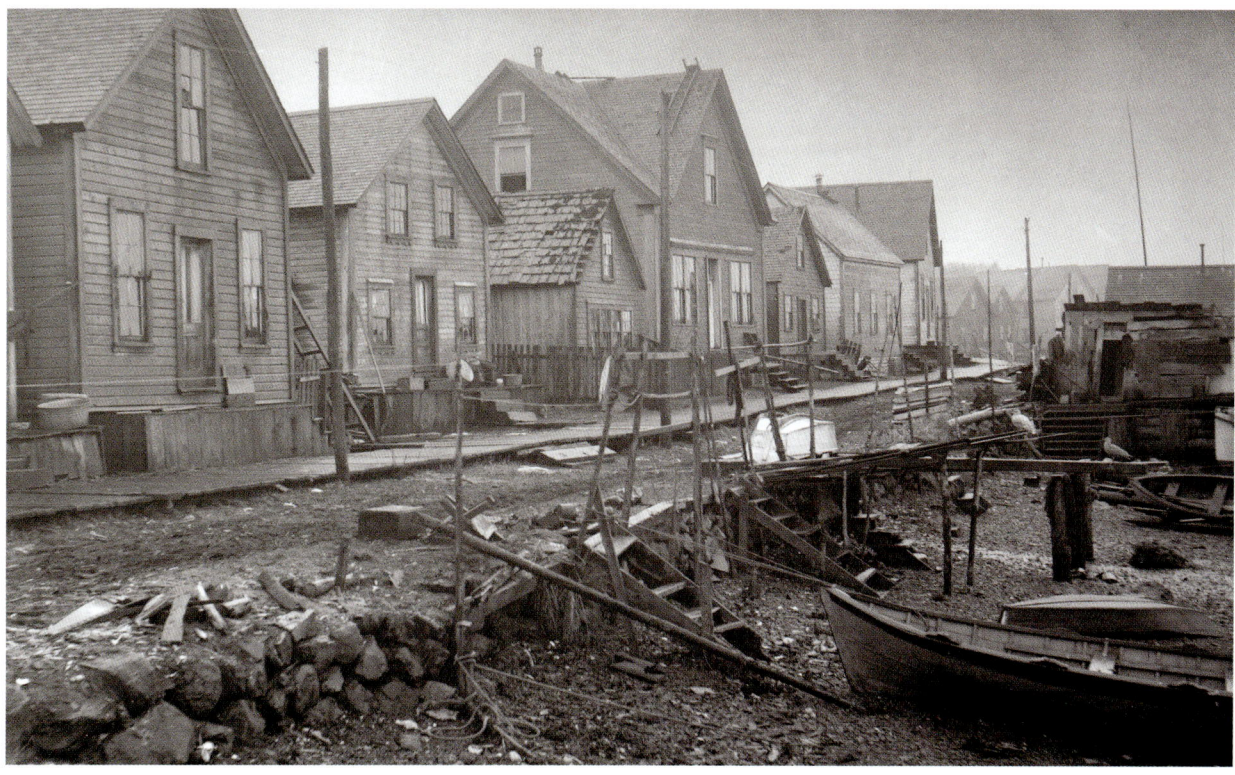

with those of the Kaagwaantaan clan and several other clans of the Eagle moiety. Each lineage and clan had its and crests depicted on their totem poles, house screens, ceremonial attire and important material objects (*at.óow*). Names or titles specific to the lineage were passed down, along with sacred traditions such as myths, songs, and dances, which often referred to the origin of the group's crests. The most important Tlingit ritual was the *k̲u.éex'*, a big feast or potlatch, which usually took place when a deceased member of the group was memorialized by the raising of a memorial or mortuary pole or the (re)building of a lineage house. By the 1900s in Sitka, such poles were being replaced with gravestones. Expensive objects commissioned from non-Native makers were often erected at the cemetery, and the ritual was followed by a memorial *k̲u.éex'*. Although in earlier times *ḵu.éex'* gifts consisted mainly of food and furs, in Merrill's day they were replaced with blankets, store-bought valuables, and even cash (see Kan 2016).

In 1799 the first Russian fort was built in the area. It was destroyed by the Tlingit three years later. Finally in 1804 the Russians settled there permanently, establishing the town of Novo-Arkhangelsk (New Archangel), which became the capital of Russian Alaska. It was surrounded by a palisade and guarded by soldiers. Despite the Native people's resentment of this occupation, the Russians were forced to trade with them, bartering some household and food items for badly needed fresh fish, meat, and berries. A few Tlingit women married Russian men and moved into the Russian town. Russian Orthodox missionaries attempted to convert the local Natives, with some success: several hundred agreed to be baptized. However, their understanding of and commitment to Christianity was minimal and had been encouraged by gifts offered to converts (see Kan 1999: 89–174).

In 1867 the Russia-American Company, which operated Russia's Alaska colony, transferred the ownership of its property in Alaska to the United States. Novo-Arkhangelsk's Russian population departed over the next couple of years, while most of the Creoles remained. The American population gradually grew and by 1900 numbered about 230. The Creoles, referred to locally as the Russians, numbered about 200, while the Tlingit numbered 750 or so. The Tlingit material culture and economy had already been affected by the Russian and especially the American colonial presence. In addition, a deep division had emerged within the Native community between a group of about fifty more-Americanized people—who had studied at the Sitka Industrial and Training School and on graduation settled down with their immediate kin in a group of cottages constructed near the school and with the school's help—and a much larger community of the more traditionally oriented Tlingit residing in the old Indian Village on other side of town. While the former were Presbyterian, most of the latter had become committed members of the Russian Orthodox Church (see Kan 1999: 245–367) (fig. 16).

Although by 1900 the material culture of the Tlingit people had changed a great deal, most of them continued to pursue traditional subsistence activities alongside part-time work in the non-Native town and sold food (especially fish), furs, and curios to non-Natives. Similarly, while some of the lower-ranking Native families had become richer through their interaction with the whites, and some high-ranking families had suffered a decline because of epidemic diseases, the basic traditional social structure and system of rank remained in place. Most lineages (houses) and clans continued to host potlatches whenever they lost a member or built a new house.

FIGURE 16. Unidentified photographer (possibly Merrill). Bishop Innokentii Pustynskii (center, with staff) with other Russian Orthodox clergymen and members of the St. Michael's (Native) Brotherhood in front of Bishop's House, Sitka, 1905–7. Michael Z. Vinokouroff Collection, Alaska State Historical Library P243-1-047.

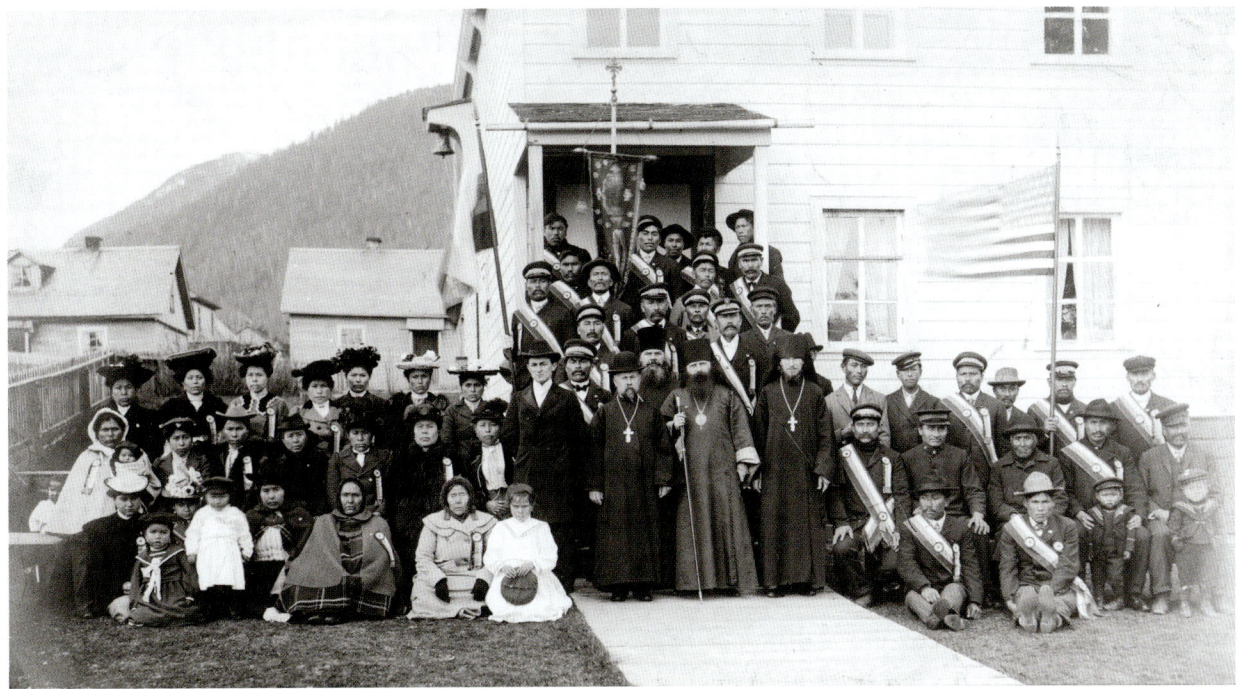

Yet pressure from local American authorities and missionaries (especially the Presbyterians) forced them to minimize public displays of traditional dancing, singing, and ceremonial regalia.

The 1904 memorial *ku.éex'*, sponsored by the Wolf House of the Kaagwaantaan clan, came to be known as the "last great potlatch" of Sitka (Preucel and Williams 2005; Kan 2022). The main hosts of that ceremony were Jacob Yarkon (Yaakwan, Xeitxut'ch, Stoowukáa) and Paddy Parker (Wooshkeenaa, Yaanaxnahoo) (fig. 17). The event involved several clans from several villages outside Sitka who arrived in town in their canoes and participated in a series of feasts, culminating with one hosted by the Wolf House of James Jackson (Annahootz), which began on December 23, 1904, and lasted for four weeks. In connection with this *ku.éex'*, the Wolf House commissioned and dedicated a Multiplying Wolf screen and two Multiplying Wolf house posts (carved by Silver Jim [Kichxook]), as well as the Panting Wolf post, which for the duration of the ceremony was displayed on the front of the house, having been raised by pulleys and attached to the house. In addition, two other Wolf posts, carved by Rudolph Walton of the Kiks.ádi clan, were placed inside the Eagle House, headed by another high-ranking Kaagwaantaan leader, Augustus Bean (K'alyaan Éesh) (Preucel and Williams 1995; Kan 2022). An article in the local paper published soon after the 1904 *ku.éex'* describes the lavish distribution of gifts at the ceremony. One of the key guests, Chilkoot Jack, received $270 in cash, one hundred blankets, ten large boxes of provisions, and seven oil cans containing candlefish oil (*Daily Alaskan*, January 13, 1905). Being affiliated with the local Presbyterian church, the Kaagwaantaan hosts of the 1904 ceremony promised Governor Brady that they would no longer perform such ceremonies. However, my research in the records of the Sitka Presbyterian Church indicates that at least some of them continued to do so in a more discreet manner (see Preucel and Williams 2005; Kan 1979–2021; Kan 2022).

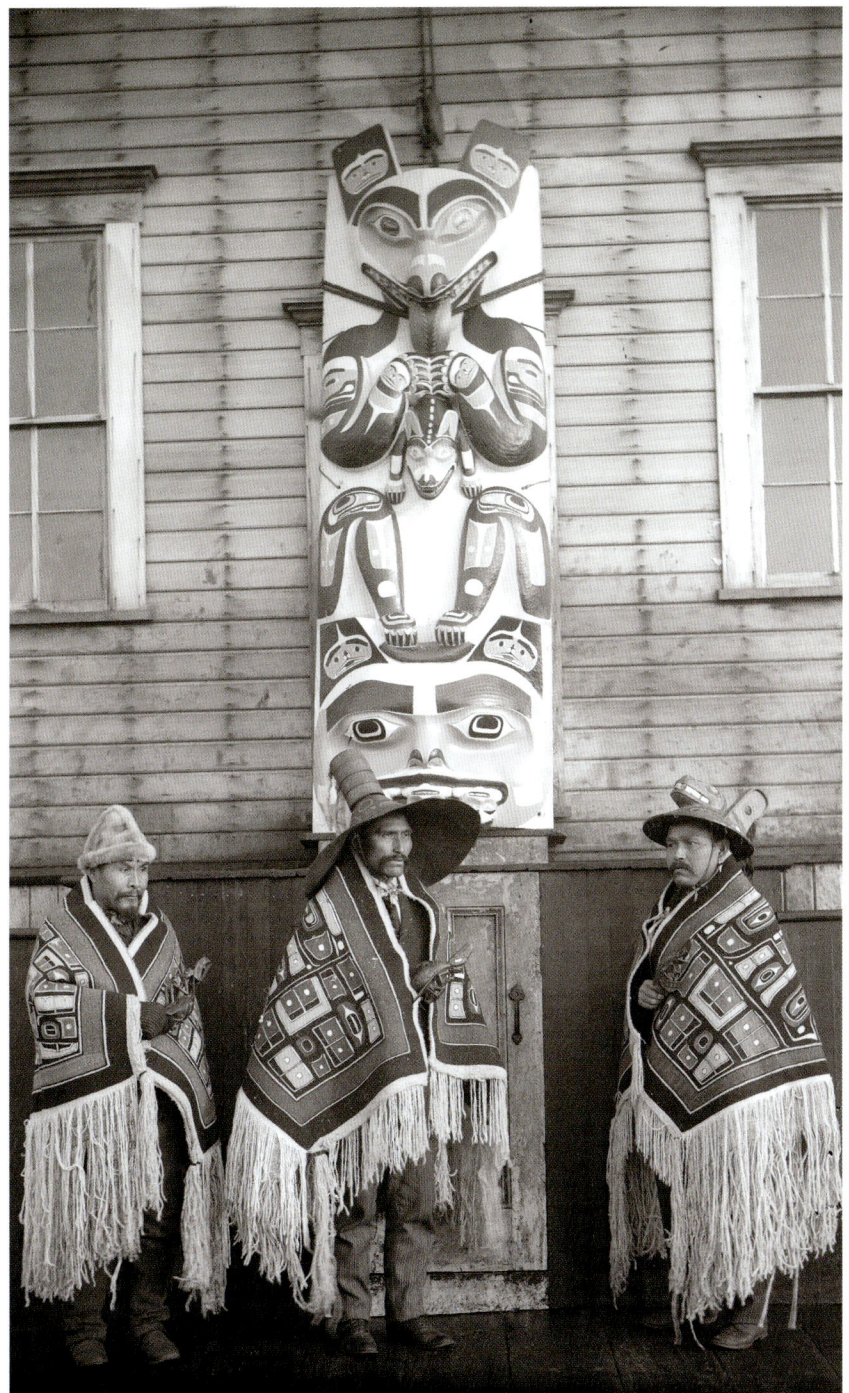

FIGURE 17. Elbridge W. Merrill. Key sponsors and hosts of the 1904 ḵu.éex' (potlatch), hosted by the Wolf House (G̱ooch Hít) of the Kaagwaantaan clan, standing in front of the Panting Wolf house post, Sitka. For the names of the men portrayed, see plate 1. Courtesy of the National Park Service, Sitka National Historical Park, 03674.

While the entire population of the Indian Village was involved in the 1904 festivities, only some of the Presbyterian Tlingit residing in dwellings known as "the Cottages" next to the Sitka Industrial and Training School participated. The majority had internalized the missionaries' negative view of the old customs. Some of the younger members of that community also preferred to speak English to their children to ensure their quicker assimilation into the dominant society. Despite these attitudes, the Cottages' residents eventually came to resent the heavy-handed and paternalistic control the Presbyterian church and the school exerted over their lives. While committed to becoming Americanized, the leaders of the cottage community wished to do so on their own terms. Along with several younger Tlingit members of the Russian Orthodox Church, they organized the Alaska Native Brotherhood (ANB), dedicated not only to "Native progress" but also to fighting for equality with whites. After the ANB's first camp was established in Sitka, camps in most other Tlingit communities were opened as well. The organization and its women's auxiliary, the Alaska Native Sisterhood, conducted its regular meetings according to *Robert's Rules of Order* and met annually for the Grand Camp meeting. Such gatherings, along with visits by Native church choirs, basketball teams, and other social groups, replaced to some degree the traditional intervillage winter visiting.

The school played a significant role in the lives of the Tlingit and other Alaska Natives from the 1880s through the 1940s. It offered its Indigenous students a solid basic American education, better than that provided by the local Indian day school. It also taught the boys boatbuilding, carpentry, and other useful skills, while the girls were instructed in "domestic arts." Of course, there was a good deal of paternalism in that education, based on the assumption that the young Natives were not receiving any useful education at home. Yet many of the teachers seem to have been dedicated to their work and to have cared deeply about their students. Having spoken in 1979 and 1980 to many of the elders who had graduated from the school, I heard very few stories of physical or sexual abuse but a good deal of praise of the school's teachers (Yaw 1985; Kan 1979–2021). At the same time, the prohibition on speaking Tlingit or other Native languages and on taking part in the ceremonies taking place in the Indian Village obviously had a strong negative effect on the students. In fact, some of the graduates could barely speak Tlingit and had to relearn it from their relatives (fig. 18).

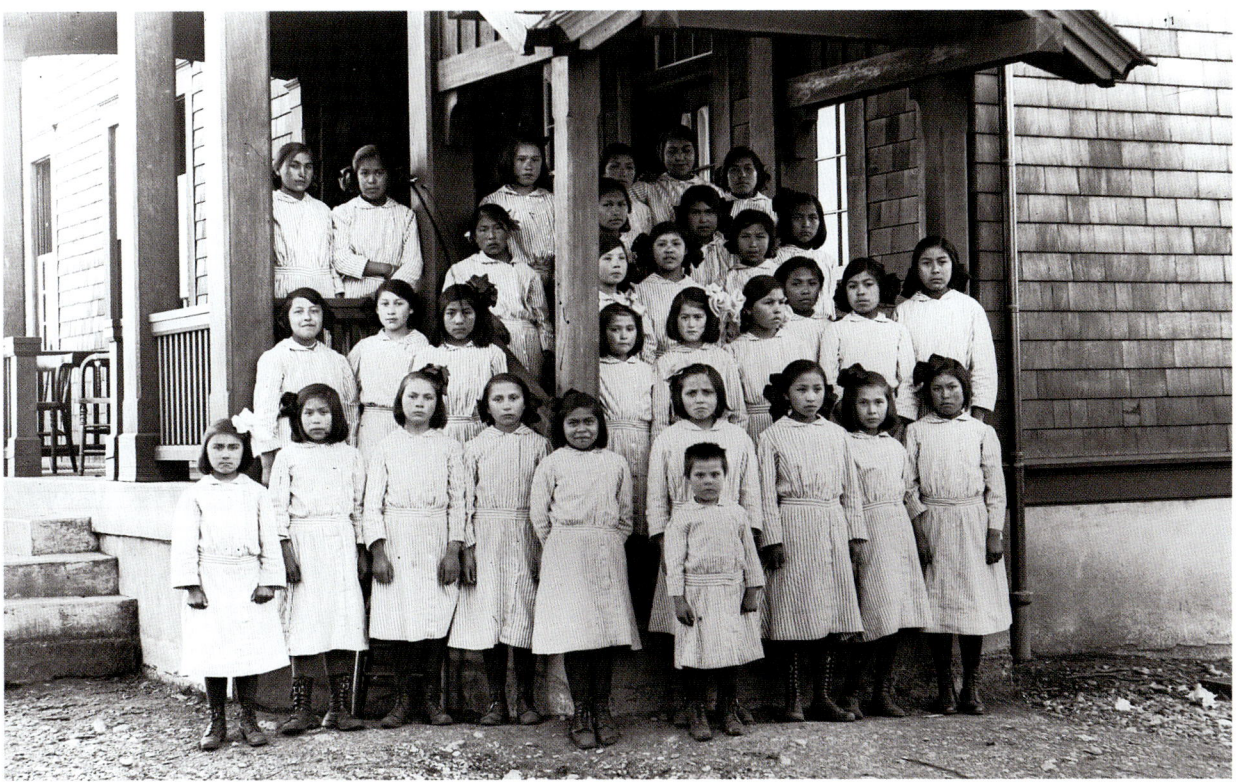

As for the Creoles, they constituted a kind of intermediate layer between Sitka's Tlingit and white communities. To begin with, the Creoles attended the same church as the majority of the local Tlingit, and a few of them acted as godparents to Tlingit children. A handful of the Creoles married into the Tlingit community or socialized with its members. At the same time, the memories of the enmity between the Russians and the Tlingit during the Russian colonial era, as well as the Creoles' desire to differentiate themselves from the "wild Indians" looked down upon by most of the local Euro-Americans, resulted in a certain tension between them and the Tlingit. Moreover, many of the Creoles resented the fact that by the late nineteenth century, the Tlingit outnumbered them in the St. Michael's Orthodox parish.

A small group of the more affluent Creoles, such as the Kostrometinoffs and the Kashevaroffs, were able to integrate themselves into the white community fairly early following the transfer of Alaska to the United States (Kan 1999, 2013a, 2023). A number of Creole women married Euro-American men and thus raised their own status as well as that of their children. Nonetheless, at least during the first few decades after 1867, many Creoles suffered from poverty as well as from being viewed by many of the local whites as "uncivilized half-breeds" (Kan 2020, 2021, 2023). During Merrill's lifetime, however, a number of Creoles, especially those whose fathers were Euro-American, managed to become fully integrated into the town's economic and social life. By the late 1920s many people of Creole descent were part of the town's Euro-American working-class and even middle-class communities.

Still, during the thirty years Merrill spent in Sitka, the Creole community retained its distinct identity and culture. Much of that culture centered on the Russian Orthodox Church and its holy days. Creoles also maintained their own cuisine and folk customs. White the older members of the Creole community continued to speak Russian with each other, the younger Creoles preferred English or used a mixture of the two languages. Some of the Creole children attended the local parish Sunday school. There was also a small orphanage for Orthodox children, mostly boys, from Sitka and other parts of Alaska, which was housed in the same building as the Orthodox bishop's quarters. In the early 1900s a small seminary was reestablished in the same building and attended by some of the older boys from the orphanage. As the principal city of the Alaska Russian Orthodox diocese, Sitka was where the bishop of Alaska tended to live, or at least visit on a regular basis. Such visits were occasions for processions and other festive events. Russian Church members, both Creoles and Tlingit, also paraded through the town during major religious holidays and in funeral processions to the Orthodox cemetery. *Sviatki*, the week following the Russian Orthodox Christmas and New Year (thirteen days after the Western Christian observances), was a time of celebration. Over the years, even some of the town's non-Orthodox residents began celebrating the "Russian New Year." Unfortunately quite a few of the Creoles were afflicted by the infamous "Russian disease," alcoholism. Of course, many Euro-Americans were not immune to that disease either.

Sitka's Euro-American population consisted of a small group of wealthy businesspeople, the most prominent among them being W. P. Mills; a relatively small middle-class segment; and a large group of working-class people employed in mining, timber cutting, and commercial fishing. When Merrill settled in Sitka, it had a small unit of US Marines and an Army Signal Corps in charge of the military cable and telegraph system. For the first seven years of Merrill's sojourn in Sitka, it remained the capital of the Territory of Alaska, but in 1906 the capital was moved to Juneau.

Despite living on an island, Sitka's residents did not feel particularly isolated from the rest of the country. Ships called regularly with mail, goods, provisions, and visitors. In the late nineteenth century the town was a major stop for tour boats operating out of Seattle. Like other small American towns, Sitka had its share of saloons, social clubs, and civic organizations. It organized annual Fourth of July celebrations and marked other American holidays in a typical small-town fashion. Taking advantage of the town's location, many white men engaged in recreational hunting and fishing, while white women tended their vegetable and flower gardens. Many residents owned small boats, and their homes followed the latest American fashions both outside and inside. One of the biggest events in the town's history was a visit in 1923 by President William G. Harding. This was the first time a sitting American president had come to town, and it was Merrill who photographed that auspicious occasion.

MERRILL'S DEATH AND THE HISTORY OF MERRILL'S PHOTOGRAPHIC COLLECTION

In late October 1929, while recuperating from influenza at his home on Jamestown Bay, Merrill caught pneumonia. By the time he checked into the local hospital on October 25, it was too late to save him. Two days later he died, at the age of fifty-nine. According to Gmelch (1995: 169–70), he must have known that he was going to die, as he dictated his will in the hospital. His funeral arrangements were handled by Elizabeth Barron, her daughter Frances, and Frances's husband, Henry Redman. Many of the town's residents turned out for the occasion. Here is how the *Daily Alaska Empire* eulogized Merrill on October 29: "The death at Sitka of E. W. Merrill, Alaska scenic artist, removes one who has done a lot of good for Alaska and for all the lovers of beauty who have been fortunate enough to study his work. Mr. Merrill was an authentic artist. He loved art, he loved the beauty of Nature, he loved Alaska. All these things are evident to those who have so long admired his pictures." The paper did not mention Merrill's exquisite photographs of Alaska's Indigenous people.

In December 1929 Elizabeth Barron, who had inherited Merrill's collection of glass negatives and was the administrator of his estate, petitioned the court to sell his six cameras and enlarger—as well as other photographic equipment, his boat, and his shotgun—in order to pay his outstanding debts and to cover the costs of administering the estate. In May 1930 Frances Redman petitioned to allow her mother to have prints made from Merrill's negatives and to sell them and any other negatives she wished. It is not known whether Elizabeth did make any prints or how many she might have sold (Gmelch 1995: 170).

After Elizabeth's death in 1933, Frances became the executor of the Merrill estate and inherited the negatives. They ended up in the hands of Ernest E. Jacobson, who in 1962 sold them to the Sitka National Historical Park (SNHP). In 1969 the SNHP purchased 203 additional glass negatives by Merrill from Peter Nielsen, a local Tlingit resident. (We do not know how he came to possess them.) That collection was labeled "the Original SNHP Collection" (SITK-00079). Nine years later the SNHP and Alaska State Historical Library commissioned the creation of two copies of the negatives of the Nielsen collection in 4 × 5-inch format, with one set deposited at the park and another in Juneau at the State Library. In 2002 that collection was digitized and made available to the public for educational and research purposes. In 2007 Sheldon Jackson College requested that the SNHP provide museum storage for its own collection of 961 glass negatives by Merrill. The college closed down later that year because of cash-flow problems. In 2015 the trustees of the college signed a resolution officially transferring its collection of Merrill negatives to the Merrill Project, Inc., an entity created explicitly to take over legal ownership of the negatives once the college ceased to exist. The former Sheldon Jackson College collection was labeled SITK-00598. Later that year the SITK-00598 collection was officially transferred to the SNHP, and the park's staff completed an inventory of this collection, which was renamed SITK-00687. Also in 2015, photography conservators conducted an item-level condition survey and digitized all plates from SITK-00079 and SITK-00687. A year later, as part of the celebration of the centennial of the National Park Service, SNHP completed the task of digitizing all of the 1,100 images from the two Merrill collections. (Over the years, a handful of negatives have been lost to breakage or theft.) The Alaska State Library owns a few Merrill photographs that I was unable to locate in the SNHP collection, and so does the Sitka Historical Society. A few of Merrill's prints can also be found in the collections of the Isabella Miller Museum in Sitka, operated by the Sitka Historical Society; the Tongass Historical Society; the Smithsonian Institution; the Special Collections unit of the University of Washington library; the Bancroft Library of the University of California, Berkeley; the Mystic Seaport Museum in Connecticut; the University of Pennsylvania Museum; and the Anchorage Museum of History and Art (Gmelch 1995: 170). I have reproduced a few of them here. In addition, a handful of the Merrill images in this book—most of them portraits—come from private individuals and families. Some were shared with me by the owners, while others were found in the archive of the Sealaska Heritage Institute.

Three years after Merrill's death, the local American Legion post sponsored a public subscription and commissioned a Seattle artist to cast a bronze plaque bearing Merrill's portrait and the following inscription: "Elbridge W. Merrill, who dedicated his life and artistic attainments toward picturing the scenic beauties surrounding Sitka Alaska, 1930" (fig. 19). Mounted on a large boulder, this plaque sits on small promontory overlooking Sitka Bay and the surrounding

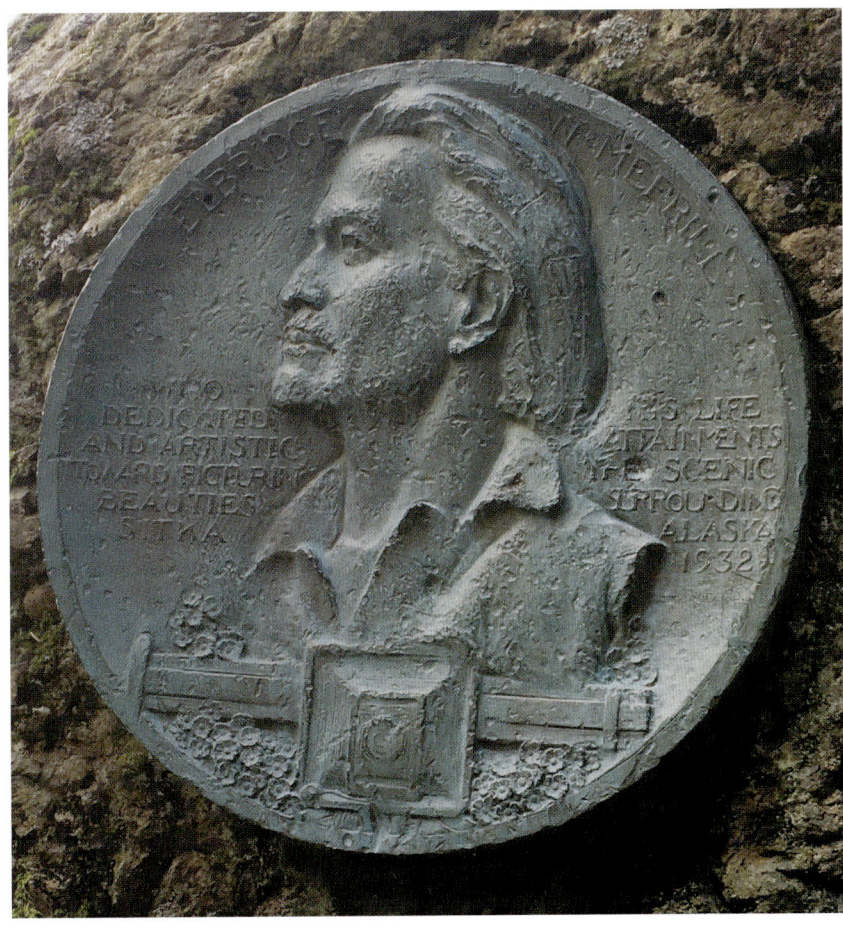

FIGURE 19. Sergei Kan. Plaque commemorating Merrill near the Sitka National Historical Park, 2021.

mountains. It is a fitting memorial to a talented man who left behind an invaluable collection of high-quality photographs of the local scenery and, most importantly, of its Tlingit, Creole, and Euro-American inhabitants.

NOTES

1. Some sources list the year of Merrill's birth as 1868. Some of the information on the early years of Merrill's life comes from the work of Sharon B. Gmelch (1995, 2008). Zollo et al. (1989) contains additional information on this subject.

2. All the Merrill photographs listed under the SITK designation are located in the Sitka National Historical Park. Photographs from the Alaska State Historical Library bear the designation ASL.

3. Gmelch (2008: 139) features a photograph of Merrill relaxing on a beach with a Tlingit boy and a Tlingit woman. The picture might have been taken by a Tlingit photographer Merrill had taught.

4. The word *clootch* comes from the Chinook jargon of the Northwest Coast and is akin to the word *squaw*. Used to refer to the local Indigenous women, it was somewhat derogatory at the time and is definitely considered offensive today.

5. Merrill was not the only photographer at that famous 1904 Sitka potlatch. Case and Draper also produced several images of the participants, dressed in spectacular costumes (see, for example, ASL-P39-0123 and ASL-P39-0786). However, they created far fewer images, and their quality is inferior to that of Merrill's photographs.

6. *Creoles* was a term introduced by the Russian-American Company in the eighteenth century to refer to the persons of mixed Russian and Alaska Native descent. During the Russian colonial era, the Creoles constituted a separate estate. They were educated in Russian schools and then worked for the Russian-American Company in various capacities (see Kan 2013). In Sitka, most of the Creoles were of Russian-

Alutiiq or Russian-Aleut (Unangan) descent. Their descendants remained after Alaska was "transferred" by Russia to the United States.
During Merrill's time, they were usually referred to as "the Russians."
A few of the local Creoles had a combination of Russian and Tlingit
ancestry.

Photographs by
Elbridge W. Merrill

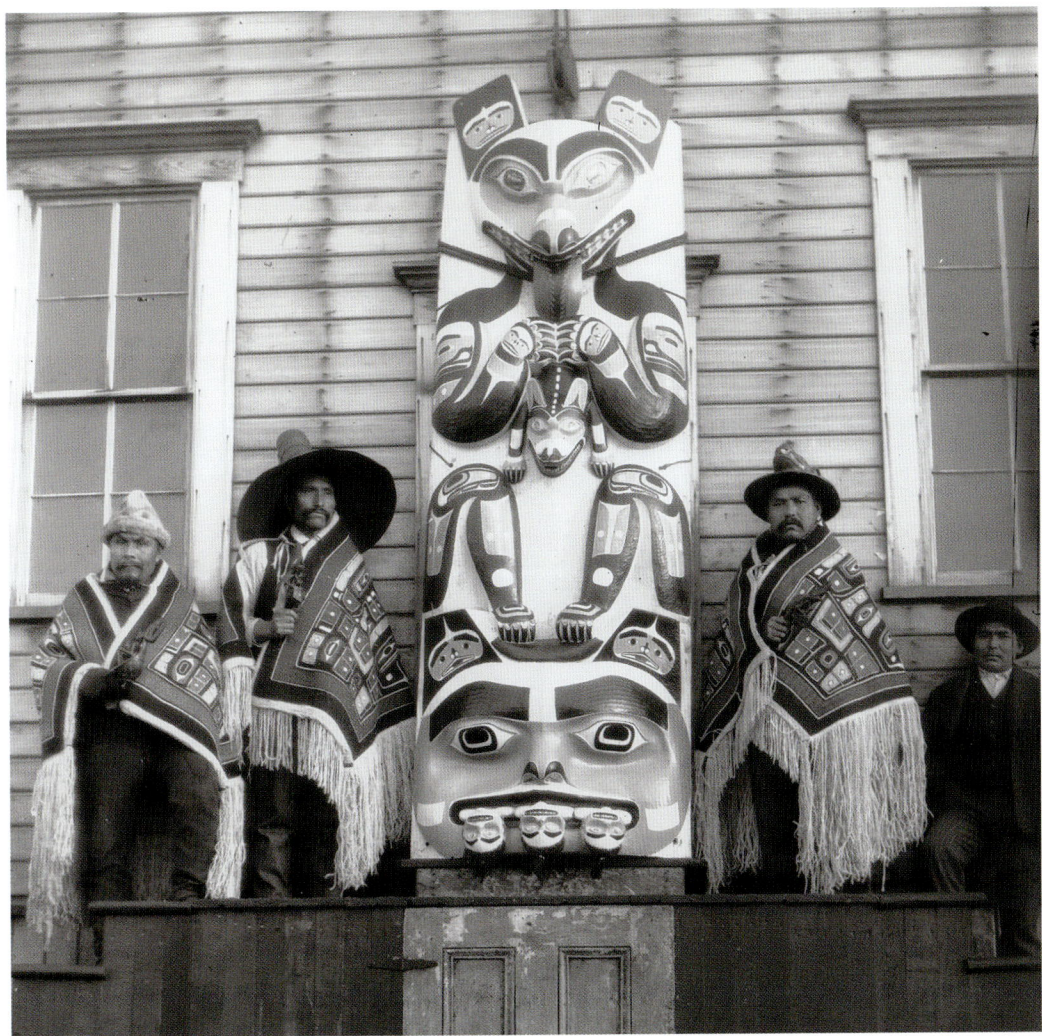

PLATE 1. Key sponsors of the potlatch (ḵu.éex') hosted by the Wolf House (G̱ooch Hít) of the Kaag-waantaan clan, beside the Panting Wolf house post (Kaawashag̱i G̱ooch Hít) of the Wolf House. Left to right: Shkeinch (Kaaxwaatli), Eagle's Nest House (Ch'áak' Kúdi Hít); Jacob Yarkon (Yakwaan, Xeitxut'ch, Stoowuḵáa) (d. 1918), Wolf House; Paddy Parker (Wooshkeenaa, Yaanaxnahoo) (d. 1906), Wolf House; David Konkedaa(?) (b. 1866). Identifications by Harold Jacobs, 2021. See also Swanton 1908: 406. Courtesy of the National Park Service, Sitka National Historical Park, 03765.

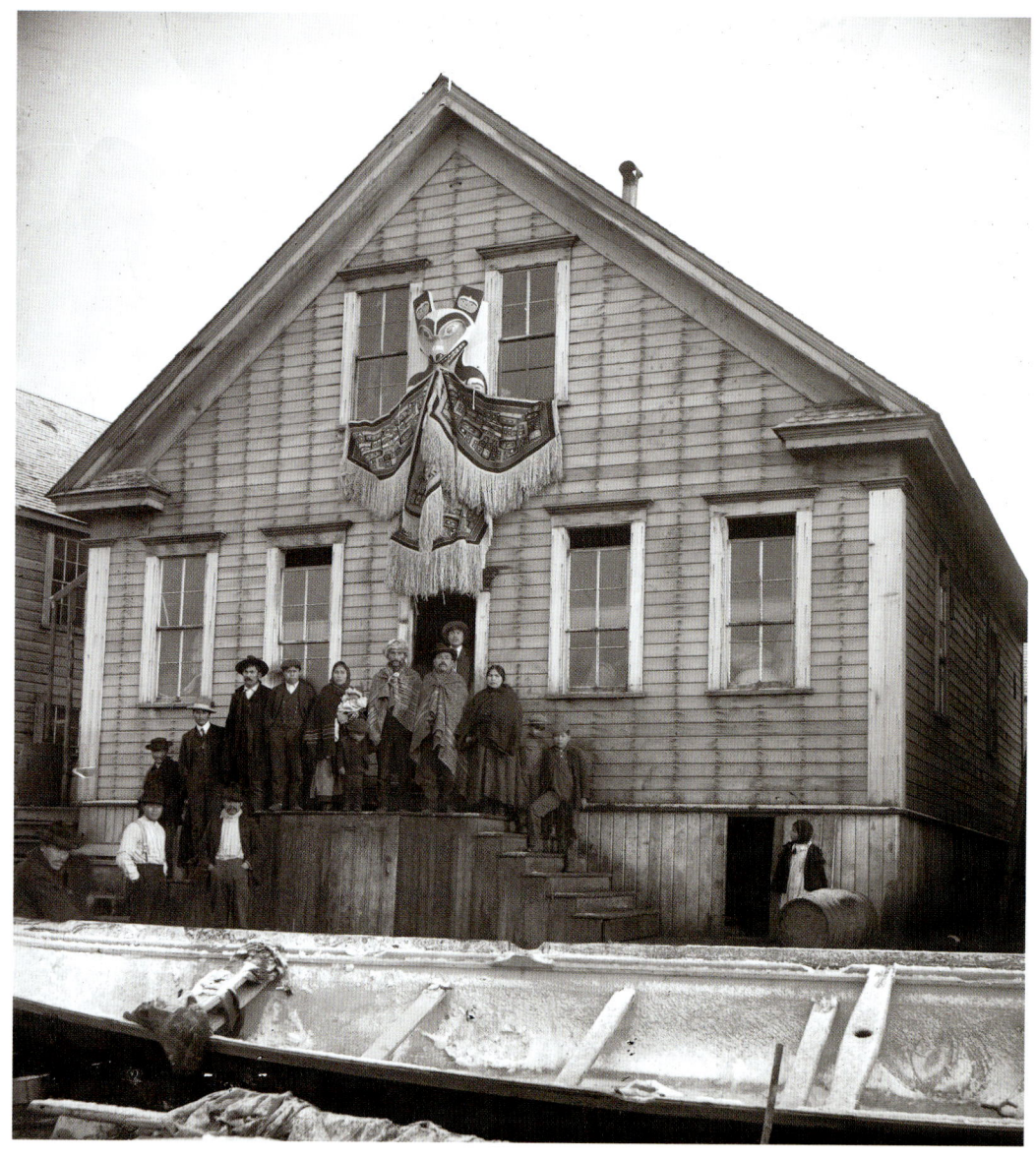

PLATE 2. Hosts of the 1904 ḵu.éex' and their families in front of Wolf House (Ḡooch Hít). Three Chilkat blankets are attached to the Panting Wolf post (Ḵaawashaḡi Ḡooch Hít). Courtesy of the National Park Service, Sitka National Historical Park, 25428.

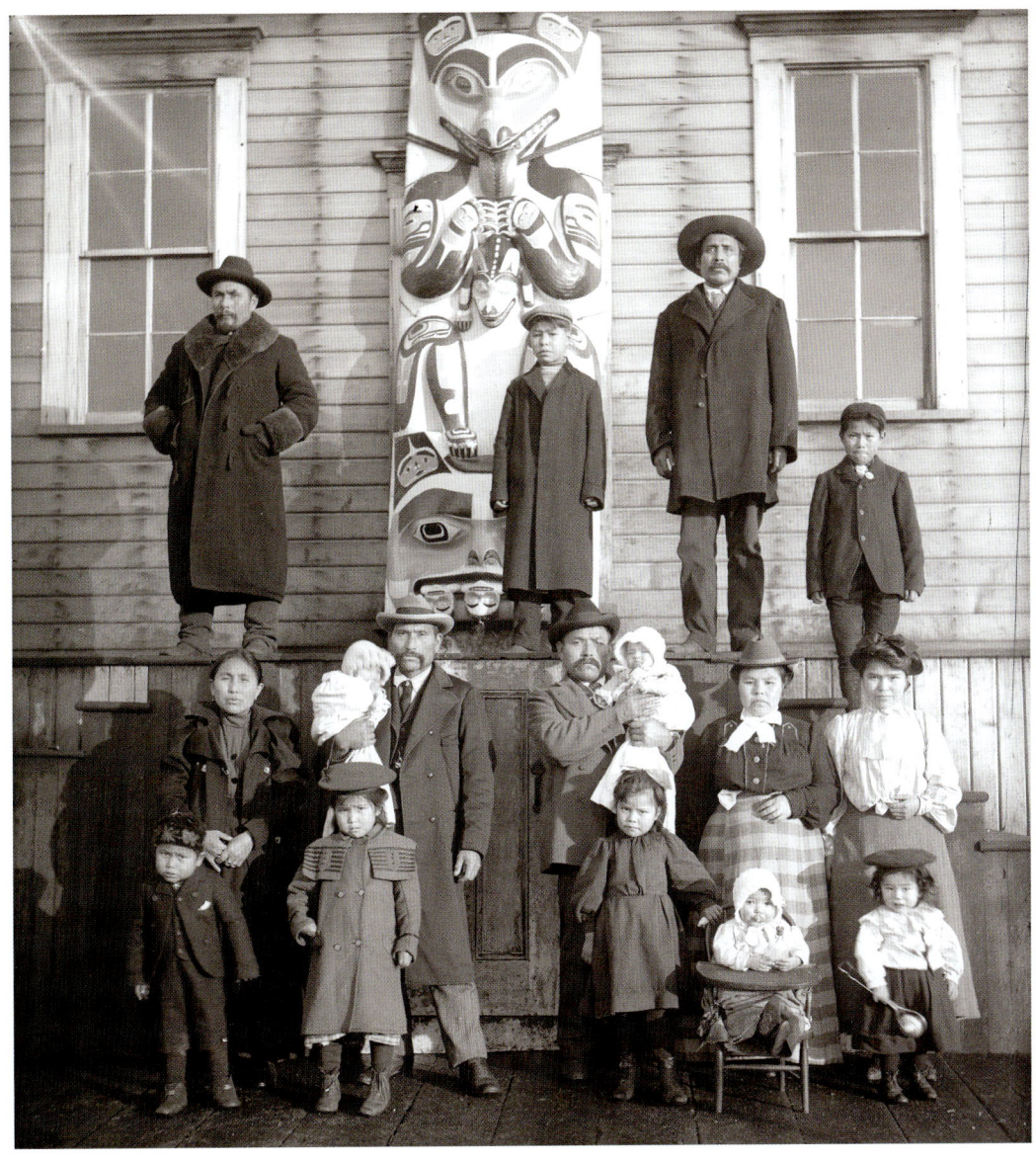

PLATE 3. Kaagwaantaan clan leaders (sponsors of the 1904 ḵu.éex') and their families in front of the Panting Wolf post (Kaawashagi Ḡooch Hít) of the Wolf House (Ḡooch Hít). Center front, holding babies, are Jacob Yarkon (Yakwaan, Xeitxut'ch, Stoowuḵáa) and Paddy Parker (Wooshkeenaa, Yaanaxnahoo) (d. 1906). The man to the left of the pole is Kaaxwaatli or Shkeinch, Eagle's Nest House (Ch'áak' Kúdi Hít). Courtesy of the National Park Service, Sitka National Historical Park, 25429.

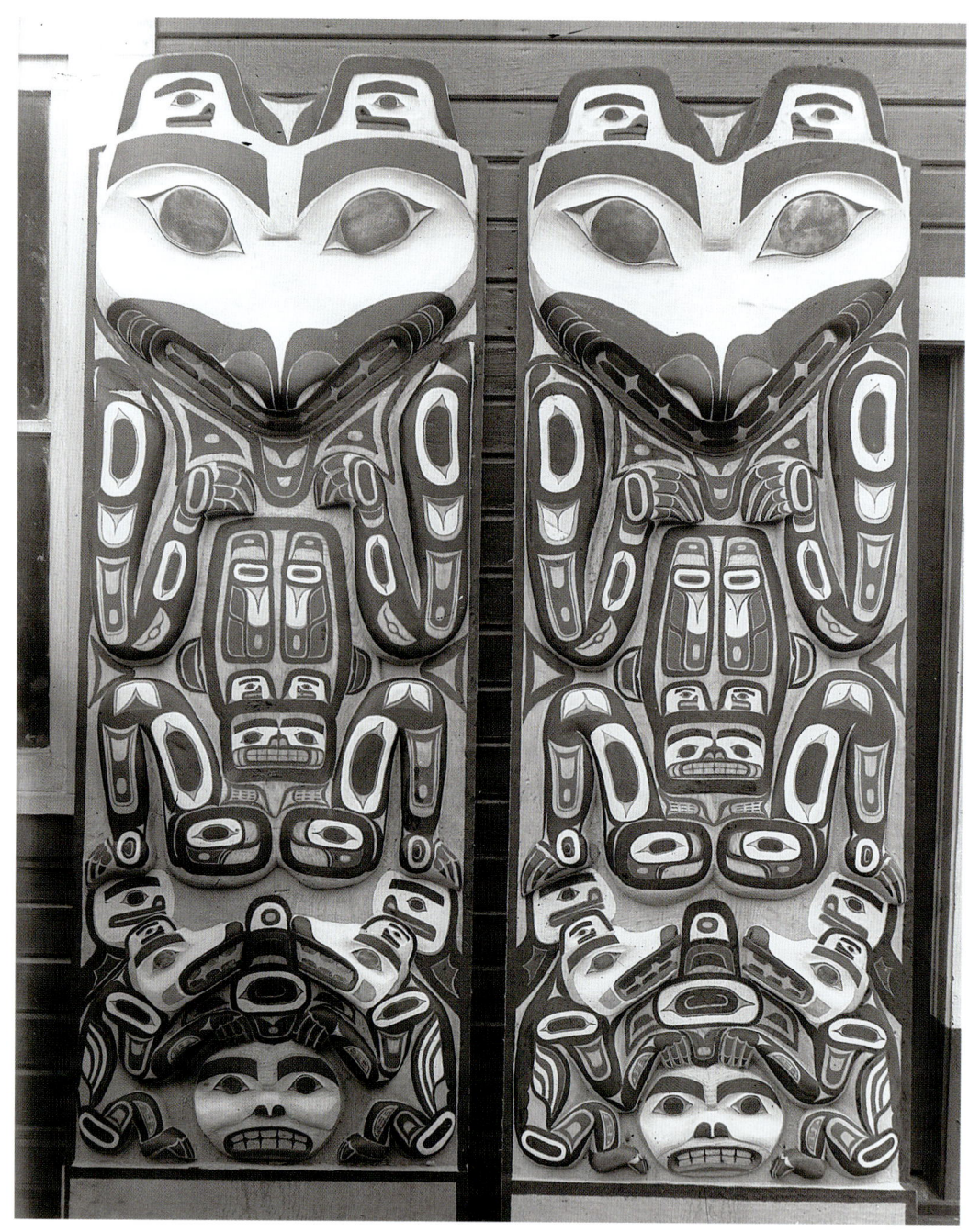

PLATE 4. Two Multiplying Wolf (Wudzix̱eedi G̱ooch) posts from the house of Annahootz, currently on loan to the Sitka National Historical Park. Courtesy of the National Park Service, Sitka National Historical Park, 03832.

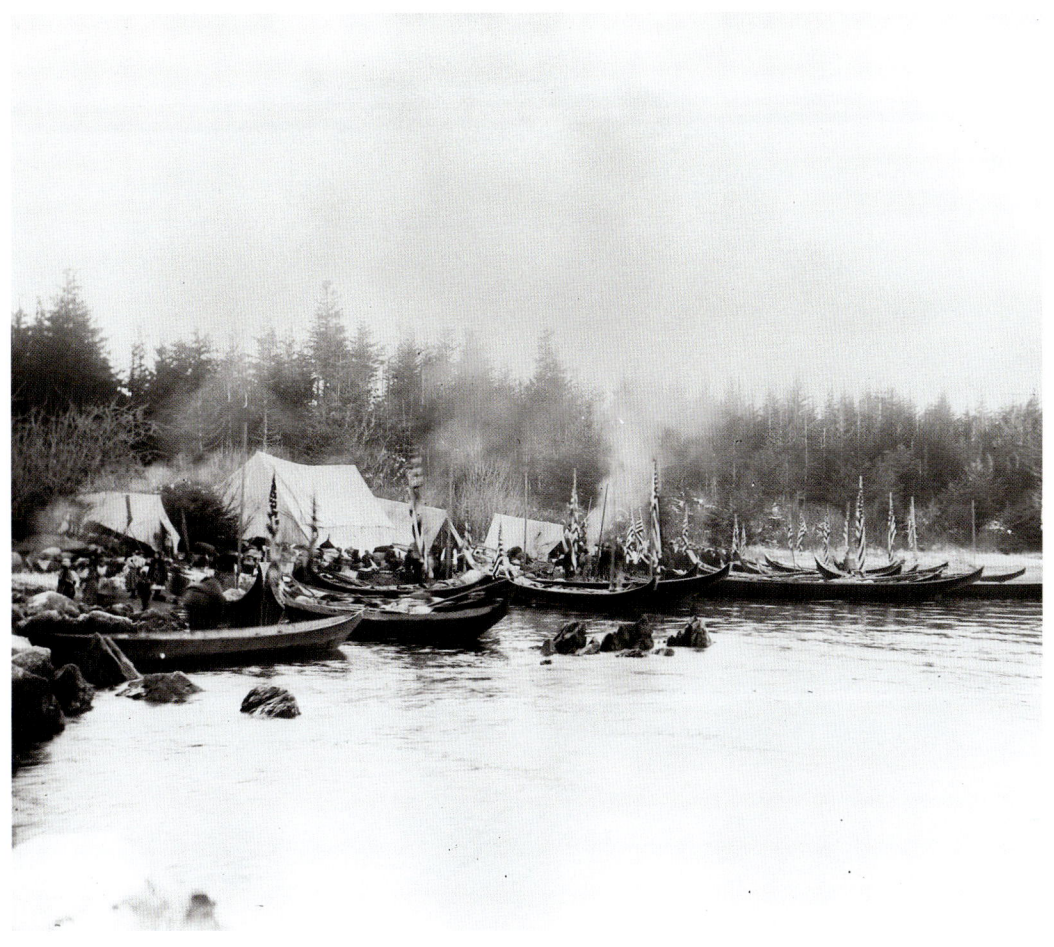

PLATE 5. Guests of the 1904 ḵu.éex' camping outside Sitka on their way there. Courtesy of the National Park Service, Sitka National Historical Park, 03761.

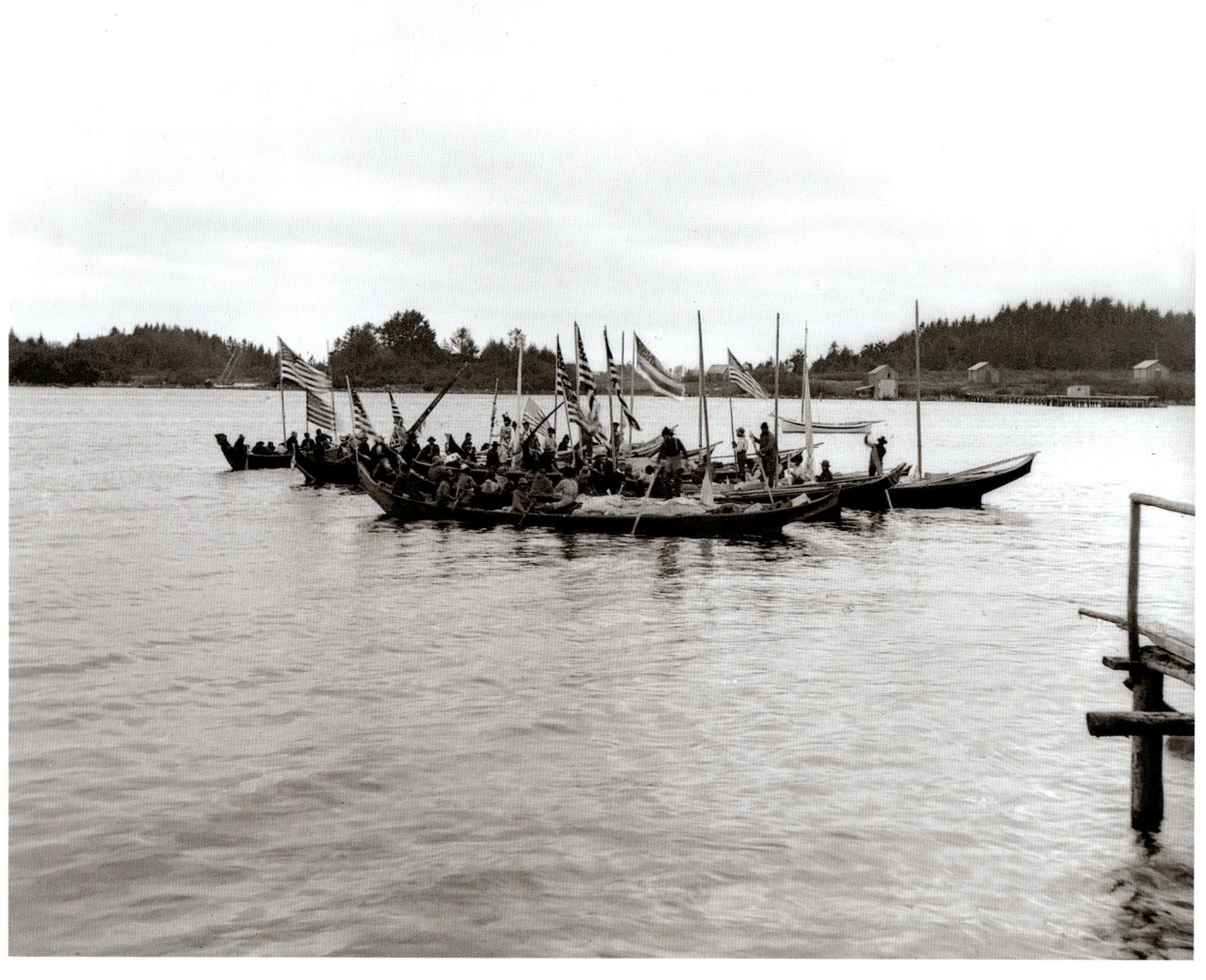

PLATE 6. Guests approaching the Sitka Indian Village for the 1904 ḵu.éex'. Most of the canoes are flying the US flag, thus appropriating the powerful symbol ("crest") of the dominant society. Courtesy of the National Park Service, Sitka National Historical Park, 03763.

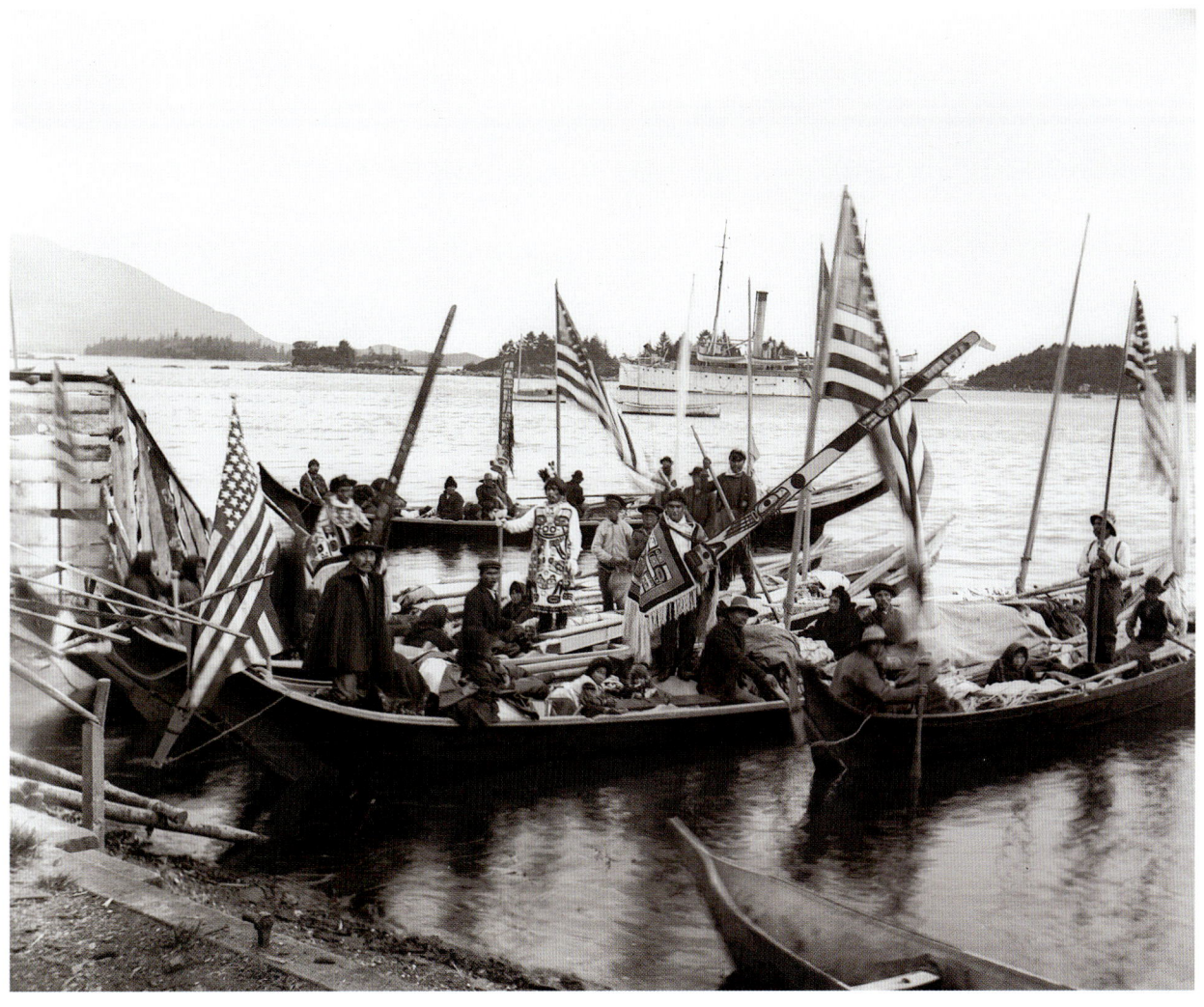

PLATE 7. Guests arriving on the beach of the Sitka Indian Village for the 1904 ḵu.éex'. A US Navy ship is in the background. Courtesy of the National Park Service, Sitka National Historical Park, 3762.

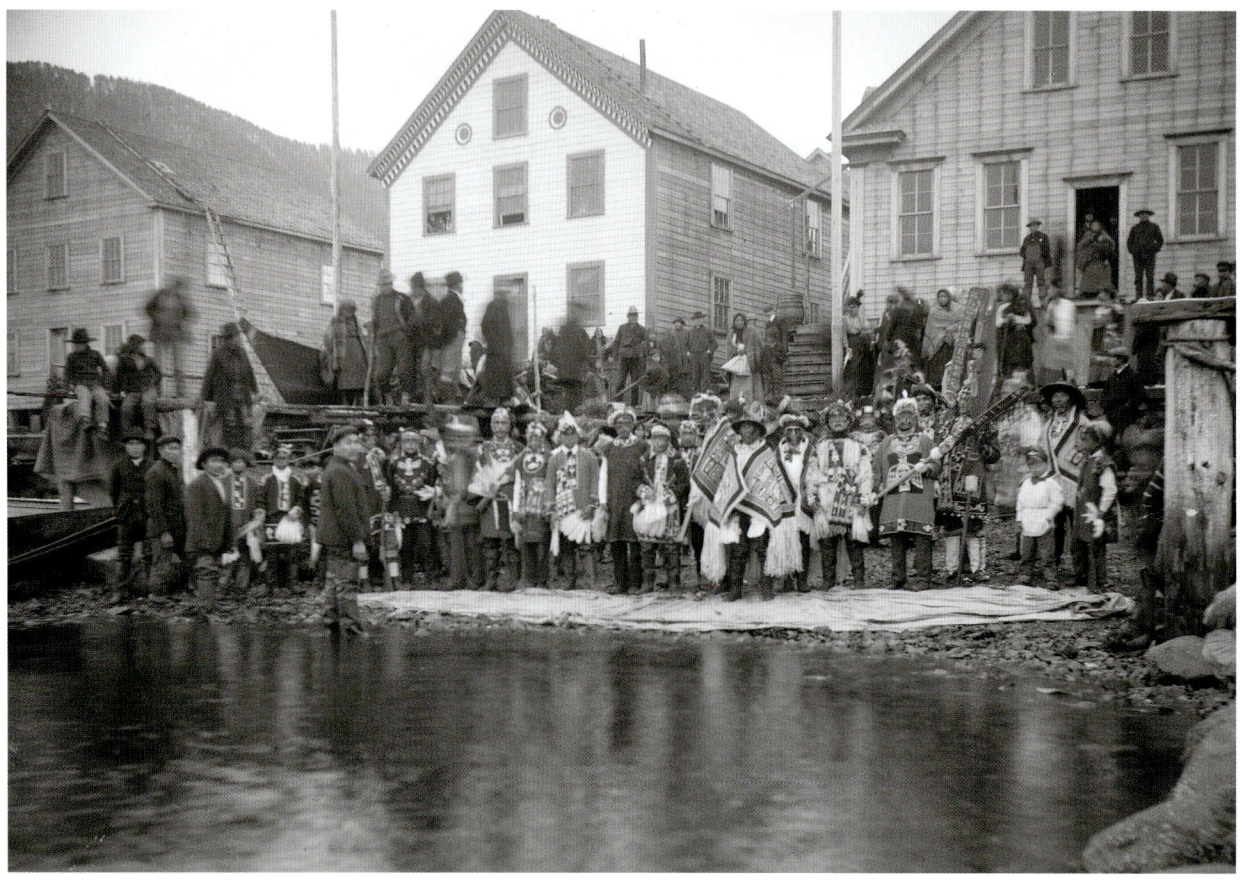

PLATE 8. A group of Sitkans, most of them of the Ľuknax̱.ádi clan, on the beach in front of the Sitka Indian Village, greeting guests arriving from Angoon. Harold Jacobs (personal communication, 2021) suggests that a preliminary Ľuknax̱.ádi ḵu.éex' might have preceded the big Kaagwaantaan ceremony. Courtesy of the National Park Service, Sitka National Historical Park, 03767.

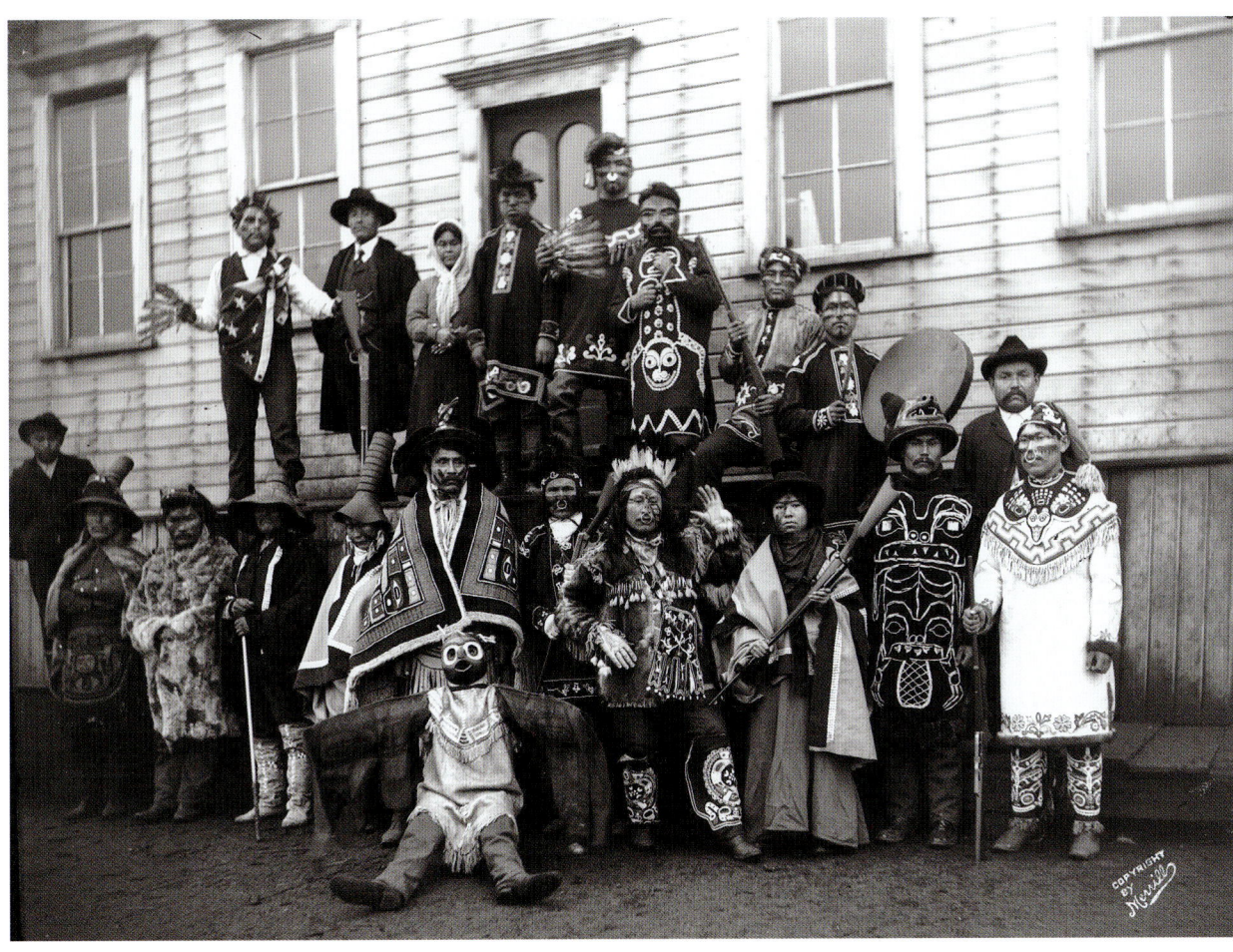

PLATE 9. Guests of the 1904 ḵu.éex', most of them from the village of Klukwan, in front of the Wolf House (Ḡooch Hít).

The man sitting on the ground in front of the front row is wearing an Owl mask. Front row, first on the left, is Gushtlein (K'eich), Frog House (Xixch'i Hít), Ḡaanaxteidí clan of Klukwan, wearing a Frog hat and a Beaver apron. The fourth man from the left is wearing a Whale hat with rings. On his left, wearing a Chilkat blanket and a Raven headdress, is George Shotridge (Yeilgooxú) (b. 1852), hereditary head of the Whale House (Yáay Hít) of the Ḡaanaxteidí clan and the father of Louis Shotridge. The second man from the right in the front row is wearing a Sun Dog hat and a Beaver tunic.

Second row, first on the right, is Paddy Parker (Wooshkeenaa, Yaanaxnahoo), one of the chief hosts of the Kaagwaantaan ḵu.éex', whose father was of the Ḡaanaxteidí clan. Fourth from the right is a man wearing a Frog tunic and a mask.

Identifications by Harold Jacobs, 2021. Courtesy of the National Park Service, Sitka National Historical Park, 3769.

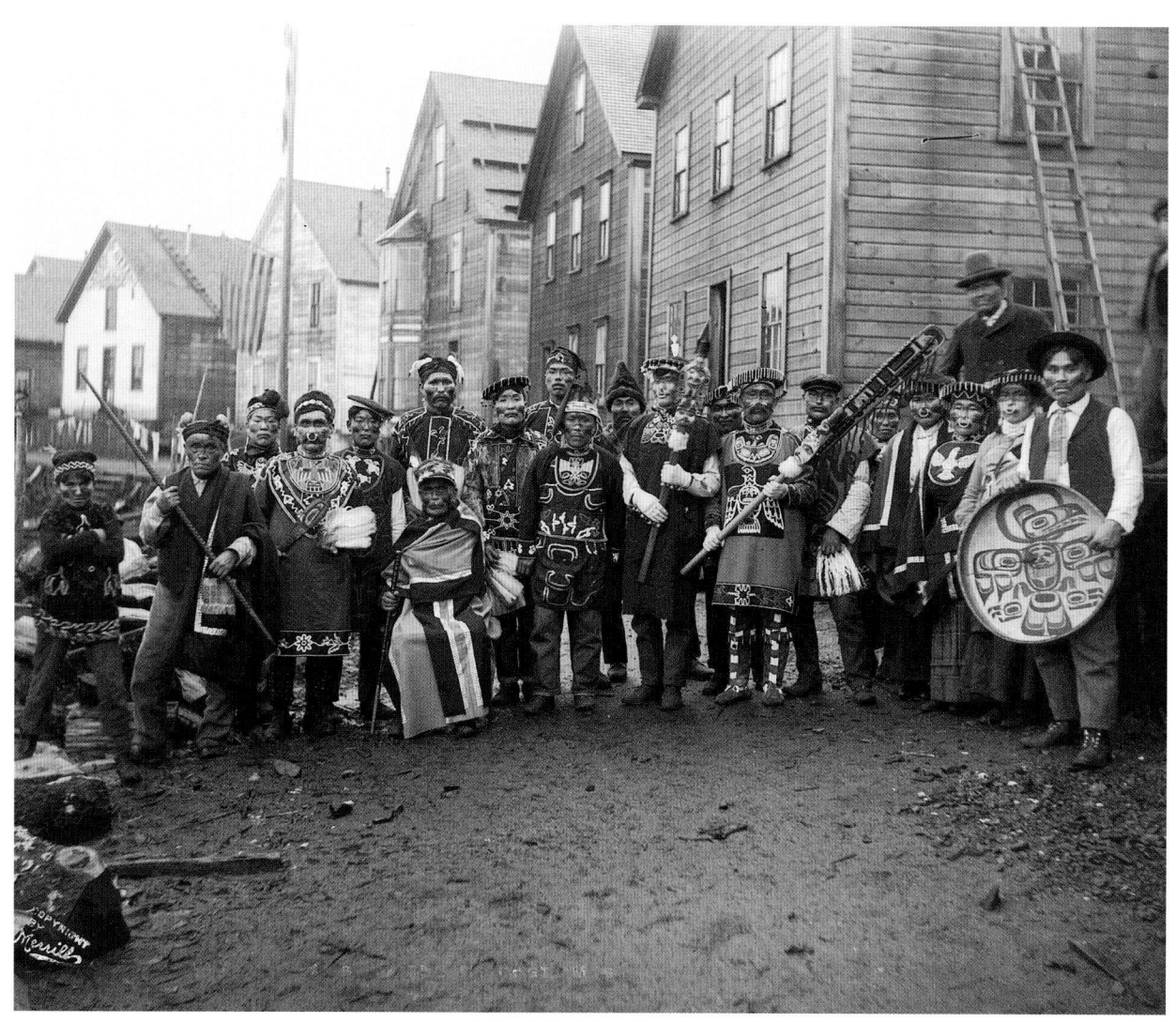

PLATE 10. Several Sitkans and a number of guests from Yakutat, many of them belonging to the Ḻuknax̱.ádi clan, on the Sitka Indian Village front street, December 9, 1904. They are attending a ḵu.éex' hosted by the Teiḵweidí. One of the houses behind them is flying a US flag.

Front row, left to right: Jack Ellis (Ḵaajaaḵw) (1892–1952), Ḻuknax̱.ádi clan of Yakutat; Sitka Jack (Katseix̱, Ldax̱éen), Whale House (Yáay Hít), Ḻuknax̱.ádi clan of Sitka, carrying a Devilfish cane; Jim Blaine (Naats' Kéek') (1885–1952), Ḻuknax̱.ádi clan, wearing a Raven bib; T. G. Henry (Duksa. áat'), Frog House (Xixch'i Hít), Ḻuknax̱.ádi clan, wearing a nose ring; John Smith (Yandás.éesh) (ca. 1886–ca. 1931), Whale House (Yáay Hít), head of the Ḻuknax̱.ádi clan of Sitka and brother of Sitka Jack, sitting and holding a cane; Ned James (Staagwáan), Frog House, Ḻuknax̱.ádi clan; Charlie White (Yaaneeḵee) (1882–1964), Whale House (Yáay Hít), Ḻuknax̱.ádi clan; a man of the Ḻuknax̱.ádi clan; Paul Henry (Kawóotk'), Frog House, Ḻuknax̱.ádi clan, wearing a bib with a double bird upside down; Howard Daanax̱.ils'eiḵ, holding a song leader's pole; Sitka Charlie (X'aasooká) (1865–1948), Whale House (Yáay Hít), Ḻuknax̱.ádi clan, holding a song leader's paddle; two unidentified men; Mrs. Sitka Ned (Achkwéi) (d. 1926), Kwaashk'iḵwáan clan of Yakutat; Mrs. Joseph Abraham (Emma Suwanee, Ḵaatootwu.oo) (1867–

1950), Ḻuknax̱.ádi, wearing a Raven bib; Moses Teet Milton (Deitx̱óon, Ḵ'a.oo) (1878–1920), Teiḵweidí clan of Yakutat, holding a drum depicting Raven. Behind the women are Situk Harry (Ḵ'ax̱oo Éesh?), Teiḵweidí clan, host of this ḵu.éex', wearing ordinary clothes; Fanny Bremner (Skwan) (1889–1934), wife of Moses Teet Milton, Kwaashk'iḵwáan clan of Yakutat.

Houses in the background, from left to right: an unidentified house; Eagle's Nest House (Ch'áak' Kúdi Hít) of the Kaagwaantaan clan (with an Eagle painted on the front); Outwards House (Daginaa Hít, also known as Out in the Ocean Salmon Box House) and Sleep House (Ta Hít) of the Ḻuknax̱.ádi clan; Burnt Timbers House (Kaawagaani Hít) of the Kaagwaantaan clan; and Sea Lion House (Taan Hít) of the Ḻuknax̱.ádi clan.

Identifications of individuals by Minnie John, recorded by Frederica de Laguna in the late 1940s (1972: 1136–37), Devlin Anderstrom of the Sealaska Heritage Institute, 2023, and Harold Jacobs, 2021, 2024.

Identification of the houses by Harold Jacobs, 2021. Courtesy of the National Park Service, Sitka National Historical Park, 03770.

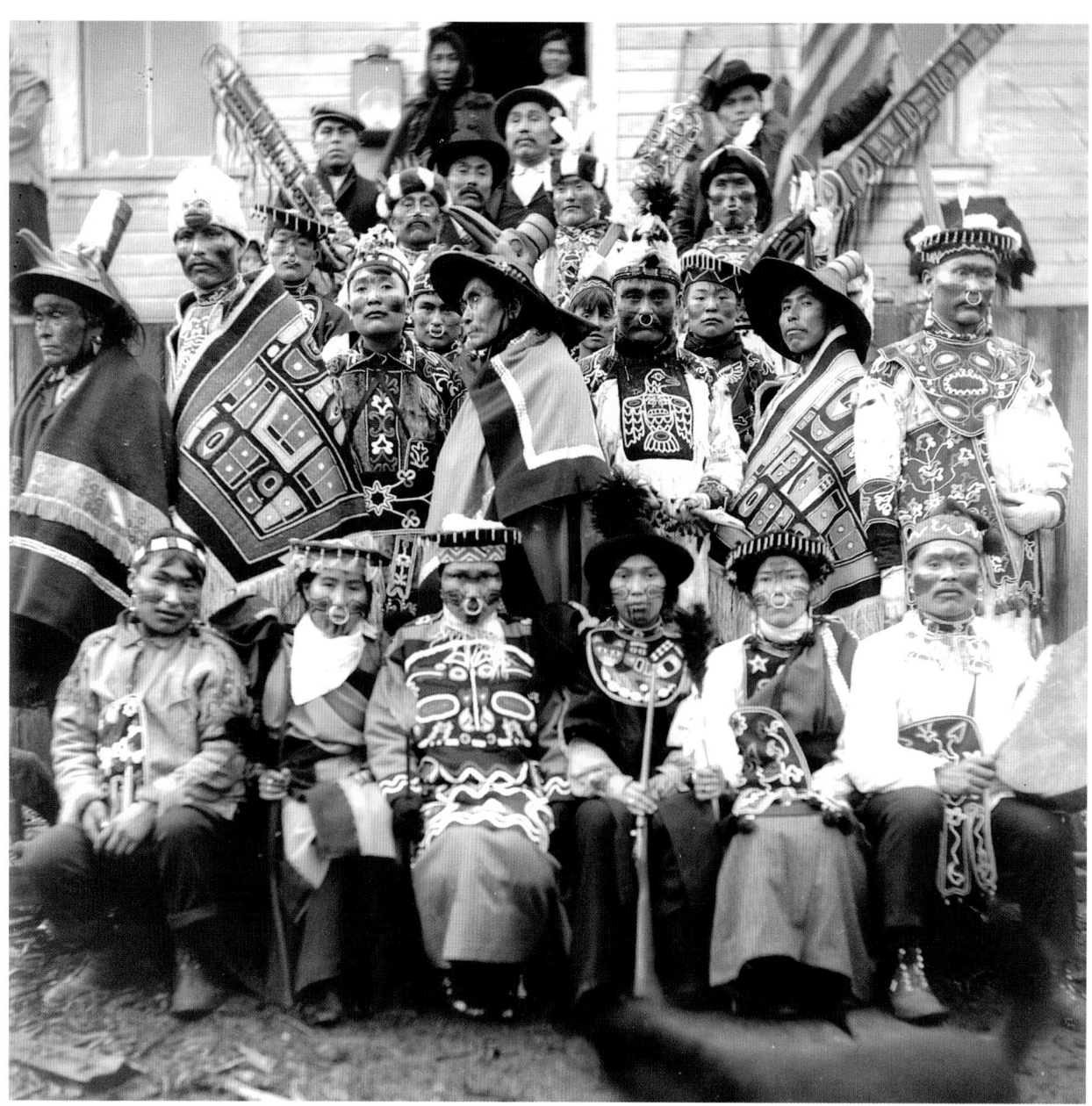

PLATE 11. Hosts and Yakutat guests at the Sitka ḵu.éex' of December 9, 1904.

Front row, left to right: Jack Reed (Kaakeindaḵín, Shkoowuyéil) (1880–1953), Ĺuknax̱.ádi clan; unidentified young woman; Jennie Kardetoo (Tlei.aan) (1872–1951), Kwaashk'iḵwáan clan of Yakutat, wearing a Raven shirt; Kitty (Xéel'i), Ĺuknax̱.ádi clan of Yakutat, wearing a bib with a Whale and a man's hat, holding a gun; Fanny Bremner (Kuwóox̱', Daax̱taan) (1889–1934), wife of Moses Teet Milton, Ḵwáashk'iḵwáan clan of Yakutat; Moses Teet Milton (Deitxóon, Ḵ'a.oo) (1878–1920), Teiḵweidí clan of Yakutat.

Middle row, left to right: Sitka Jack (Katseix̱, Ldax̱éen), Whale House (Yáay Hít), Ĺuknax̱.ádi clan of Sitka, wearing a Raven hat; Ned James (Sdaagwáan) (ca. 1860–1921), Ĺuknax̱.ádi clan of Sitka, wearing a shaman's white feather headdress with a small mask on the front; young man wearing a nose ring; Charlie White (Yaaneeḵee) (1882–1964), Ĺuknax̱.ádi clan; Ḵexix̱ (1865–1948), head of the Sitka Whale House (Yáay Hít) of the Ĺuknax̱.ádi clan and a brother of Sitka Jack, in profile, wearing a Raven hat and glasses; Billy Jack, wearing a Raven bib and a nose ring; James Willard (Deix̱.udu.oo), Sea Lion House (Taan Hít), Ĺuknax̱.ádi clan of Sitka, wearing a Chilkat blanket and a hat with three rings; Tashaa, brother of George Dick, wearing a Raven bib.

Back row: standing to the left of the American flag is Ḵ'ax̱oo Éesh(?); in front of and to the left of the US flag, holding a long Raven pole and wearing a nose ring, is T. G. Henry (Duksa.áat'), Ĺuknax̱.adí clan of Sitka. Behind and to the right of Ḵexix̱ is George Dick (Donnaisht?), Sea Lion House (Taan Hít), Ĺuknax̱.adí clan, holding a Raven pole and wearing a striped fur hat.

Tentative identifications by De Laguna's Yakutat consultants in the late 1940s to early 1950s (De Laguna 1972: 1138–39). Additional identifications by Harold Jacobs, 2021, 2024. Courtesy of the National Park Service, Sitka National Historical Park, 03779.

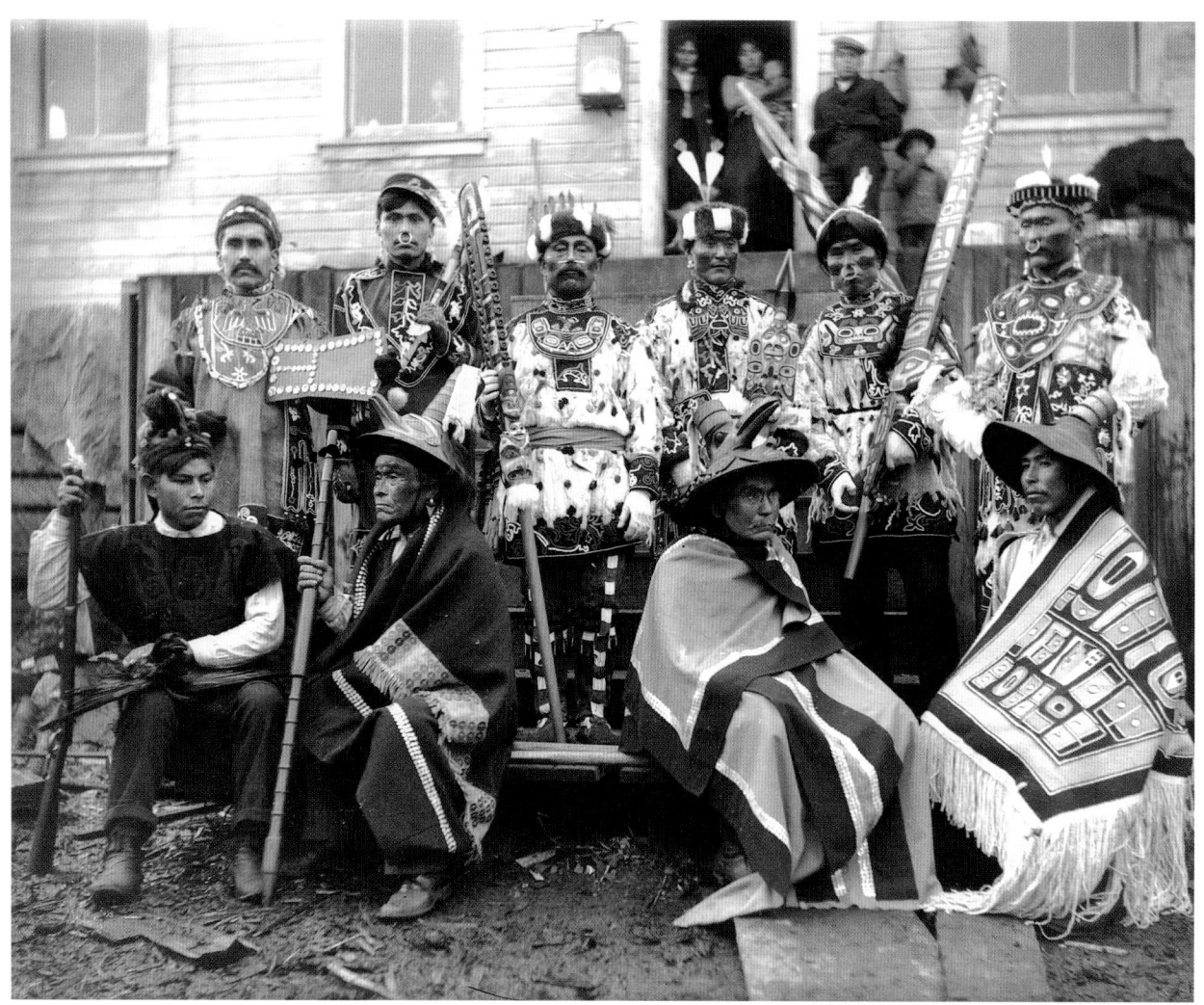

PLATE 12. Sitka and Yakutat Ĺuknax̱.ádi clan guests at the Kaagwaantaan clan ḵu.éex'.

Front row, second from left: Sitka Jack (Katseix̱, Ldax̱éen), Whale House (Yáay Hít), Ĺuknax̱.ádi clan of Sitka, holding a staff; third from left: Ḵex̱ix̱, head of the Sitka Whale House of the Ĺuknax̱.ádi clan, wearing a Raven hat and glasses; fourth from left, James Willard (Deix̱.udu.oo), Sea Lion House (Taan Hít), Ĺuknax̱.ádi clan of Sitka, wearing a Chilkat blanket and a hat with three rings.

Back row, third from left: Sitka Charlie (X'aasooká), Whale House (Yáay Hít), Ĺuknax̱.ádi clan of Sitka; fourth from left: possibly George Dick (Daanáak'w Éesh); fifth from left: T. G. Henry (Duksaat), Ĺuknax̱.ádi clan of Sitka, holding a long Raven pole. Sitka National Historical Park, 3778.

Identifications by De Laguna's Yakutat consultants in the late 1940s–early 1950s (see De Laguna 1972: 1134–37). Courtesy of the National Park Service, Sitka National Historical Park, 03778.

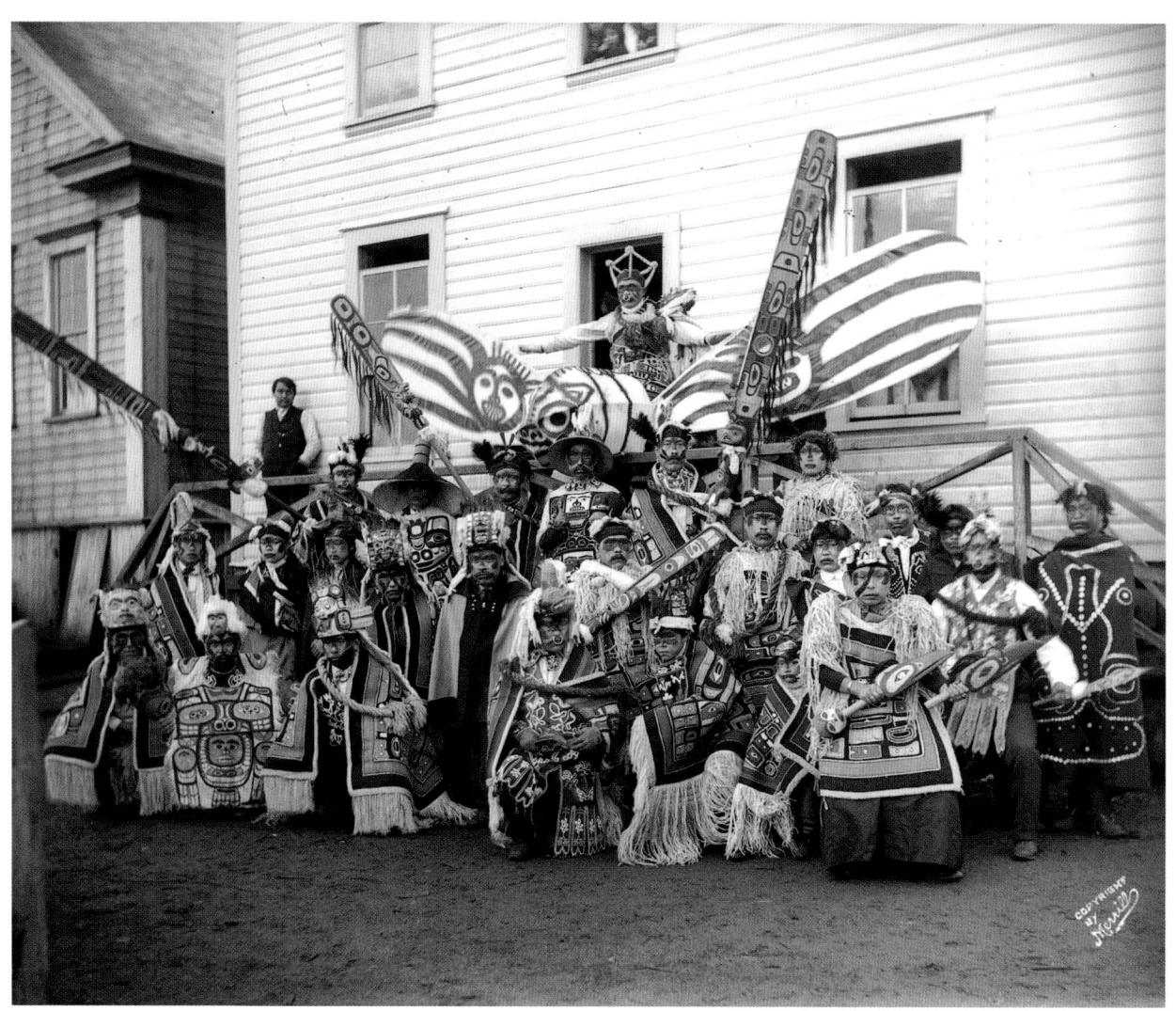

PLATE 13. Guests from Angoon at the 1904 Kaagwaantaan k̲u.éex' in front of the Wolf House (G̲ooch Hít) of the Kaagwaantaan clan. Most are from the Deisheetaan clan of Angoon. Behind the group is a giant dragonfly. When moved it was supported by three people, one under the body and one under each wing.

First row, left to right: unidentified man; George Johnson (Kashaxaaw), Raven House (Yéil Hít), Deisheetaan clan, wearing a Sleeping Man headdress; Kaatéenaa, Arch House (Kaak̲áak'w Hít) of the Basket Bay subdivision of the Deisheetaan clan, wearing a Dragonfly shirt; Jimmy Hanson (Kwaal Éesh), Steel House (Shdeen Hít), Deisheetaan clan, wearing a Dragonfly headdress; Little Jack (Woolshook), Freshwater Spring House (Goon Hít), Deisheetaan clan, wearing a Bear hat; Andrew Dick (K̲aakájee) (1877–1940), Arch House (Kaak̲áak'w Hít) of the Basket Bay subdivision of the Deisheetaan clan, holding a dance paddle; Larry Jackson (Keelt') (b. 1898), Killer Whale House (Kéet Hít), Dak̲l'aweidí clan (the child wearing a Chilkat blanket); unidentified child; Annie Jack (Yaxlahaat), Valley House (Shaanáx̲ Hít), Teik̲weidí clan, dressed as a *naa k̲áani* (a person commissioned to take part in a k̲u.éex' who belongs to a clan from the moiety opposite to that of the hosts); John Fred (Kootla.aa) (1872–1926), Fort House (Noow Hít), Wooshkeetaan clan, dressed as a *naa k̲áani*.

Second row, left to right: Tom Phillips (Deiyikt'aa), Strong House (At.uwaxiji Hít), Kiks.ádí clan of Sitka, wearing his grandparents' Beaver hat; unidentified woman; X'aaw (K'aaw), Brown Bear House (X̲óots Hít), Teik̲weidí clan; Samuel John-son (Aayaax) (1889–1976), Raven House (Yéil Hít), Deisheetaan clan, wearing a Hawk headdress; Yéilk', Steel House (Shdeen Hít), Deisheetaan clan, wearing a Raven headdress; Harry Scott (Skein), Dog Salmon House (Teel Hít), L'eeneidí clan.

Back row, left to right: Billy Jones (L.aangooshu) (1865–1967), Raven Bones House (Yéil S'aag̲í Hít), Deisheetaan clan, with a song leader's paddle showing Raven married to Killer Whale; Klillisnoo Jake (Kichnaalx) (ca. 1840s–1908), Steel House (Shdeen Hít), Deisheetaan clan, wearing Sheltered Area under a Tree (At Seiy̲í S'áaxw) headdress and the Multiplying Wolf Chilkat tunic; John Paul Jr. (K̲áa Tlein) (1865–1933), Needlefish House (Tuk̲ká Hít), Deisheetaan clan, with Beaver song leader's paddle; Dick Yetlma (Yeilnaawú), Raven House (Yéil Hít), Deisheetaan clan, wearing a Beaver Chilkat shirt; Jimmie Albert (L'axkéik'w), Freshwater Spring House (Goon Hít), Deisheetaan clan, holding a Bear song leader's paddle; Mary Albert (Shaawat Goox̲), Killer Whale Tooth House (Kéet Oox̲ú Hít), Dak̲l'aweidí clan, dressed as a *naa k̲áani*; Kaaxoo.át'ch, End of the Trail House (Deishú Hít), Deisheetaan clan, wearing Bear's Ears and a Raven shirt; Charlie John (Took'), Standing Sideways House (Tl'aadéin Hít), Deisheetaan clan, wearing a Floating Island robe. The man in the doorway wearing a crown-like headdress is Peter Johnson (Aanx'isx̲áa), Raven's Bones House (Yéil S'aag̲í Hít), Deisheetaan clan.

Identifications by Harold Jacobs, 2021, based on information provided in 1980 by his grandmother Annie (Paul) Jacobs, who attended this k̲u.éex', and by Mary (Thom) John in 1983. Alaska State Historical Library P57-028.

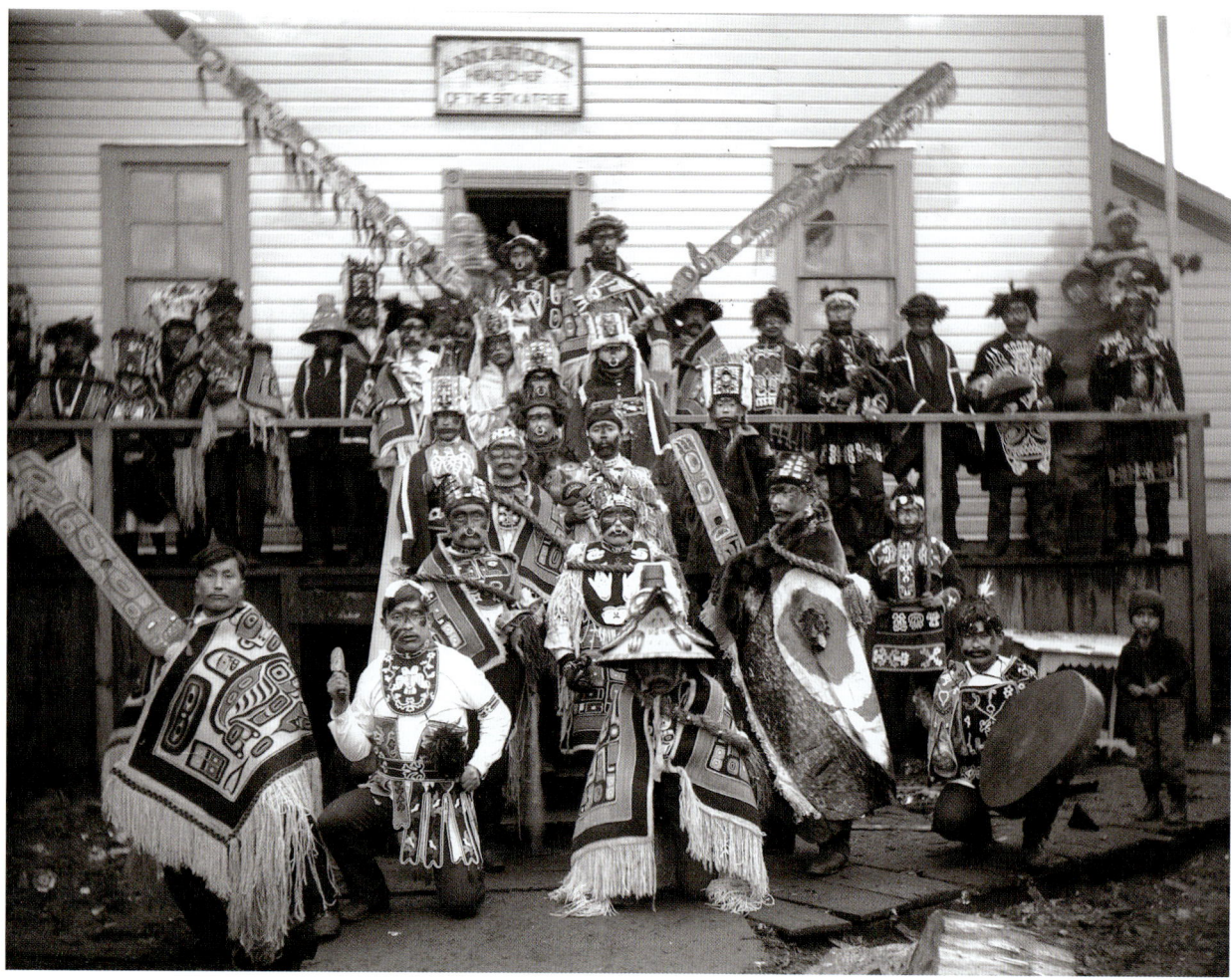

PLATE 14. A group of guests, mostly from Hoonah, in front of the house of James Jackson (Annahootz), head of the Wolf House (G̲ooch Hít), Kaagwaantaan clan.

Front row: First on the left, wearing a Killer Whale blanket and holding a dance paddle, is David Lawrence (1879–1935), Chookaneidí clan of Hoonah. The third man from the left wears a Raven hat of the T'ak̲deintaan clan. The man in the back row on the right-hand side, under and to the right of the dance paddle, wearing a brass hat, is Archie White (Yook̲is'kook̲éik, Tuk̲k̲'ax̲aaw) (ca. 1857–1939), Mount Fairweather House, T'ak̲deintaan clan of Hoonah.

Identifications by Harold Jacobs, 2021. Courtesy of the National Park Service, Sitka National Historical Park, 3773.

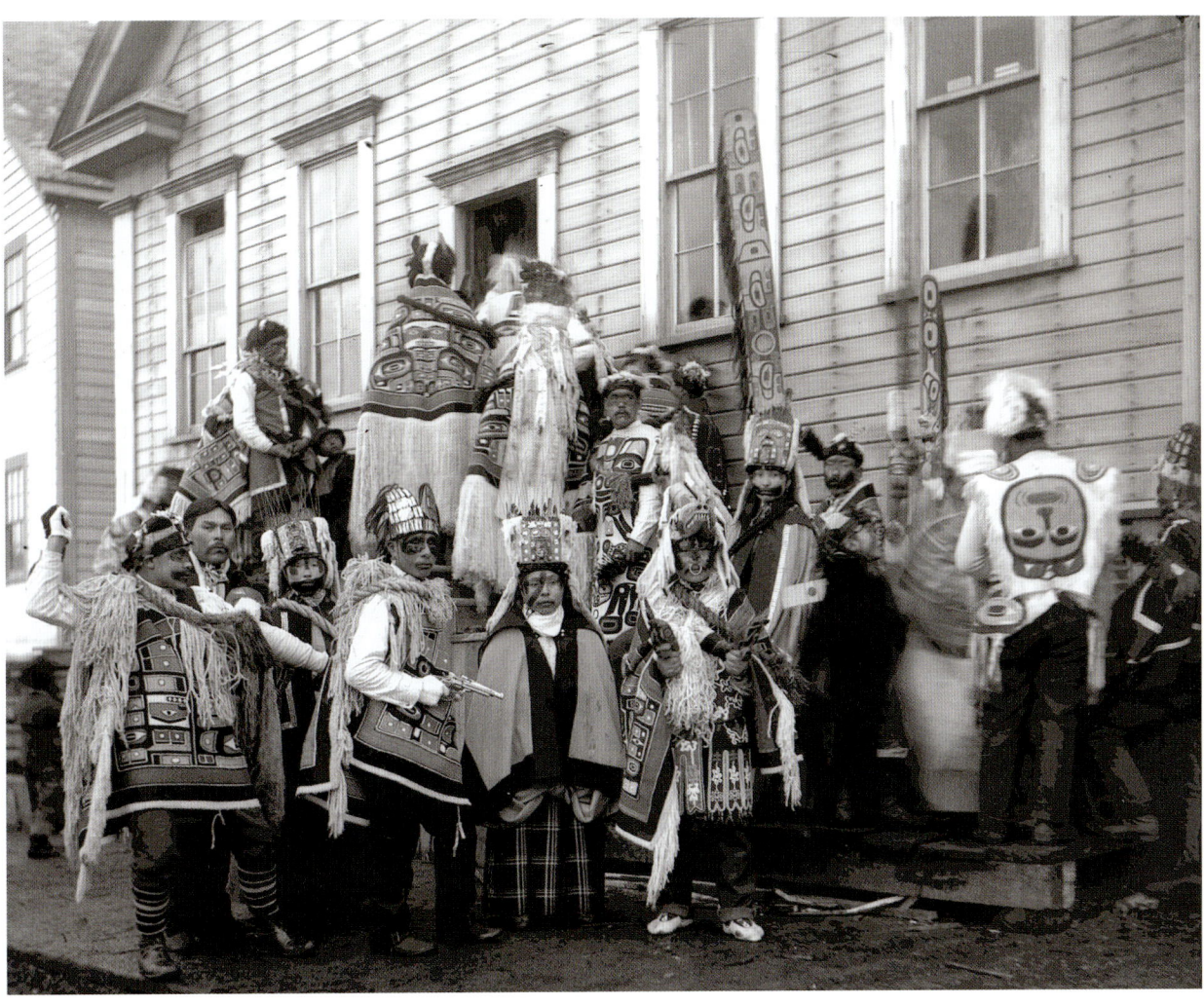

PLATE 15. 1904 Ḵu.éex' guests, most of them from the Deisheetaan clan of Angoon, entering the Wolf House (Ḡooch Hít) of the Kaagwaantaan clan.

Front row, second from left (bareheaded), is William Peters (Kaalḵáawu) (1859–1936), Arch House (Kaaḵáak'w Hít), of the Basket Bay subdivision of the Deisheetaan clan. Fourth from left is Little Jack (Woolshook), wearing a Tsimshian Bear's Ears hat (given to the Tlingit as a gift) and holding a pistol. He was from the Freshwater Spring House (Goon Hít) of the Deisheetaan clan. Fifth from the left might be Annie George Jack (Yaxlaháat), Valley House (Shaanax Hít), Teiḵweidí clan.

Second row, fourth from the right, wearing a *shakee.át* headdress, might be Kaaxkwei (Lottie [Plotnikov] Peters) (1879–1955), Box House (Ḵóok Hít), Kaagwaantaan clan of Sitka. Back row, standing between two paddles, is Jimmie Albert (Ĺaxkéik'w) (b. 1882), Freshwater Spring House (Goon Hít), Deisheetaan clan.

Identifications by Harold Jacobs, 2021. National Park Service, Sitka National Historical Park, 03774.

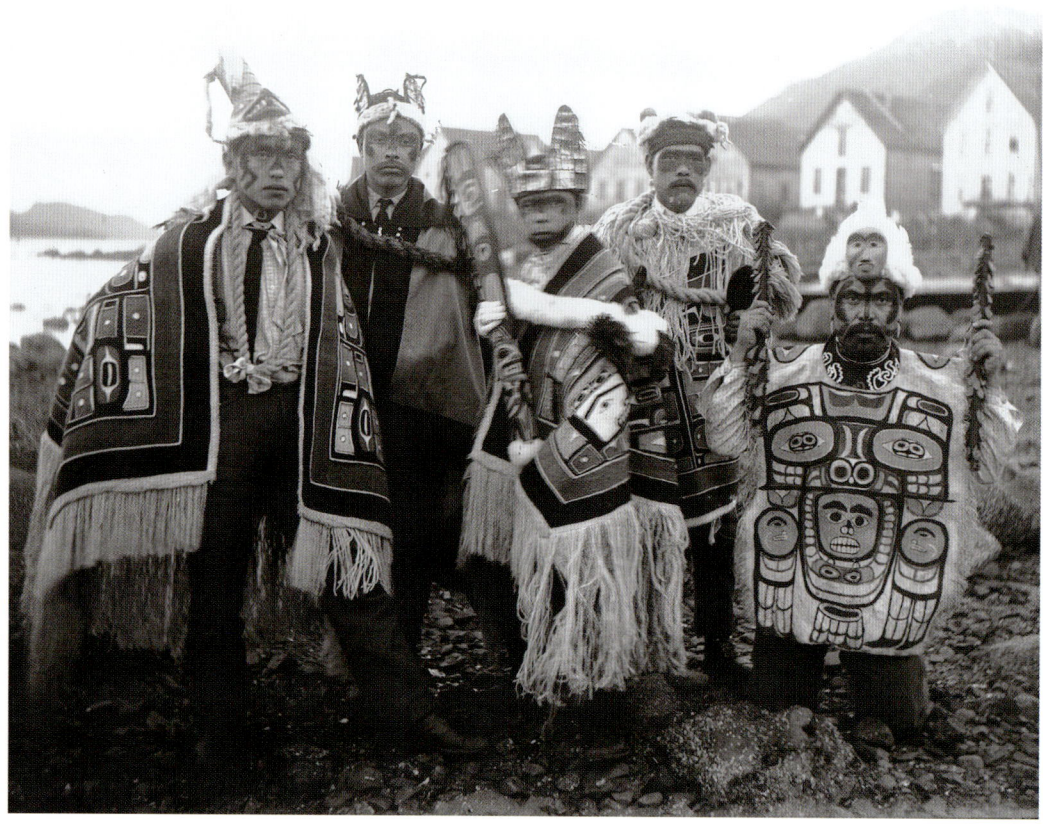

PLATE 16. Participants in the 1904 Sitka ḵu.éex' in the Sitka Native Village, with lineage houses visible in the background.

Front row, left to right: Tom Phillips (Deiyikt'aa), Strong House (At.uwaxiji Hít), Kiks.ádi clan of Sitka, wearing his grandparents' Beaver hat; Alfred Perkins (Kwaléwah), Needlefish House (Tuḵká Hít), Deisheetaan clan of Angoon, wearing Bear's Ears; Peter [?] Dick (Kaatéenaa), Arch House (Kaaḵáak'w Hít), of the Basket Bay subdivision of the Deisheetaan clan, wearing a Mosquito moosehide shirt.

Back row, left to right: Charlie Ondaynahot (Aandéina.áat) (1859–1934), Steel House (Shdeen Hít), Deisheetaan clan, wearing Western clothes; Yéilk, Steel House (Shdeen Hít), Deisheetaan clan, wearing Bear's Ears and a cedar bark ring. The ceremonial bark rings were called *kaseekw* (collars) and were obtained from the Kwakwakawak'w.

Courtesy of the National Park Service, Sitka National Historical Park, 03781. Identifications by Harold Jacobs, 2021.

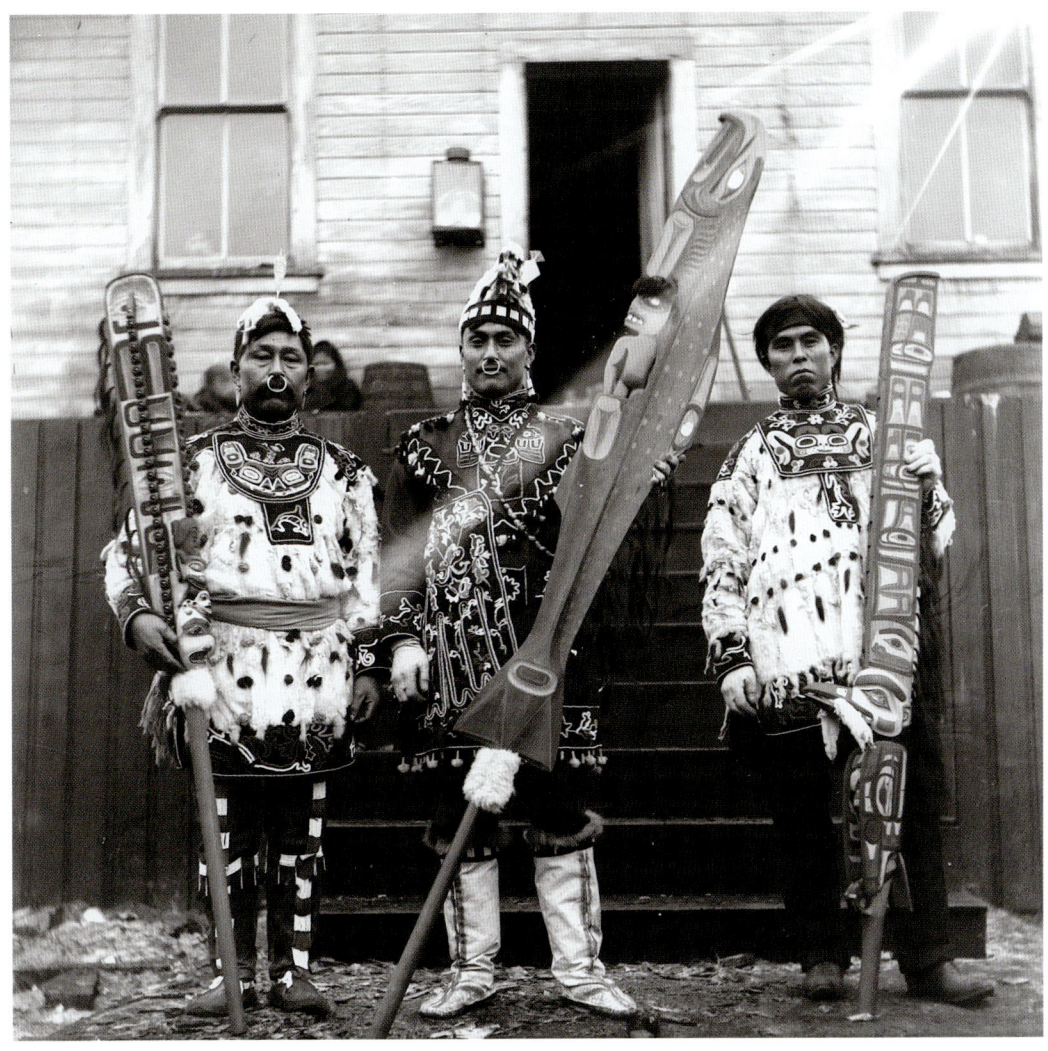

PLATE 17. Participants in the 1904 Sitka ḵu.éex': three men from the Ľuknax̱.ádi clan of Sitka. Left to right: Sitka Charlie (X'aasooká) (1865–1948), Whale House (Yáay Hít) Ľuknax̱.adí clan, holding a dance leader's paddle; unidentified man, Ľuknax̱.adí clan(?), holding a Salmon dance paddle (still in the clan's possession); T. J. Henry (Duksa.áat), holding a Raven dance leader's paddle (see plate 11). Identifications by Harold Jacobs, 2021. Courtesy of the National Park Service, Sitka National Historical Park, 03782.

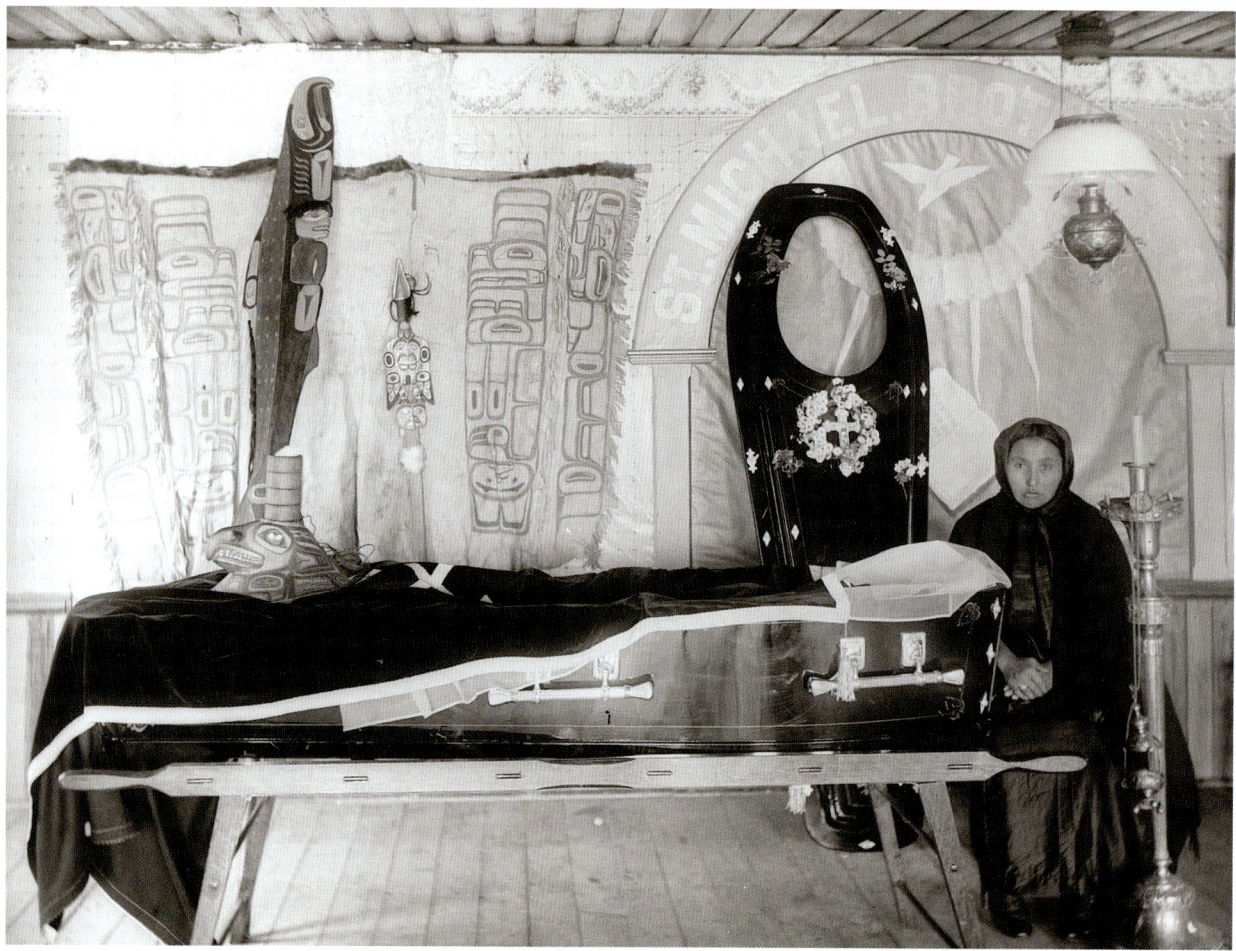

PLATE 18. A body lying inside a coffin in the Little Coho House (Ľook Hít Yádi) of the Ľuknax̱.ádi clan, Sitka, ca. 1900–1920. The leader of this house was Harold (Peter) Bailey (Goox̱ Éesh) (1877–1941), who was also the head of the St. Michael's Brotherhood of the Russian Orthodox Church. The house was used for weekly brotherhood meeting (the words "St. Michael Brotherhood" are painted on the wall to the right). The presence of a candle holder and an incense burner from the church indicate that a memorial service has been held here. Several major Ľuknax̱.ádi *at.óow* are displayed with the body, including the Coho headdress (still in the clan's possession) sitting on top of the casket and a Coho dance leader's staff along the wall (see plate 17). The woman sitting with the body must be the deceased man's widow. See Kan 1999: 340–41. Courtesy of the National Park Service, Sitka National Historical Park, 03790.

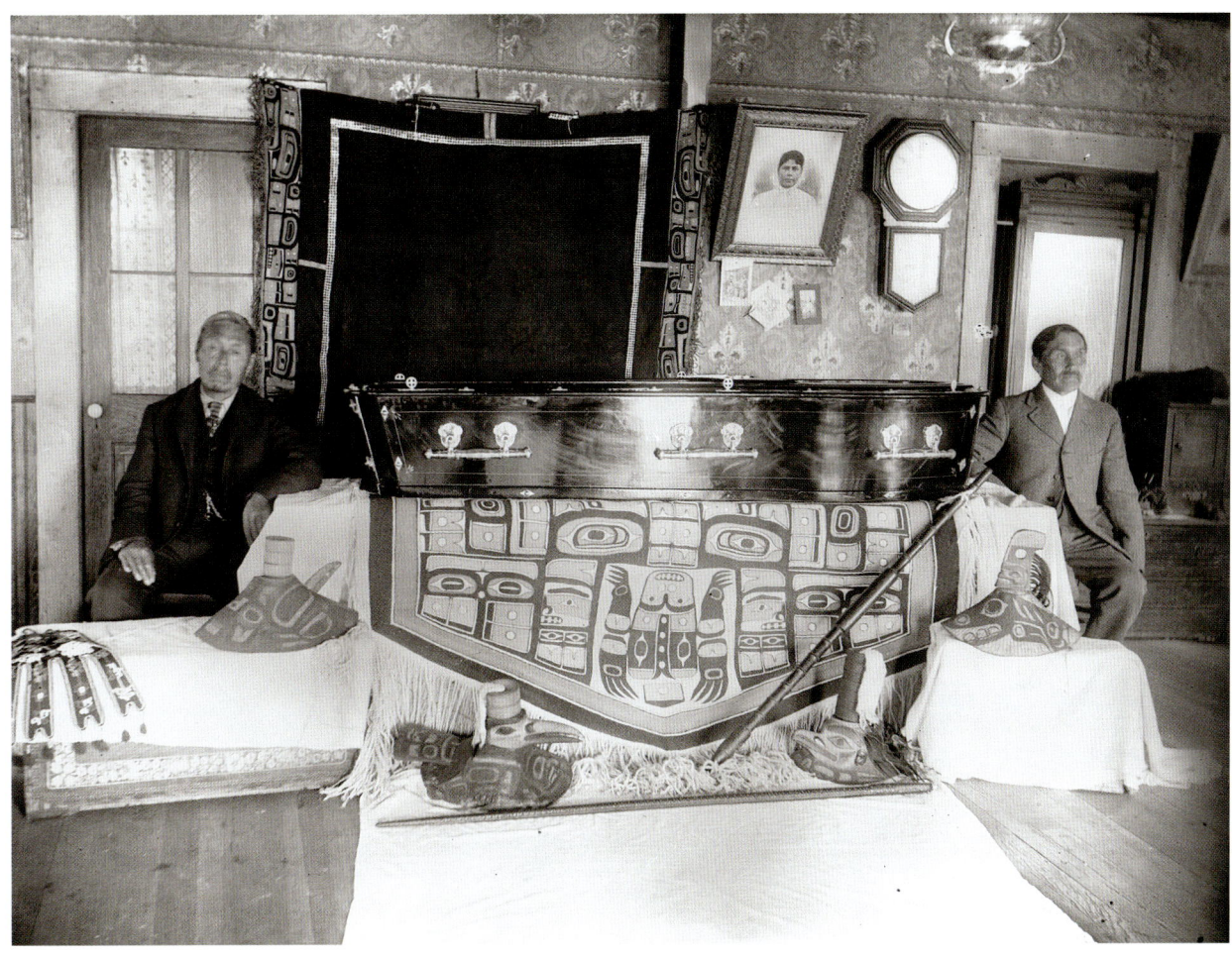

PLATE 19. A funeral scene in a house most likely belonging to the Ľuknax.adí clan, Sitka, ca. 1900–1920. Several ceremonial headdresses belonging to the clan are displayed. The wooden staff belonged to Sitka Jack (Katseix̱, Ldax̱éen), Whale House (Yáay Hít), Ľuknax̱.ádi clan. The two men sitting with the body are either of the Coho clan or members of the opposite moiety whose ritual task it was to honor and protect the body while it lay in the house. Harold Jacobs (2021) suggested that the deceased might have been Sitka Jack, who died ca. 1915. Courtesy of the National Park Service, Sitka National Historical Park, 03791.

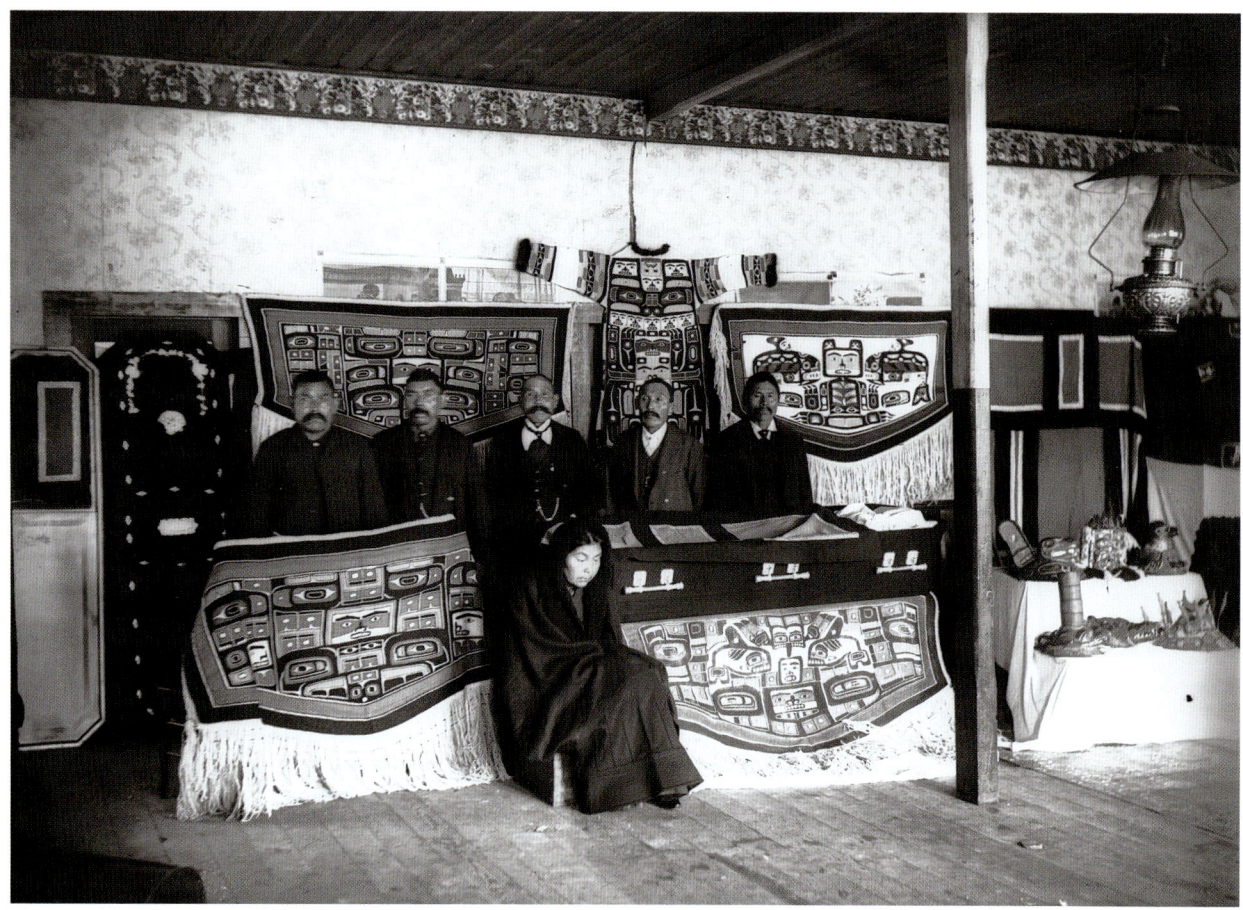

PLATE 20. A funeral scene inside a house, Sitka, ca. 1900–1920. Judging by the images depicted on the Chilkat blankets (a bear and killer whales), it belongs to the Kaagwaantaan clan. Two of the men standing behind the casket are prominent Kaagwaantaan leaders: third from the left is James Jackson (Annahootz) (1845–1934), Wolf House (G̱ooch Hít), Kaagwaantaan clan; fourth from the left is Augustus Bean (K'aleaneesh) (1856–1926), Wolf House (G̱ooch Hít). The woman sitting in front of the casket is most likely the widow. Identifications by Harold Jacobs, 2021. Courtesy of the National Park Service, Sitka National Historical Park, 03789.

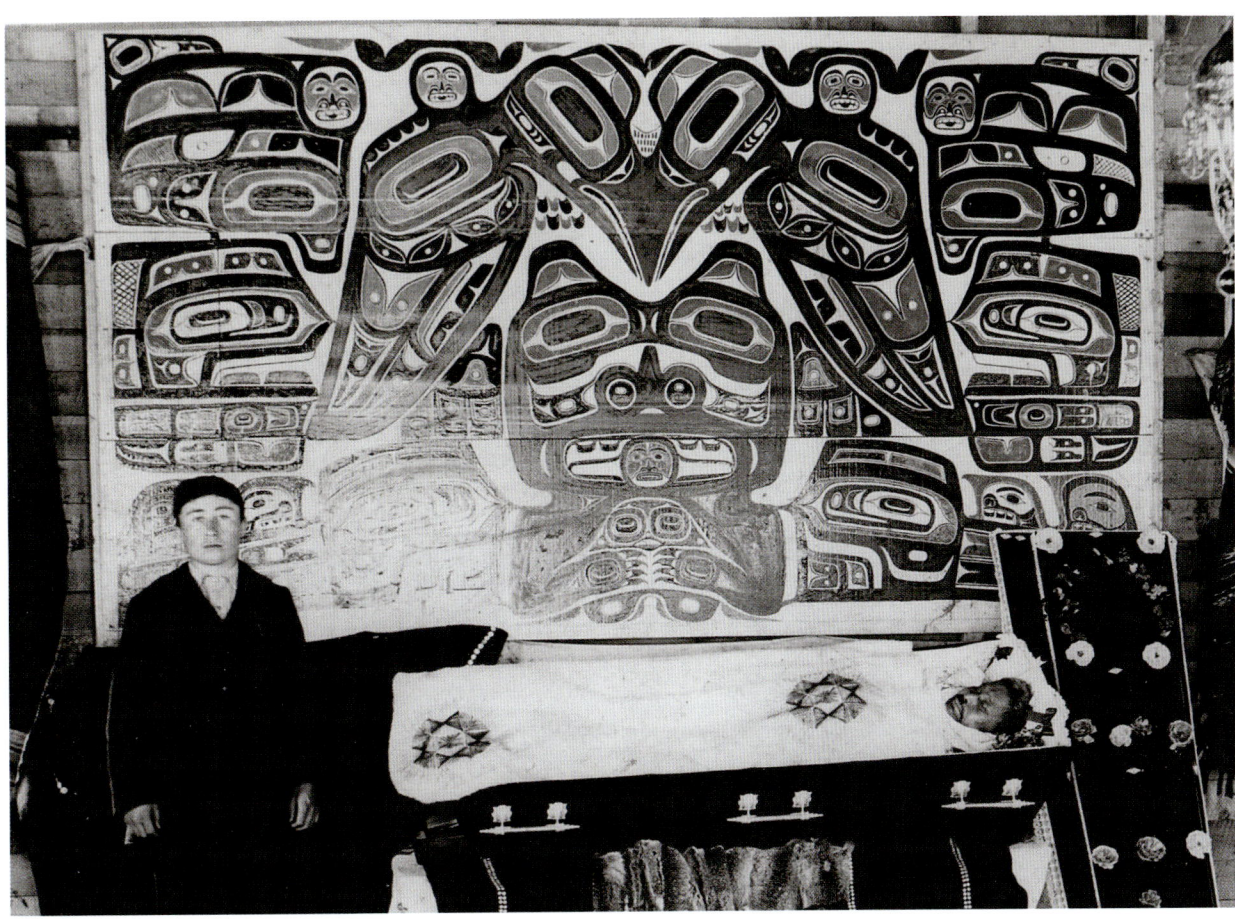

PLATE 21. Funeral of Ed Kay-Chaik (Xeijáak'w), Raven's Nest House (Yéil Kúdei Hít), T'aḵdeintaan clan of Hoonah, ca. 1895–1900. Standing by the casket is Ralph Young (Looshkát) (1877–1956), Raven's Nest House (Yéil Kúdei Hít), T'aḵdeintaan clan of Hoonah. On the wall is the Raven's Nest house screen, which Ralph Young eventually donated to the Sheldon Jackson Museum of Sitka (see Dauenhauer and Dauenhauer 1994: 693). Photo donated to the Sealaska Heritage Institute by Mark Jacobs Jr. and Harold Jacobs and attributed to Merrill by them.

As far as we know, this is the only photograph Merrill took in Hoonah. According to Harold Jacobs, the original print he owns has Merrill's name printed in the corner. Richard Dauenhauer Photograph Collection. P0004/006-#080. William L. Paul Sr. Archives, Sealaska Heritage Institute, Juneau, Alaska.

INDIVIDUAL AND GROUP PORTRAITS OF TLINGIT PEOPLE

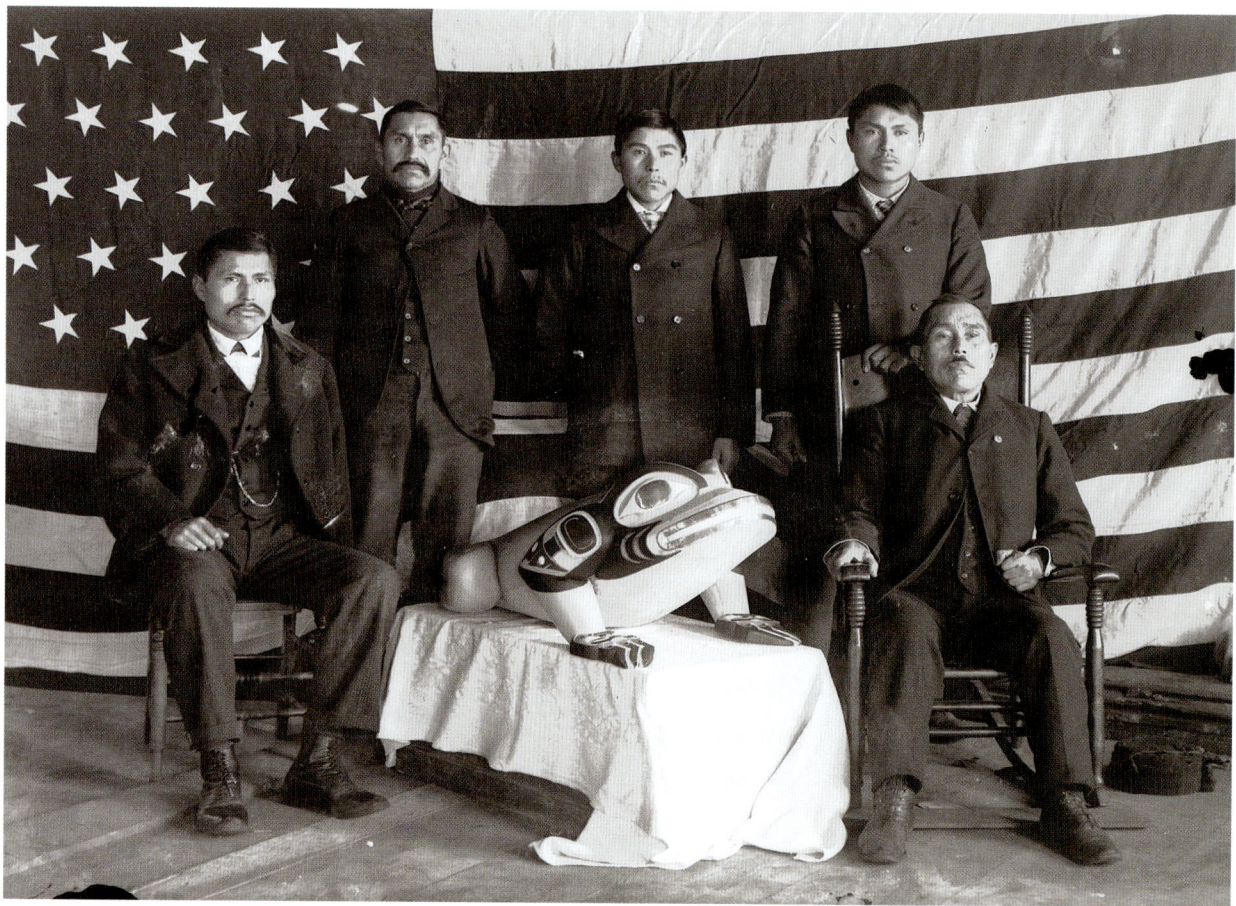

PLATE 22. A group of men of the L'uknax̱.ádi clan with one of their crests inside a lineage house, Sitka, 1902. This Frog carving is now in the SNHP building. It was carved by Daniel Benson (Daaḵoos.eich) (1874–1943), Teiḵweidí clan of Yakutat; and Yeilnaawú, the head of the Cow House (Xaas Hít), Ḵoosk'eidí subdivision of the L'uknax̱.ádi clan of Sitka. The object is currently on loan from the late Frank Kitka, Outwards House (Daginaa Hít), L'uknax̱.ádi clan.

Standing left to right: Ned James (Sdaagwáan) (1860–1921); T. J. Henry (Duksa.áat); Déix̱.wudu.oo (brother of T. Max Italio); Ḵux̱tdzináa(?); Lxeitéech.

Identifications by Frederica de Laguna, based on information provided by Harry K. Bremner and Helen Bremner of Yakutat in the late 1940s and early 1950s (see De Laguna 1972: 1132–33) and Harold Jacobs, 2024. See also https://www.nps.gov/places/sleeping-man-pole.htm. National Park Service, Sitka National Historical Park, 03806.

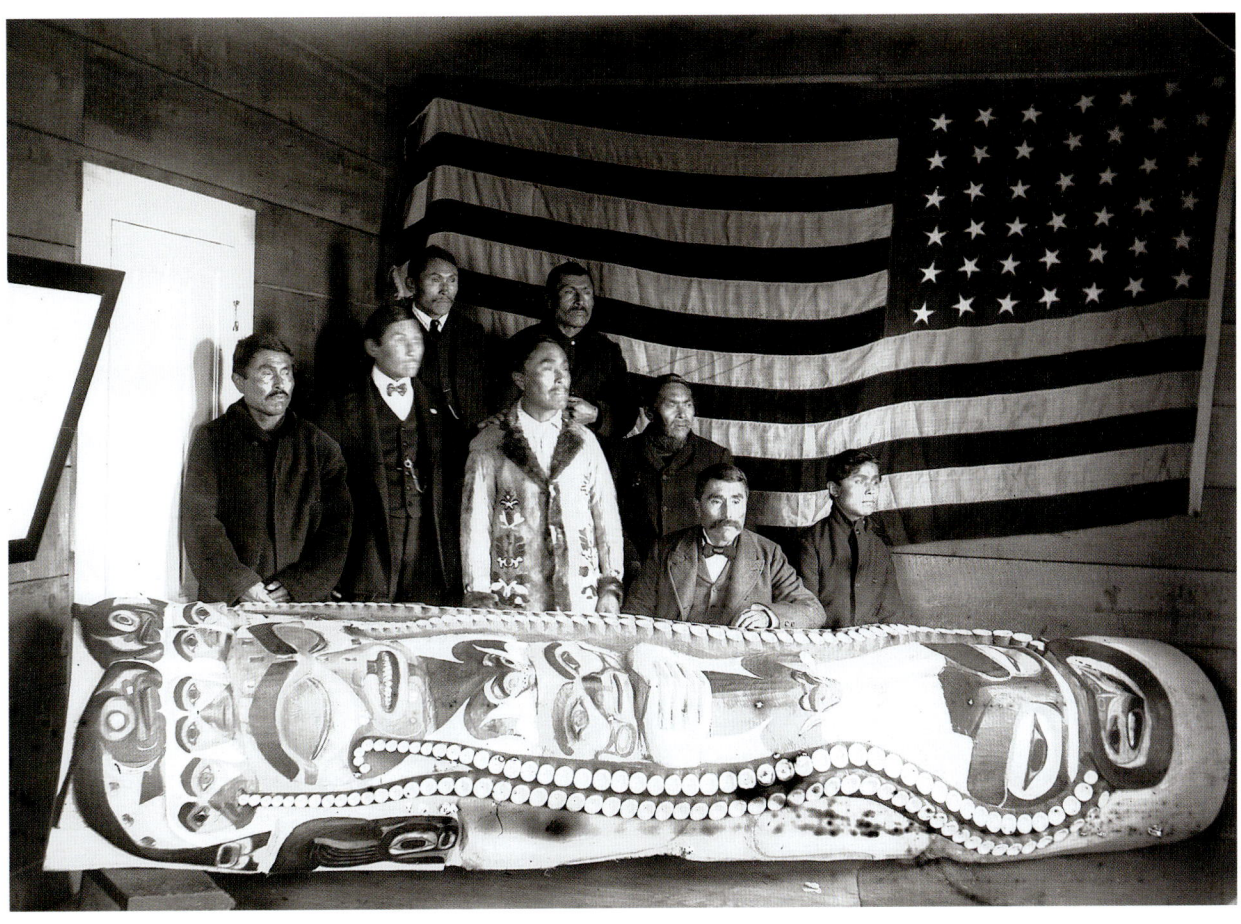

PLATE 23. The Sleeping Man and the Octopus pole of the Ľuknax̱.ádi at the Steel House (Shdeen Hít), Kiks.ádi clan, Sitka, ca. 1900–1910. X'oowhaach (whose name is written on the bottom of the photograph) was its headman. Others shown in this photograph are unidentified. The pole is currently on loan to the Sitka National Historical Park. See also https://www.nps .gov/places/sleeping-man-pole.htm. Courtesy of the National Park Service, Sitka National Historical Park, 03808.

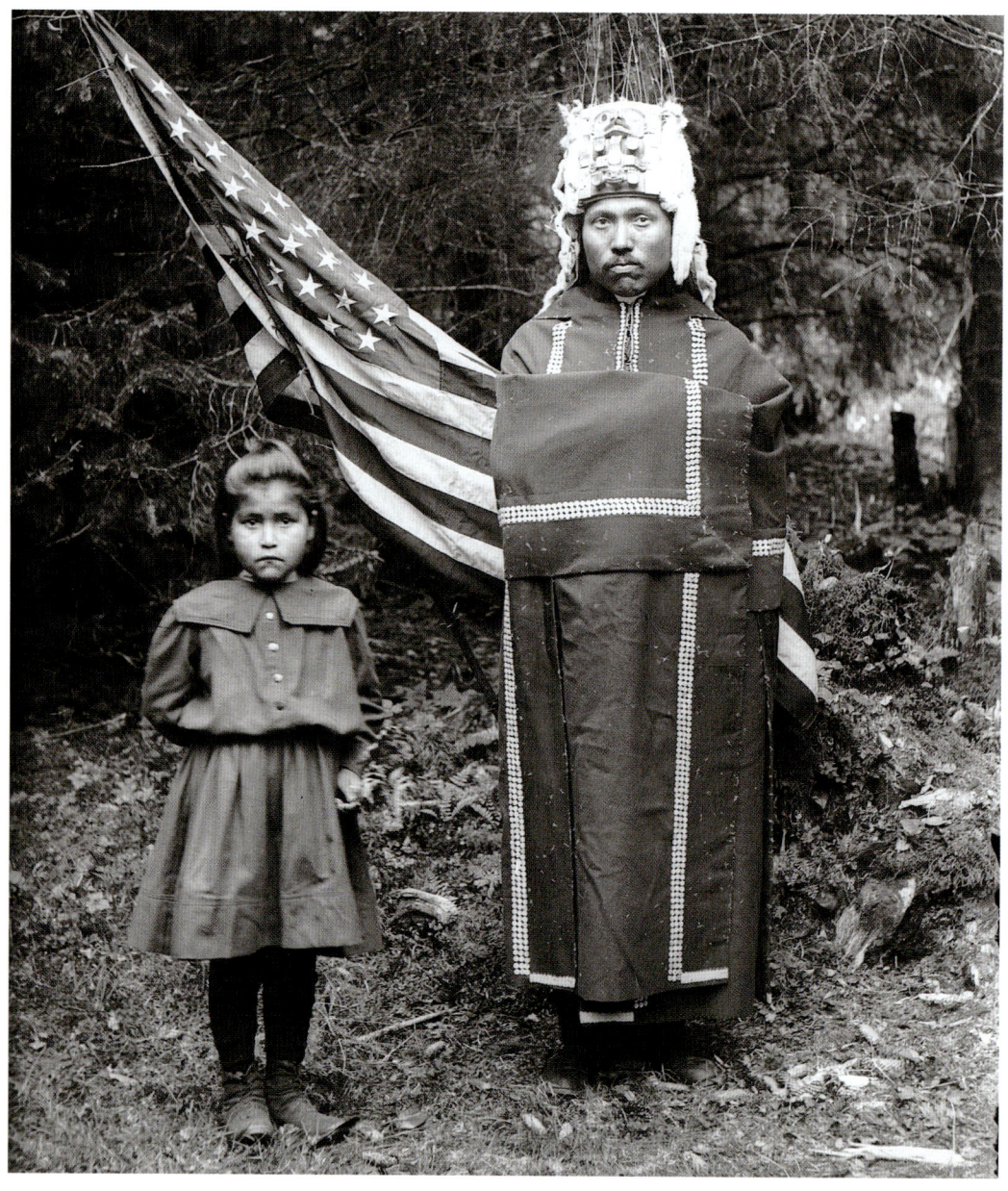

PLATE 24. Mary Marks (G̲unaa Sháa, S'eistaan Tláa) (1894–1992), Clay House (S'é Hít), Kiks.ádi clan of Sitka, with her father, Jim Andrews (Jeex'wán Éesh) (1854–1929), Chookaneidí clan, Sitka, ca. 1900. Identifications by Harold Jacobs, 2024. Courtesy of the National Park Service, Sitka National Historical Park, 03927.

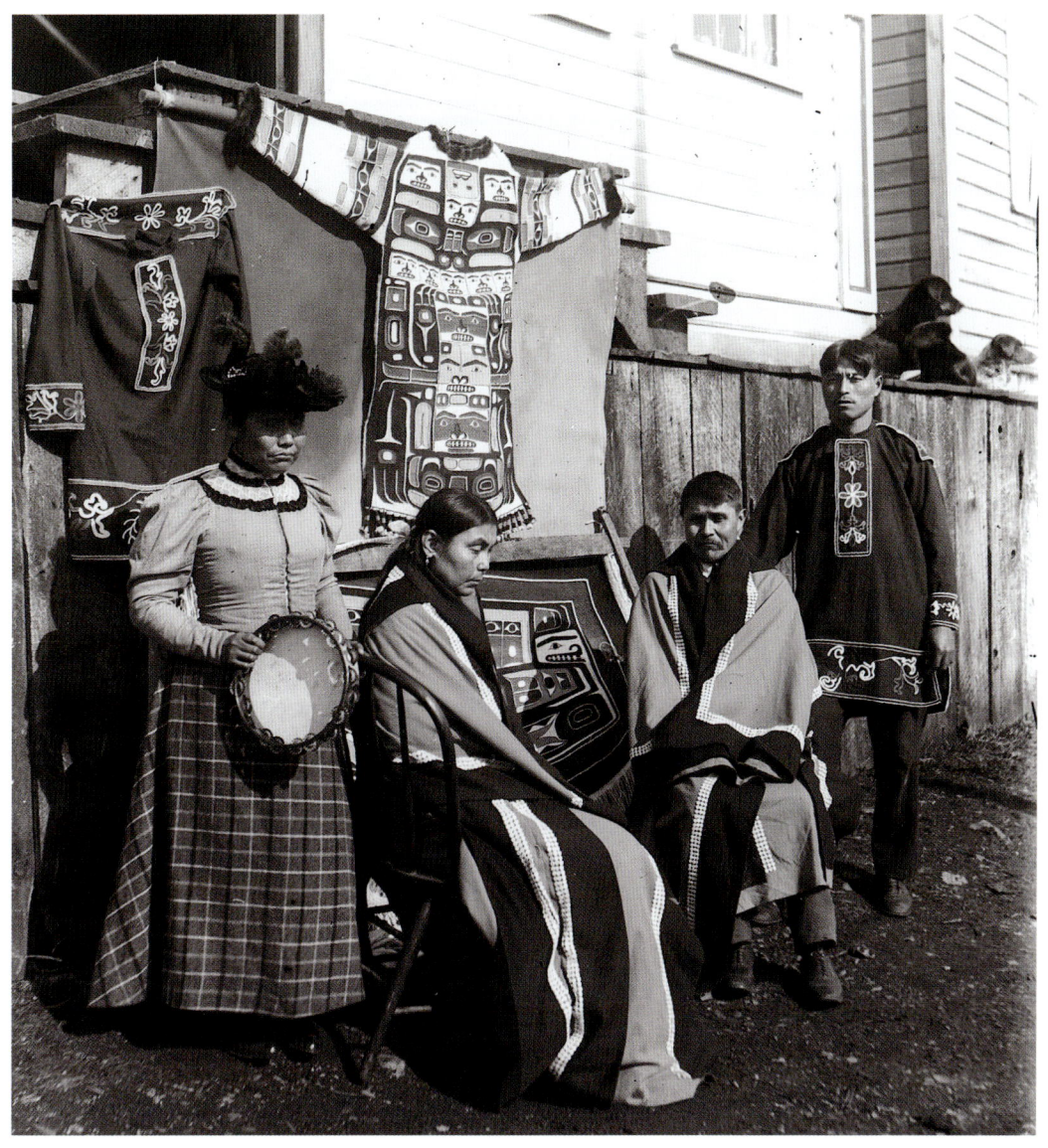

PLATE 25. Two men and two women displaying traditional regalia in front of a house in the Sitka Indian Village, ca. 1900–1929. Courtesy of the National Park Service, Sitka National Historical Park, 03934.

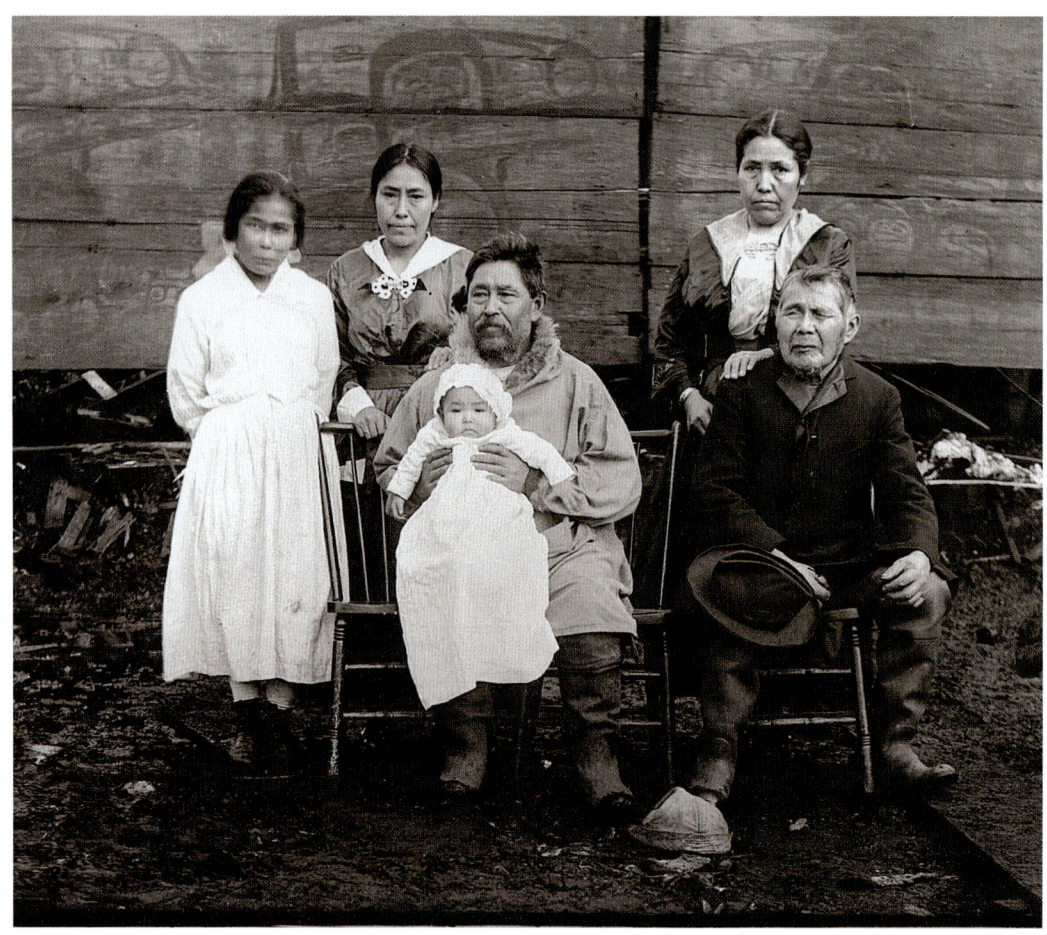

PLATE 26. A group of men and women sitting in front of the Raven screen belonging to the Whale House (Yáay Hít) of the Ľuknax.ádi clan in the Sitka Indian Village, ca. 1900–1910. At the center, holding an unidentified baby, is Sitka Charlie (X'aasooká) (1865–1948), Whale House (Yáay Hít), Ľuknax.adí clan. To his right is Sam Paul (Kaatáawu), Ľuknax.adí clan. Behind Sam Paul is his wife, Jennie Paul (Sáadoowu), Kaagwaantaan clan of Sitka, a daughter of Sitka Jack. The woman standing behind and to the left of Sitka Charlie looks a lot like Jennie Paul and might be related to her. The young woman on the far left was identified in 1980 by Lizzie Basco as Mrs. "Sweetie Pie" Benson. The women's dresses resemble the style of the early 1900s. Identifications by Harold Jacobs, 2021. Courtesy of the National Park Service, Sitka National Historical Park, 03813.

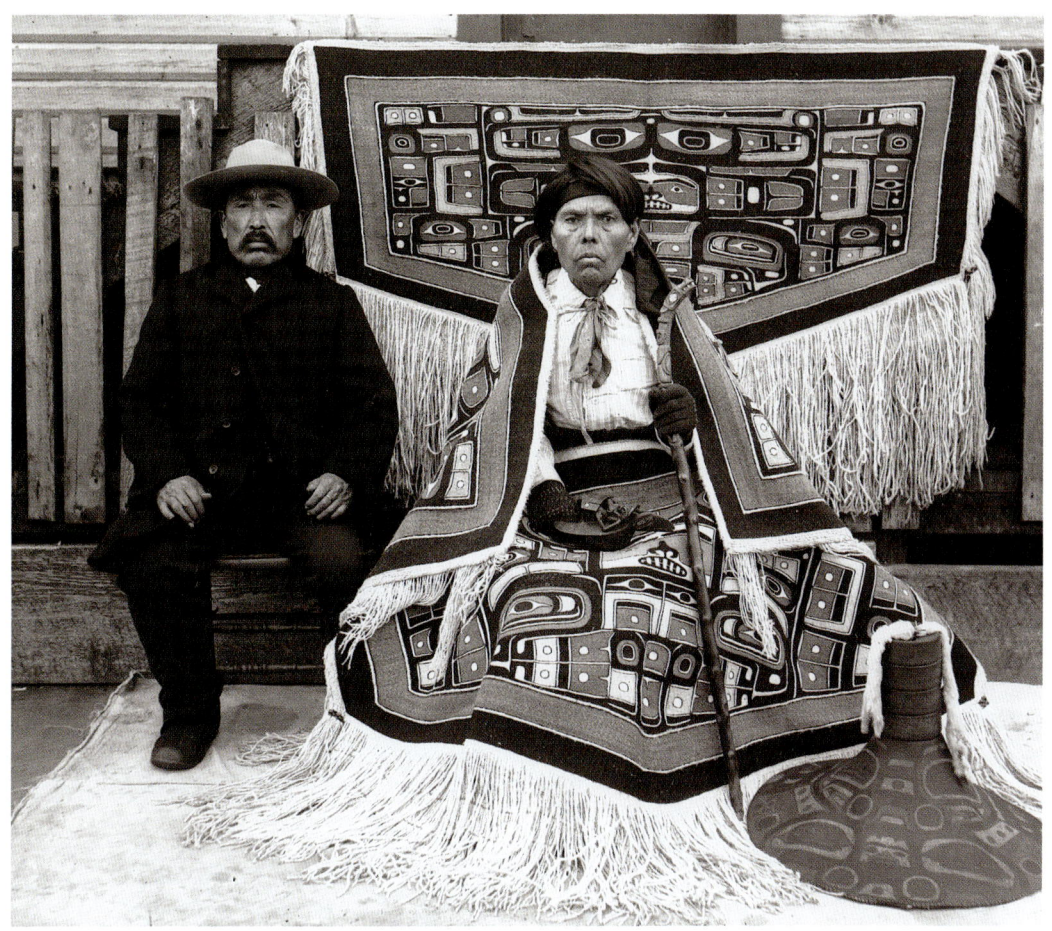

PLATE 27. Sitka Native Village, ca. 1910. The man on the right is Gushteitoowaa, Wolf House (G̲ooch Hít), Kaagwaantaan clan of Sitka, also known as Prince Tom, the husband of Princess Tom. He is wearing a wig. The woven hat in front of him is called Lingit'aaní S'áaxw (World Hat). The other man might be Jack Watson. Identifications by Harold Jacobs, 2021. Courtesy of the National Park Service, Sitka National Historical Park, 03857.

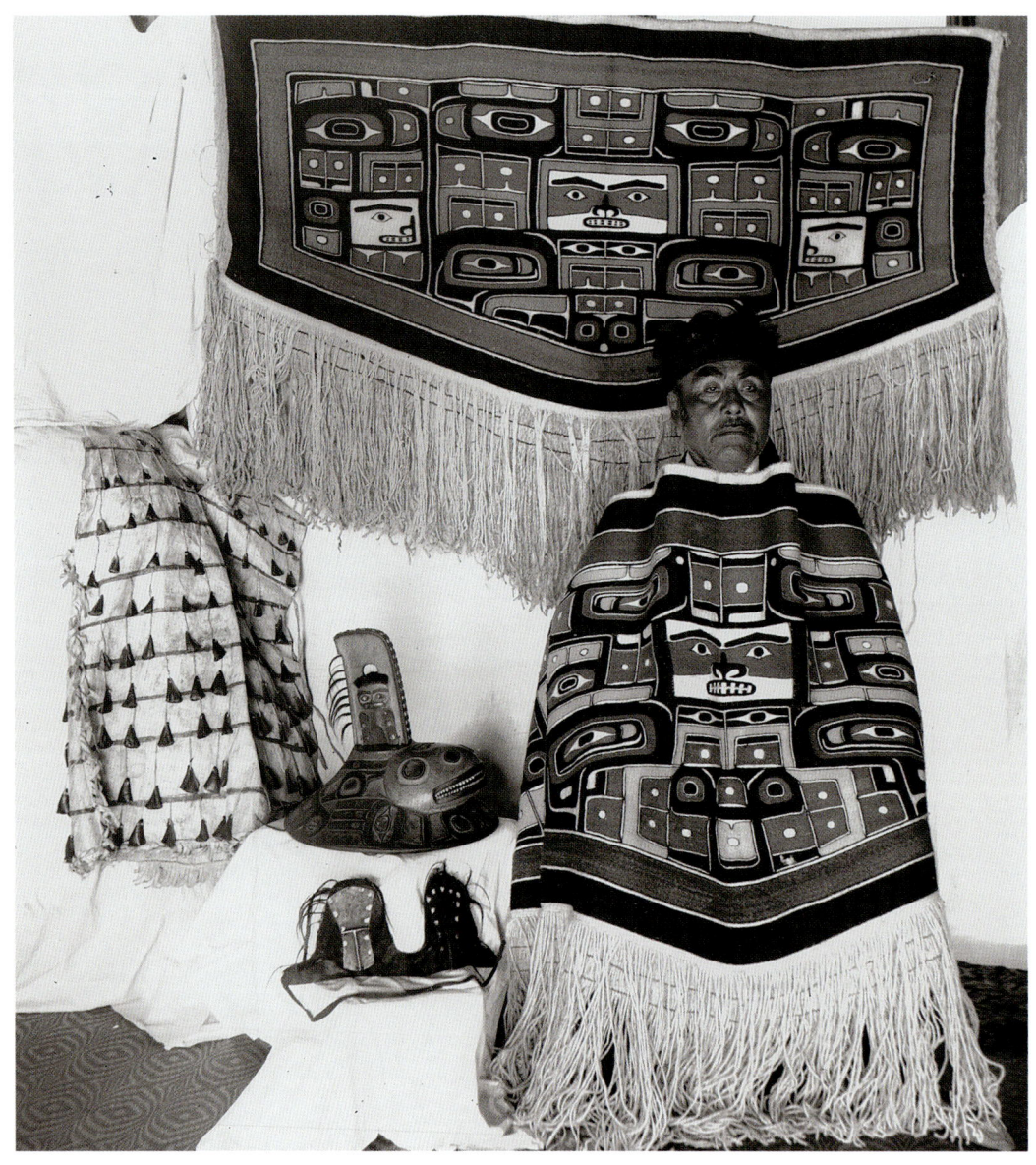

PLATE 28. L'aanteech (1843?–1908), a high-ranking man of the House with Two Doors (Déix X'awool Hít), Sitka Kaagwaantaan clan, in a house in the Sitka Native Village, ca. 1900. The headdress displayed is called Kéet Aanyádi S'áaxw (High-Caste Killer Whale Hat), a major crest object of his clan. Courtesy of the National Park Service, Sitka National Historical Park, 03858.

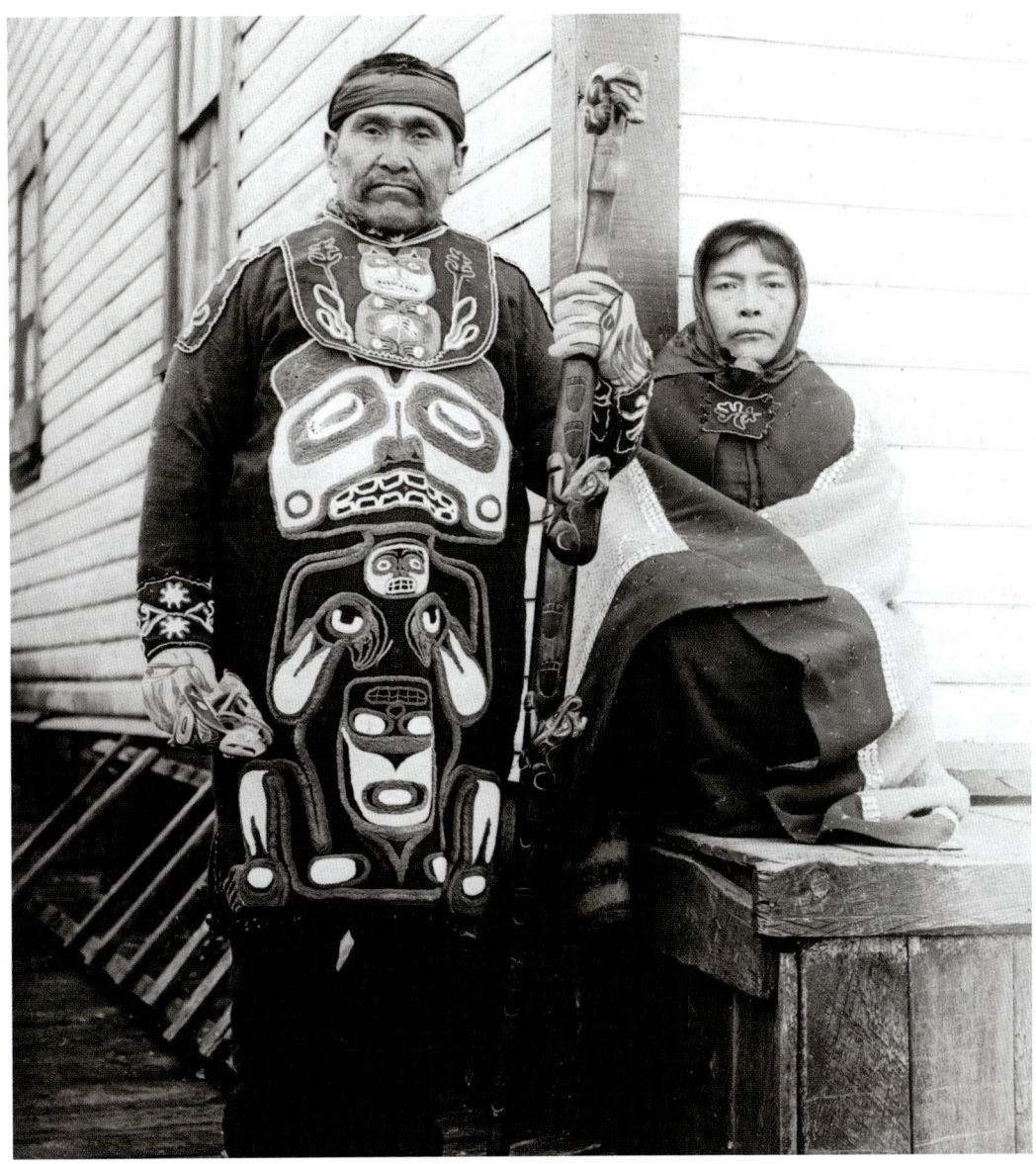

PLATE 29. Martin White (Ḵuchéin), head of one of the houses of the Box House (Ḵóok Hít) Ḵookhittaan subdivision of the Kaagwaantaan clan of Sitka, wearing a Bear tunic and holding a Bear staff, Sitka, ca. 1900–1910. To his right is his wife, Yaast'ooch, of the Canoe Trail House (Yakwdeiyí Hít), T'aḵdeintaan clan, who made the shirt. The last person to wear the shirt and use the staff was Charlie Joseph Sr. (Kaal.átk') (1895–1986), Box House (Ḵóok Hít), Sitka Kaagwaantaan clan. These at.óow are now at the SNHP. Alaska State Library, Historical Collection, Elbridge W. Merrill, Alaska State Historical Library P427-54.

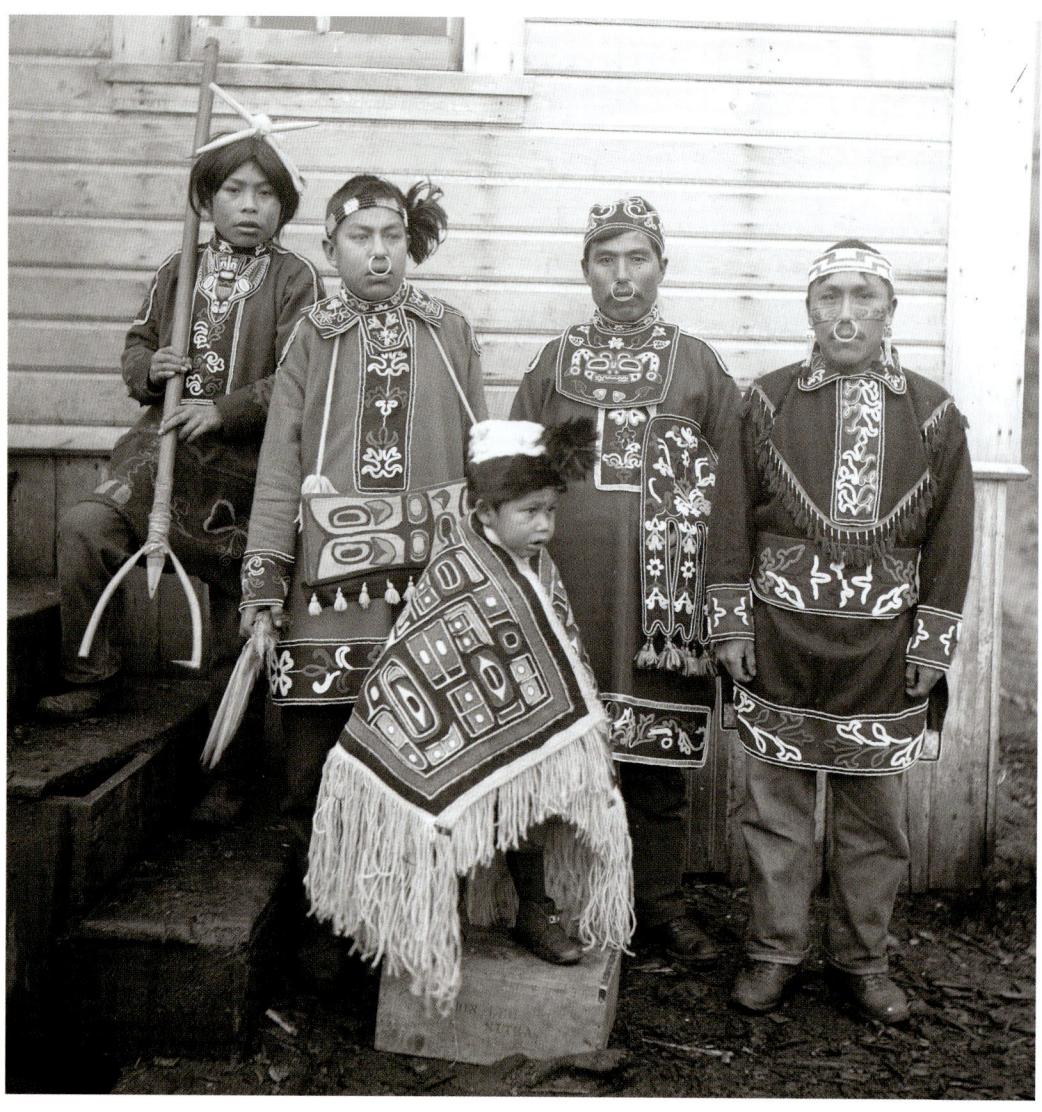

PLATE 30. A group of young men and boys in Sitka, ca. 1910. The youngest is Jacob Yarkon (Yakwaan) Jr. (1903–44), Outwards House (Daginaa Hít), Lʼuknax̱.ádi clan of Sitka. His father was Jacob Yarkon (Yakwaan, Xeitxutʼch, Stoowuk̲áa). Judging by the Raven and Frog bibs worn by two of the young men, all are probably members of the Lʼuknax̱.ádi clan. Identifications by Cecilia Kunz. Courtesy of the National Park Service, Sitka National Historical Park, 03784.

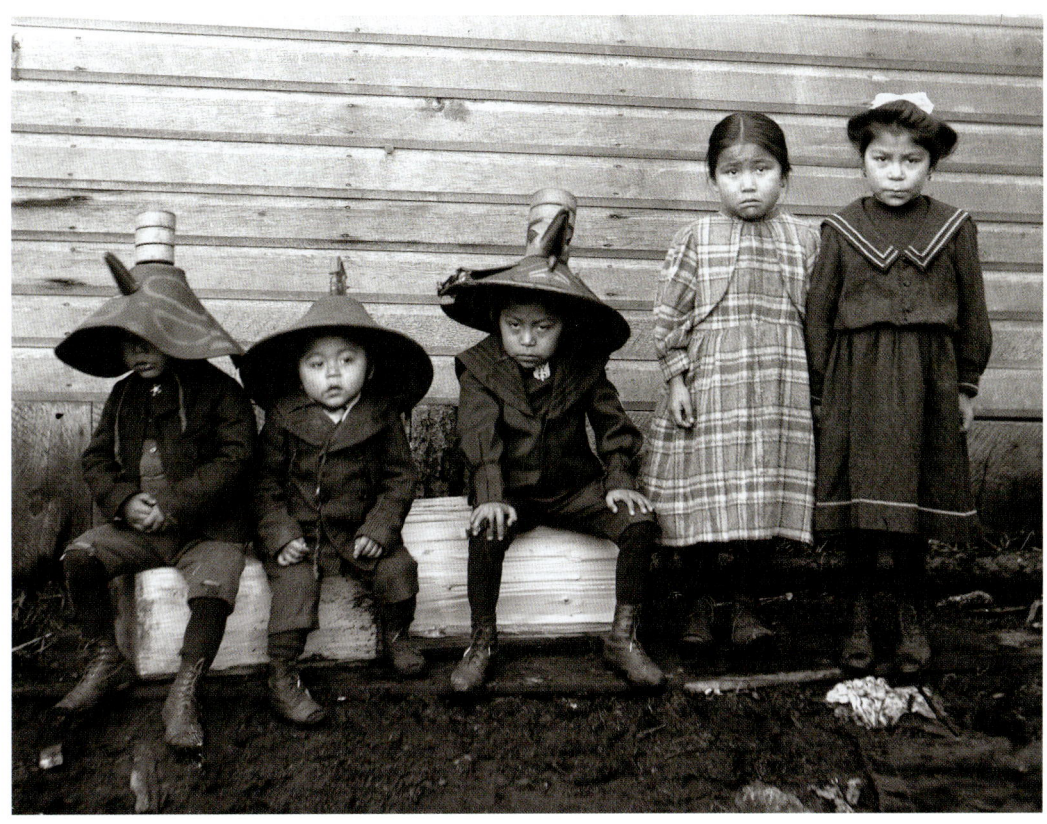

PLATE 31. Tlingit children dressed in Western clothing. The three boys are wearing ceremonial hats, Sitka, ca. 1900–1920. Courtesy of the National Park Service, Sitka National Historical Park, 26257.

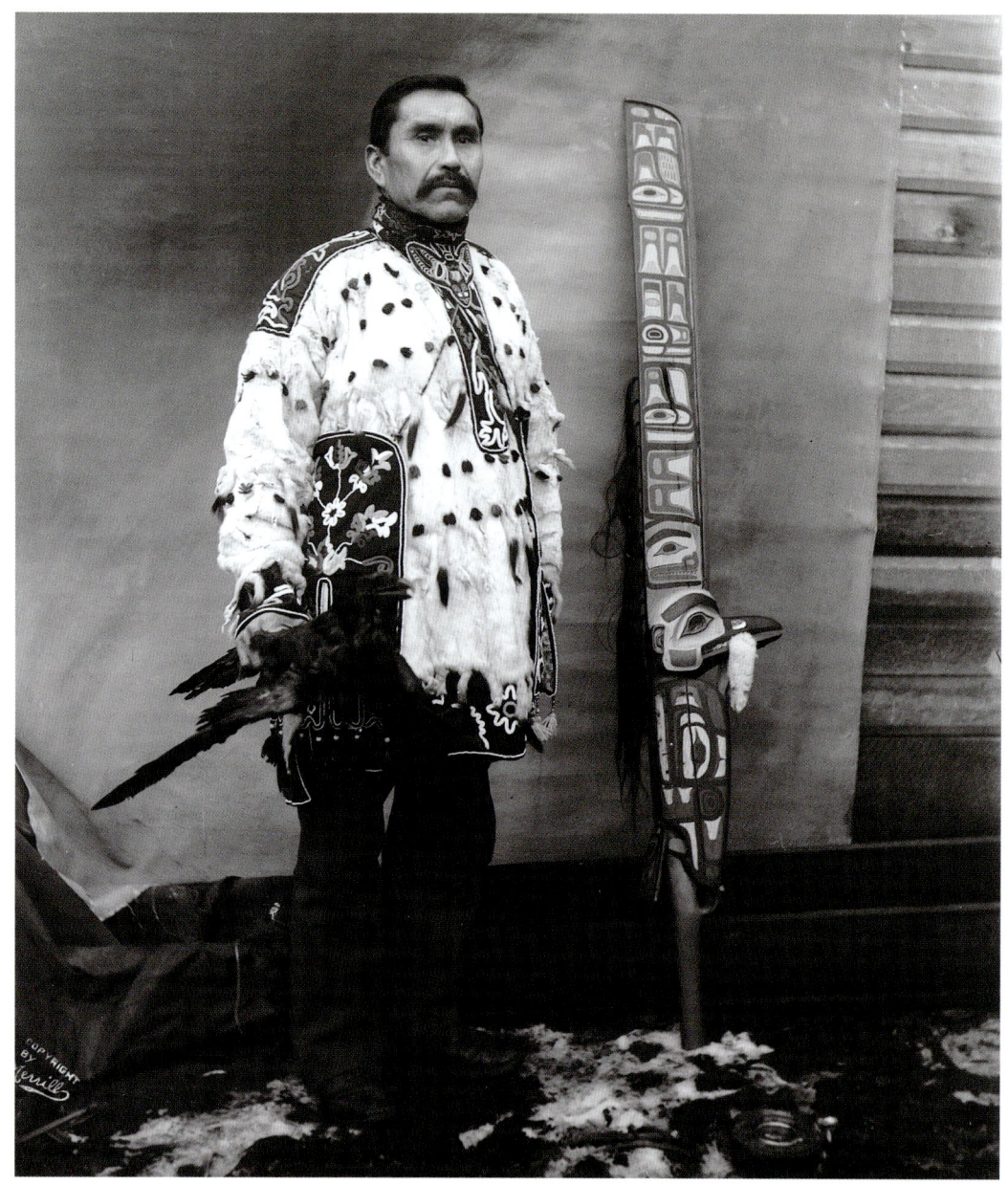

PLATE 32. A formal portrait of Silver Jim (Kichx̱ook̲), Cow House (Xaas Hít), K̲oosk'eidí subdivision of the L'uknax̱.adí clan of Sitka, ca. 1900–1920. He is holding a dance paddle that is identical to the one held by T. G. Henry (Duksaat) (plate 12). He is also holding a stuffed Raven representing his moiety crest and wearing an ermine beaded shirt. Identification by Harold Jacobs, 2021, 2024. Courtesy of the National Park Service, Sitka National Historical Park, 03936.

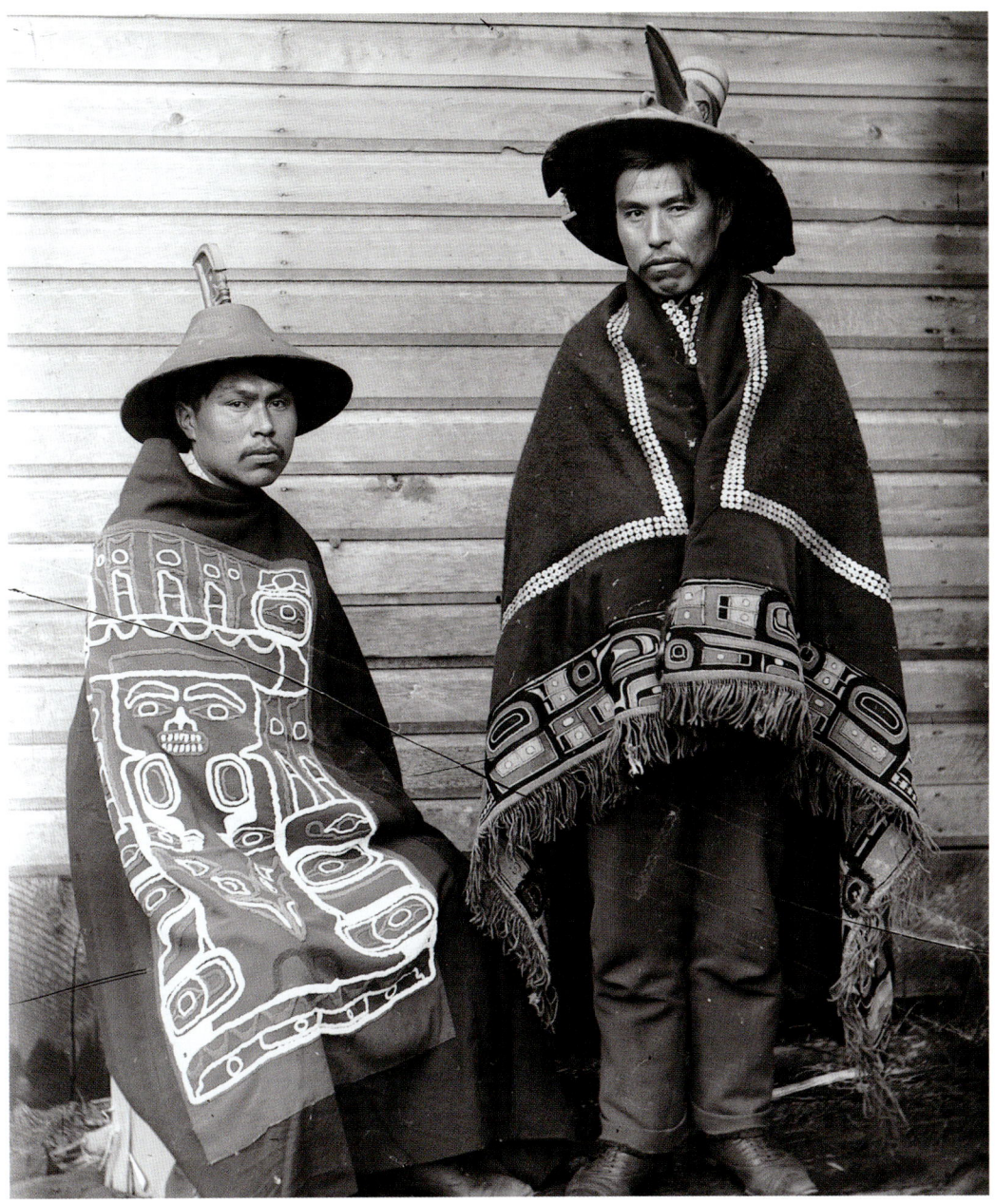

PLATE 33. A semiformal portrait of two Raven moiety (Ĺuknax̱.ádi clan?) men, Sitka, ca. 1900–1920. The man on the left wears a Whale hat, the one on the right a Raven hat. Both are crests of the Ĺuknax̱.ádi clan. Identification by Harold Jacobs, 2021. Courtesy of the National Park Service, Sitka National Historical Park, 03938.

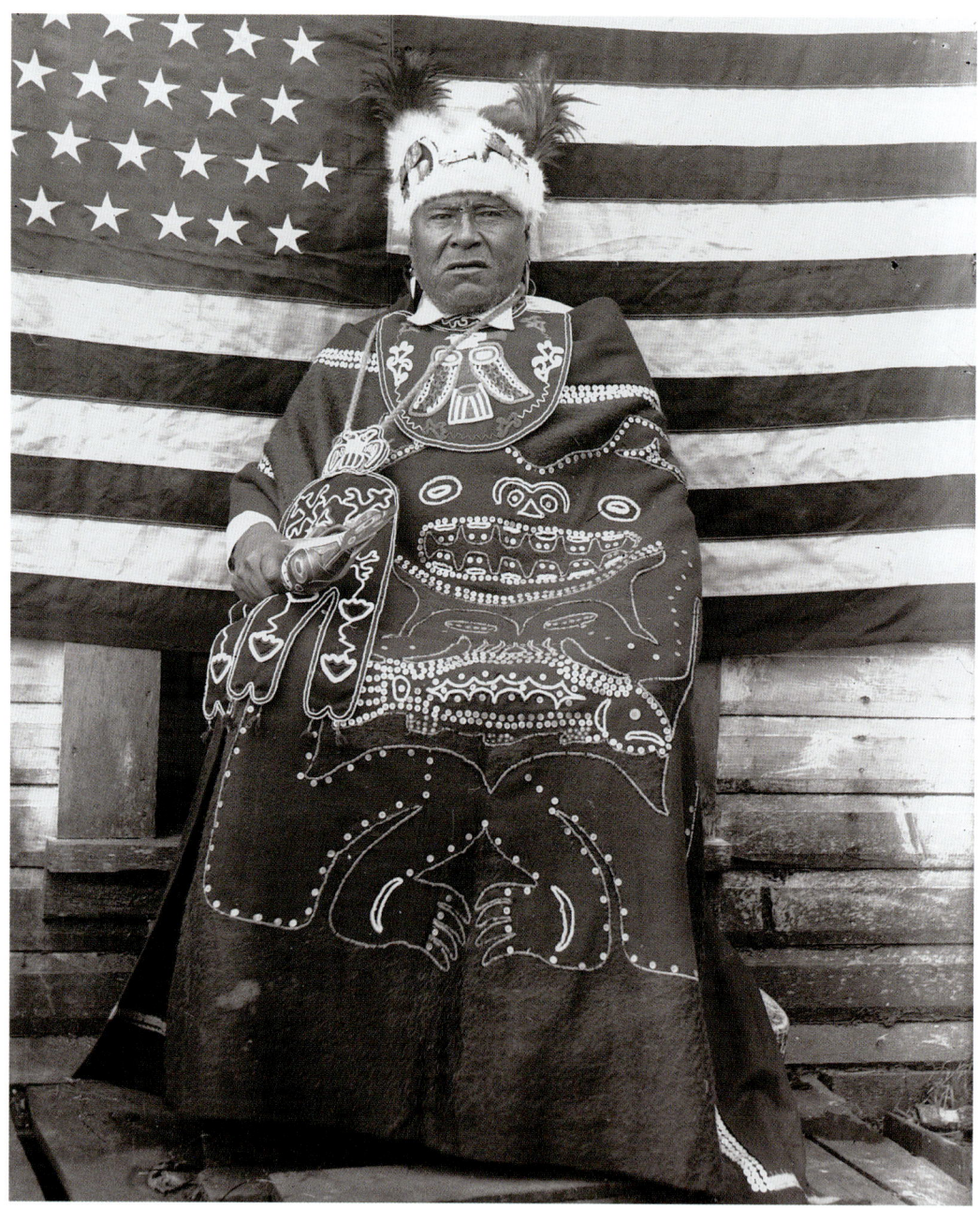

PLATE 34. A portrait of Deikeenaak'w (John Norris) (ca. 1828–1928), Box House (Ḵóok Hít), Ḵookhittaan division of the Kaagwaantaan clan of Sitka, wearing an Eagle bib and a Bear tunic, Sitka, ca. 1900–1910. Identification by Harold Jacobs, 2021. Courtesy of the National Park Service, Sitka National Historical Park, 03926.

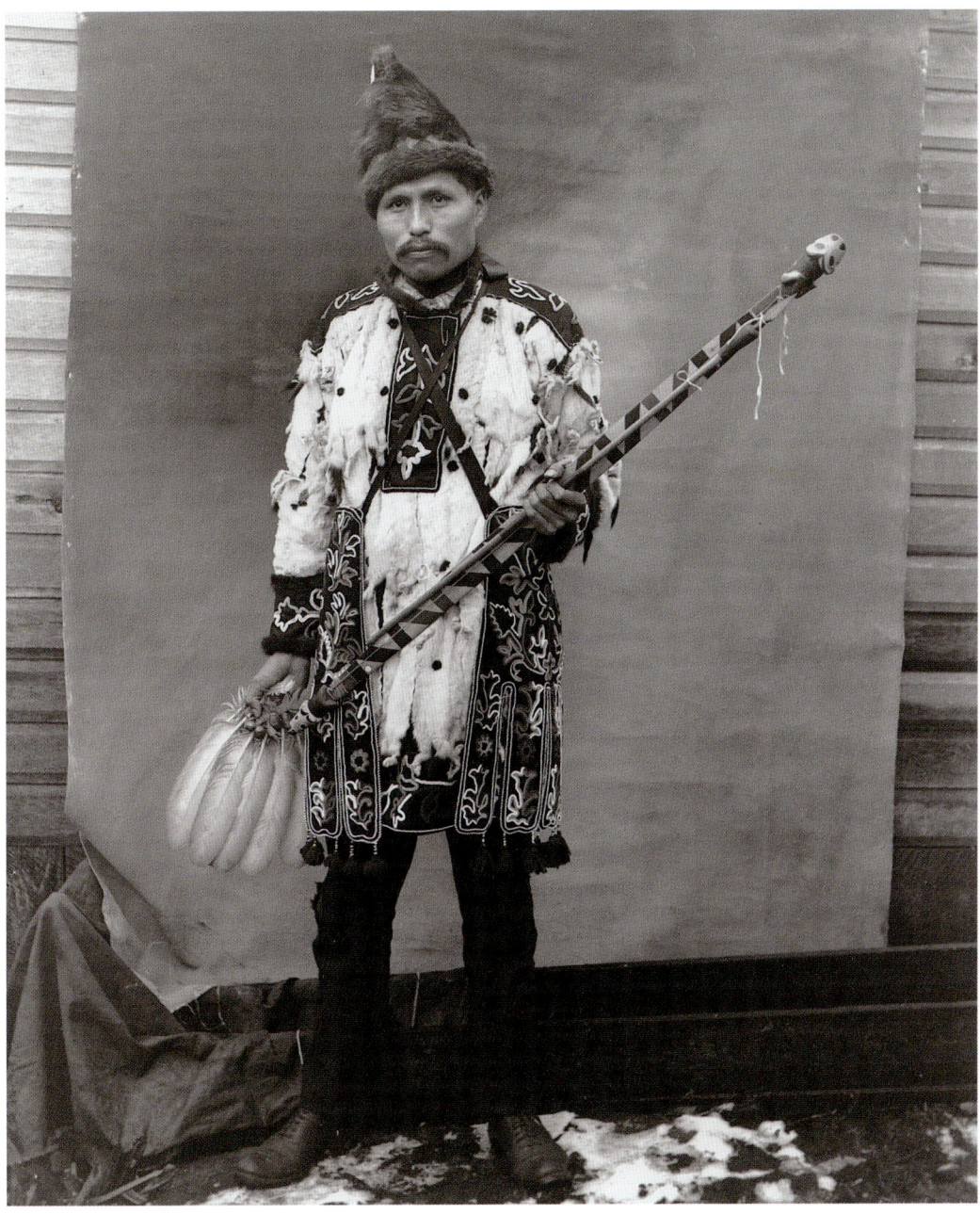

PLATE 35. A formal portrait of man dressed in an ermine coat and holding a Frog staff, Sitka, ca. 1900–1920. Courtesy of the National Park Service, Sitka National Historical Park, 3930.

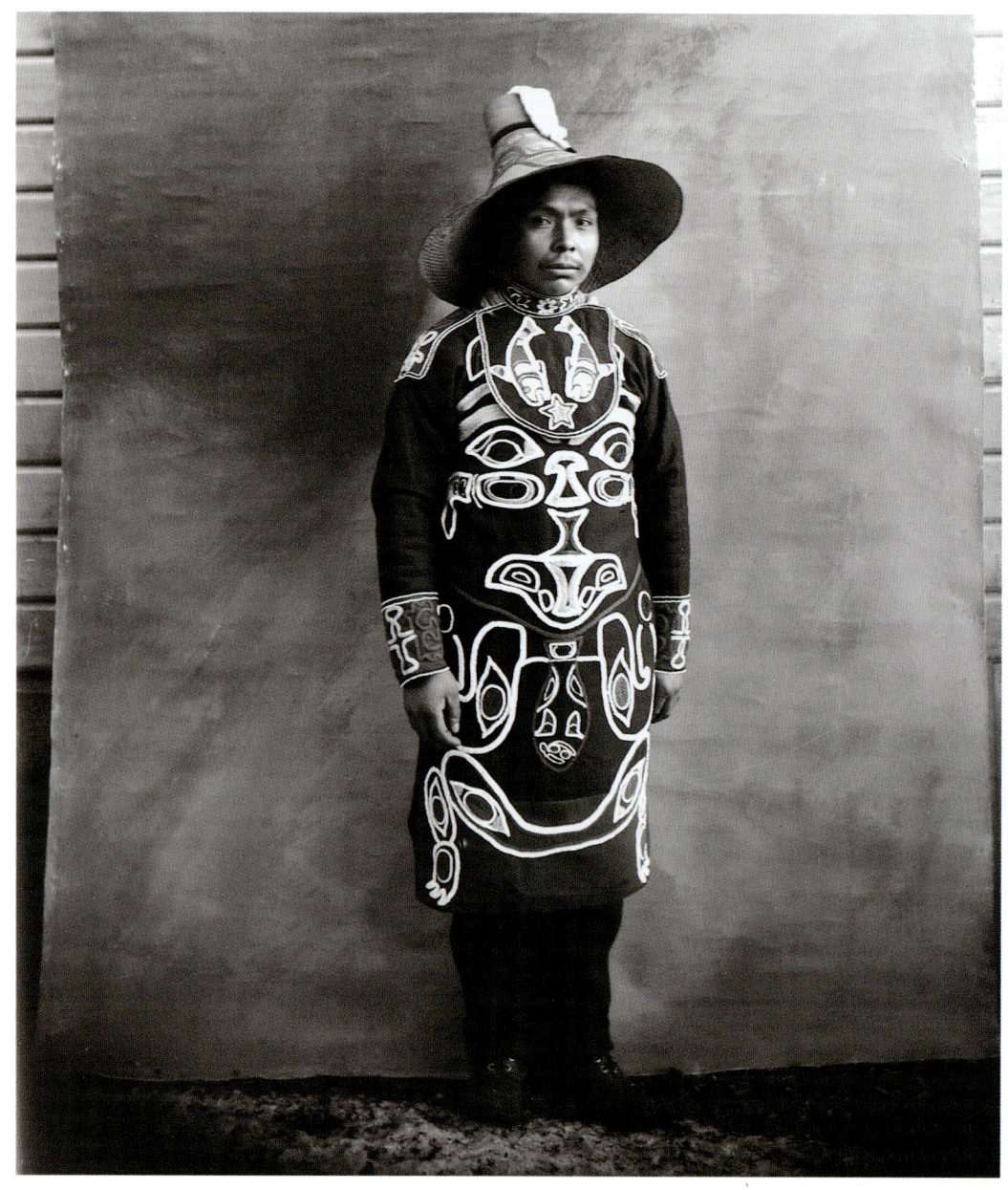

PLATE 36. A formal portrait of a young man wearing a ceremonial shirt, Sitka, ca. 1900–1920. Courtesy of the National Park Service, Sitka National Historical Park, 3932.

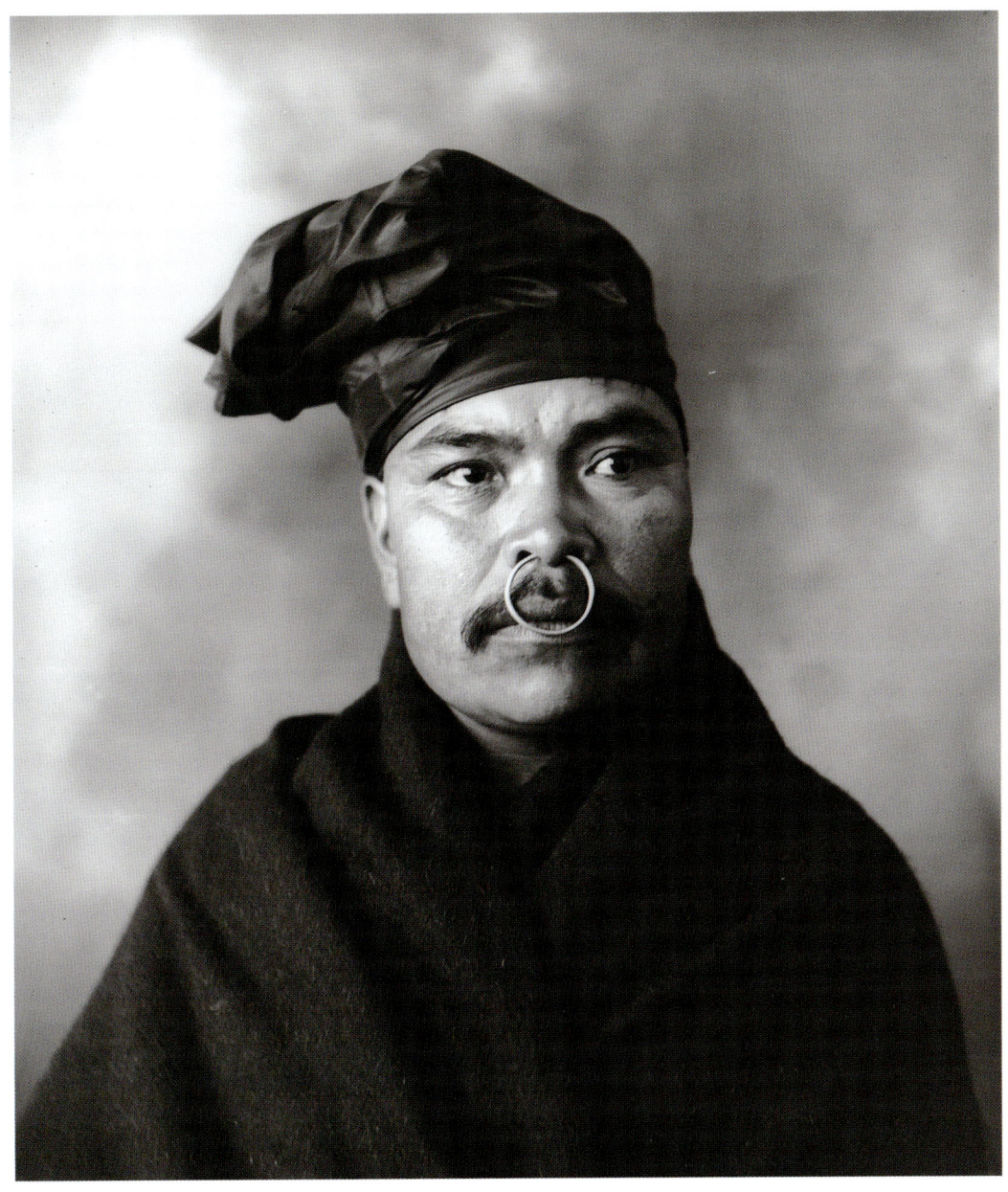

PLATE 37. A formal portrait of an unidentified Tlingit man, which might have been taken inside Merrill's studio, ca. 1900–1920. He wears a black head covering and a nose ring, common ḵu.éex' attire. Courtesy of the National Park Service, Sitka National Historical Park, 03935.

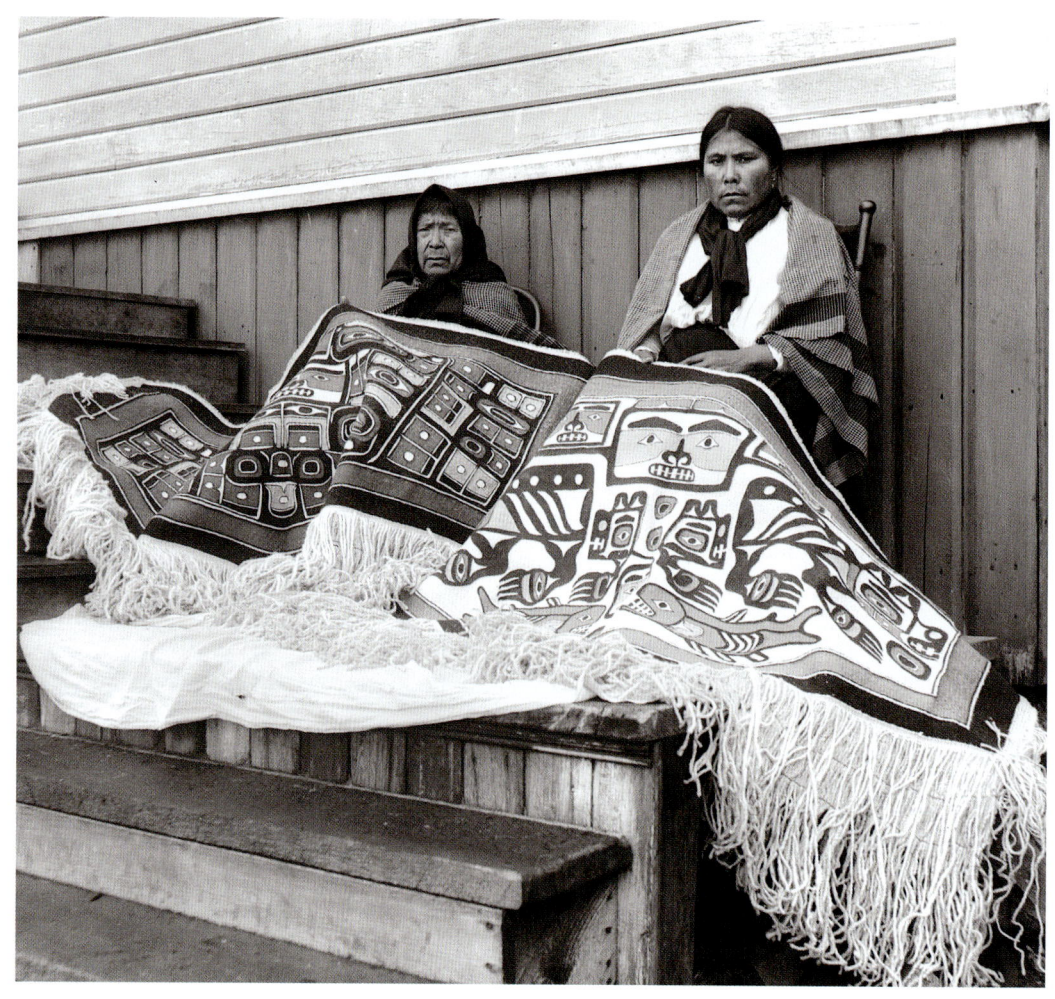

PLATE 38. An informal portrait of Mary Willard (Aaklé, Déix̲.wudu.oo) (b. 1880), Wolf House (G̲ooch Hít), Kaagwaantaan clan of Klukwan, with Saantats, her mother (at left). Mary is displaying a Chilkat blanket depicting bears and salmon. She was a well-known Chilkat blanket weaver, so these were probably blankets she had made. Mary was the wife of James Willard (b. 1880). Identifications by Harold Jacobs, 2021. Courtesy of the National Park Service, Sitka National Historical Park, 03854.

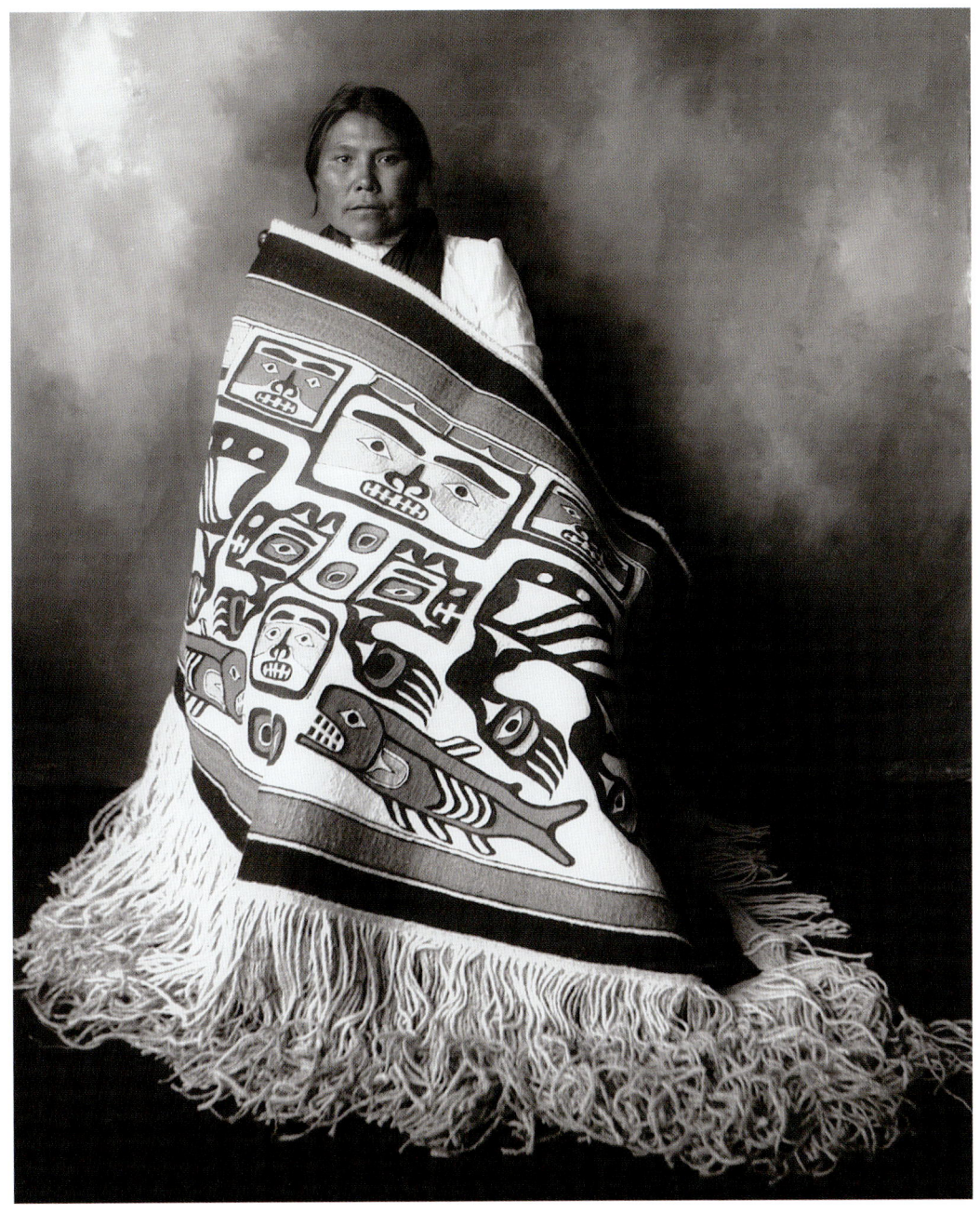

PLATE 39. A formal portrait of Mary Willard (Aaklé, Déix̱.wudu.oo), Wolf House (G̱ooch Hít), Kaagwaantaan clan of Klukwan, wearing the same blanket as in plate 38. Identification by Harold Jacobs, 2021. Courtesy of the National Park Service, Sitka National Historical Park, 3855.

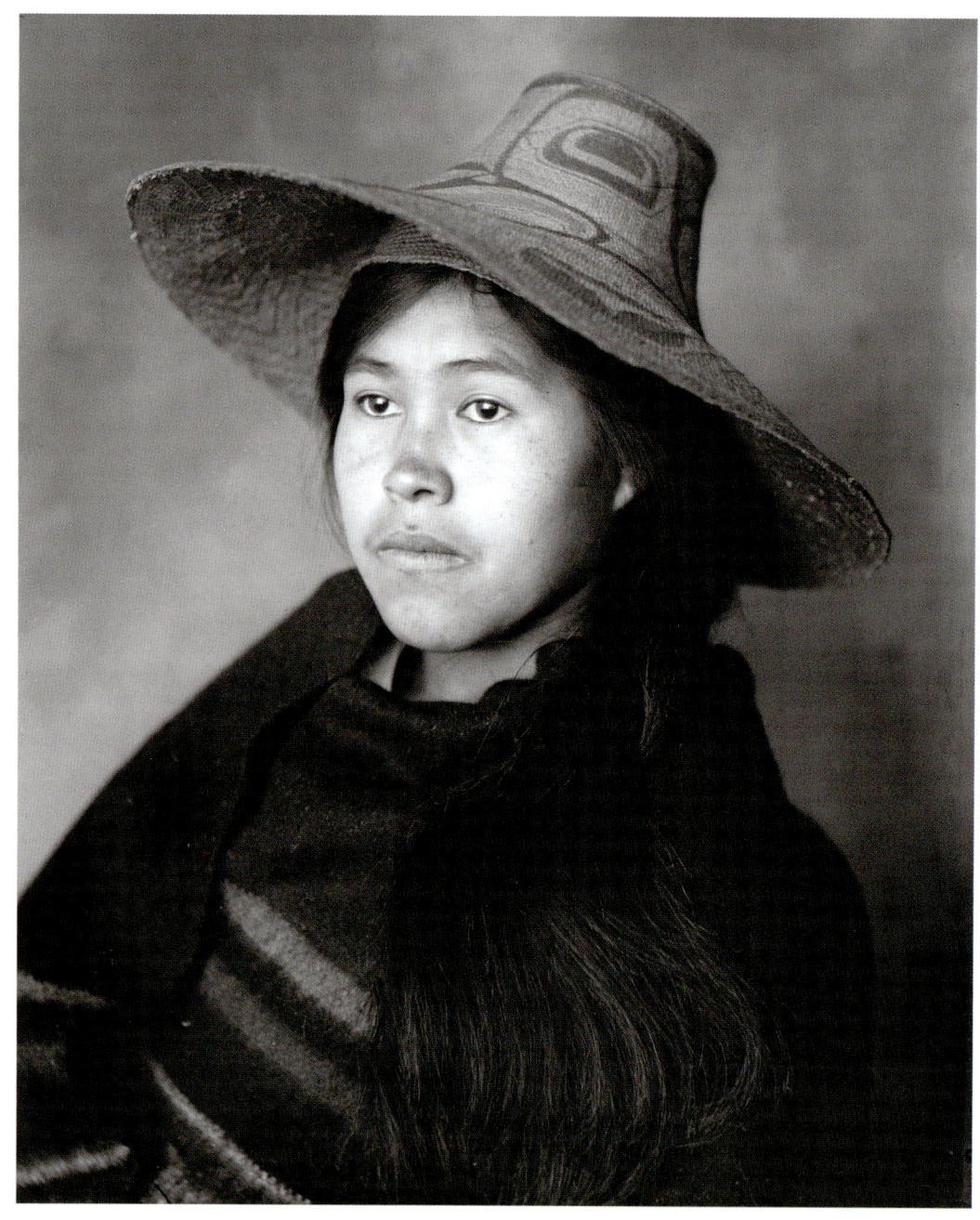

PLATE 40. Studio portrait of an unidentified Tlingit woman wearing a simple blanket and a woven spruce-root hat, Sitka, ca. 1900–1929. Courtesy of the National Park Service, Sitka National Historical Park, 26412.

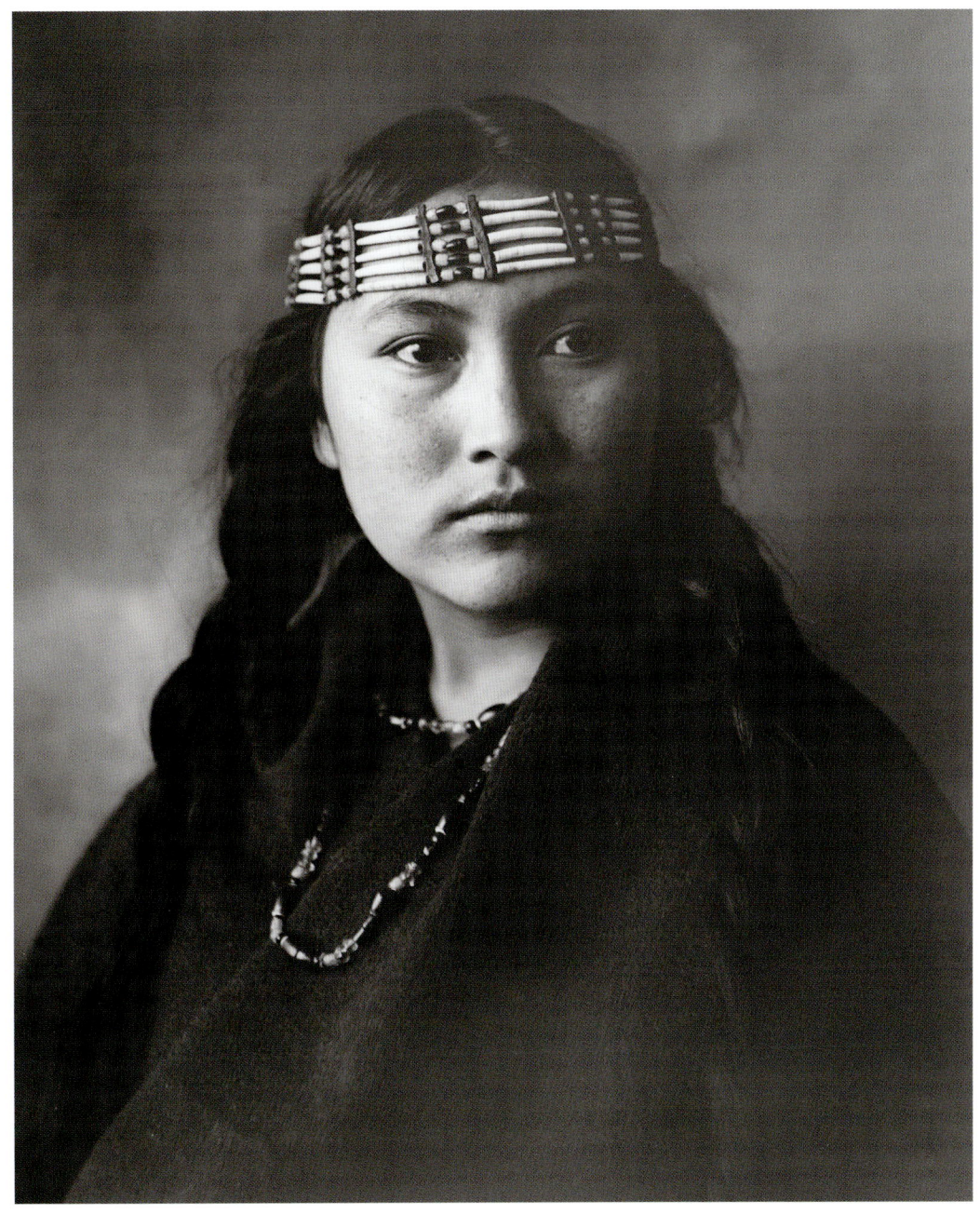

PLATE 41. Studio portrait of Lillian Cook, Little Coho House (Lʼook Hít Yádi), Lʼuknax̱.ádi clan of Sitka, ca. 1900–1929. Courtesy of the National Park Service, Sitka National Historical Park, 25426.

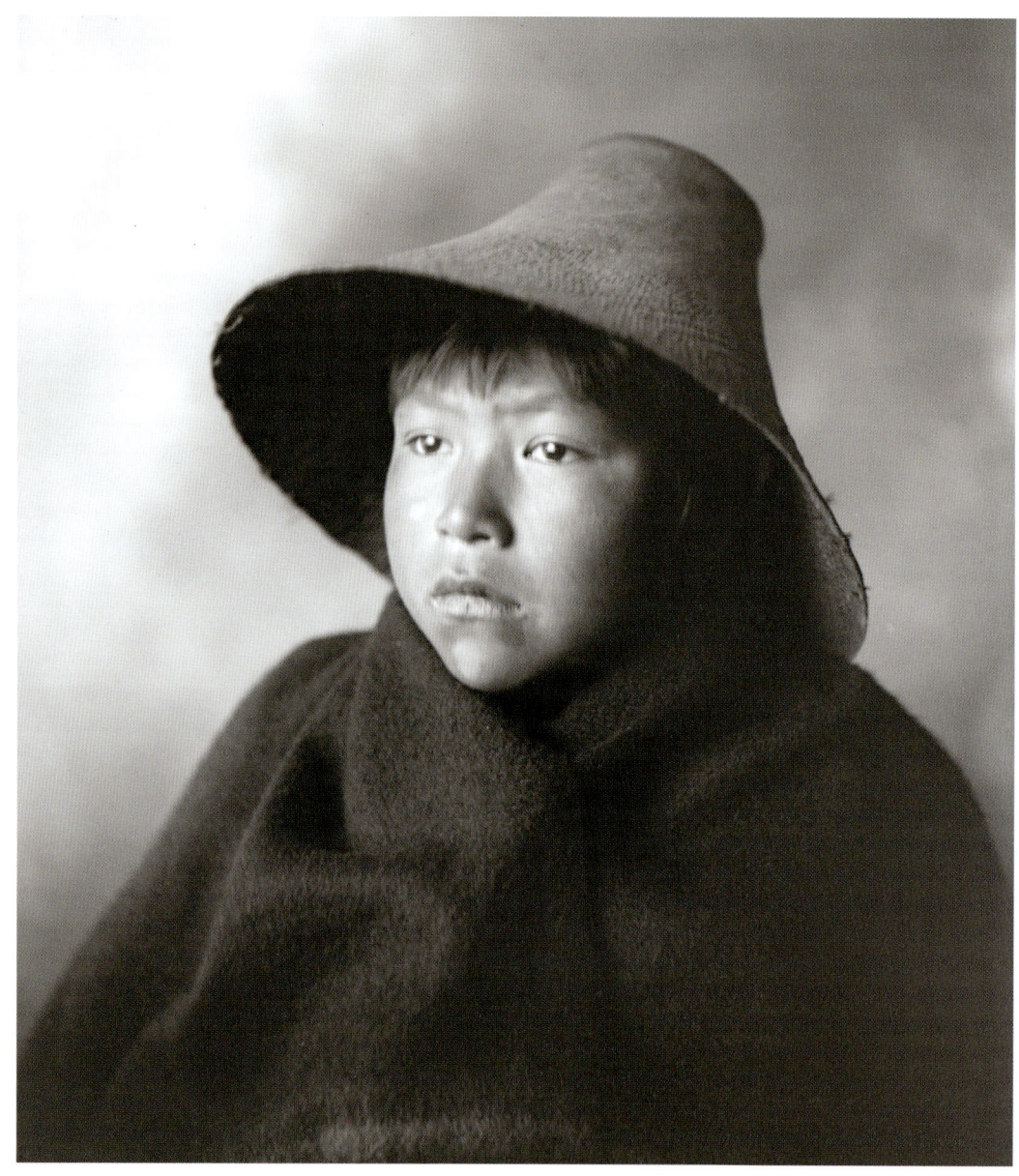

PLATE 42. Studio portrait of an unidentified Tlingit boy wearing a simple blanket and a woven spruce-root hat, Sitka, ca. 1915. Courtesy of the National Park Service, Sitka National Historical Park, 25424.

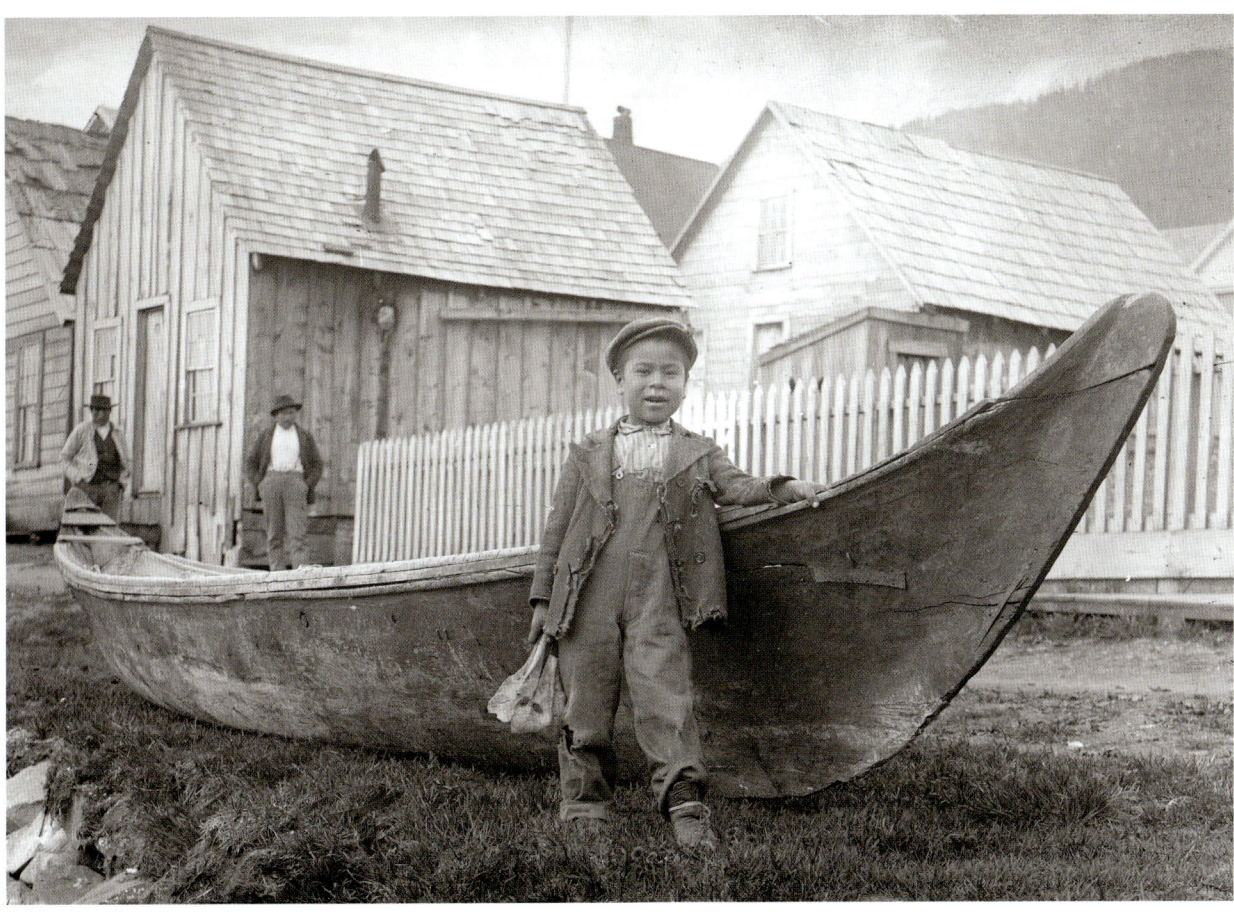

PLATE 43. Unidentified Tlingit boy in front of a canoe on the front street of the Sitka Indian Village, ca. 1900–1929. Courtesy of the National Park Service, Sitka National Historical Park, 26119.

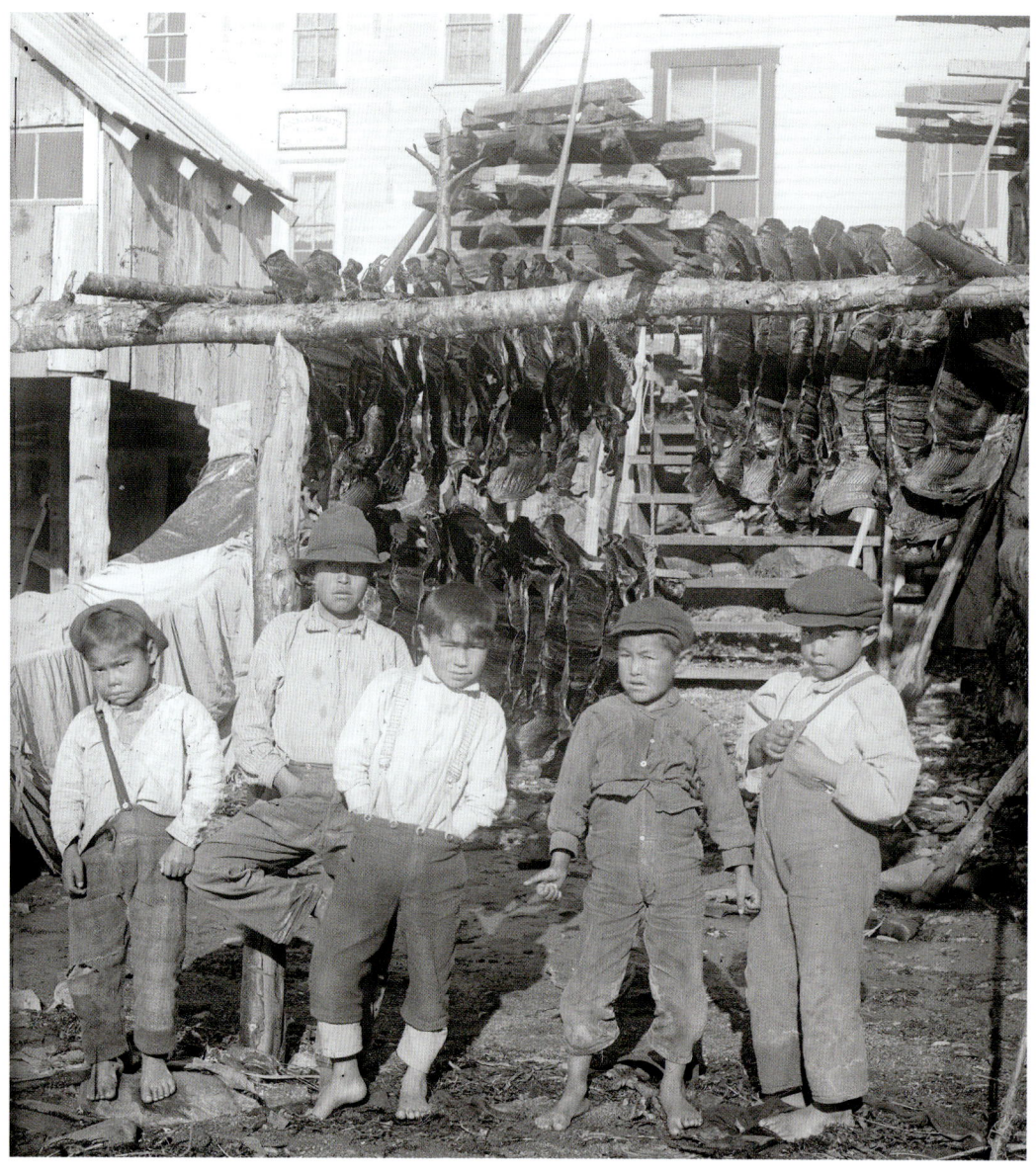

PLATE 44. Sitka, ca. 1900. Five Tlingit boys on Sitka Indian Village's front street, ca. 1900.

Left to right: unknown; Dick Harris (G̱eedei); unknown; Charles Dick (Daanax̱.ils'eiḵ) (1893–1972), Platform House (Kayaaashká Hít), L'uknax̱.ádi clan. Part of Annahootz's lineage house is visible in the upper left corner. Salmon is drying on the racks in the background.

Identifications by Sharon Gmelch (2008: 115) and Harold Jacobs, 2021. Courtesy of the National Park Service, Sitka National Historical Park, 26120.

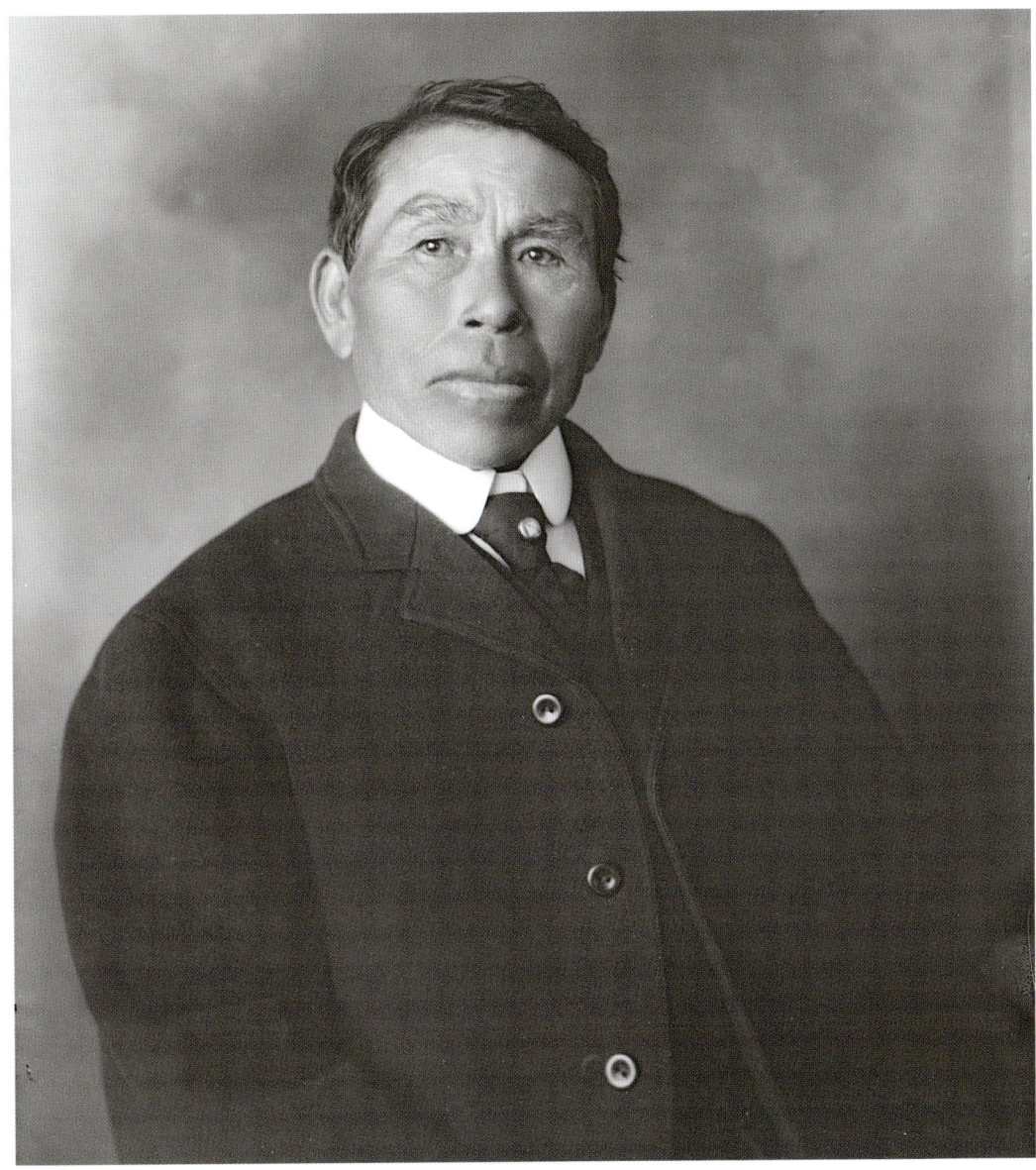

PLATE 45. Possibly Don Cameron (Daalwools'ees') (1876–1938), Kaagwaantaan clan of Klukwaan, 1920s. He was John Swanton's interpreter and consultant in Sitka (Swanton 1909: 1). Identification from an inscription on the back of the photograph and by Harold Jacobs, 2024. Courtesy of the National Park Service, Sitka National Historical Park, 26229.

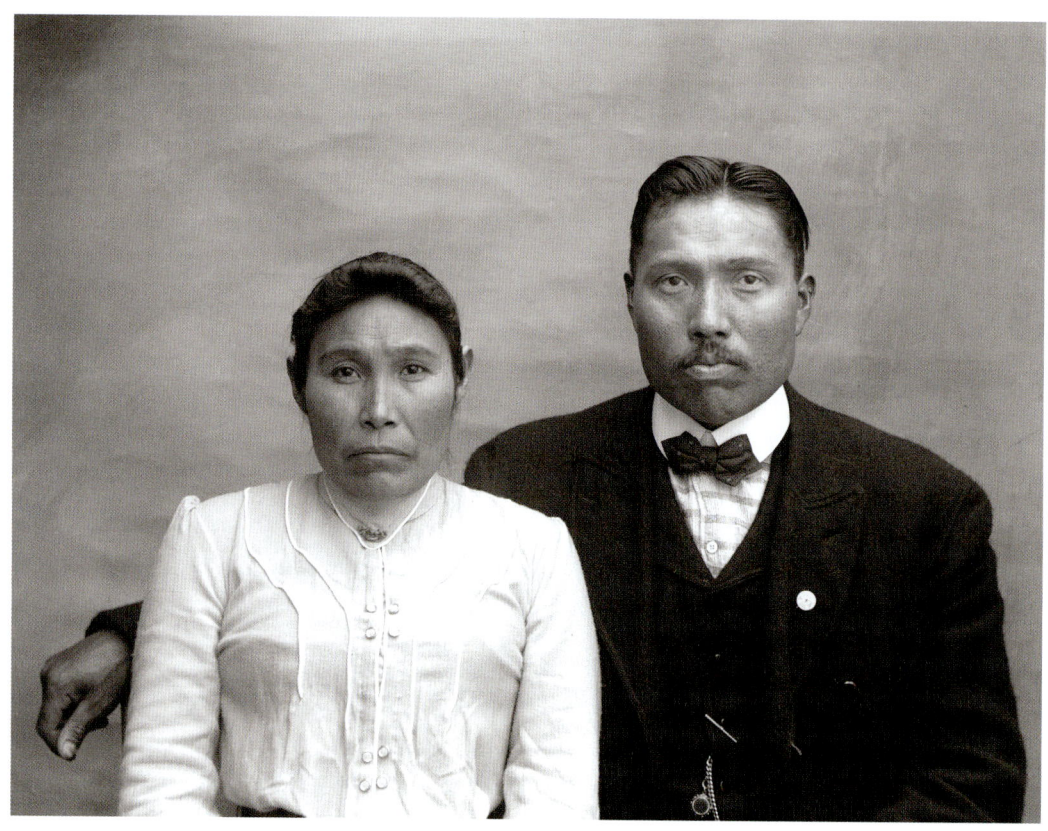

PLATE 46. An unidentified Tlingit couple, Sitka, date unknown. Courtesy of the National Park Service, Sitka National Historical Park, 26256.

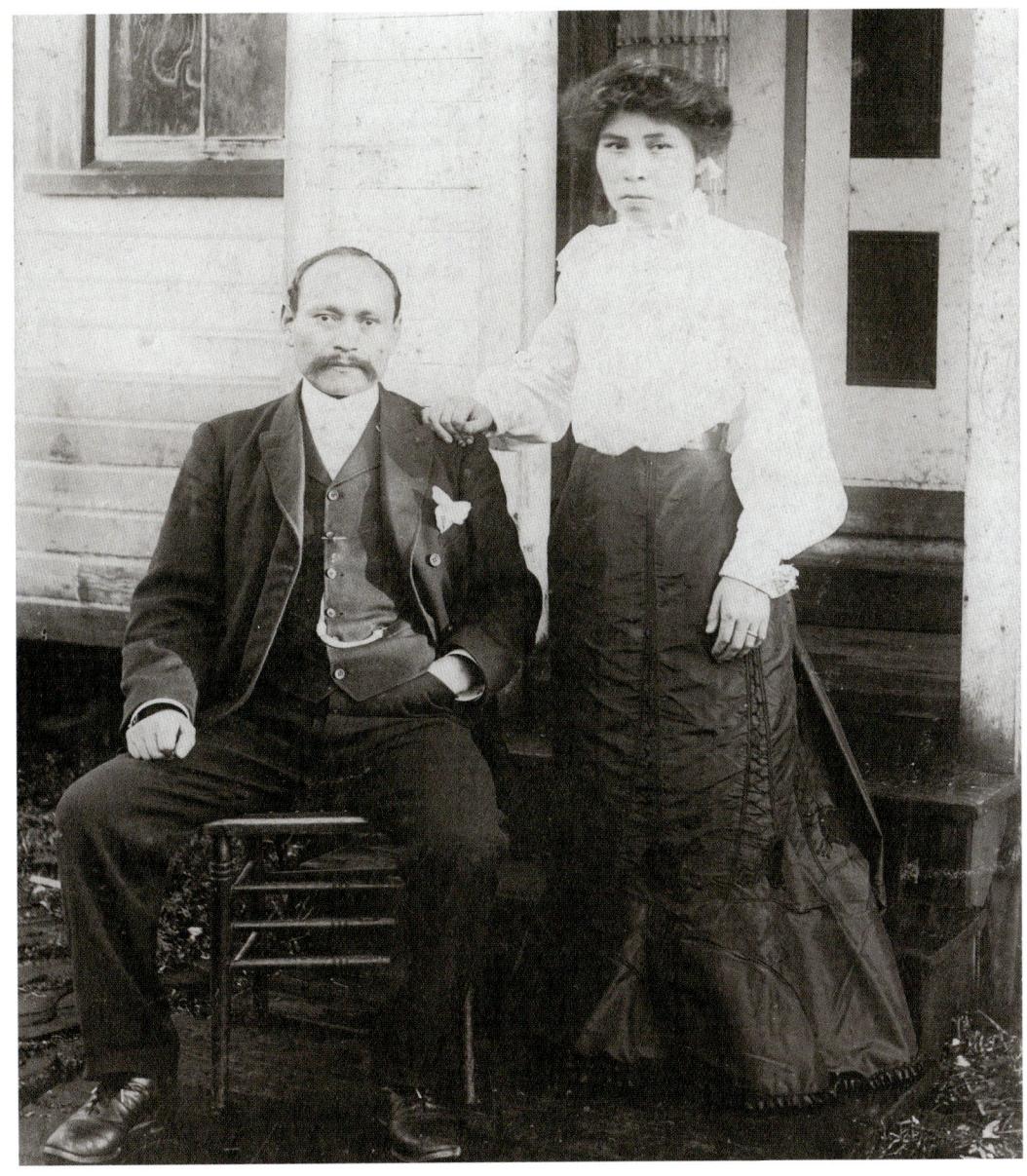

PLATE 47. George Howard Sr. (Naats'tlein) (1865–1925) and Lottie (Sloan) Howard (K̲aakaltin) (1878–1956), X̲aak̲á Hít (Point House), Kiks.ádi clan, near the Sitka Industrial and Training School, ca. 1910–15. University of Washington Library, Special Collections, Elbridge Warren Merrill Collection, PH Coll 325.22.

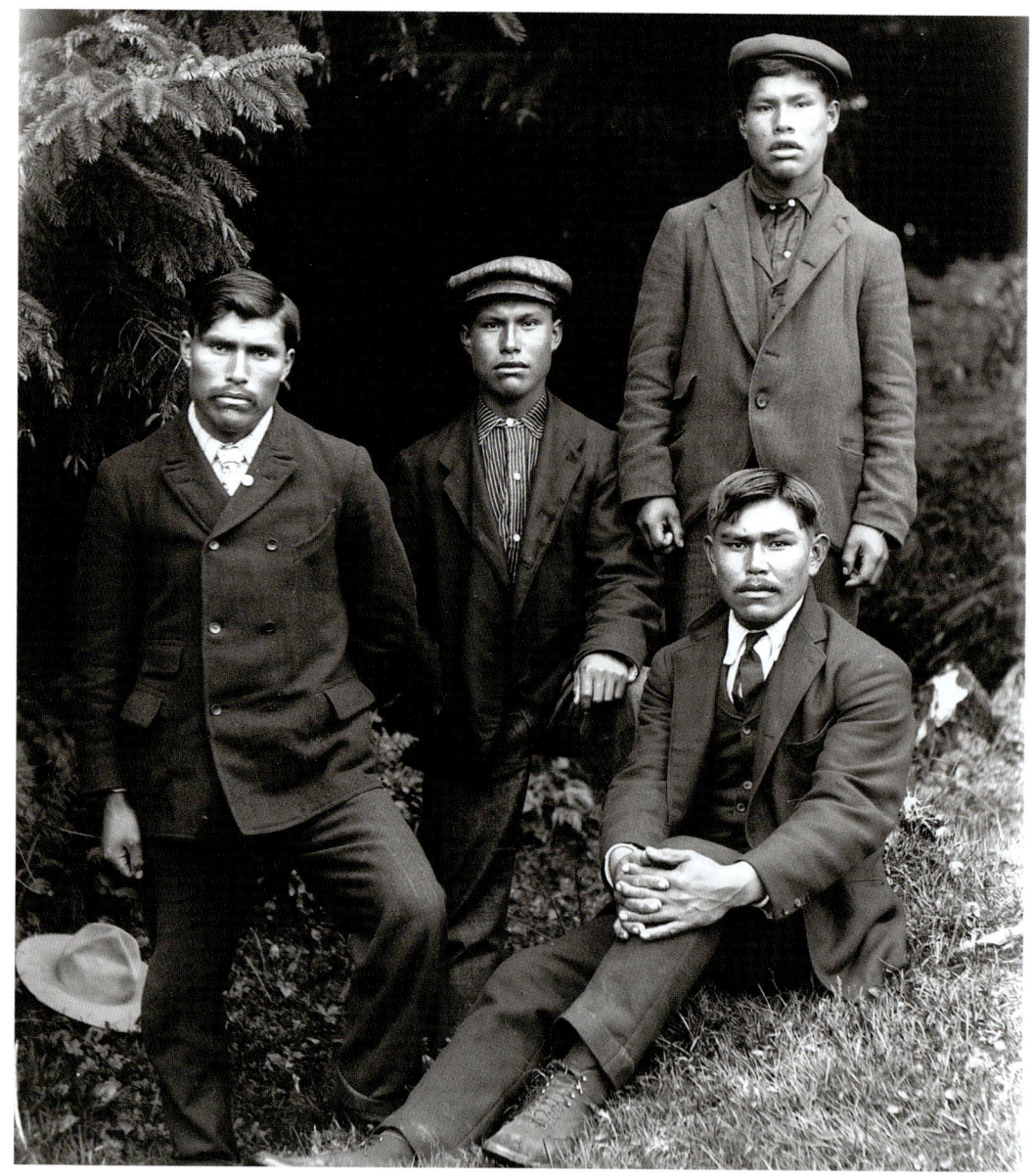

PLATE 48. Four young Tlingit men, Sitka, ca. 1910–20. On the left is Scotty James (Lʼashaa Éesh) (1886–1961), of the Tʼakdeintaan clan of Hoonah. The two other standing men might be his brothers. The seated man might be Ben Bailey (Géikʼi) (b. 1888), Little Coho House (Lʼuk Hít Yádi), Lʼuknax̱.ádi clan. Identification from an inscription on the back of the photograph and by Harold Jacobs, 2024. Courtesy of the National Park Service, Sitka National Historical Park, 03815.

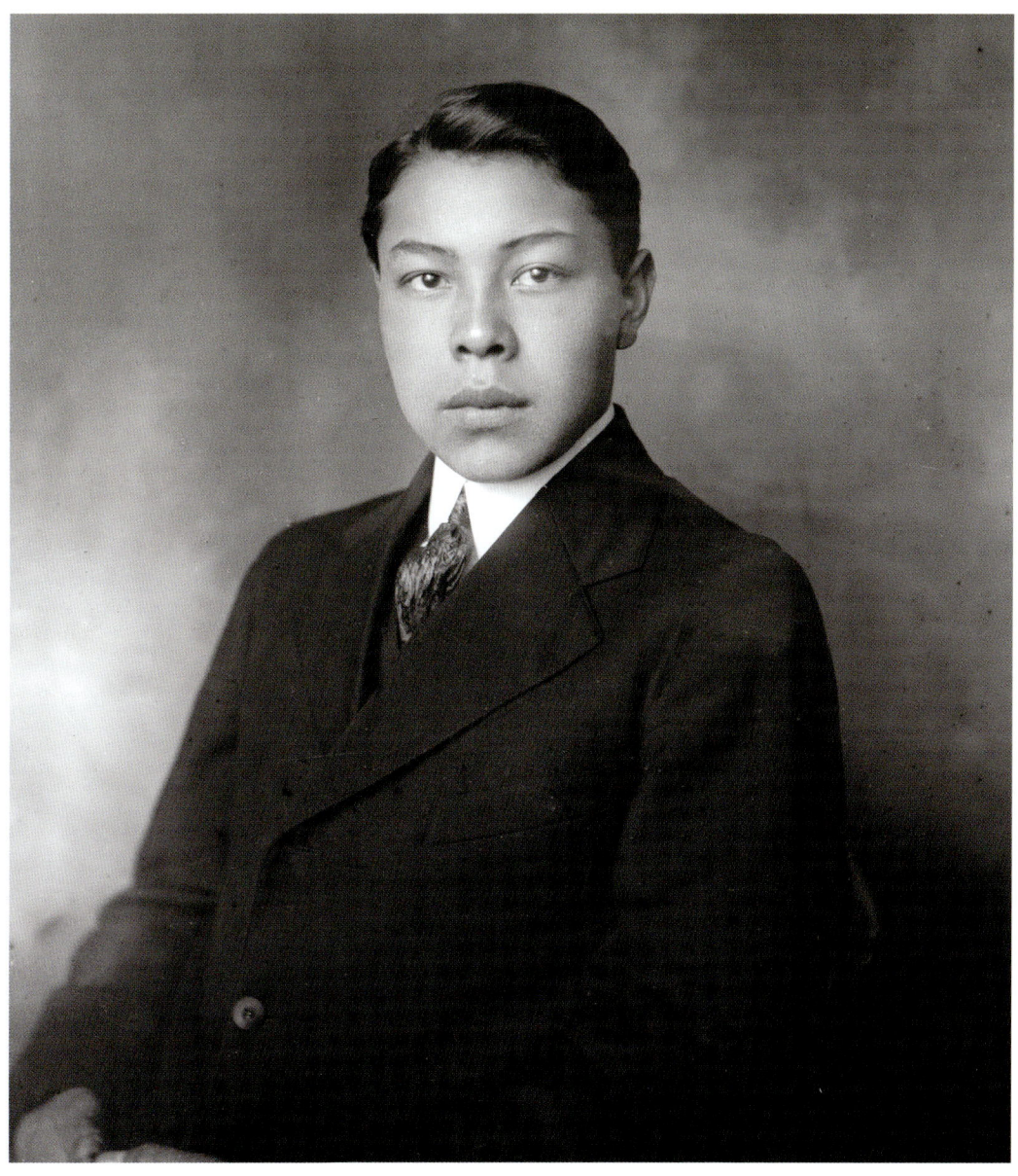

PLATE 49. Young Tlingit man, Sitka, date unknown. Courtesy of the National Park Service, Sitka National Historical Park, 26232.

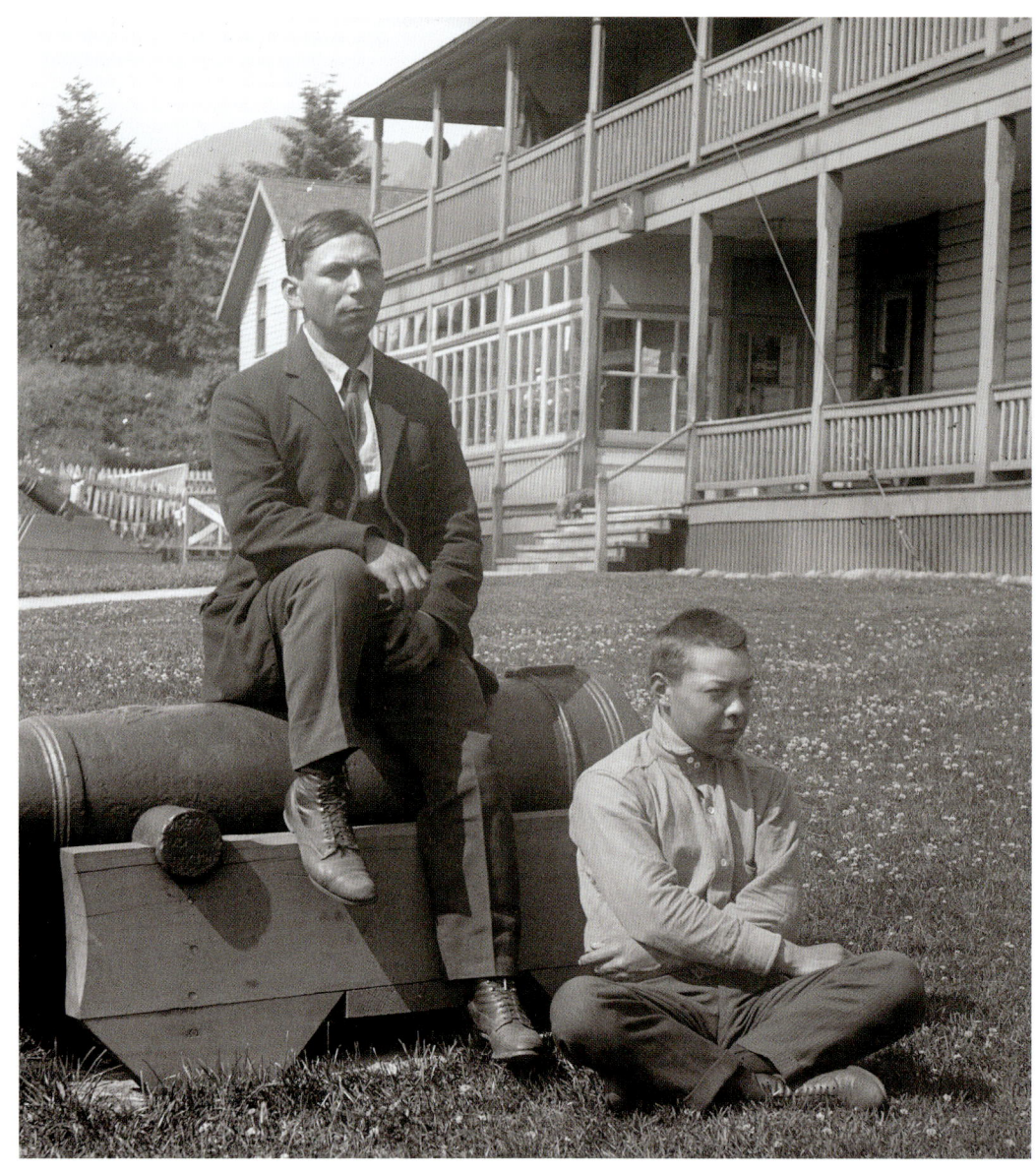

PLATE 50. On the right, Sam (Simon) Didrickson (1898–1965) (Tlákwsátaan), Shattering House (Kaxátjaa Hít), Kiks.ádi clan, with a non-Native companion (possibly his father) on the parade grounds. Sam's father, Chris (Ole Christian Gustav) Didrickson, was Norwegian; his mother, Polly Didrickson (Seexweit Tláa) (b. 1877), was Tlingit. Identification from an inscription on the back of the photograph and by Harold Jacobs, 2024. Courtesy of the National Park Service, Sitka National Historical Park, 25836.

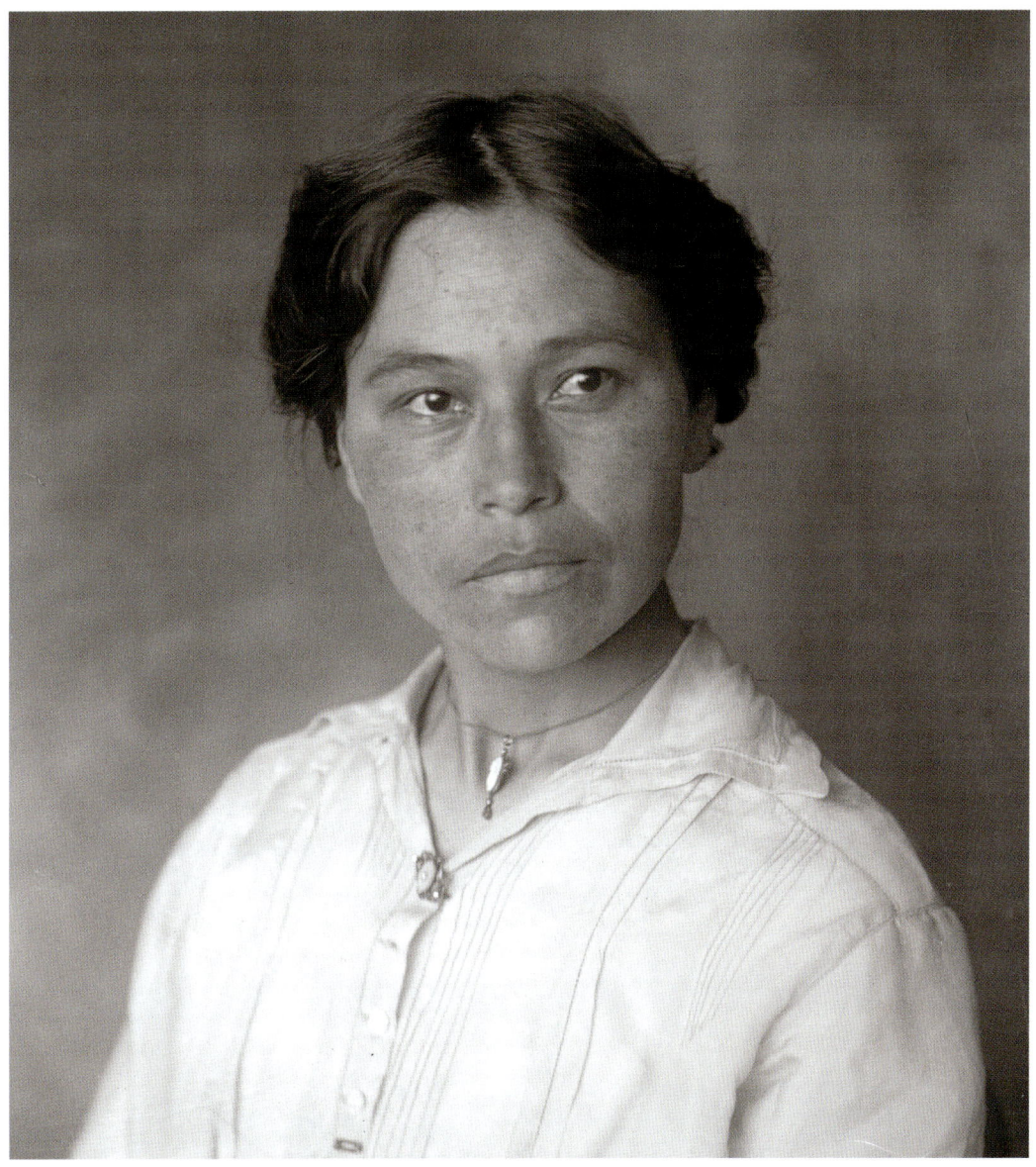

PLATE 51. Mary (Jean) (Williams) Wannamaker (Shaax̲aatk'í) (1884–1941), Cow House (Xaas Hít) of the Ḵoosk'eidí clan, or unknown house of the T'aḵdeintaan clan. She was the wife of Andrew J. Wannamaker (Shamata's, Wooshkeenaa), Eagle's Nest House (Ch'áak' Kúdi Hít), Kaagwaantaan clan of Sitka, and the adoptive mother of Elizabeth Peratrovich (1911–58). Identifications from an inscription on the back of the photograph, Dauenhauer and Dauenhauer (1994: 526), and Harold Jacobs, 2024. Courtesy of the National Park Service, Sitka National Historical Park, 26254.

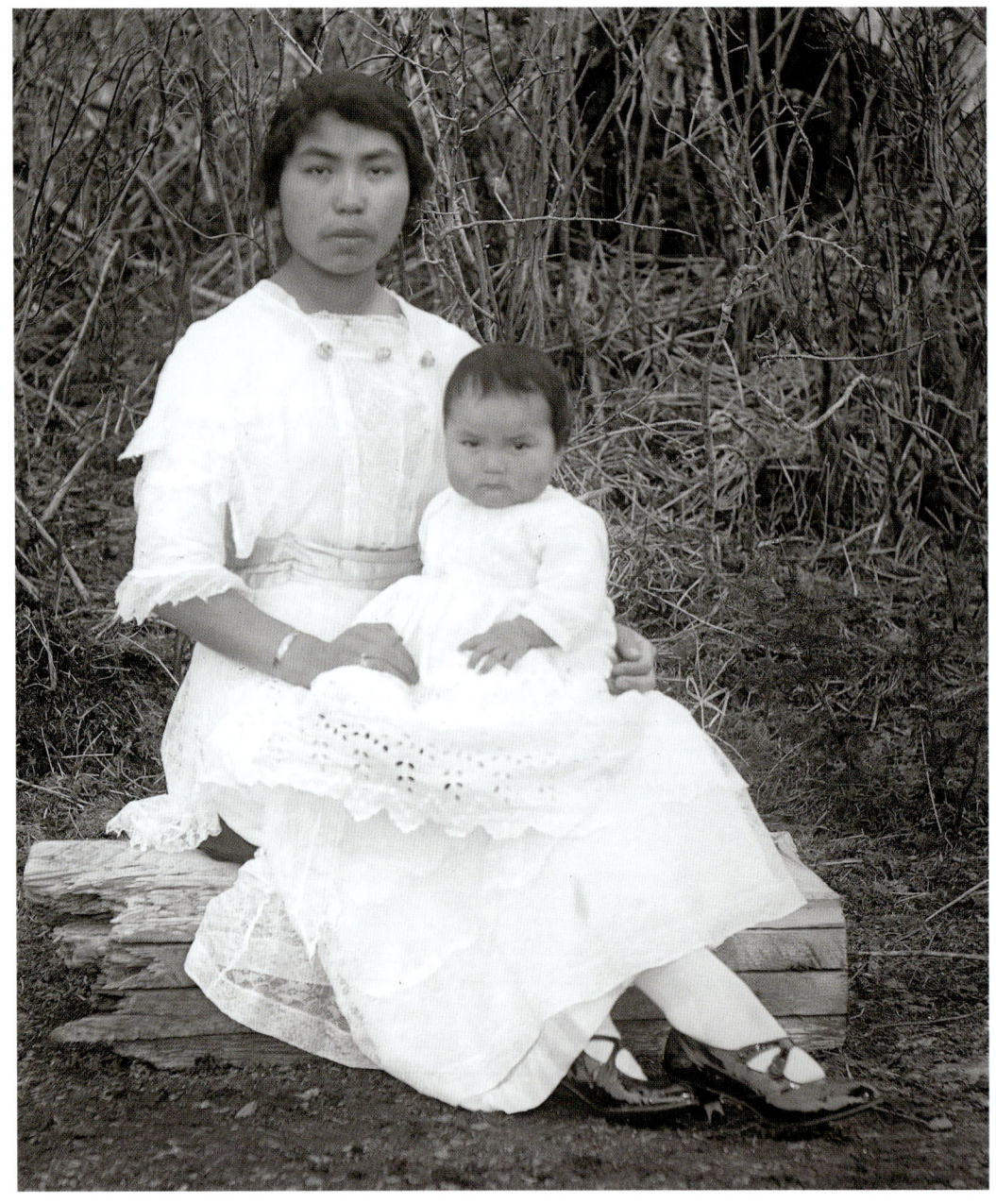

PLATE 52. Jessie Hanlon (Yanéitkwáa) (1912–89), Shark Backbone House (Toos' Díx'ee Hít), Wooshkeetaan clan, with her daughter Irene (1929–2006), Sitka, date unknown. Identification from an inscription on the back of the photograph and by Harold Jacobs, 2024. Courtesy of the National Park Service, Sitka National Historical Park, 25909.

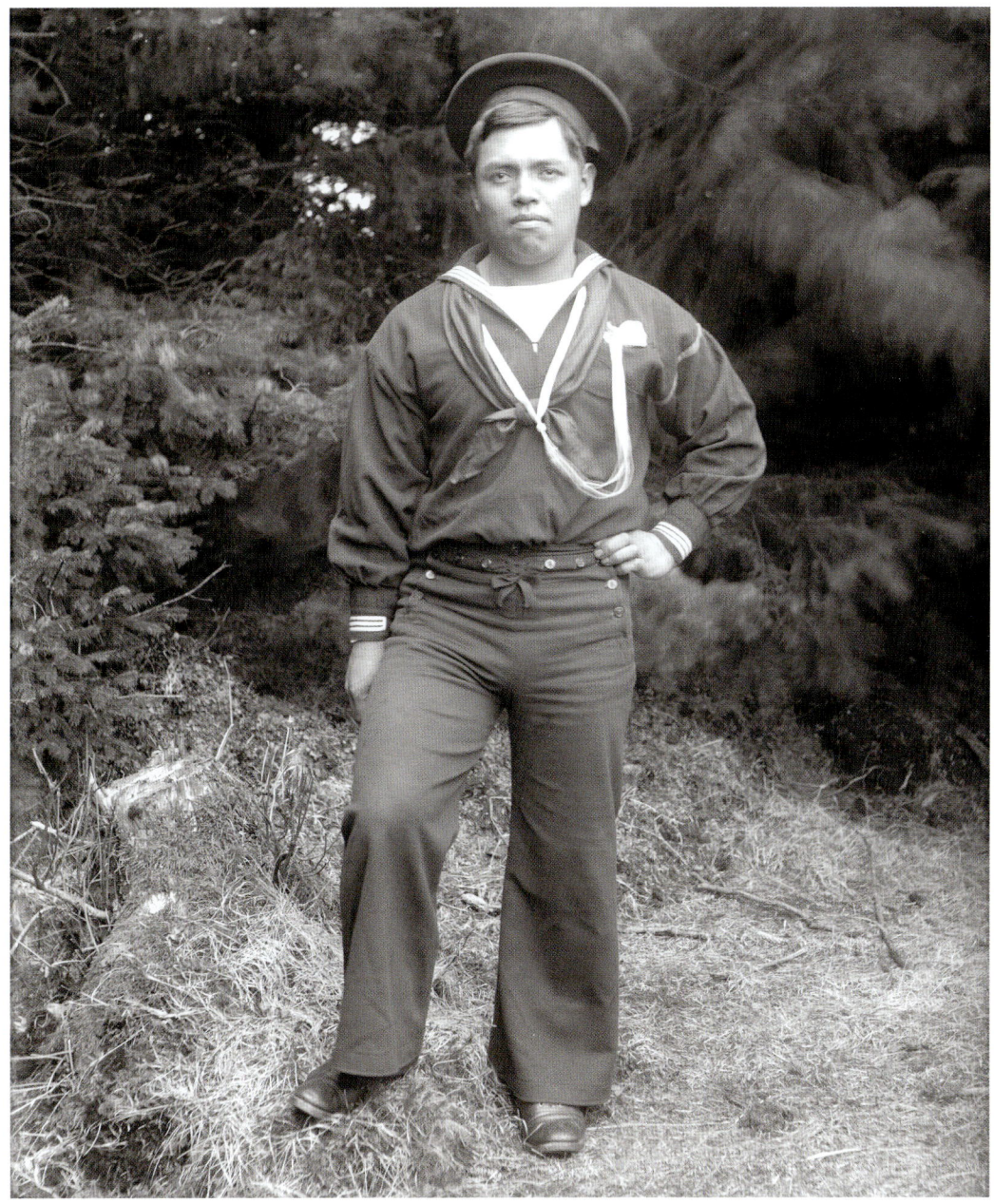

PLATE 53. Eddie Marshall (Kʼeich Éesh) (b. 1883), Big Box House (Ḵóok Hít Tlein), Ḵookhittaan subdivision of the Kaagwaantaan clan of Sitka, a sailor in the US Navy, Sitka, ca. 1910. Identification from an inscription on the back of the photograph and by Harold Jacobs, 2024. Courtesy of the National Park Service, Sitka National Historical Park, 26165.

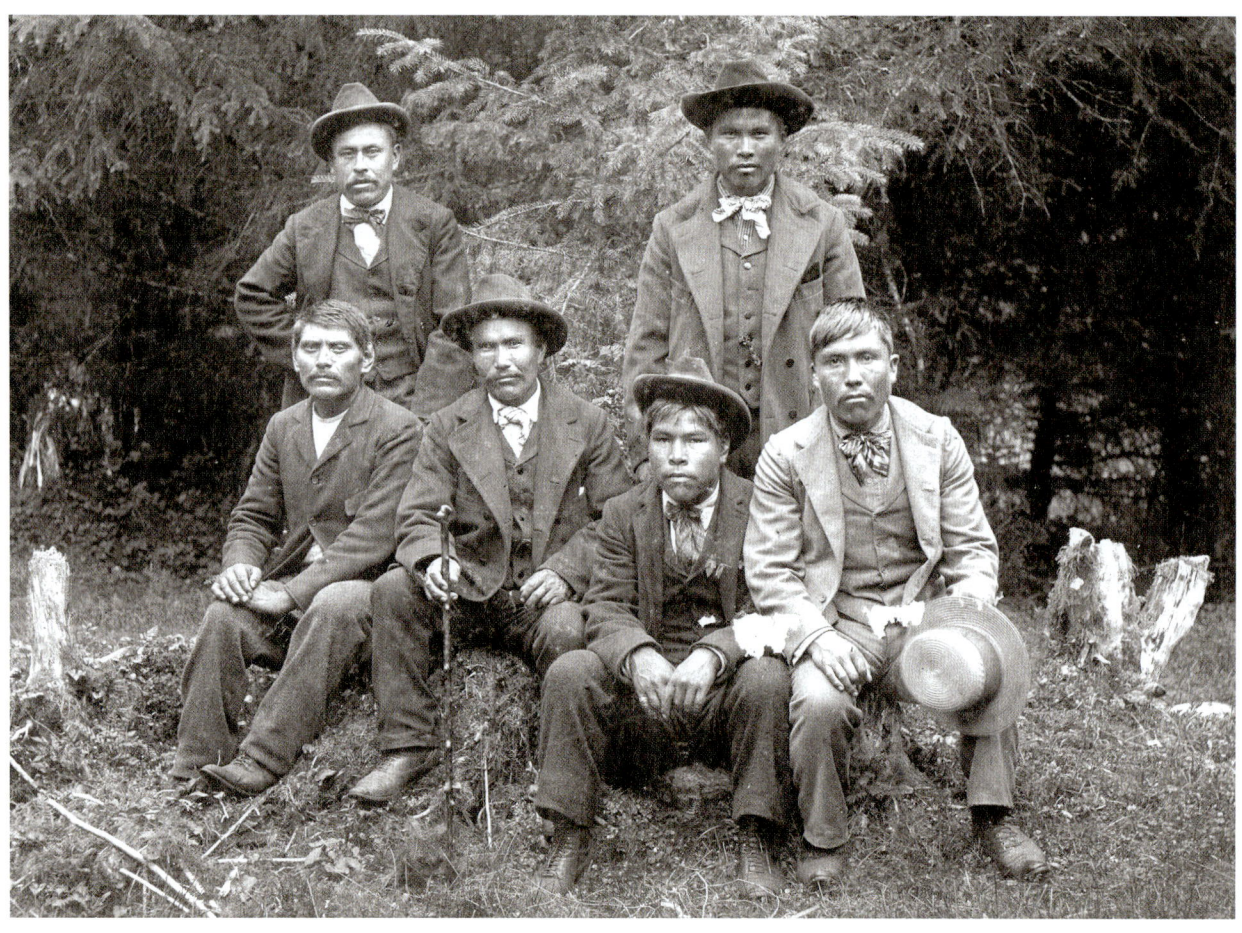

PLATE 54. A group of Tlingit men, Sitka, date unknown. Courtesy of the Sitka Historical Society, Sitka, Alaska. 83.19.19.

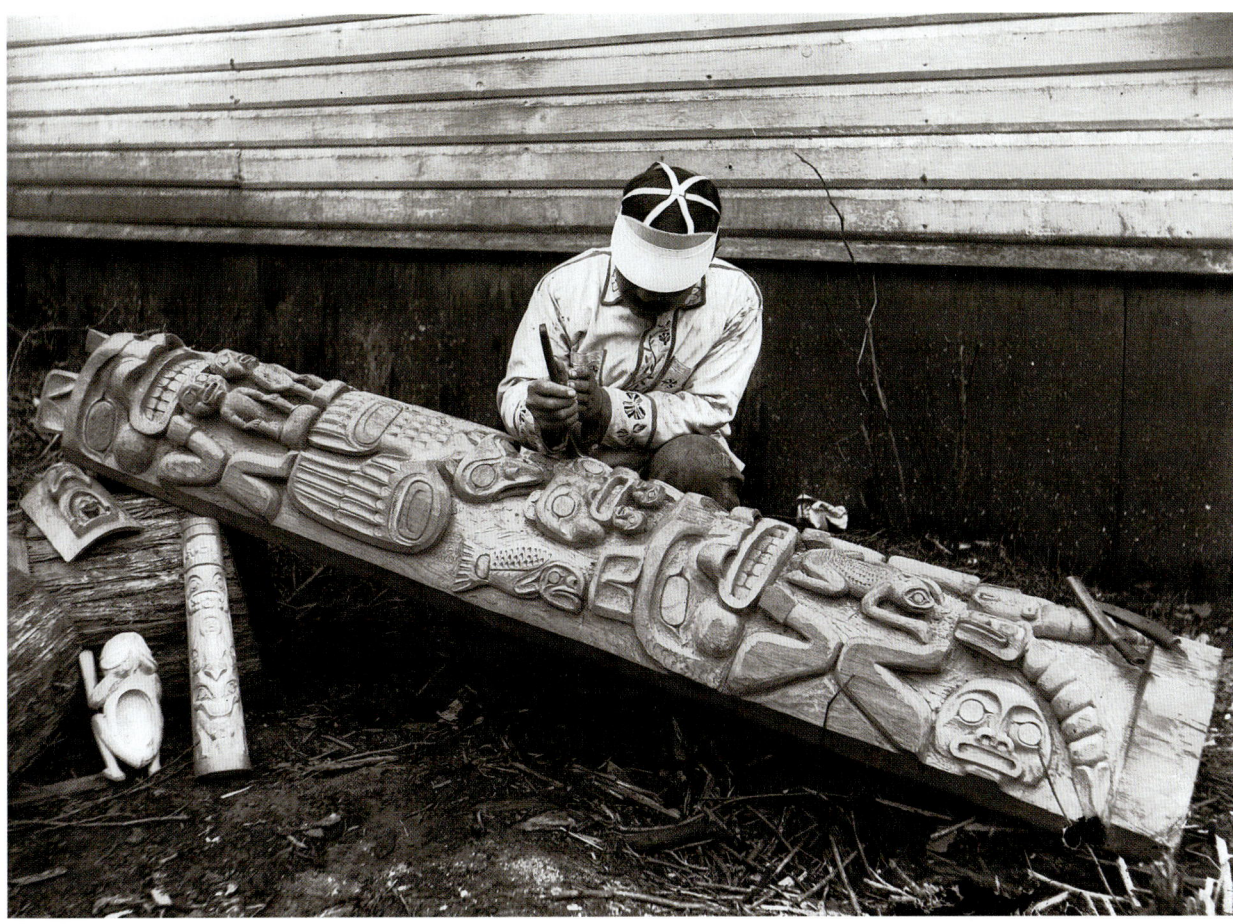

PLATE 55. The Tlingit carver William Cason (Shaayí Éesh) of the Ľuknax.ádi clan, working on a totem intended most likely for sale to non-Natives; a miniature totem pole, a Frog dish and another carving are displayed next to him. Sitka, date unknown. Identification by Harold Jacobs, 2021. Courtesy of the National Park Service, Sitka National Historical Park, 03829.

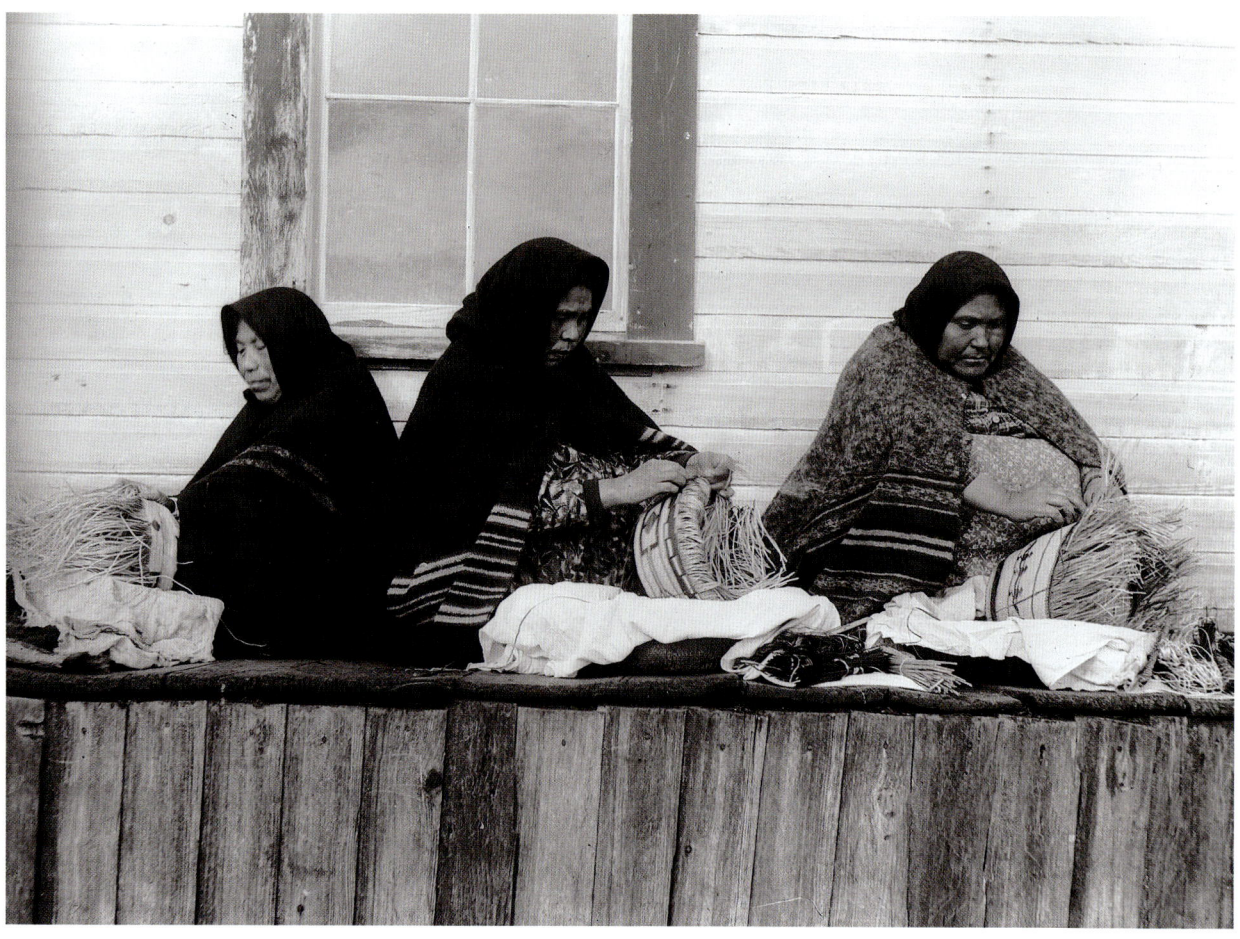

PLATE 56. Three Tlingit women sitting on a ledge in front of a house in the Sitka Indian Village, weaving spruce-root baskets, date unknown. Courtesy of the National Park Service, Sitka National Historical Park, 30852.

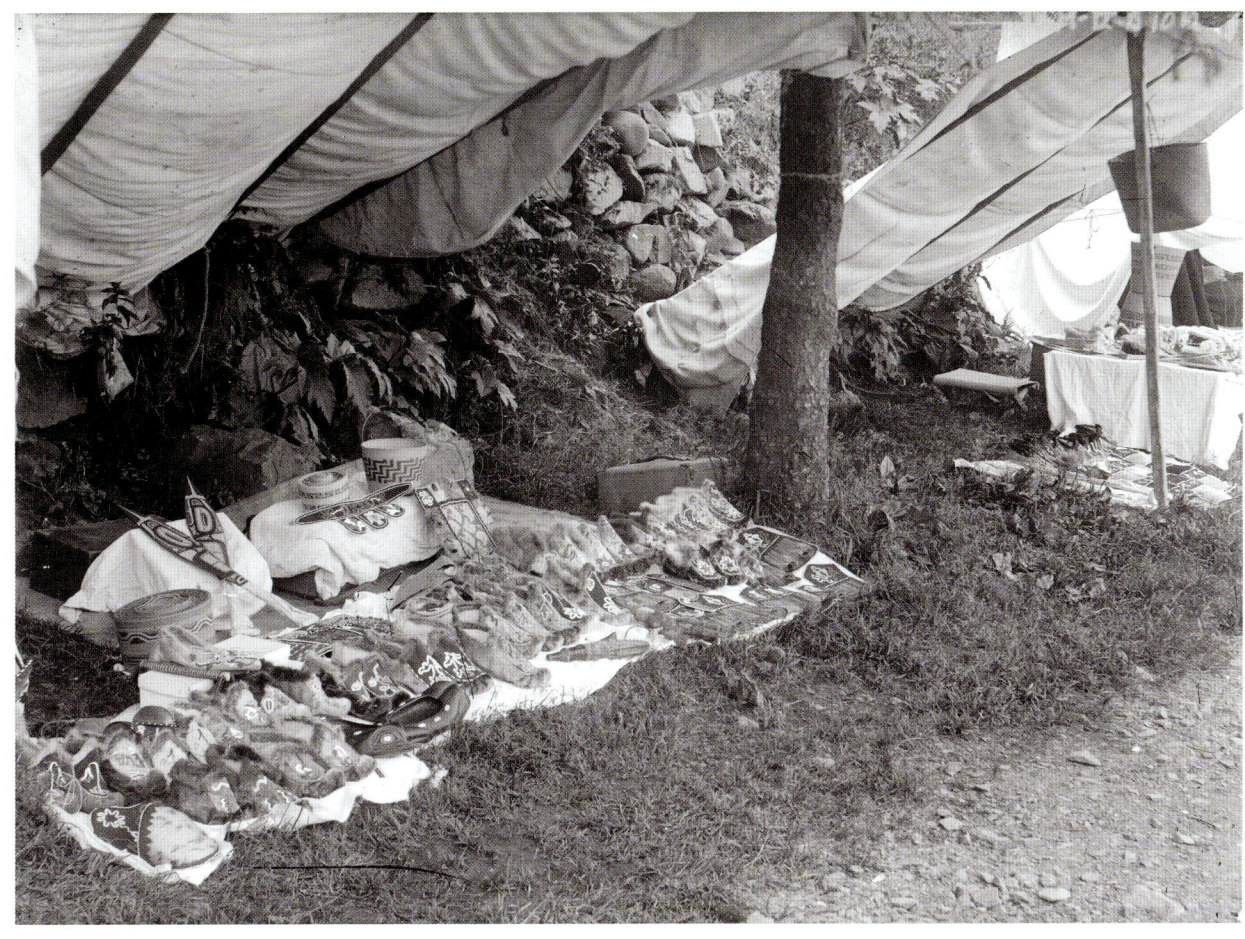

PLATE 57. Tlingit craft objects for sale to tourists, displayed under tents in downtown Sitka, date unknown. Courtesy of the National Park Service, Sitka National Historical Park, 26274.

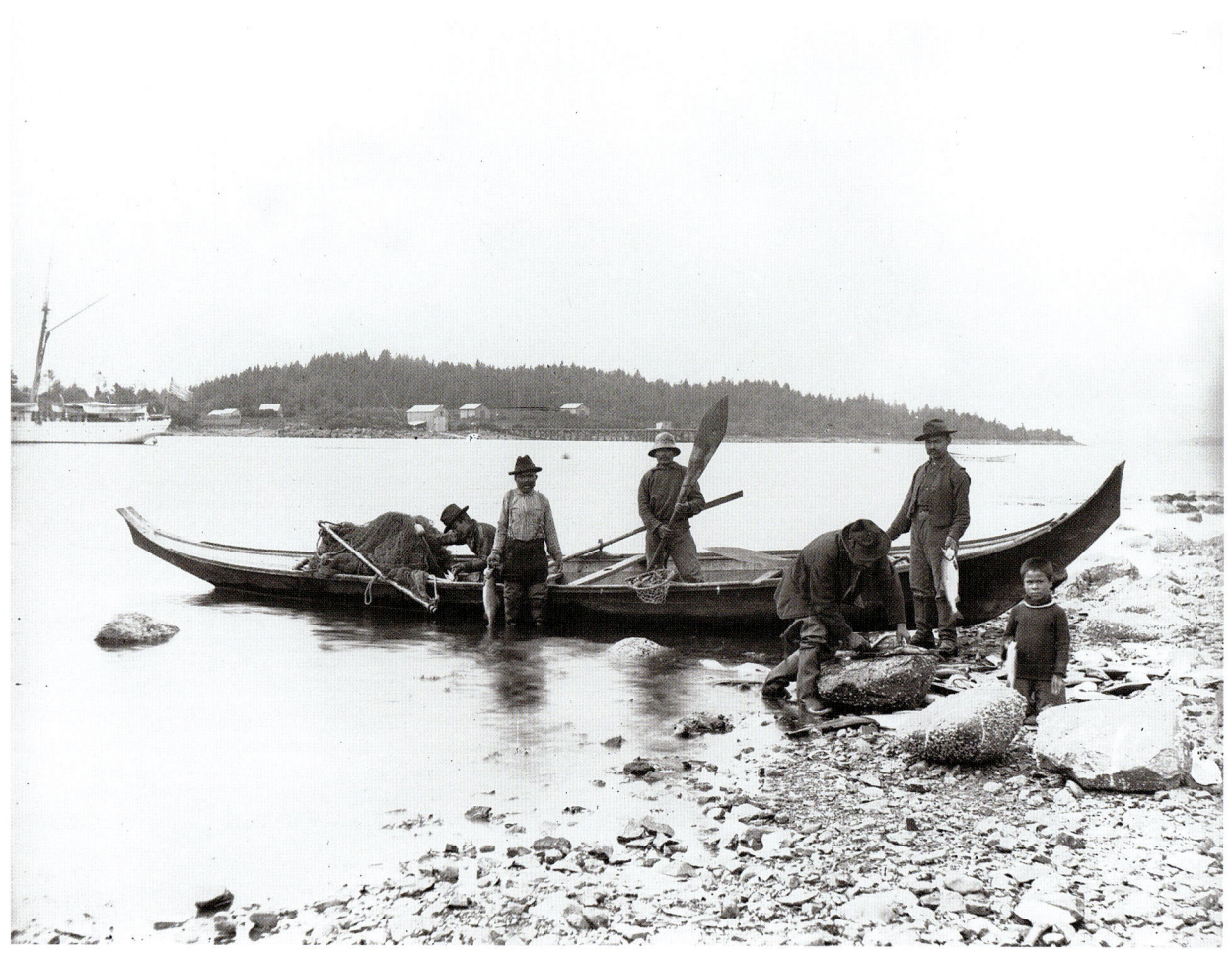

PLATE 58. Five Tlingit fishermen and a small boy with their canoe and catch on the beach near the Sitka Indian Village, date unknown. Japonski Island and a US Navy vessel are visible in the background. Courtesy of the National Park Service, Sitka National Historical Park, 03810.

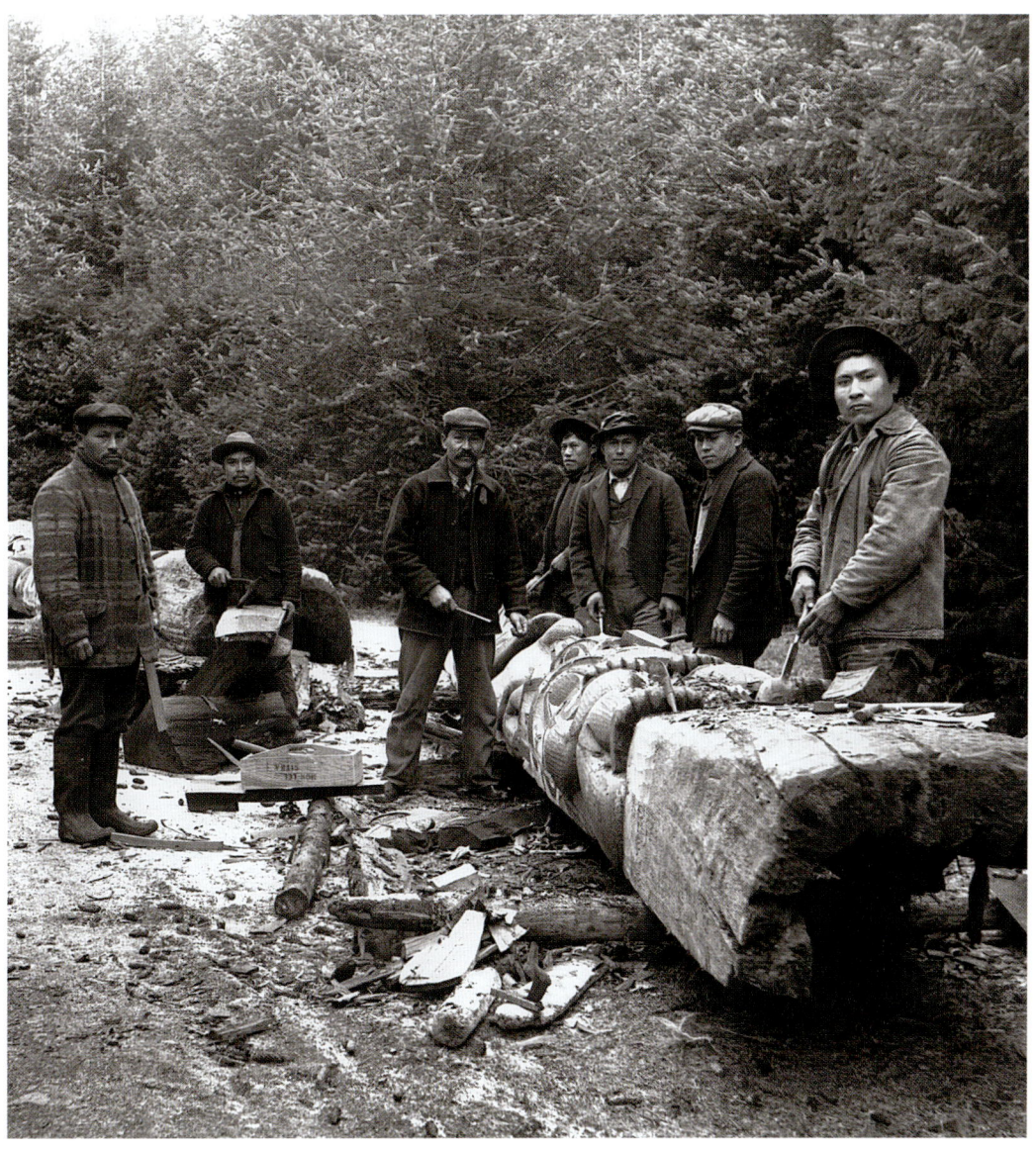

PLATE 59. Six Tlingit men repairing totem poles at the Sitka National Park, ca. 1900–1910. Left to right: John Willard (Xwaaséin) (1872–1962), Naasteidí clan; Garfield Bailey (1874–1932); Thomas Cook (b. 1870); Thomas Willis, Chookaneidí clan; Ray James Sr. (1880–1936), (Duksaa.eeh), Point House (X'aaká Hít), Kiks.ádi clan; Ray James Sr.'s brother; unidentified. Tentative identifications by Sharon Gmelch (2008: 136) and Harold Jacobs, 2024. Courtesy of the National Park Service, Sitka National Historical Park, 3816.

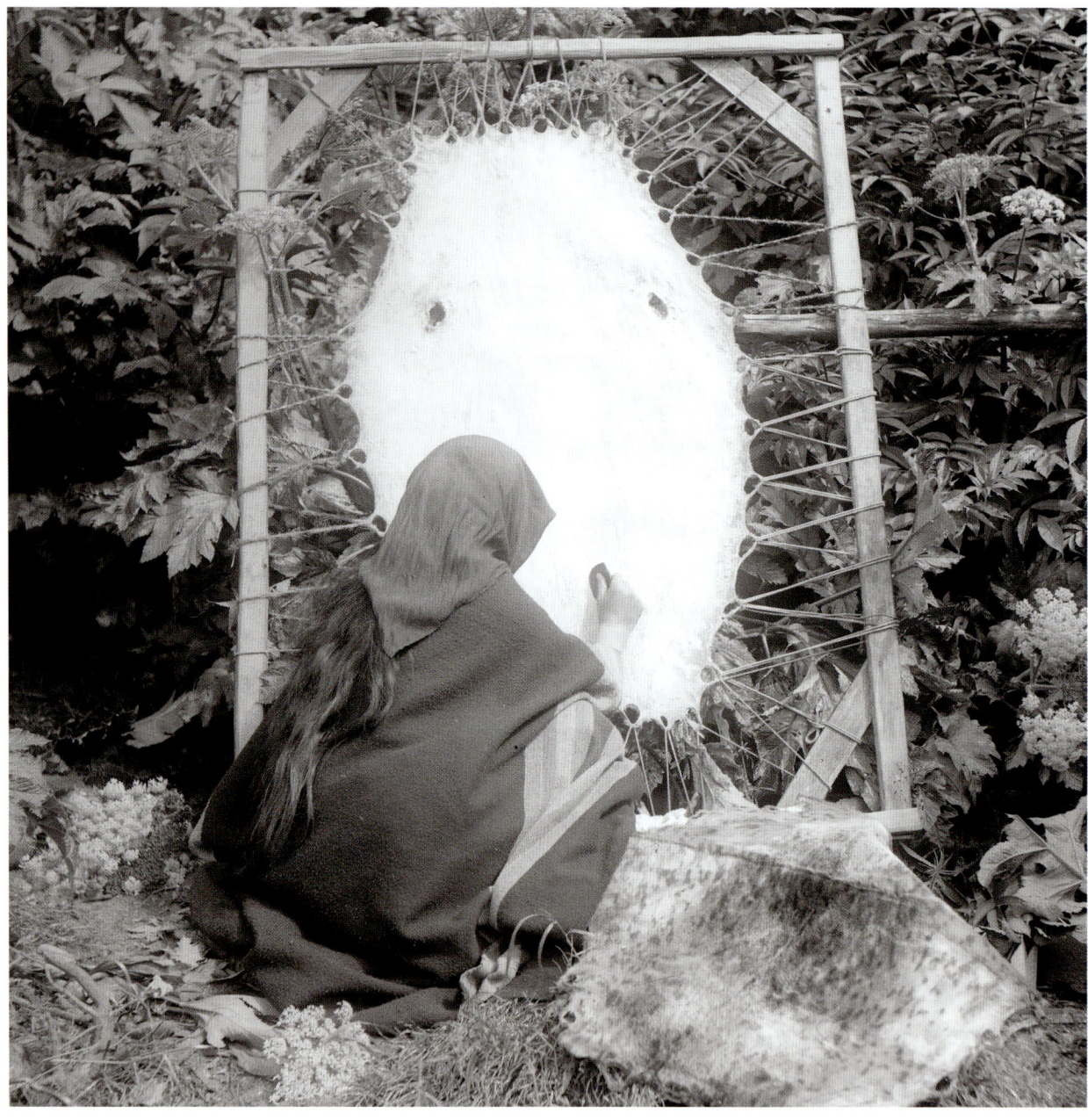

PLATE 60. A Tlingit woman scraping a seal skin, Sitka, date unknown. Courtesy of the National Park Service, Sitka National Historical Park, 25440.

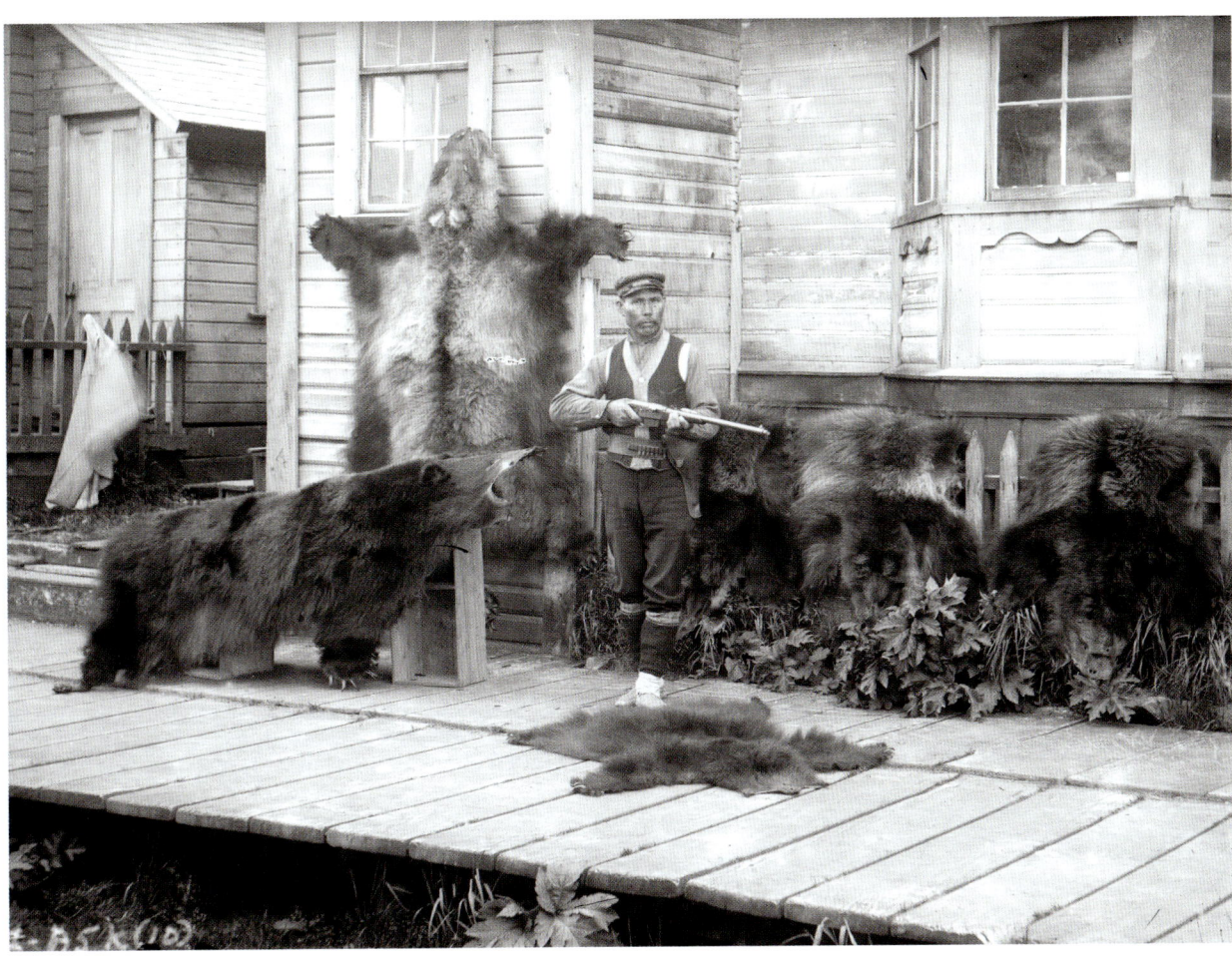

PLATE 61. The bear hunter William Kasko (Shaayi Éesh) (1875–1940), Platform House (Kayaaashká Hít), Ľuknax̱.ádi clan, Sitka Indian Village, ca. 1910. Identification from an inscription on the back of the photograph and by Harold Jacobs, 2024. Courtesy of the National Park Service, Sitka National Historical Park, 26224.

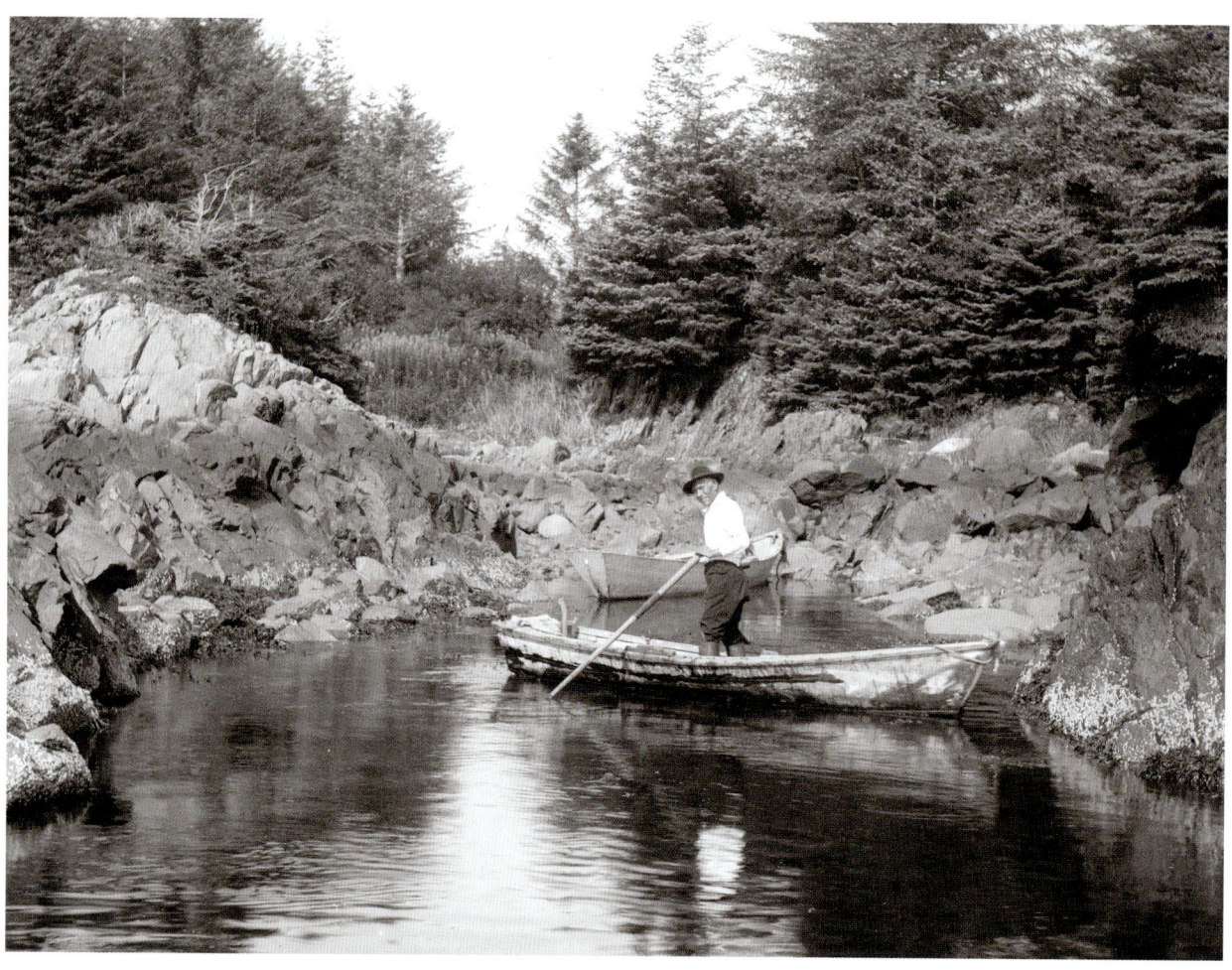

PLATE 62. Tlingit fisherman with his canoe in a small cove near Sitka, date unknown.
Courtesy of the National Park Service, Sitka National Historical Park, 25449.

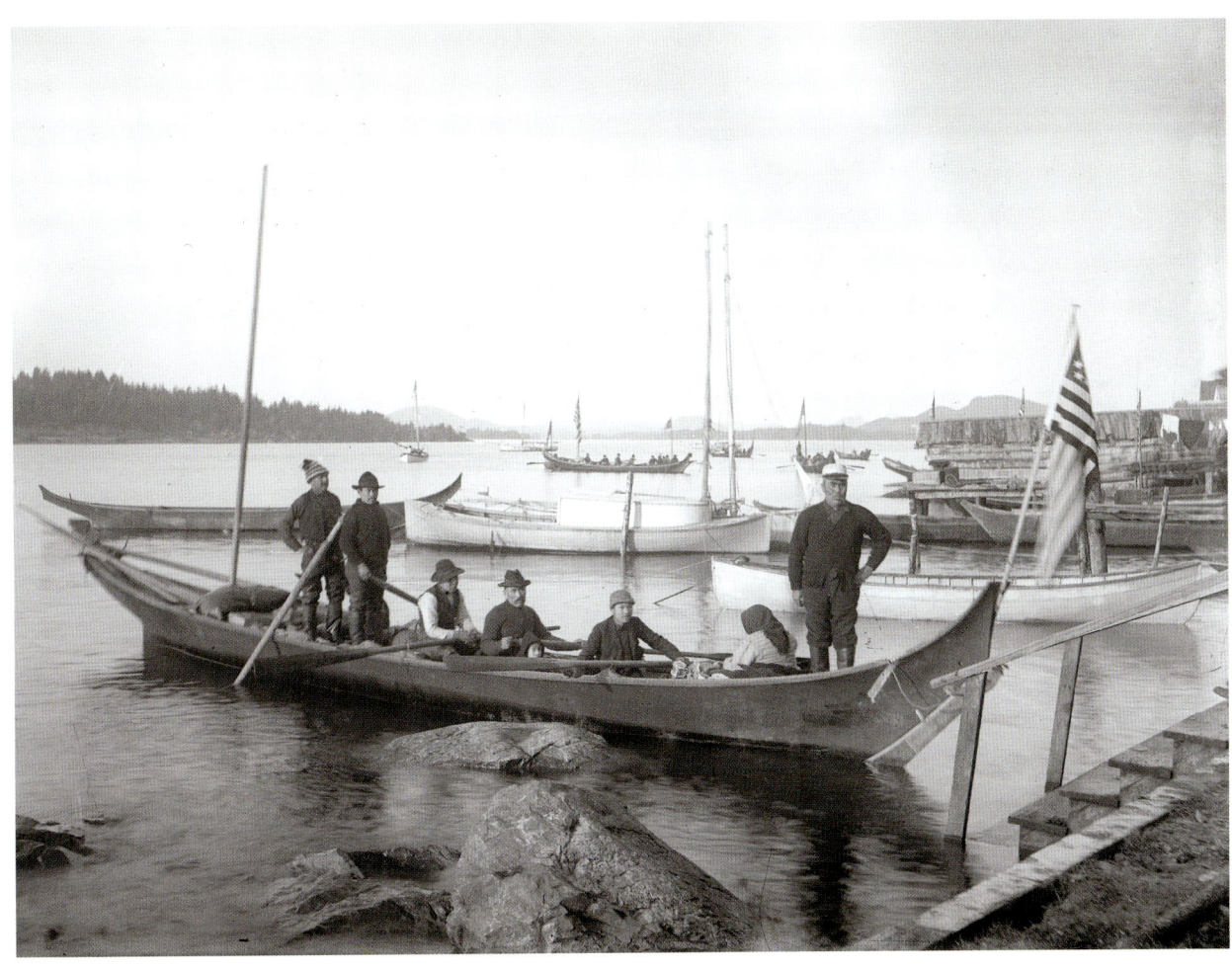

PLATE 63. Six Tlingit men and one woman in a canoe near the shore at the Sitka Indian Village, ca. 1900–1908. The man at the front of the boat is Lʼaanteech (1843?–1908), a high-ranking man of the House with Two Doors (Déix X̱ʼawool Hít), Kaagwaantaan clan of Sitka (see plate 28). Courtesy of the National Park Service, Sitka National Historical Park, 25719.

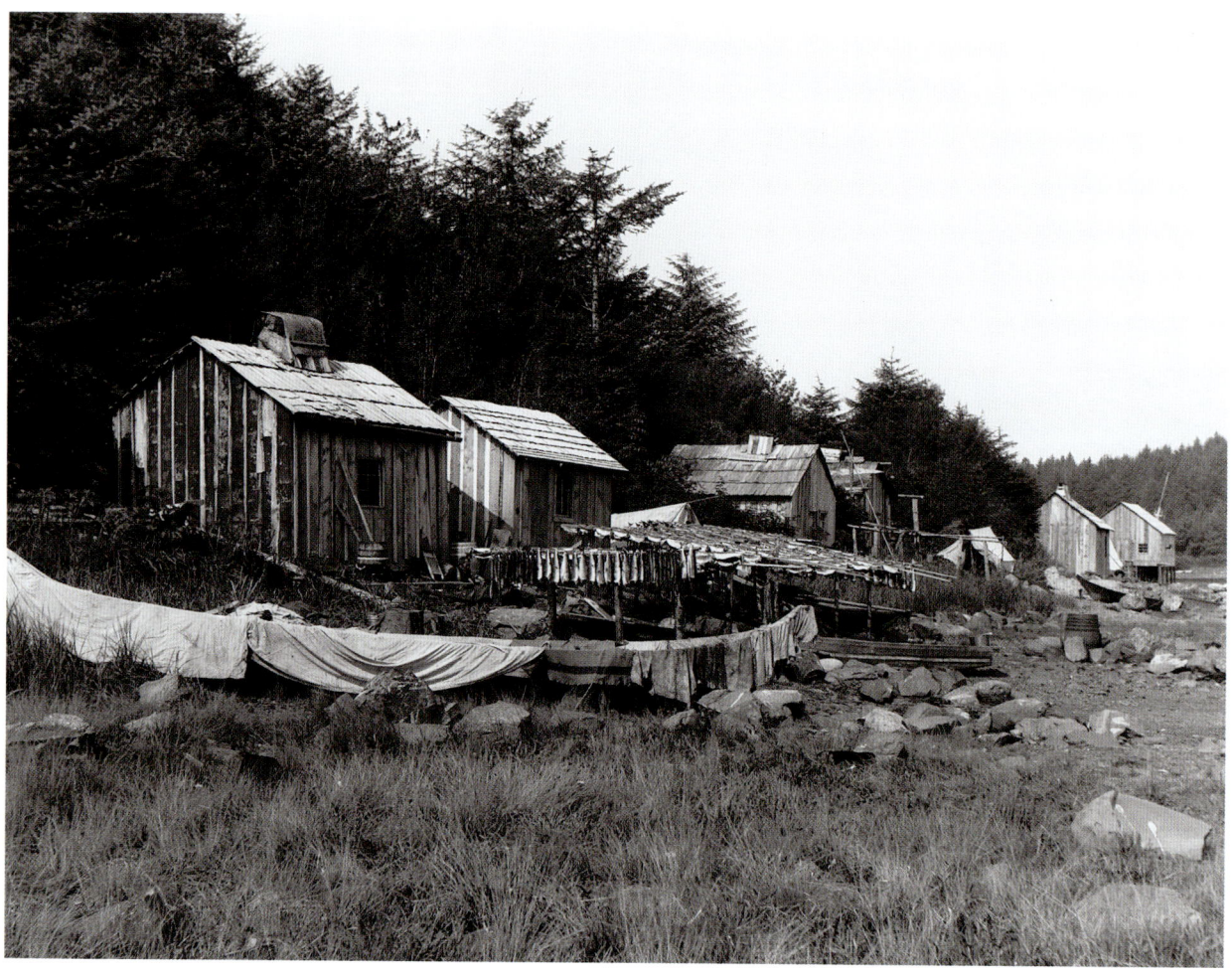

PLATE 64. A Tlingit fishing camp on Alice Island near Sitka, with several smokehouses and processed salmon drying in the sun, date unknown. According to A. P. Johnson (Íxt'ik' Éesh), the third house from the left belonged to his maternal grandmother, of the Kiks.ádi clan. Courtesy of the National Park Service, Sitka National Historical Park, 03923.

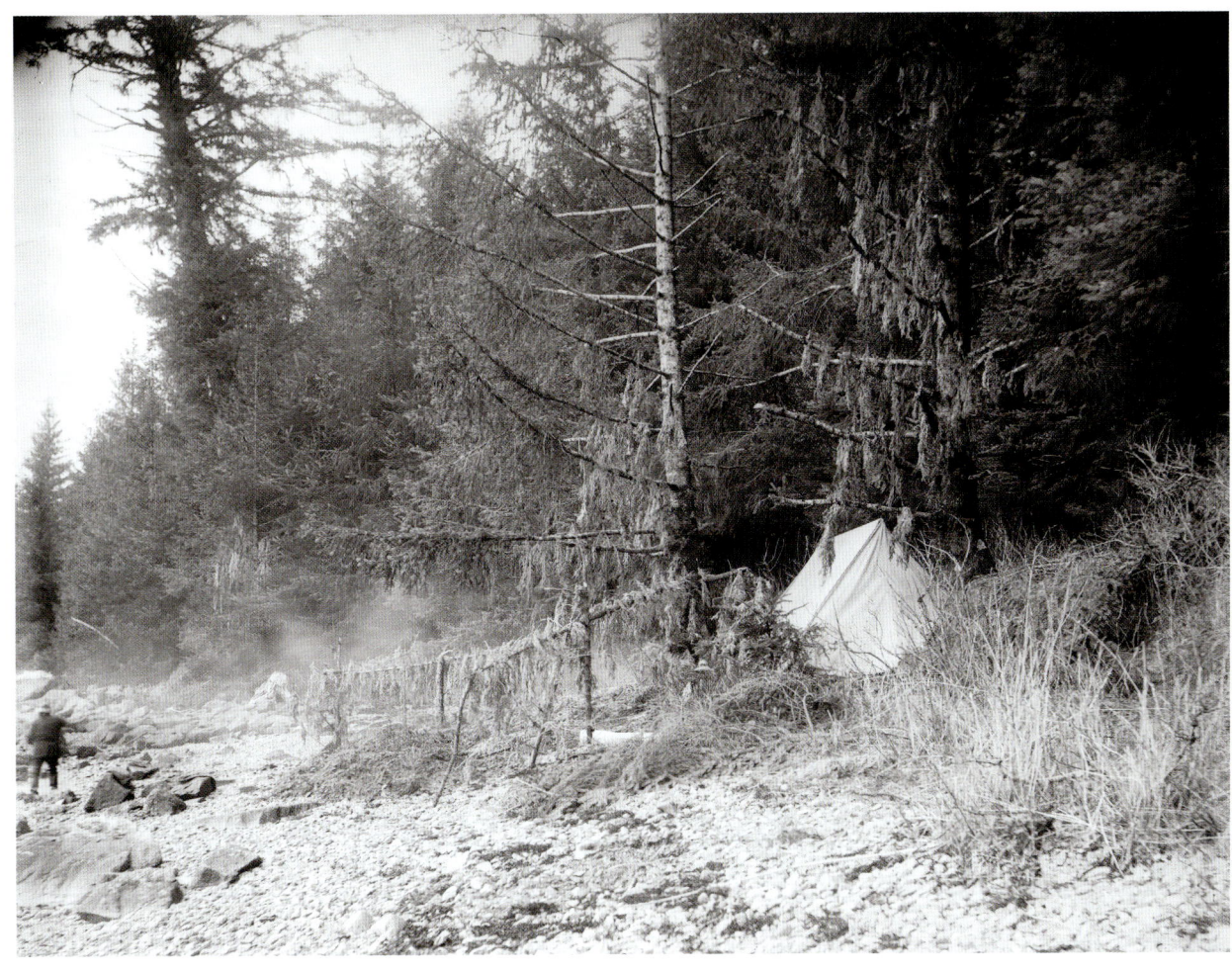

PLATE 65. A Tlingit camp in the vicinity of Sitka, with a single tent and herring roe drying on tree branches, date unknown. A man is visible in the bottom left corner. Courtesy of the National Park Service, Sitka National Historical Park, 25442.

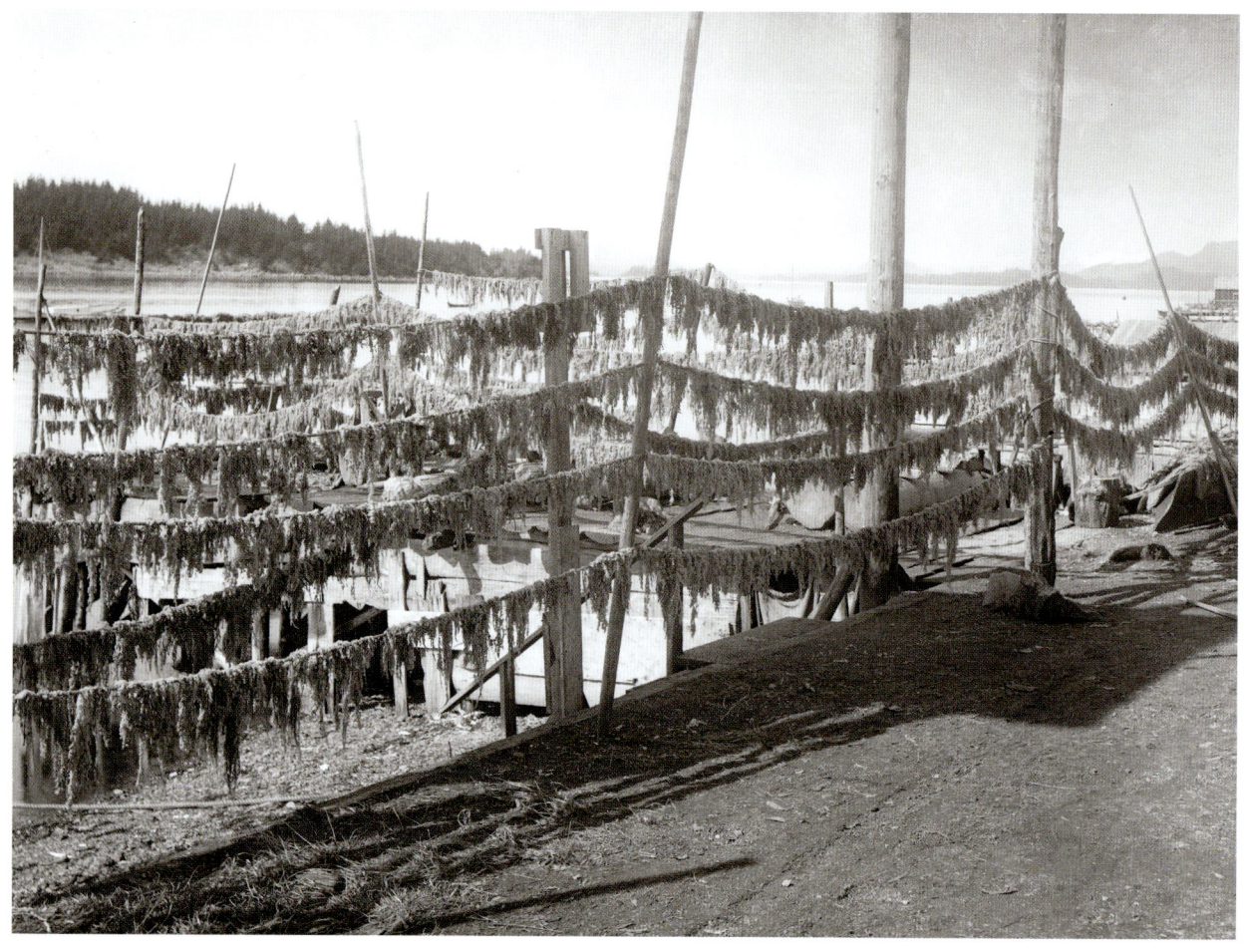

PLATE 66. Herring roe drying near the beach in the Sitka Indian Village, date unknown.
Courtesy of the National Park Service, Sitka National Historical Park, 25444.

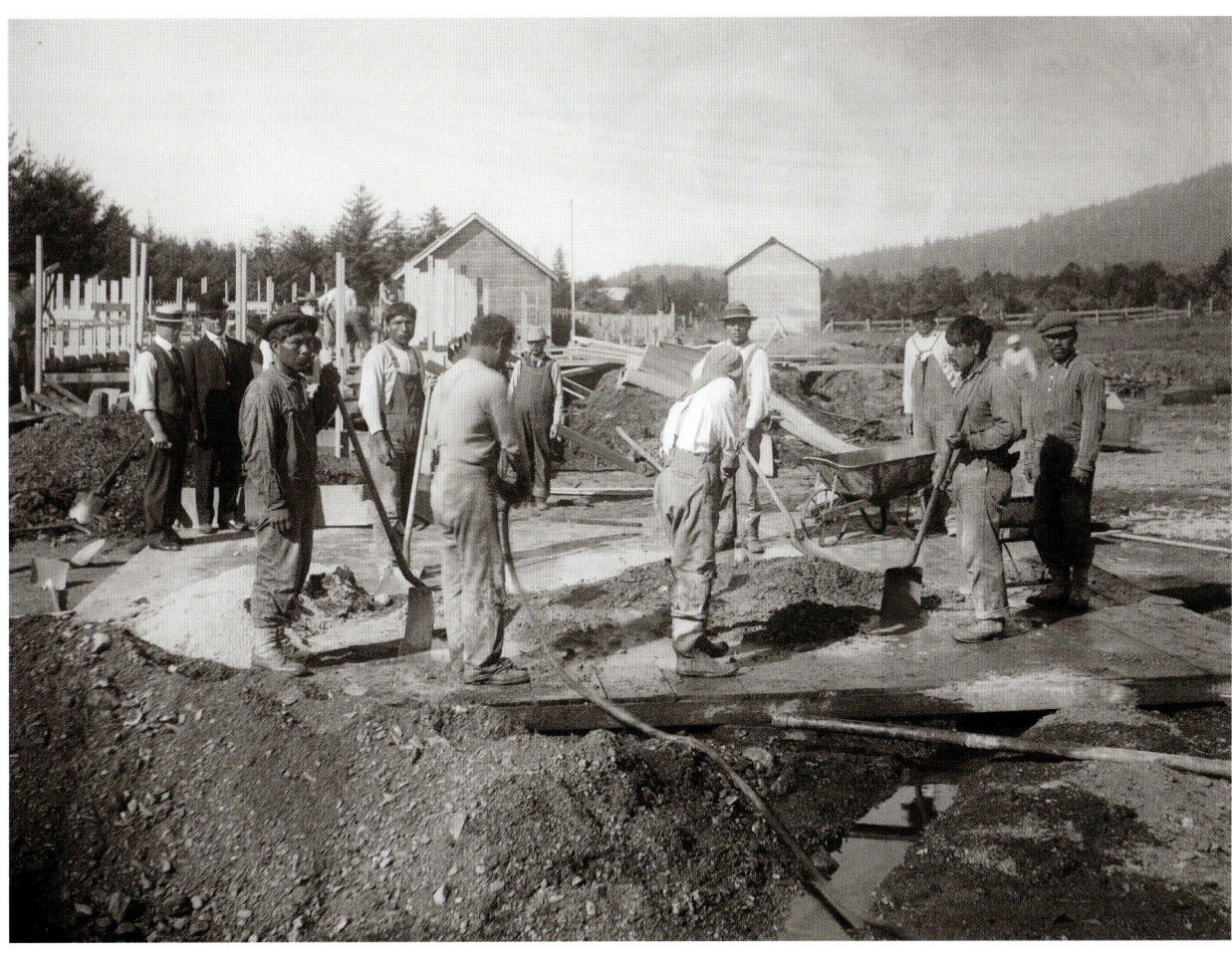

PLATE 67. Tlingit men mixing cement while doing repair work on a Sitka street, date unknown. In the back at the far left are two non-Native men, supervising or observing them. Courtesy of the National Park Service, Sitka National Historical Park, 25438.

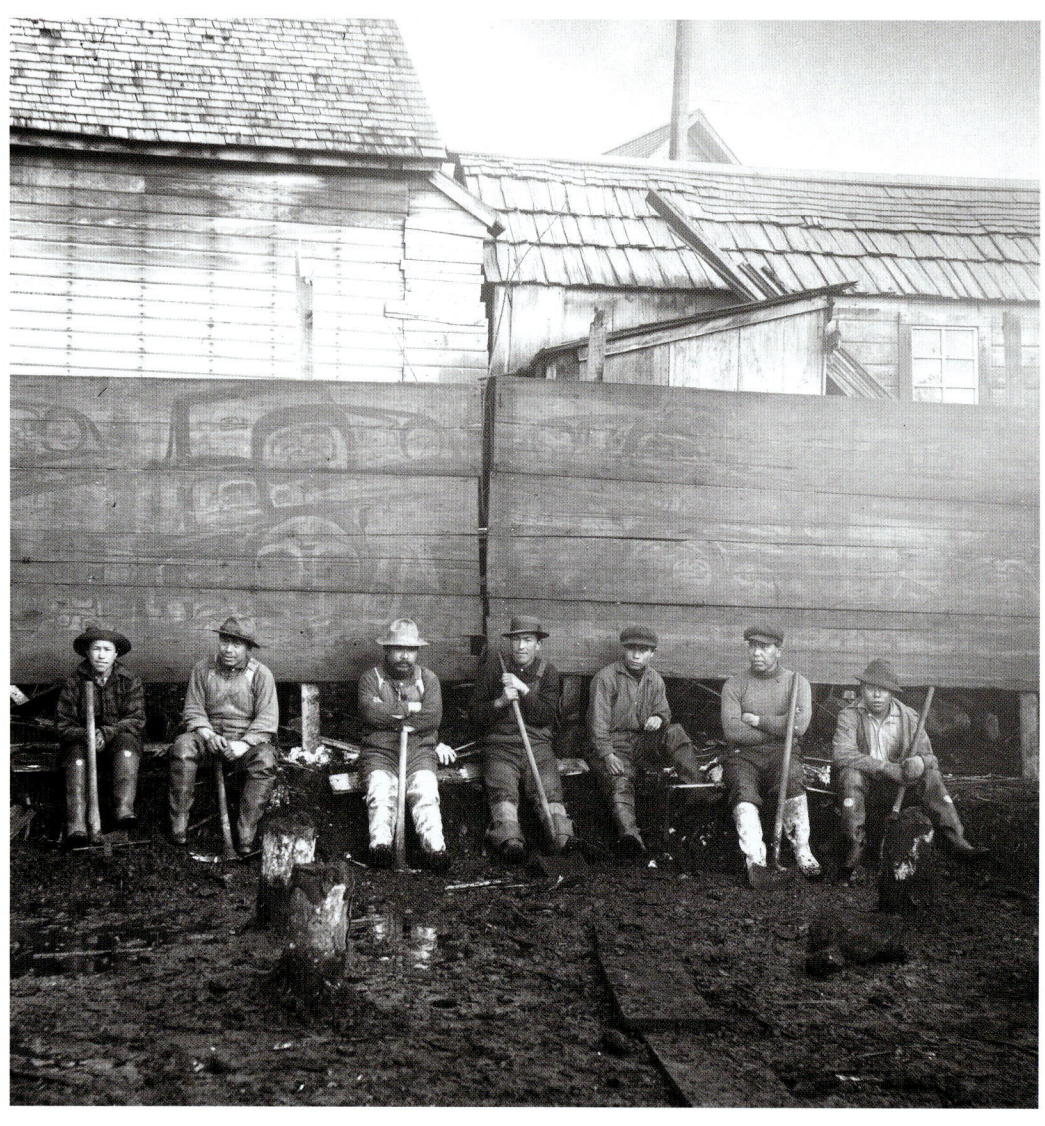

PLATE 68. A group of Tlingit men resting during a break from work in the Sitka Indian Village, date unknown. Behind them is the Raven screen also shown in plate 26. Courtesy of the National Park Service, Sitka National Historical Park, 25437.

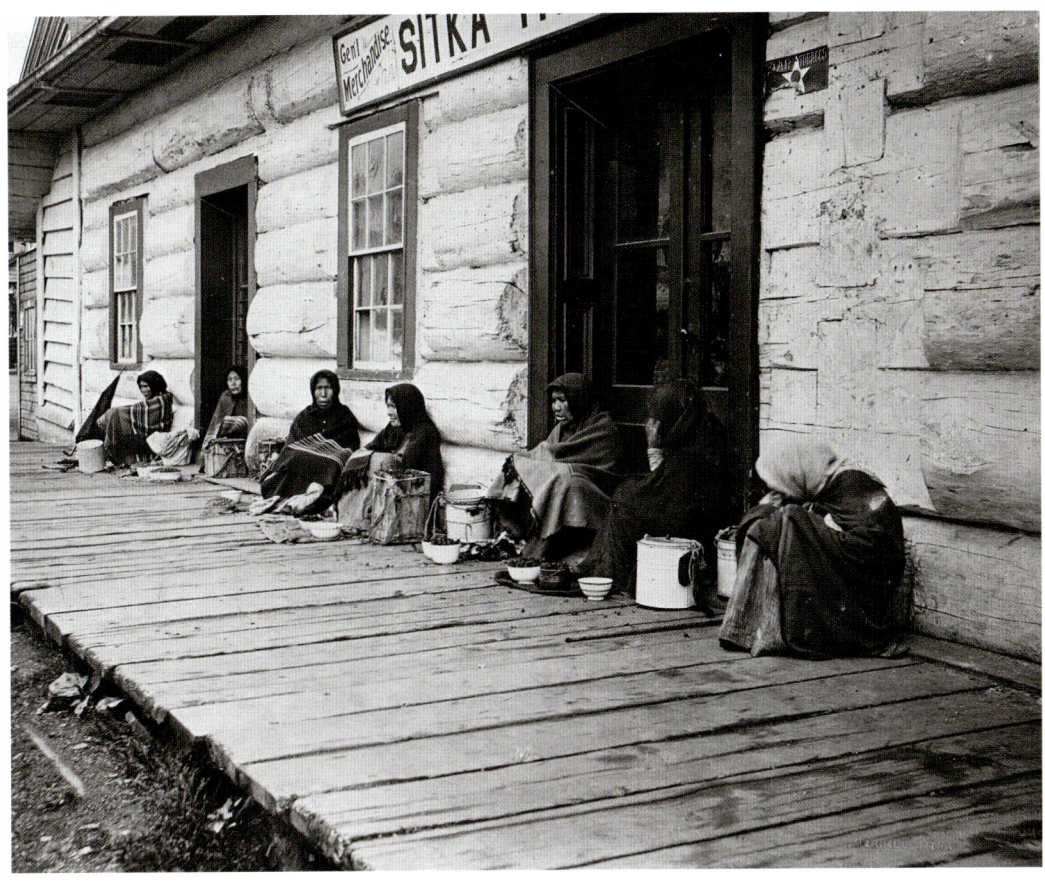

PLATE 69. Tlingit women selling berries on Lincoln Street in front of an old Russian building that was used as a general store in Merrill's times, date unknown. Alaska State Historical Library, P57-169.

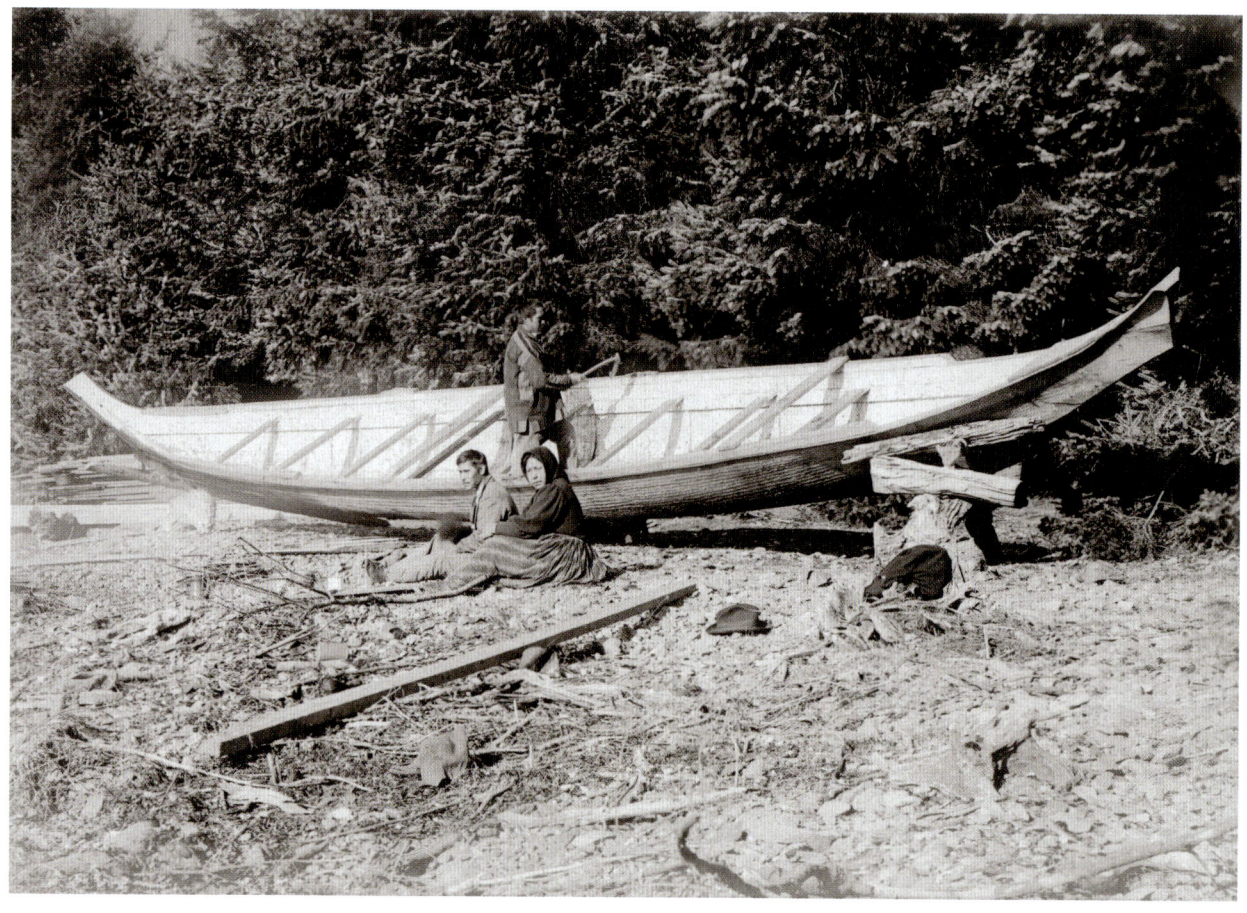

PLATE 70. A canoe maker and his friends having a meal near Sitka, date unknown.
Alaska State Historical Library, P427-12.

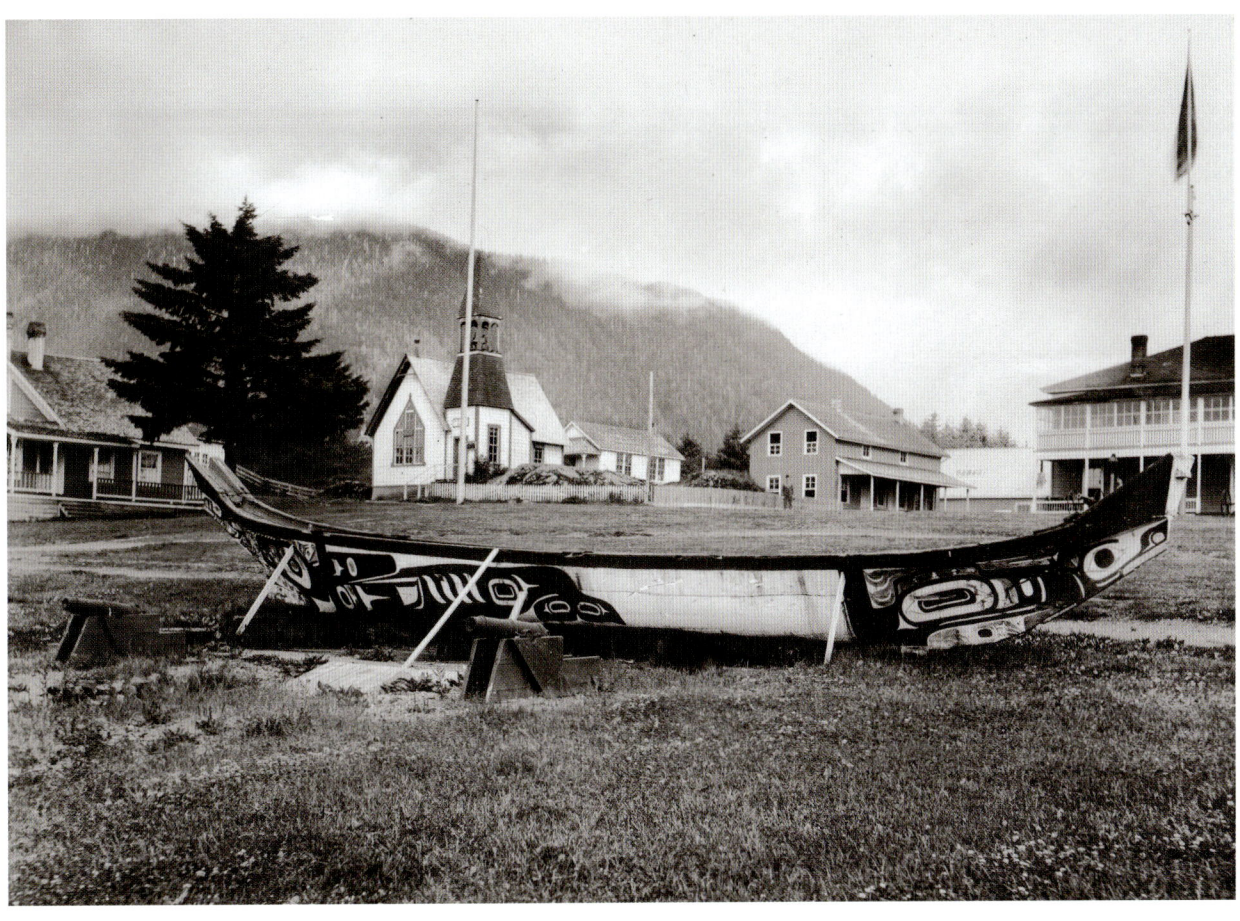

PLATE 71. A Tlingit canoe displayed at the Sitka parade grounds, ca. 1908. Alaska State Historical Library, P57-160.

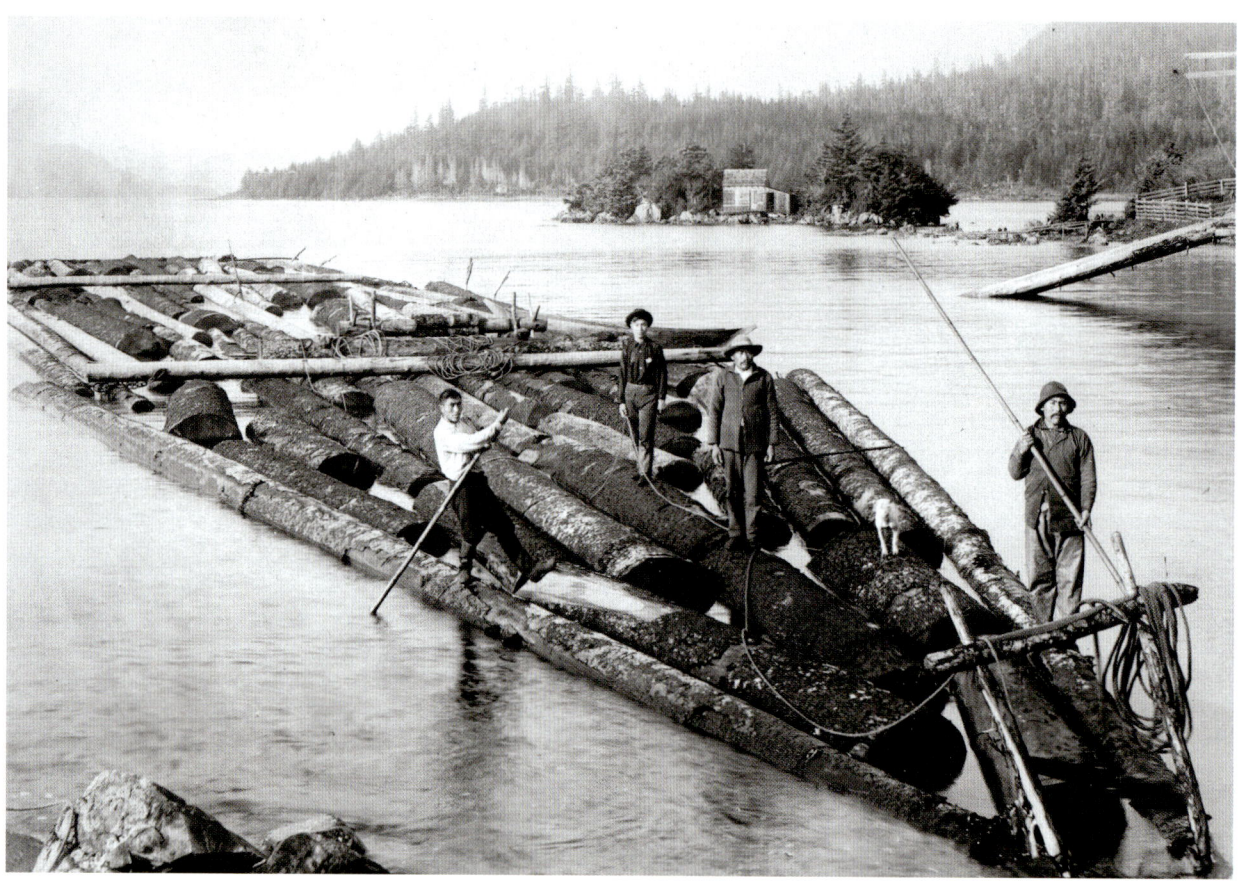

PLATE 72. Four Tlingit men on a log raft near Sitka, date unknown. Alaska State Historical Library, P427-19.

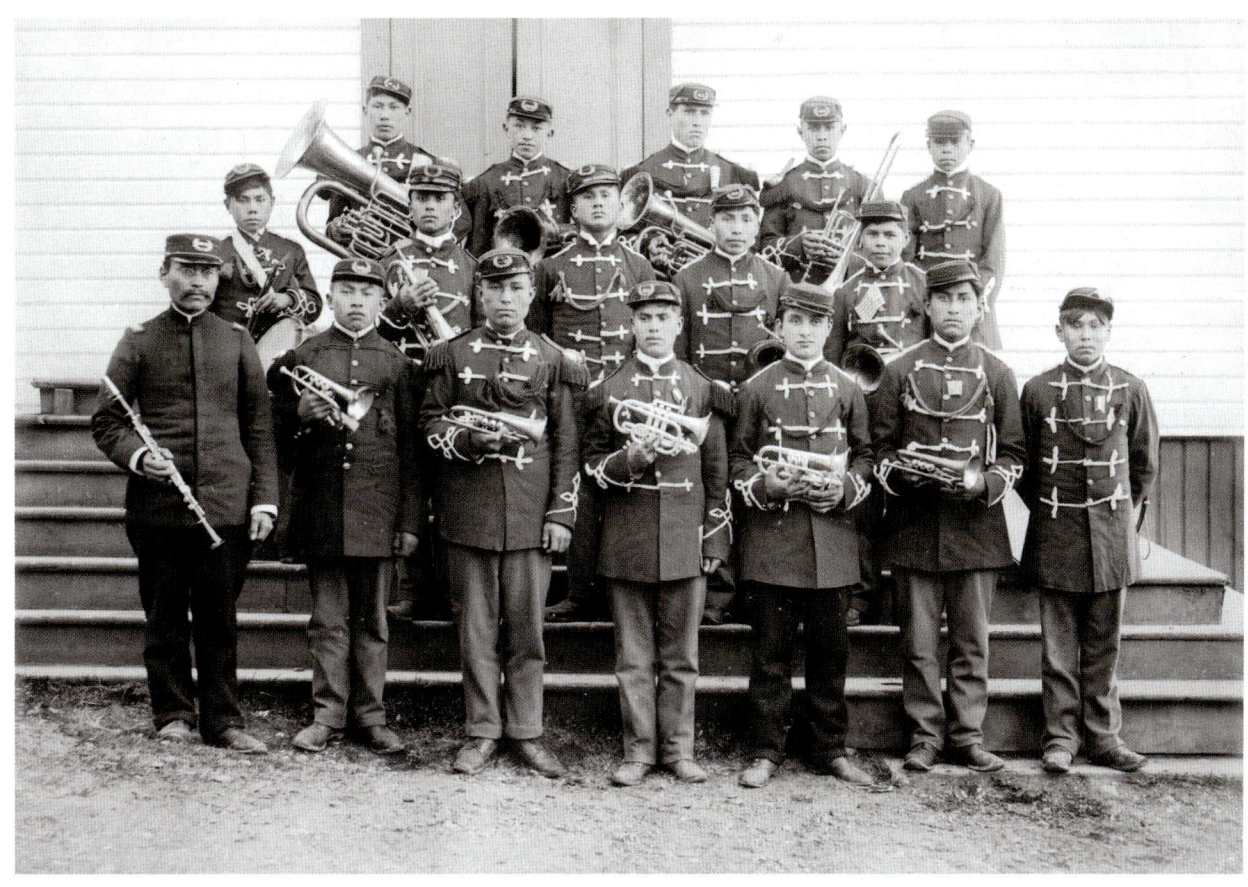

PLATE 73. A Tlingit brass band, Sitka, date unknown. Alaska State Historical Library, P427-16.

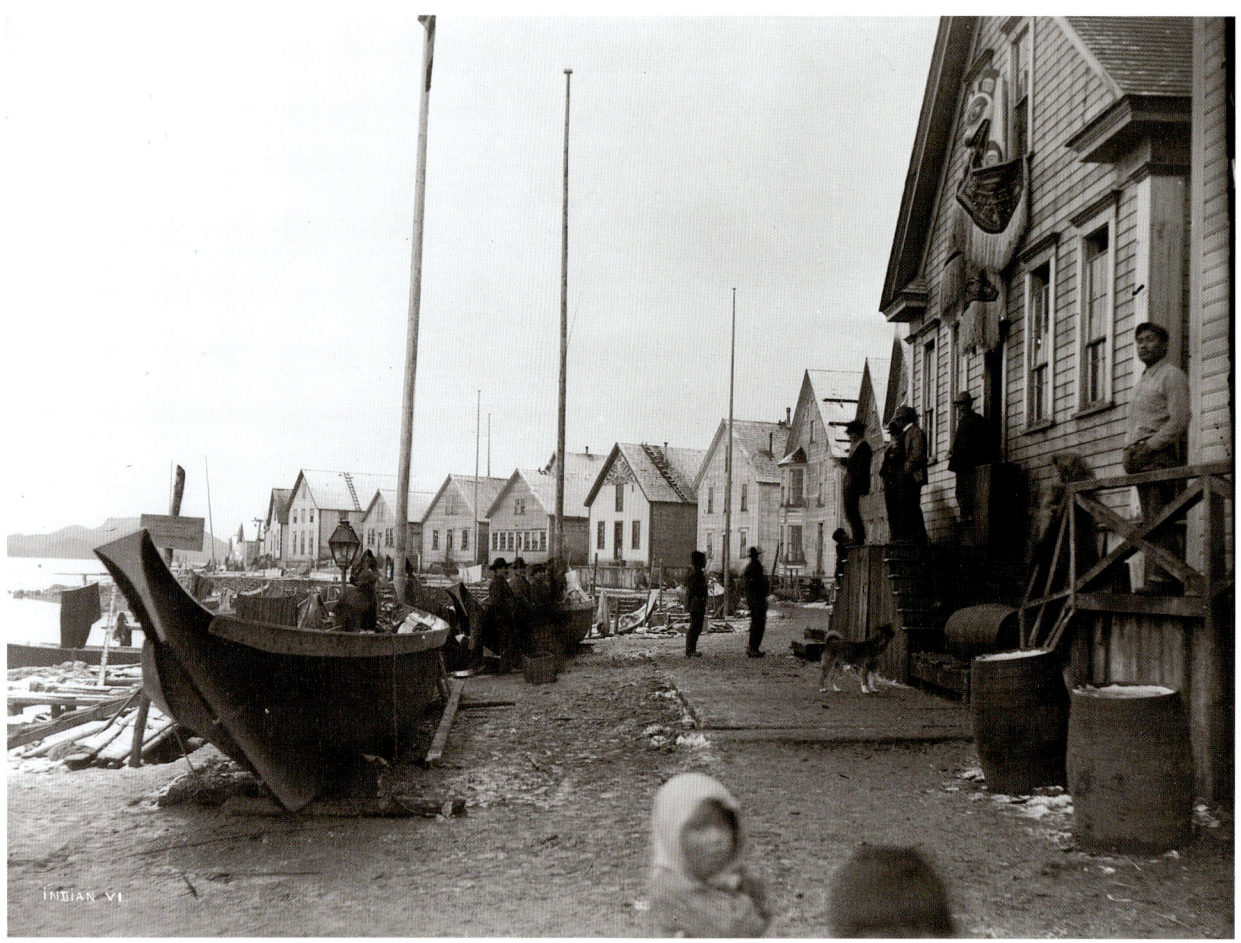

PLATE 74. Sitka Indian Village, front street. The first house on the right is Wolf House (G̲ooch Hít), with a panel showing a wolf holding Chilkat blankets in its mouth. The presence of the panel dates the photo to the 1904 Kaagwaantaan k̲u.éex'. Courtesy of the National Park Service, Sitka National Historical Park, 03915.

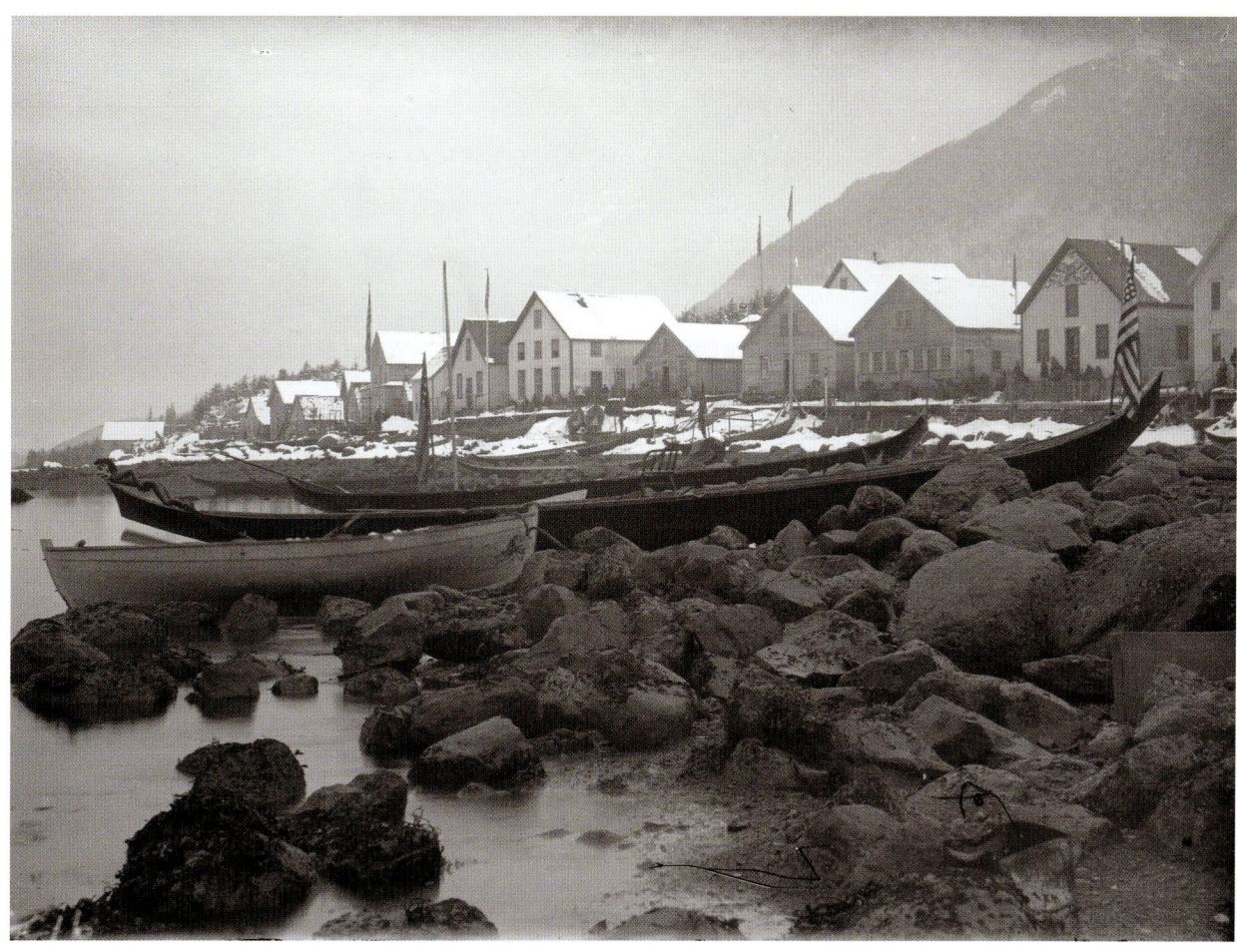

PLATE 75. Sitka Indian Village in the winter, date unknown. The second house from the right is Eagle's Nest House (Ch'áak' Kúdi Hít) of the Kaagwaantaan clan, with its crest visible on the front. Several canoes are beached. Courtesy of the National Park Service, Sitka National Historical Park, 25812.

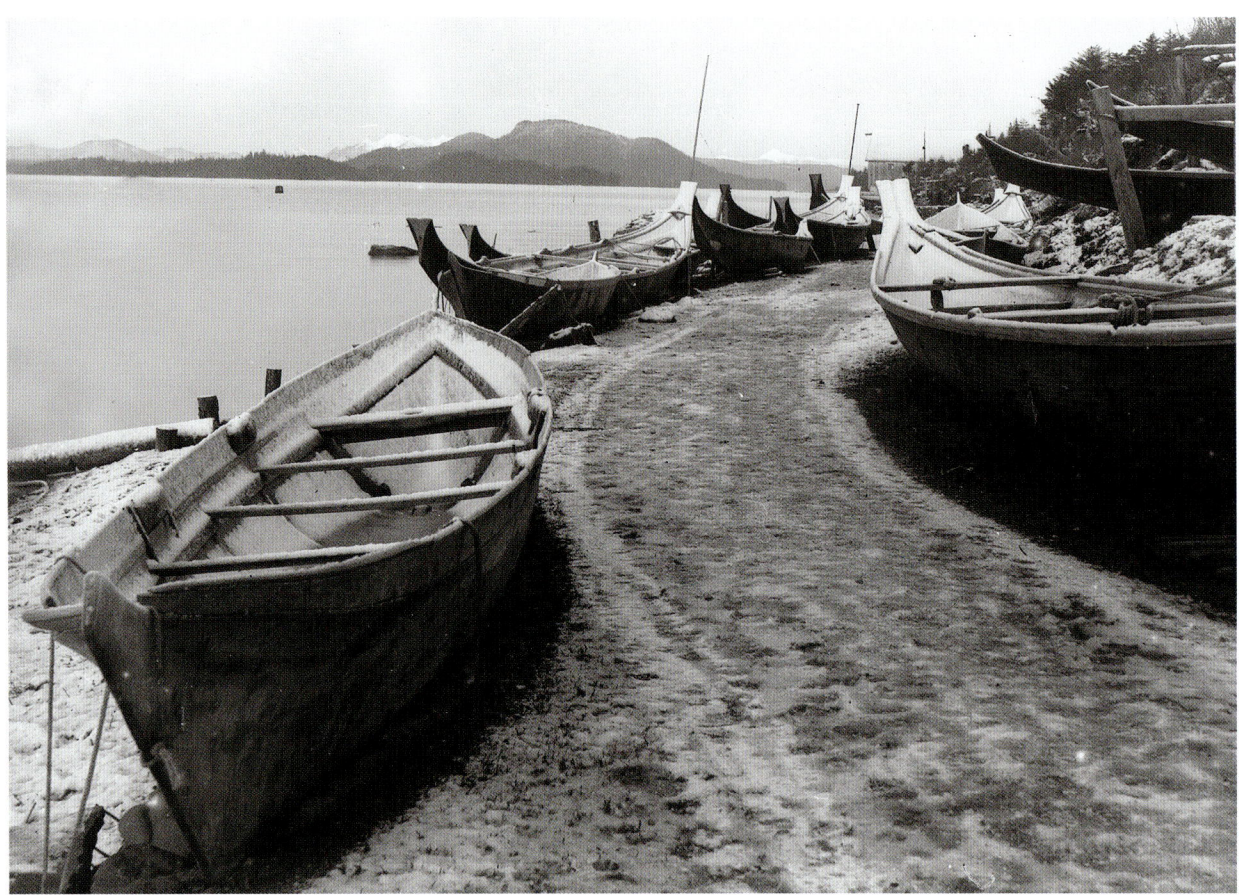

PLATE 76. Canoes on the beach in the Sitka Indian Village, date unknown.
Courtesy of the National Park Service, Sitka National Historical Park, 03920.

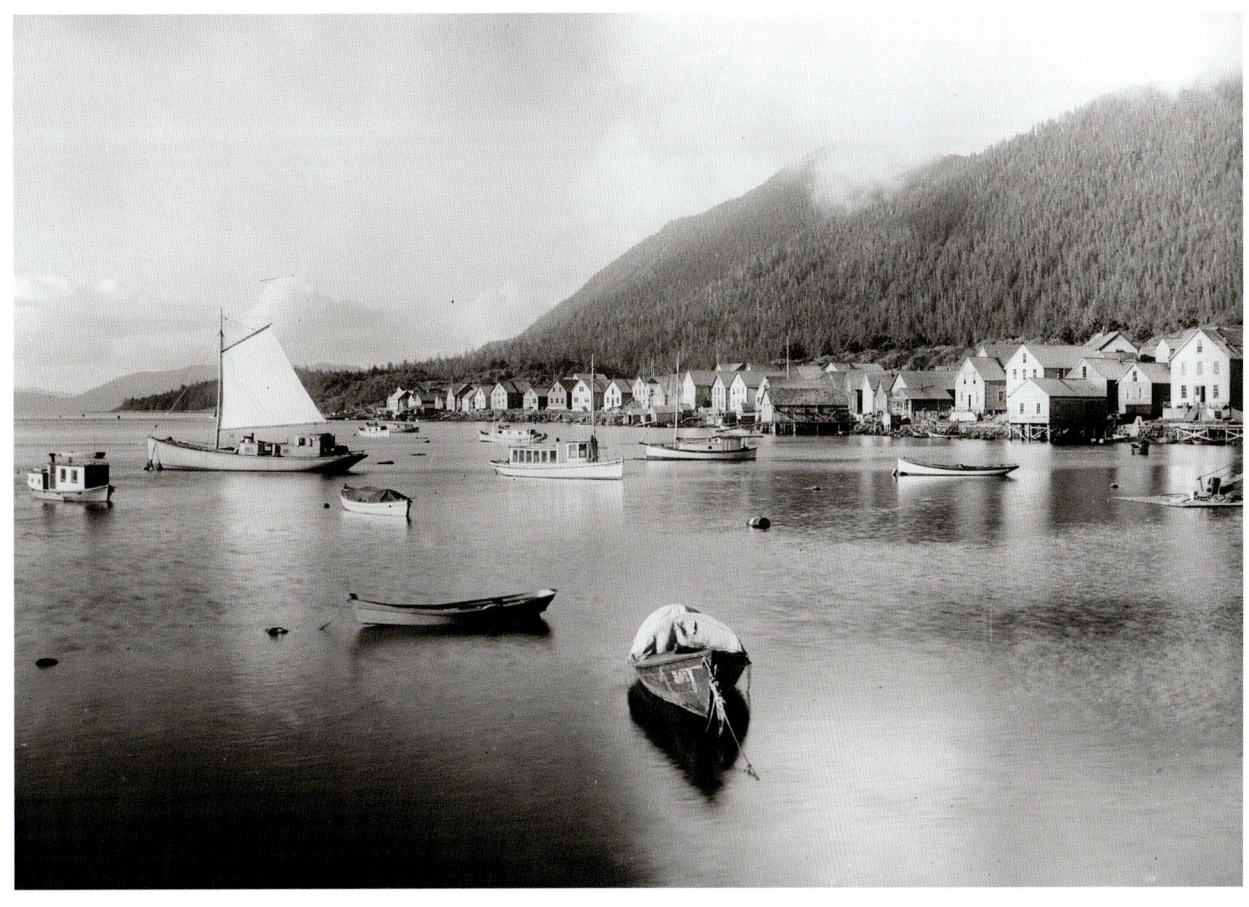

PLATE 77. Waterfront with various boats and Sitka Indian Village in the background, date unknown. Courtesy of the National Park Service, Sitka National Historical Park, 03916.

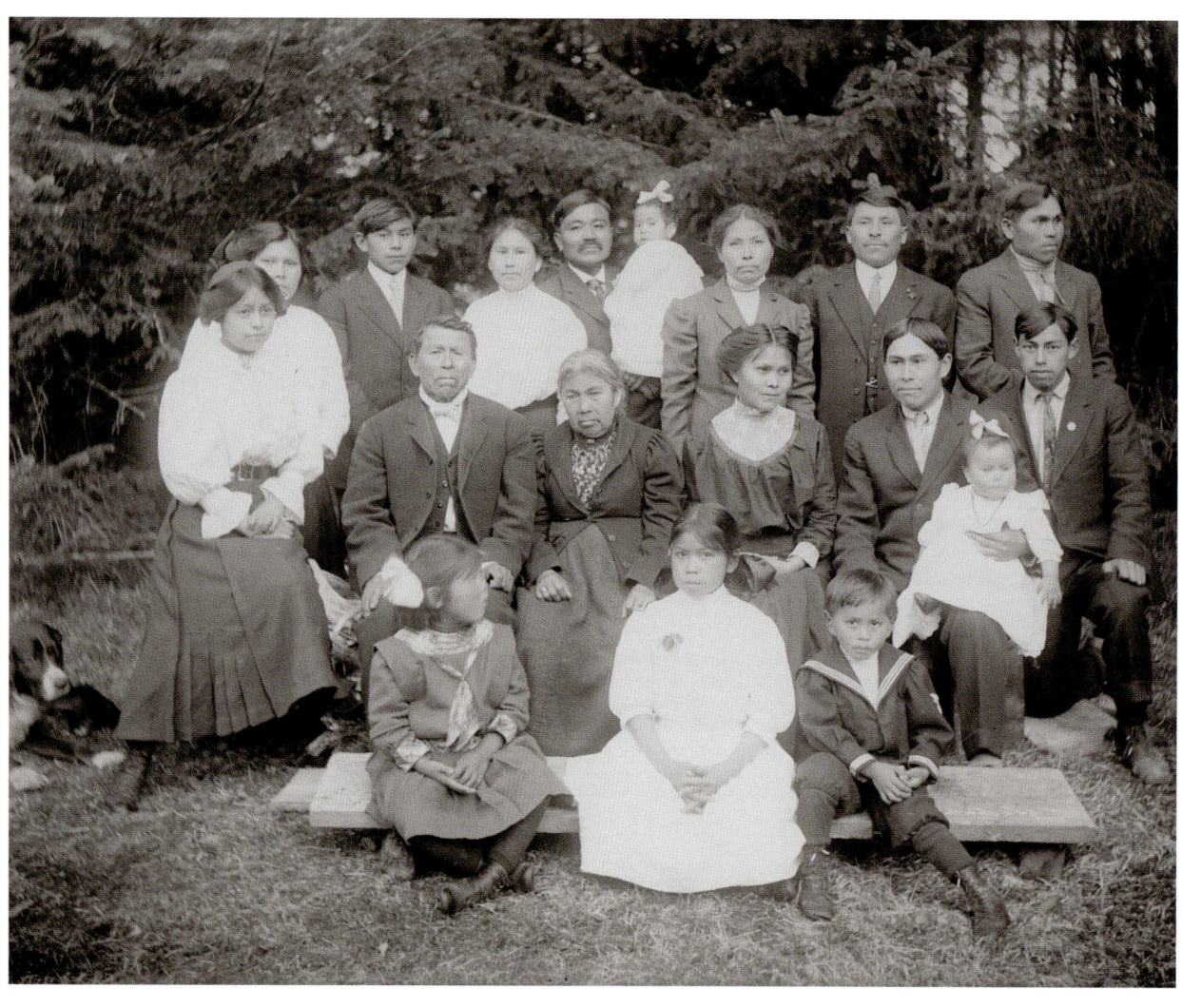

PLATE 78. Residents of the cottages (the Cottage Club), Totem Park, ca. 1910.

Front row, left to right: Dorothy (James) Truitt (Goonook) (1907–43), Fort House (Noow Hít), Wooshkeetaan clan of Sitka; Jennie (Simpson) Sing (Xáachkadu.aat) (1901–40), Point House (X'aaká Hít), Kiks.ádi clan; Ray James Jr. (Góodl.aaw) (b. 1908), Mudshark House (X'átgu Hít), Naanya.aayi clan of Wrangell.

Middle row, left to right: Tillie (Howard) Hope (Aasdakáa) (1895–1975), Point House (X'aaká Hít), Kiks.ádi clan; Don Cameron (Daalwools'ees') (1876–1938), Kaagwaantaan clan of Klukwan; Amelia (Sloan) (Yaandusgei) Cameron (1852–1947), Point House (X'aaká Hít), Kiks.ádi clan; Elizabeth (Kadashan) James (Xaatuxl.aat) (1887–1939), Mudshark House (X'átgu Hít), Naanyaa.aayi clan; Ray James Sr., Point House (X'aaká Hít), Kiks.ádi clan, holding a baby; David Howard Sr. (1893–1974),

Point House (X'aaká Hít), Kiks.ádi clan, brother of Tillie Howard Hope.

Back row, left to right: Olinda (Eldred) Bailey (Tsanákh) (1890–1978), sister of Ray James Sr.; Louis Simpson (Shḵ'awulyéil) (1896–1936), Point House (X'aaká Hít), Kiks.ádi clan; Mary (Sloan) Simpson (K'ashéech Tláa) (1875–1936), Point House (X'aaká Hít), Kiks.ádi clan; Peter Simpson Sr. (1871–1947), Tsimshian, holding a baby; Jennie Willard (Xáachkadu.aat) (1870–1956), Point House (X'aaká Hít), Kiks.ádi clan; John Willard (Xwaaséin) (1872–1962), Naasteidí clan; Albert James (Duksaa.éex) (1880–1936), Kiks.ádi clan, brother of Ray James Sr.; unidentified individual, Point House (X'aaká Hít), Kiks.ádi clan.

Identifications by Carol Brady, 1990, and Harold Jacobs, 2024. Courtesy of the National Park Service, Sitka National Historical Park, 25433.

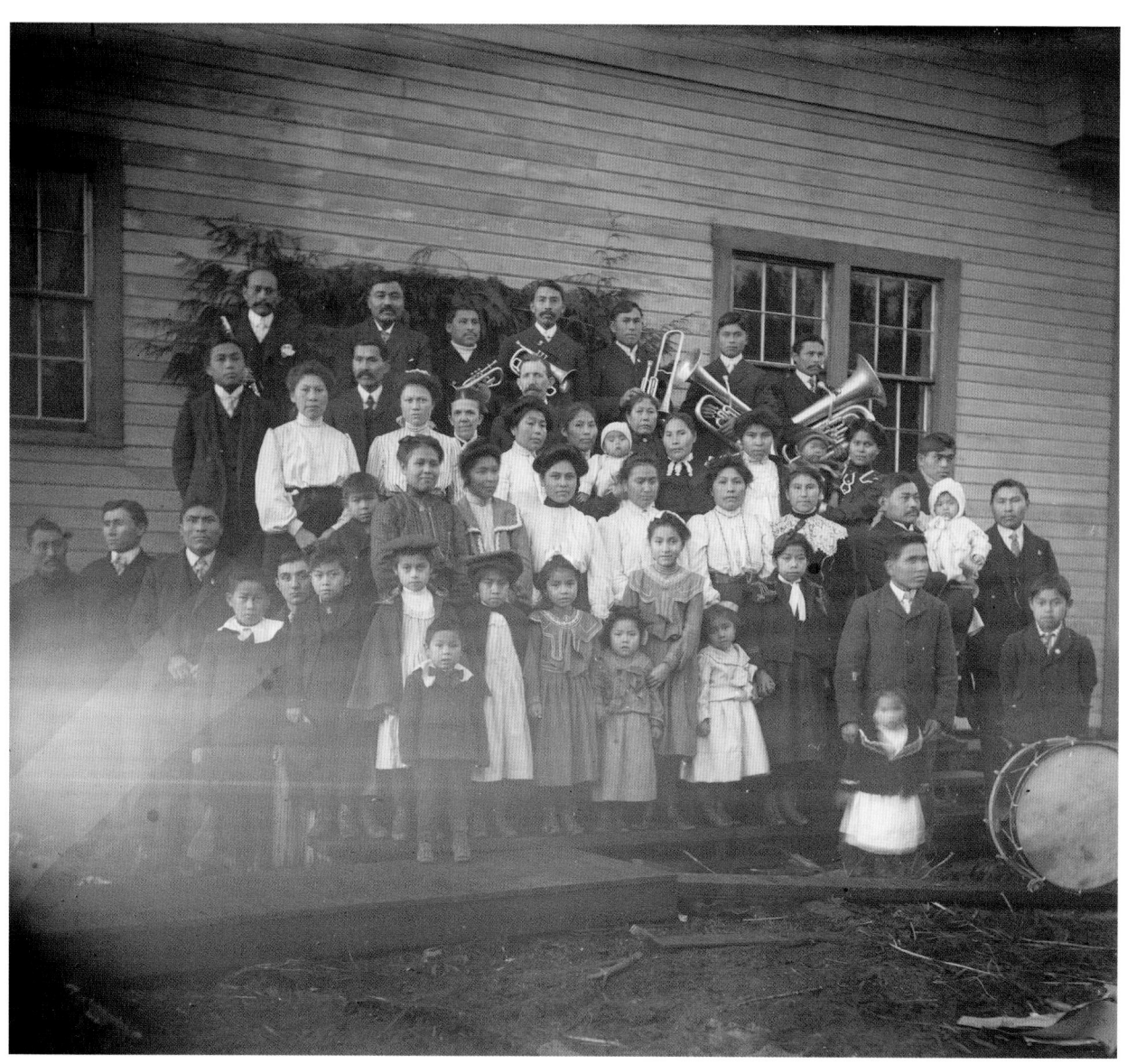

PLATE 79. Cottage Club and band in front of the Cottage Hall, Sitka, ca. 1900–1905.

Front row, left to right: Ethan "Eaton" Hunter (ca. 1865–?), House with Two Doors, Kaagwaantaan clan of Sitka; Ralph Young (Looshkát) (1877–1956), Raven's Nest House (Yéil Kúdei Hít), T'akdeintaan clan of Hoonah; possibly Don Cameron (Daalwools'ees'), Kaagwaantaan clan of Klukwan; John Cameron (Xaalgéik'w) (1895–1922), X'aaka Hít (Point House), Kiks.ádi clan; Frank Price (Saatan Éesh) (1886–1946), Eagle's Nest House (Ch'áak' Kúdi Hít), Kaagwaantaan clan of Sitka; Ben Peck (1896–?); Tillie (Howard) Hope (Aasdakáa) (1895–1975), X'aaka Hít (Point House), Kiks.ádi clan; George Howard (1901–1956), X'aaka Hít (Point House), Kiks.ádi clan; unknown; Esther Cooke (1895–?); Mary (?) Cooke; Matilda Wells Zuboff (X'akéet) (ca. 1907–73), House With Two Doors, Sitka Kaagwaantaan; Isabella Simpson (1895–?), Point House (X'aaká Hít), Kiks.ádi clan; George Bartlett (Naayiéesh) (1880–ca. 1919); Ruth Bartlett (1906–53); David Howard (Ltutéen) (1893–1974), Point House (X'aaká Hít), Kiks.ádi clan (behind the drum).

Second row up: Louis Simpson (boy) (1896–1936), Point House (X'aaká Hít), Kiks.ádi clan; Lizzie Bartlett, Box House, Kaagwaantaan clan of Sitka; Pauline James (Kaaxáni) (1884–1911), Fort House (Noow Hít), Wooshkeetaan clan; Mary (Jean) Wanamaker (Shaaxaatk'í) (1885–1941), Cow House (Xaas Hít), Koosk'eidí clan of Sitka; Louise Peck (Gaayéitli) (1875–?), Murrelet House, Kaagwaantaan clan of Sitka; Maud Wells (ca. 1875–?); Mary (Sloan) Simpson (K'ashéech Tláa) (1875–1936), Point House (X'aaká Hít), Kiks.ádi clan; John Newell (ca. 1870–

?) (Koohúk), Yeíl Kúdei Hít (Raven's Nest House), T'akdeintaan clan; Lila (Newell) Strand (child); John James.

Third row up: Mrs. Ralph Young, Dakl'aweidí clan; Elsie (Holler) Newell (ca. 1887–?); unknown; Mrs. John James; Jennie Willard (1870–1956) (holding a baby); Amelia (Sloan) Cameron (1852–1947), X'aaka Hít (Point House), Kiks.ádi clan, Mattie Cooke (1875–?); Lottie (Sloan) Howard (Kaakaltin) (1878–1956), Xaaká Hít (Point House), Kiks.ádi clan; Mrs. Ray James (holding Ray James Jr.), Albert James (Duksaa.éex) (1880–1936), Kiks.ádi clan.

Second row from top: Edward Grant (1885–?); Thomas Cooke (1870–?); John E. Gamble. Top row: George Howard Sr. (Naats'tlein) (1865–1925); Peter Simpson (1871–1947); John Willard (Xwaaséin) (1872–1962), Nasteidí clan; Willie Wells (Kaads'aati) (1866–?), L'uknax.ádi clan; Ray James Sr.; Andrew J. Wanamaker (Chalyee Éesh, Wooshkeenaa, Shamata's) (1886–1969), Eagle Nest House, Kaagwaantaan clan of Sitka; Cyrus E. Peck Sr. (X'anaxtáan) (1870–1922), Log Jam House, L'eeneidi clan of Auk Bay.

First on the right (the boy in front of a drum): David Howard Sr. (Ltutéen) (1893–1974), Point House (X'aaká Hít), Kiks.ádi clan.

Back row, second from left, Peter Simpson (1871–1947).

Identifications by Sergei Kan, based on other Merrill photographs (2023). See also https://www.sjvoices.org/the-cottages.html. Courtesy of the National Park Service, Sitka National Historical Park, 25434.

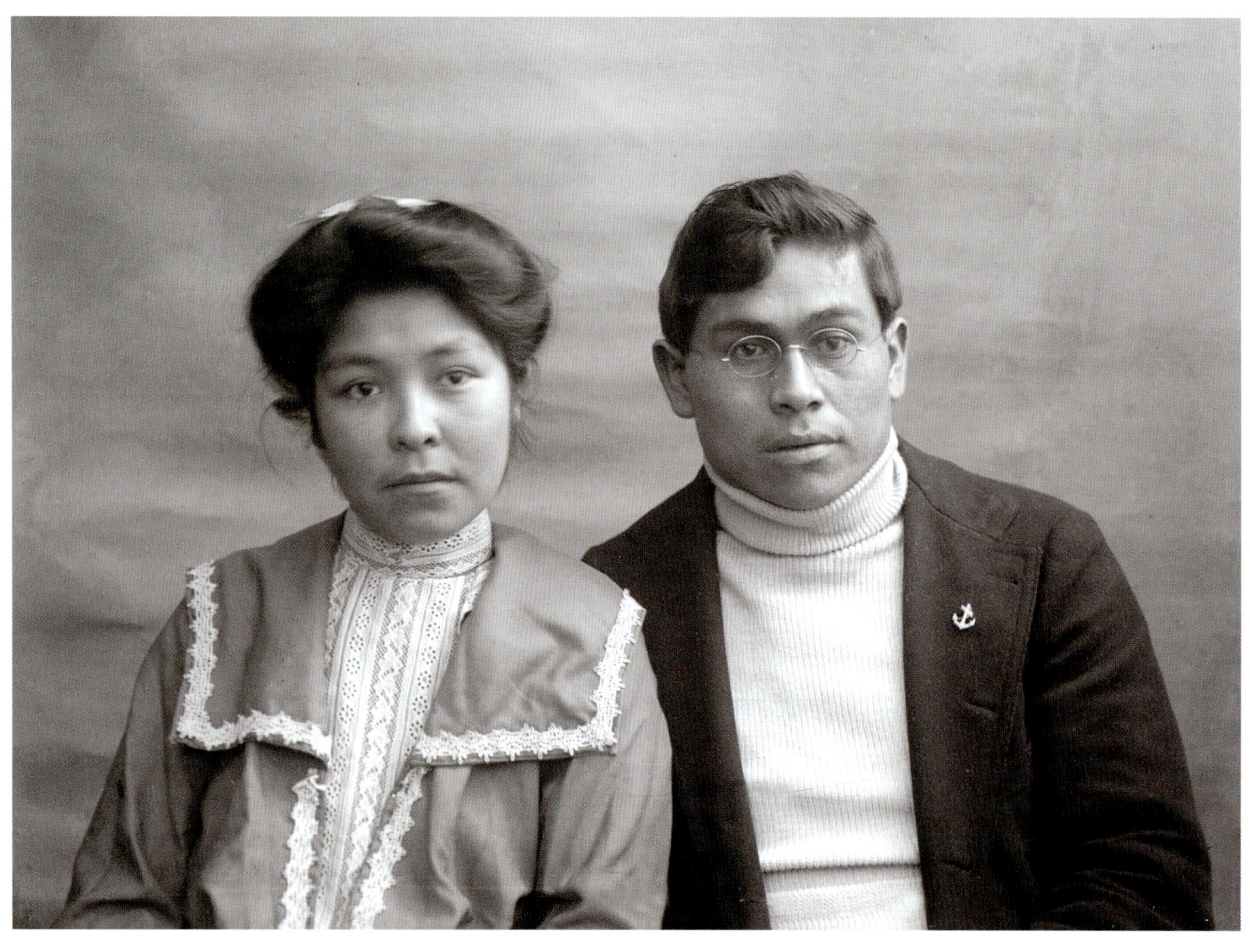

PLATE 80. Pauline James (K̲aax̲áni) (b. 1884-1911), Fort House (Noow Hít), Wooshkeetaan clan of Sitka and Albert James (Duksaa.éex) (1880–1936), Kiks.ádi clan, date unknown. Both were graduates of the Sitka Industrial and Training School and the maternal grandparents of Gilbert Truitt (Yeeshx̲á) (1927–2020). Identifications by Gilbert Truitt (2015). Courtesy of the National Park Service, Sitka National Historical Park, 25841.

SITKA INDUSTRIAL AND TRAINING SCHOOL
(LATER THE SHELDON JACKSON SCHOOL)

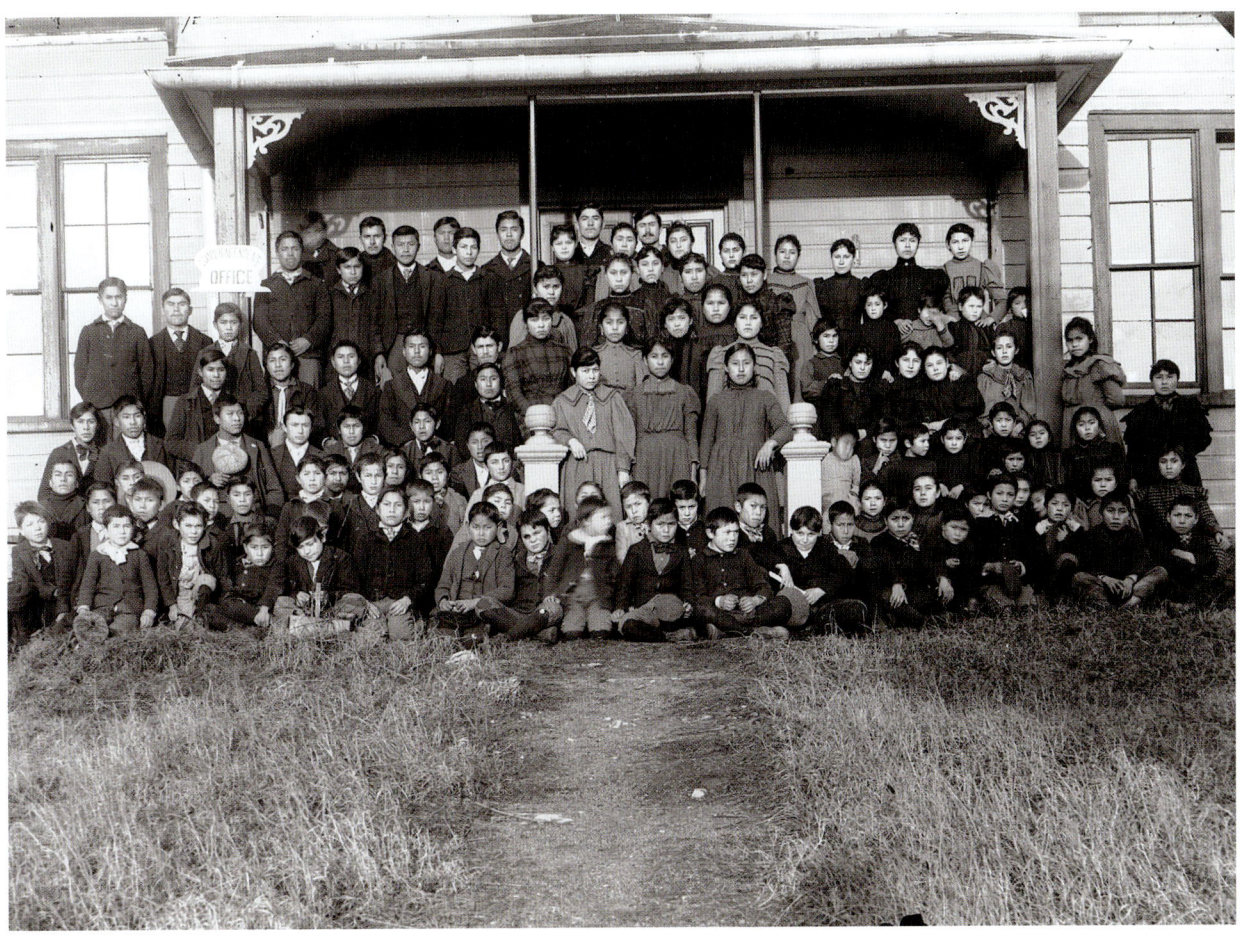

PLATE 81. An early photograph (ca. 1900) depicting Native boys and girls standing in front of an office building on the campus of the Sitka Industrial and Training School. Courtesy of the National Park Service, Sitka National Historical Park, 03752.

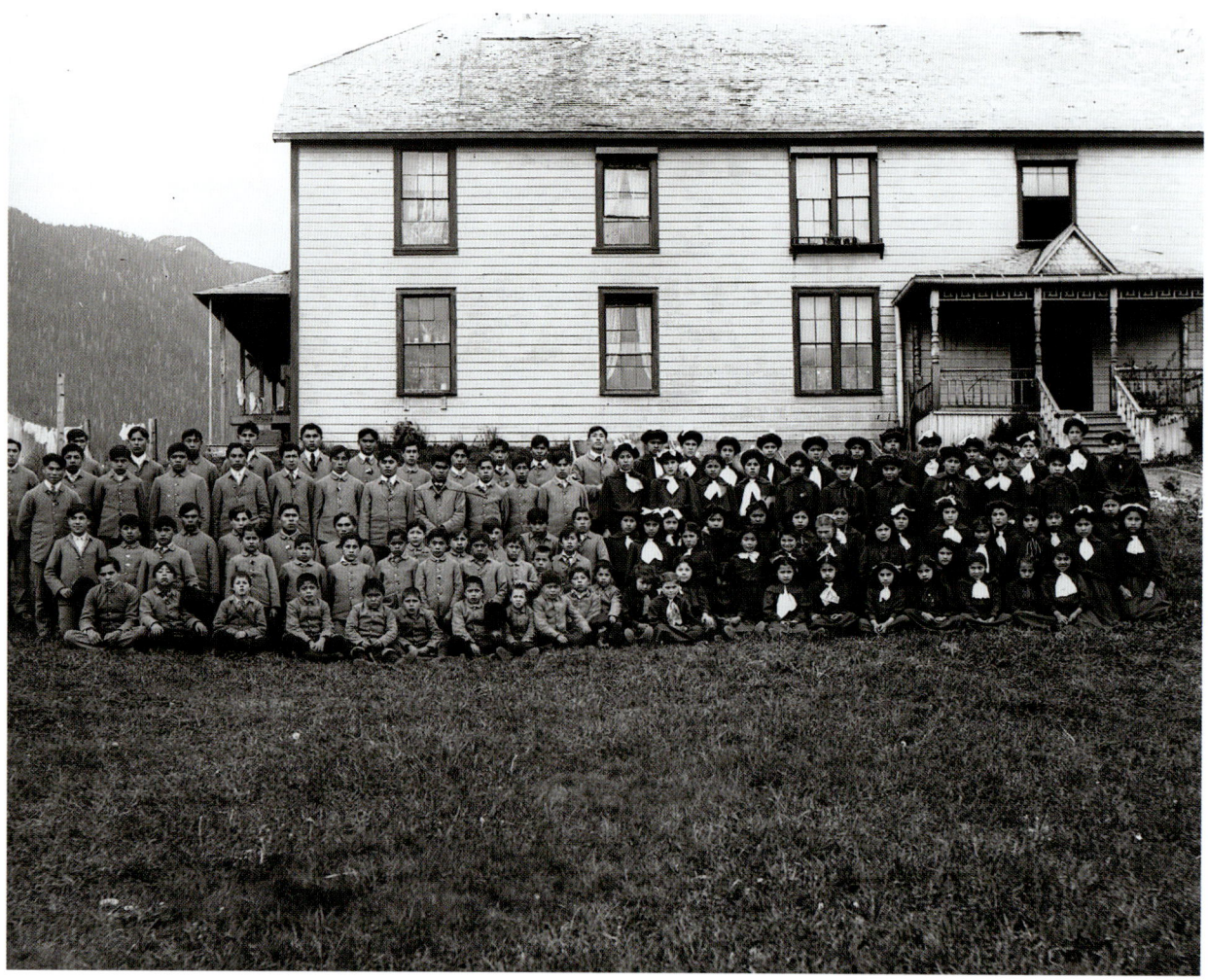

PLATE 82. Another early photograph (1900–1910) depicting students at the Sitka Industrial and Training School, with boys in military uniforms and girls in formal dresses. The building behind them was built in 1882 and razed in 1910. Courtesy of the National Park Service, Sitka National Historical Park, 03760.

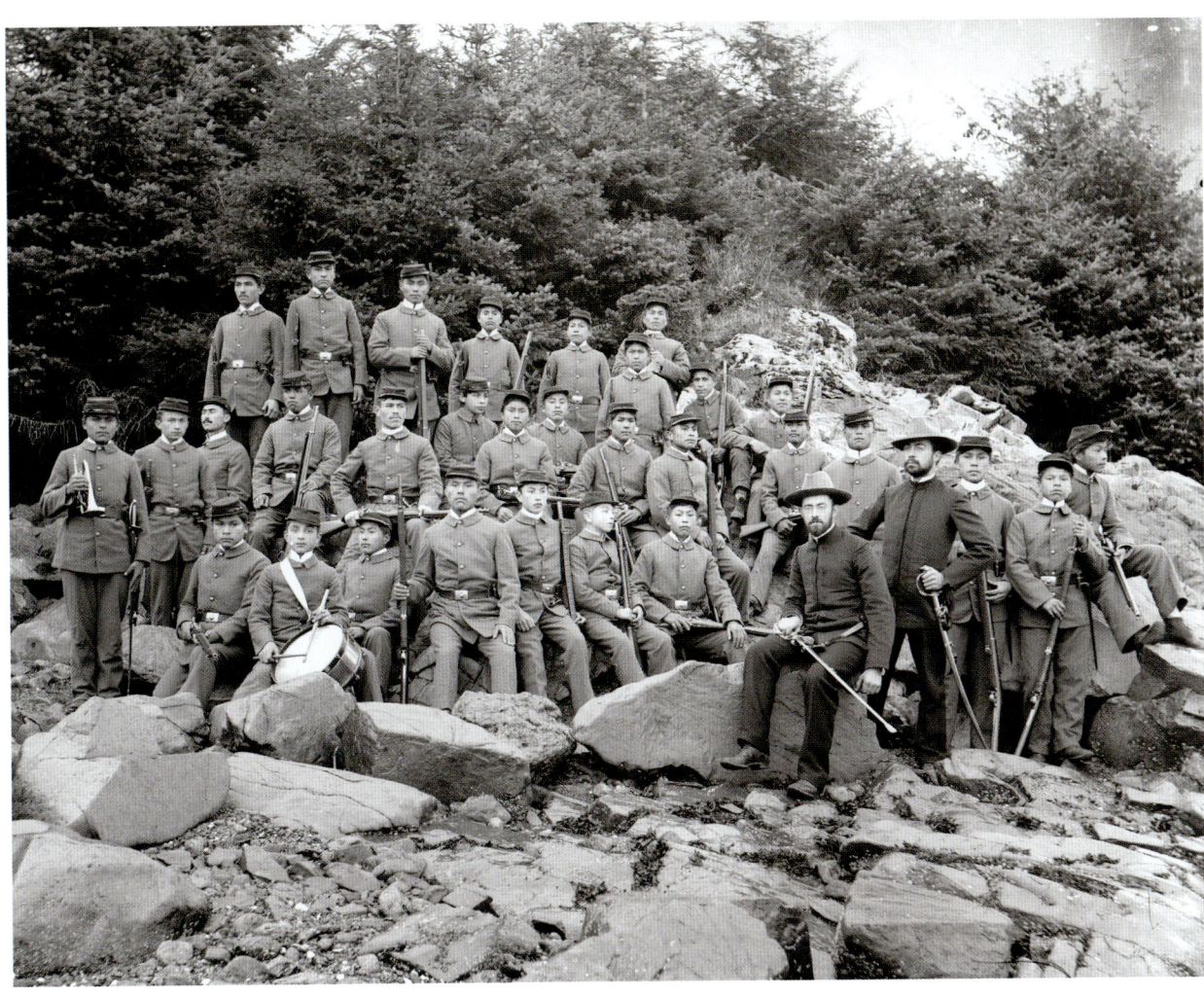

PLATE 83. An early photograph of a group of Sitka Industrial and Training School male students dressed in military uniforms and carrying rifles, with two teachers (at the front) acting as their commanding officers. On the right is Bertrand Wilbur, MD (1870–1945); on the left is Mr. Sharp. The drummer is Frank Price (Saatan Éesh) (1886–1946), Eagle's Nest House, Kaagwaantaan clan of Sitka. The picture was taken between 1899 and 1904, as Wilbur left the school in 1904. Courtesy of the National Park Service, Sitka National Historical Park, 25788.

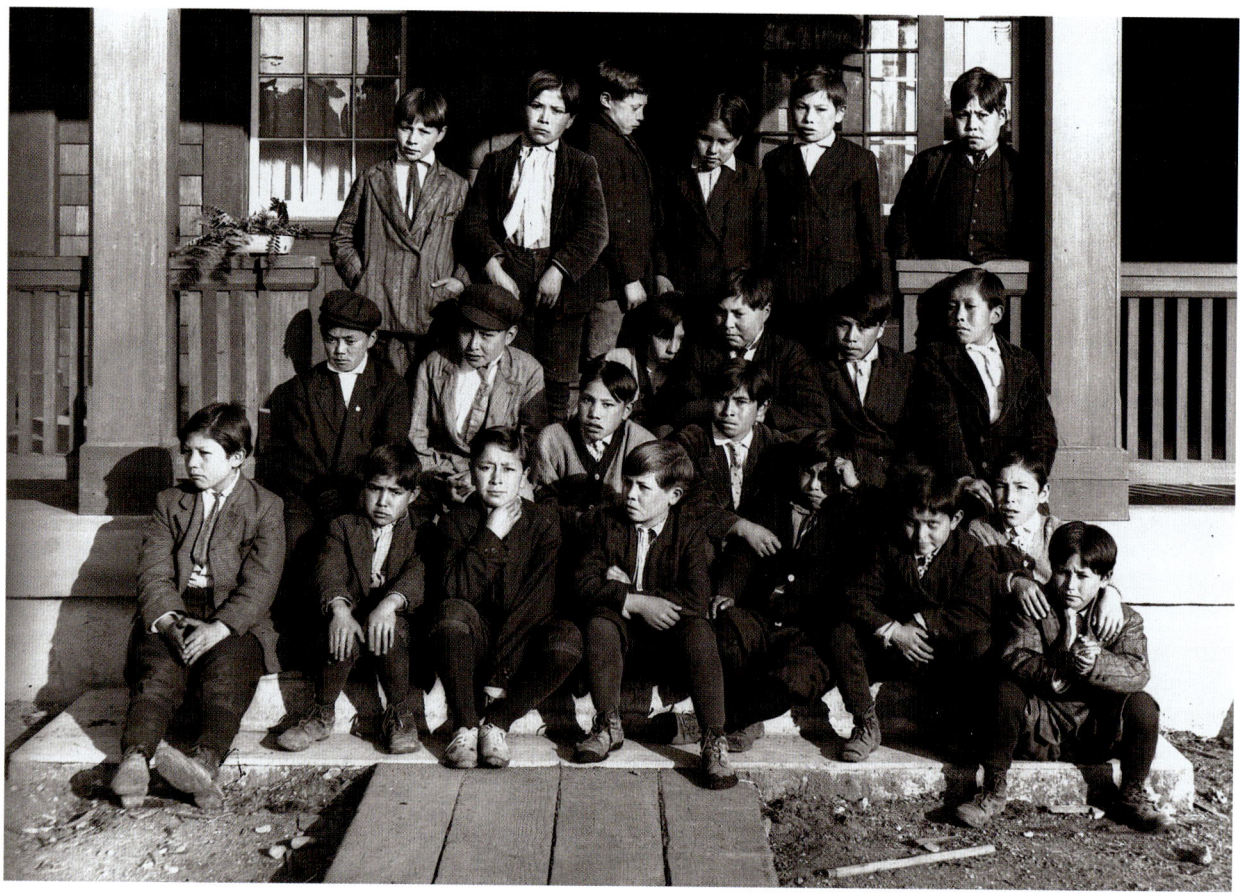

PLATE 84. A group of Native boys on the porch of a campus building, Sitka Industrial and Training School, ca. 1900–1910. Courtesy of the National Park Service, Sitka National Historical Park, 03749.

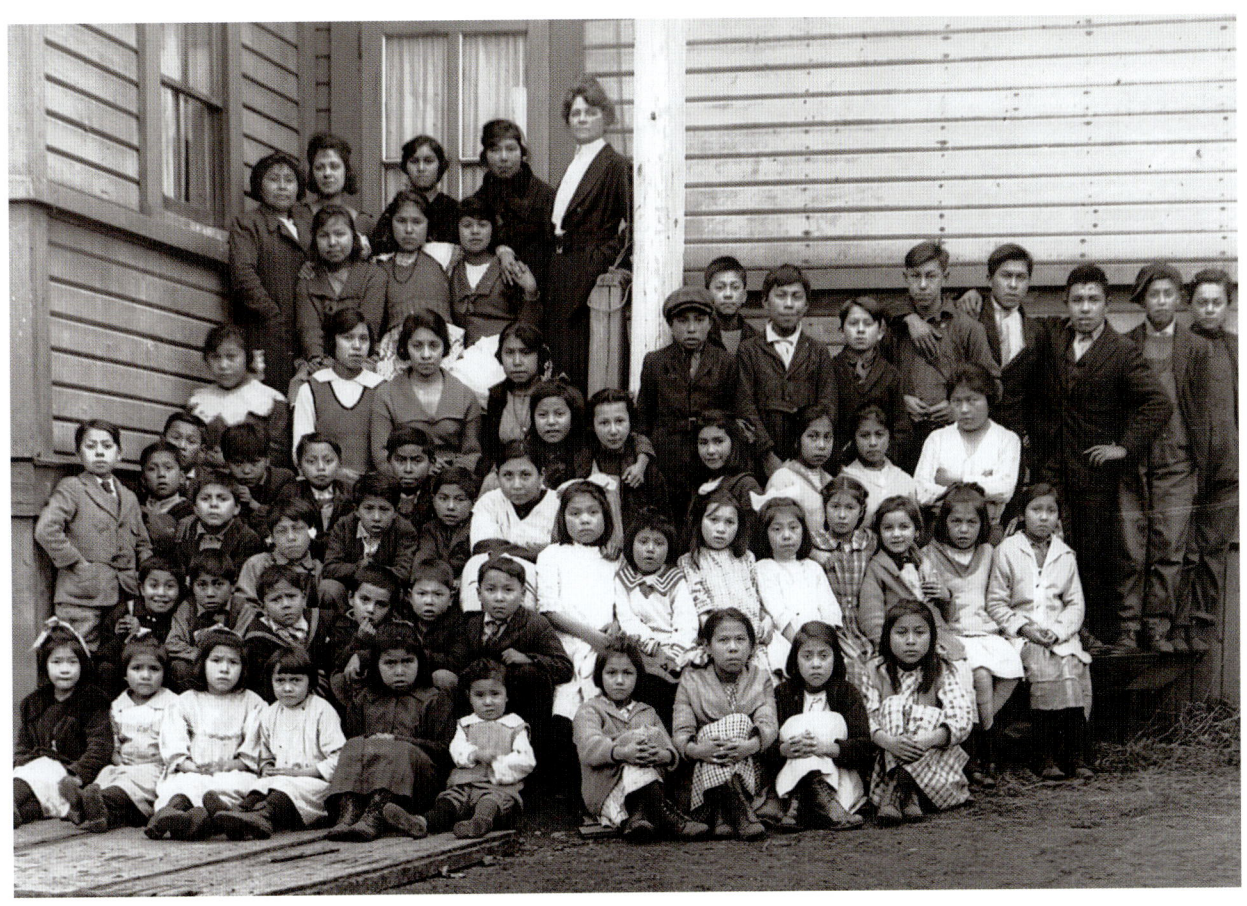

PLATE 85. Native boys and girls with a teacher at the Sitka Industrial and Training School, ca. 1900–1910. Courtesy of the National Park Service, Sitka National Historical Park, 3744.

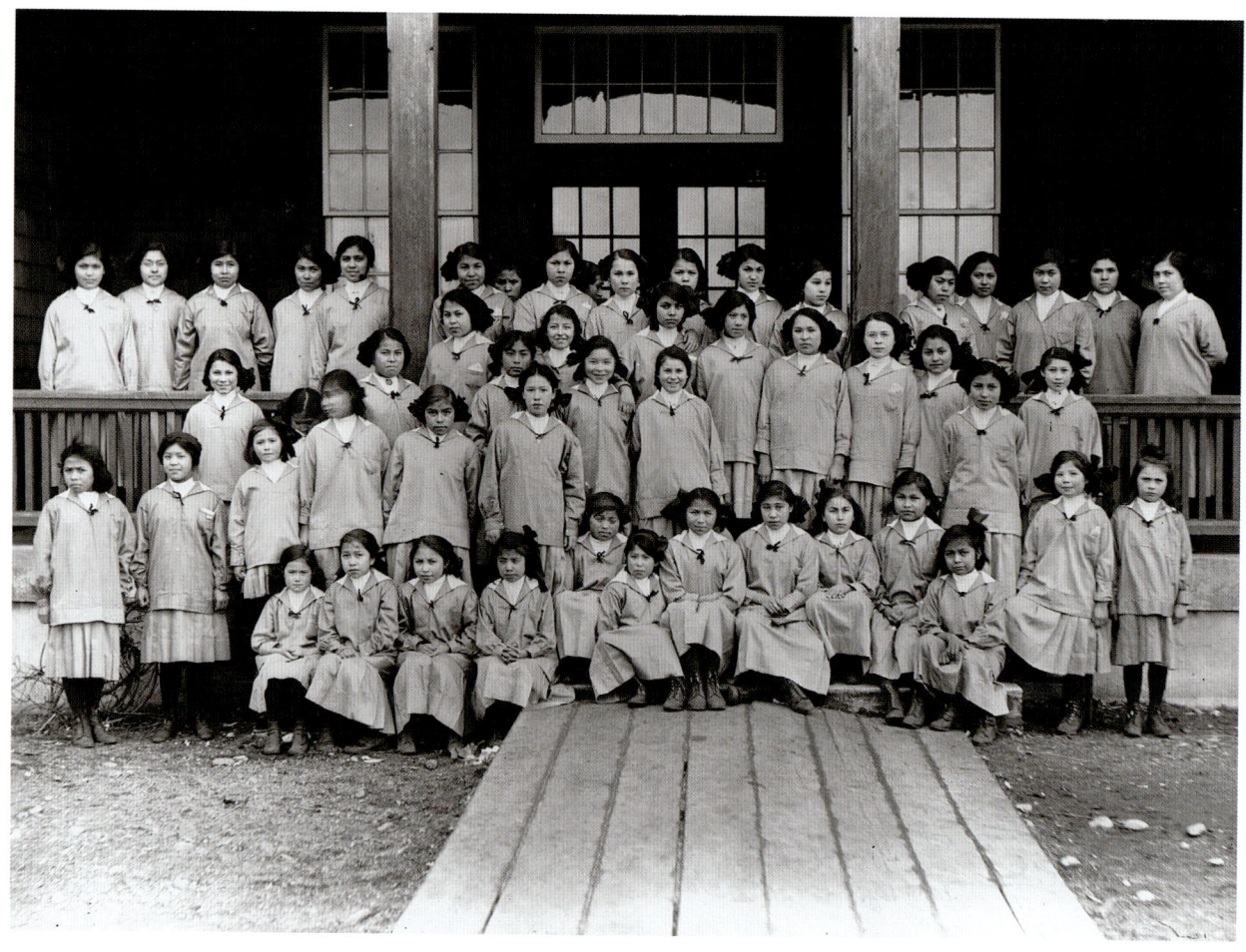

PLATE 86. Sitka Industrial and Training School, ca. 1900–1910. Native girls dressed in uniforms. Courtesy of the National Park Service, Sitka National Historical Park, 03756.

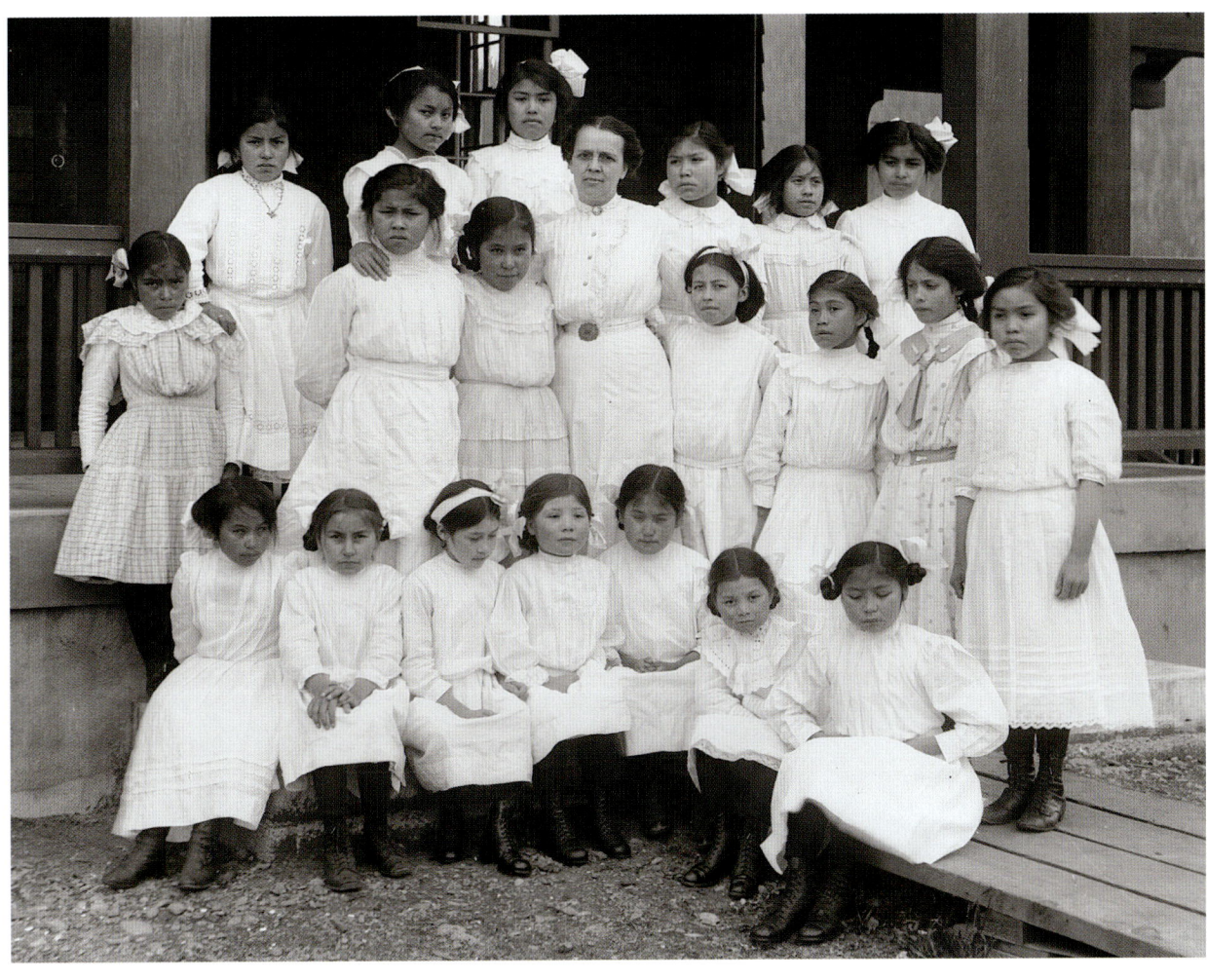

PLATE 87. Sitka Industrial and Training School, ca. 1910. Girls with a teacher. Front row, fourth from left, is Lucy Widmark (1902–57). Courtesy of the National Park Service, Sitka National Historical Park, 03745

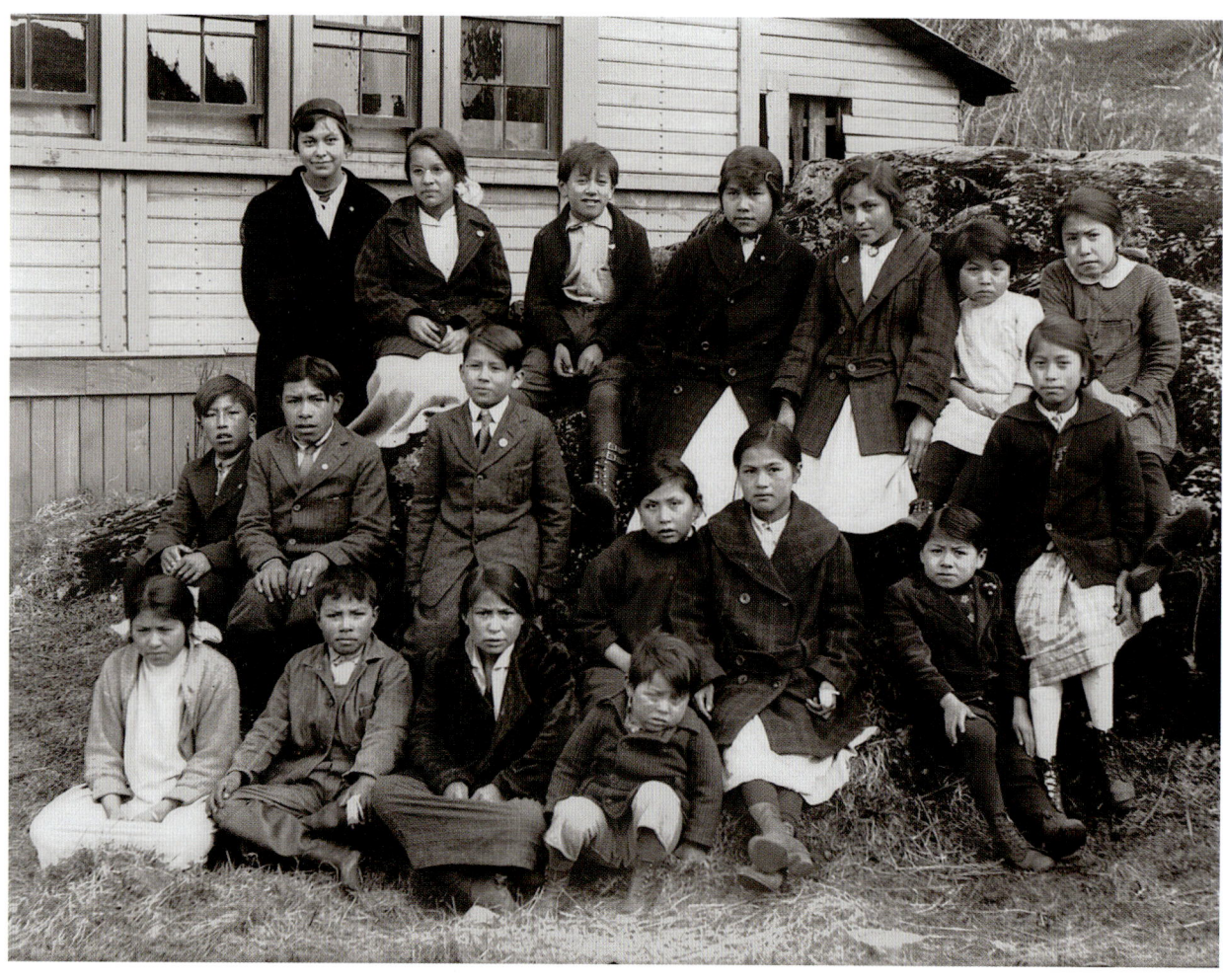

PLATE 88. A teacher at the Sheldon Jackson School (formerly the Sitka Industrial and Training School) with a group of Native boys and girls, late 1910s. Back row, fourth from left, is Katherine Mills (Yakwx̱aan Tláa), Tʼax̱deintaan clan of Hoonah; fifth from left is Annie (Davis) Dick (X̱áasenax̱) (1904–93), Iron House (G̱ayes' Hít), Chookaneidí clan of Hoonah. Courtesy of the National Park Service, Sitka National Historical Park, 03753.

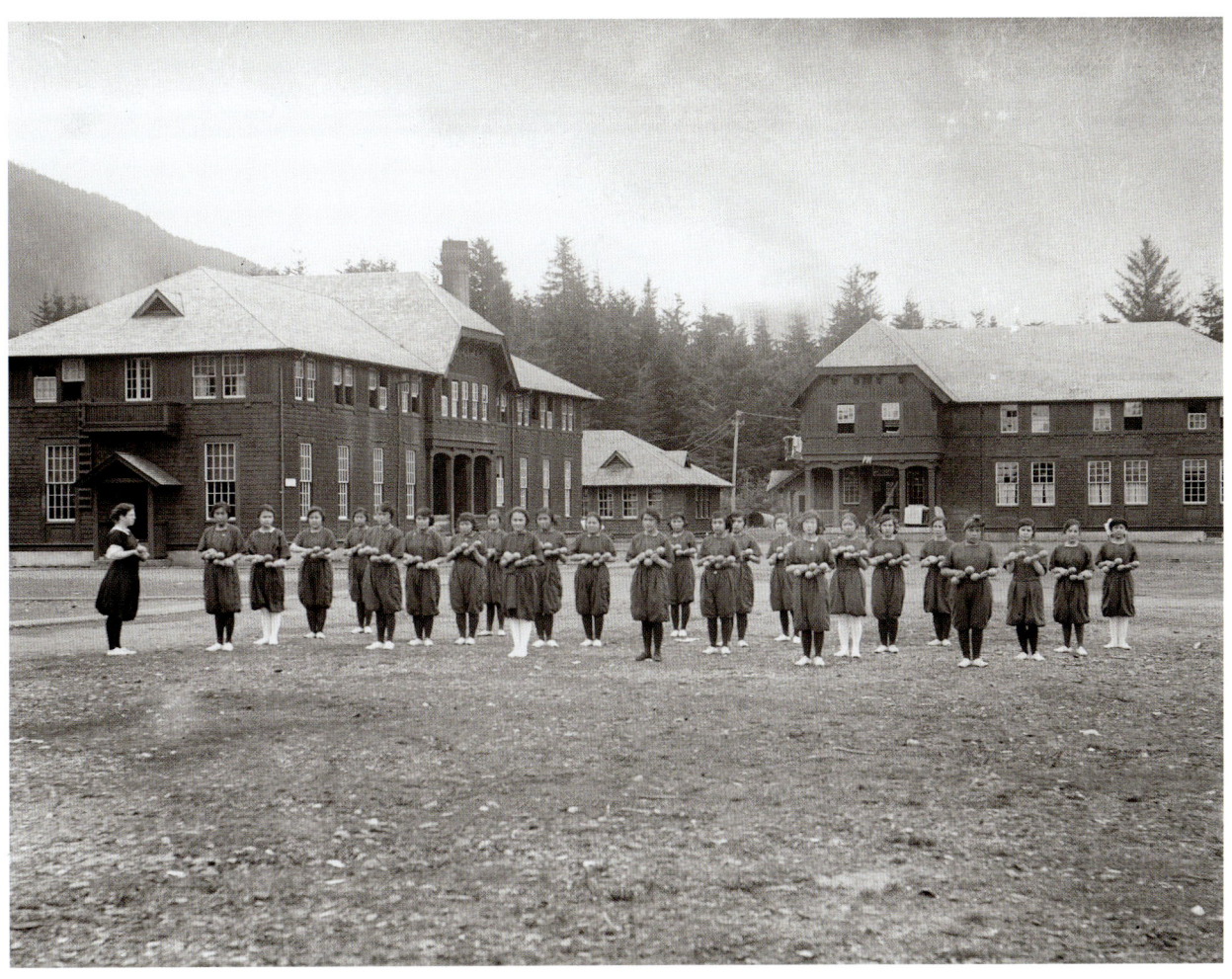

PLATE 89. A group of older female students at the Sheldon Jackson School doing athletic exercises, ca. 1915. The instructor is Ms. Ranson. Courtesy of the National Park Service, Sitka National Historical Park, 25902.

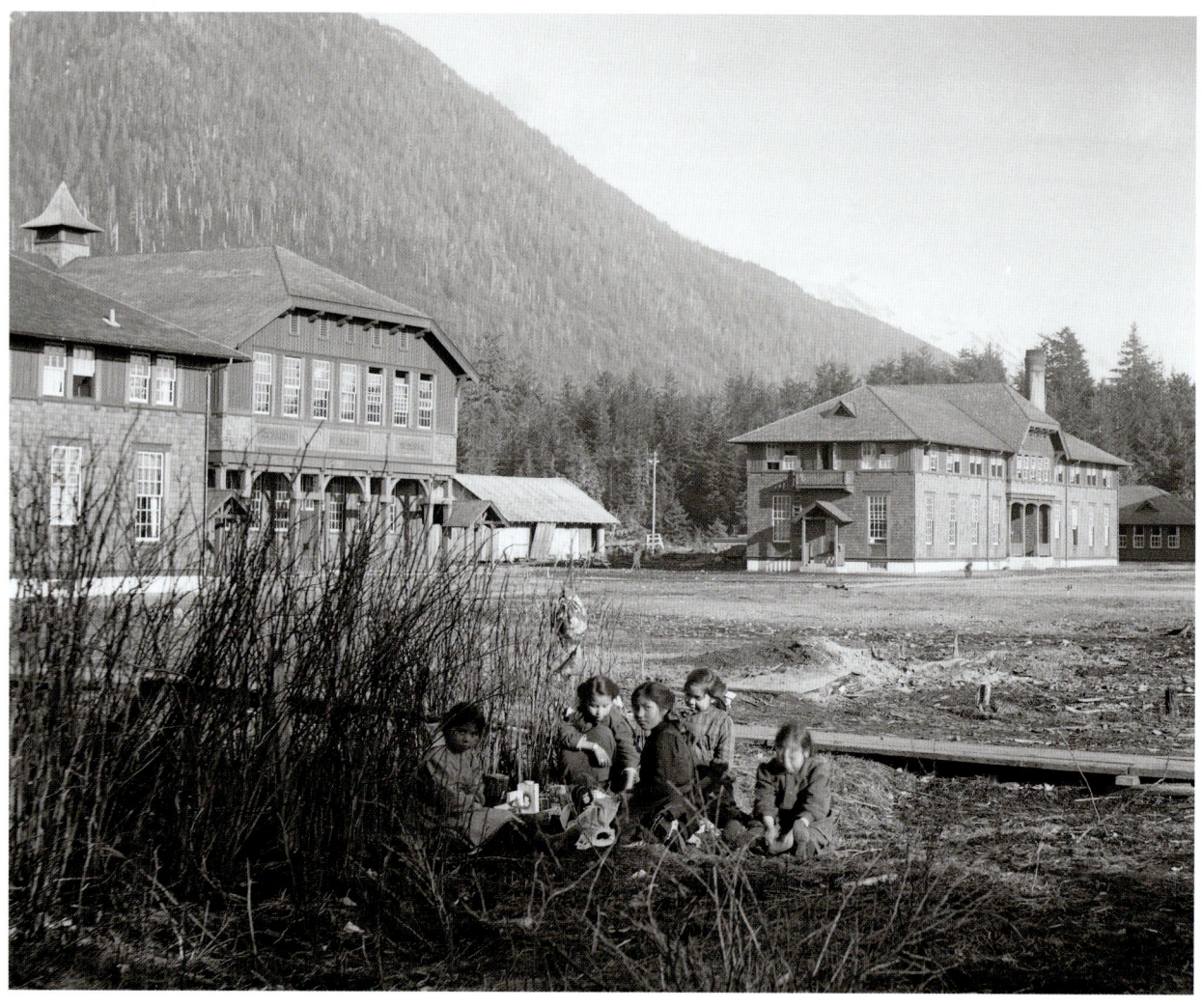

PLATE 90. An informal photo of a group of Native students at the Sitka Industrial and Training School, date unknown. Courtesy of the National Park Service, Sitka National Historical Park, 25780.

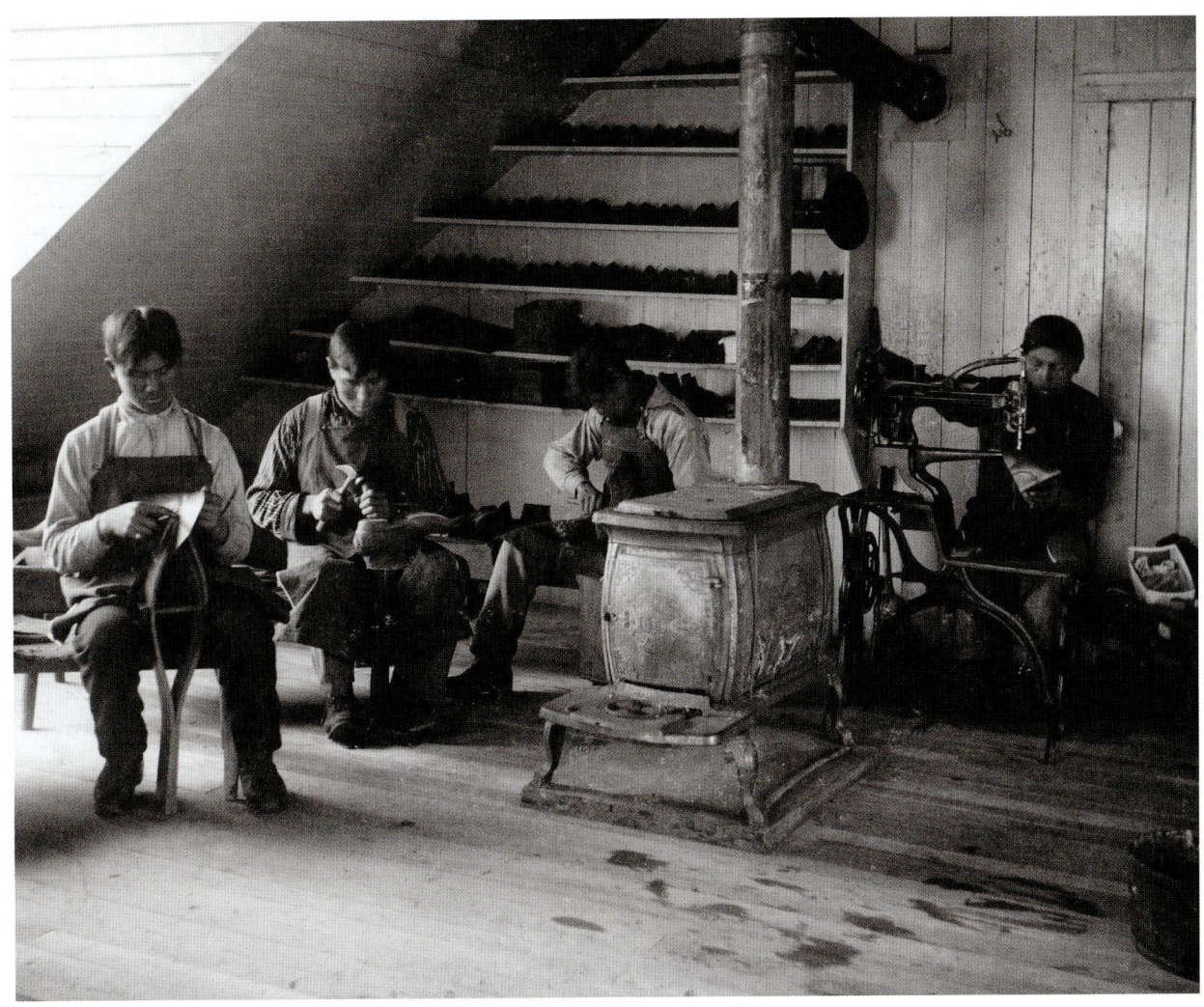

PLATE 91. Sitka Industrial and Training School students in the cobbler shop, date unknown. Alaska State Historical Library, P427-70.

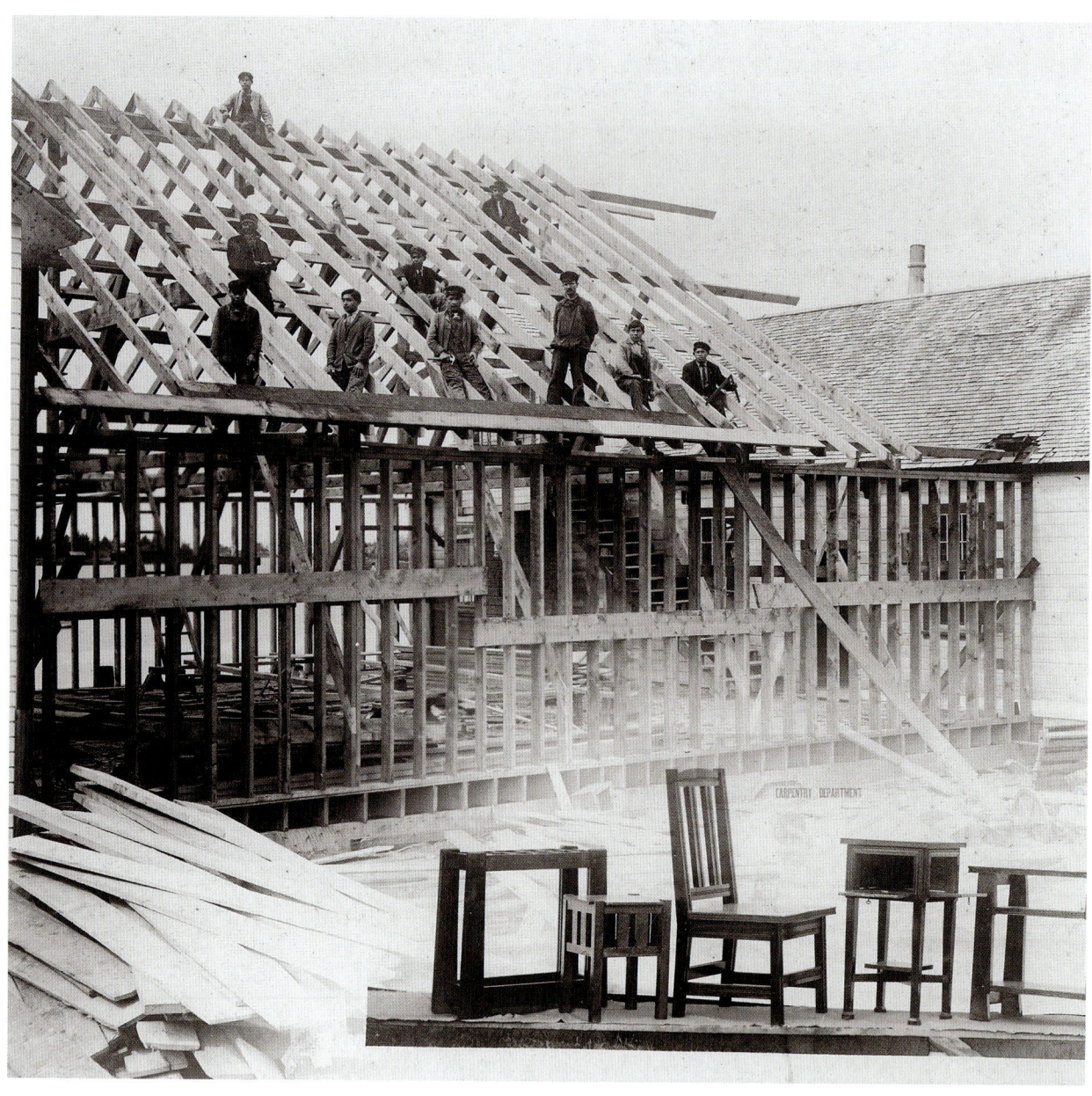

PLATE 92. Sitka Industrial and Training School boys building a house frame, ca. 1910–15.
University of Washington Libraries, Special Collections, Elbridge Warren Merrill Collection. PH Coll 325.31.

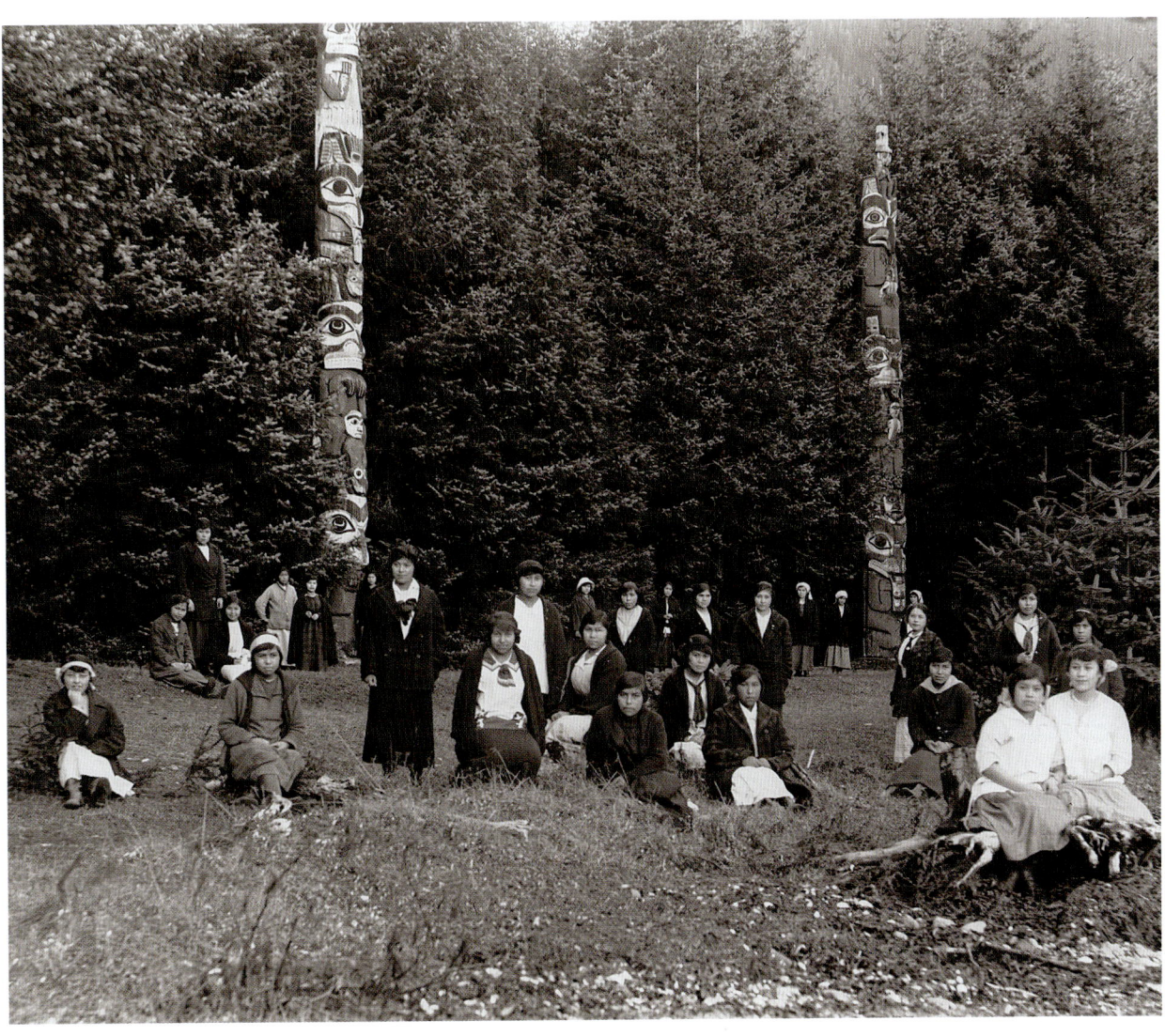

PLATE 93. Older female students of the Sheldon Jackson School on an outing in the Sitka National Park. Judging by their clothing, the photograph was taken in the 1920s. Courtesy of the National Park Service, Sitka National Historical Park, 03754.

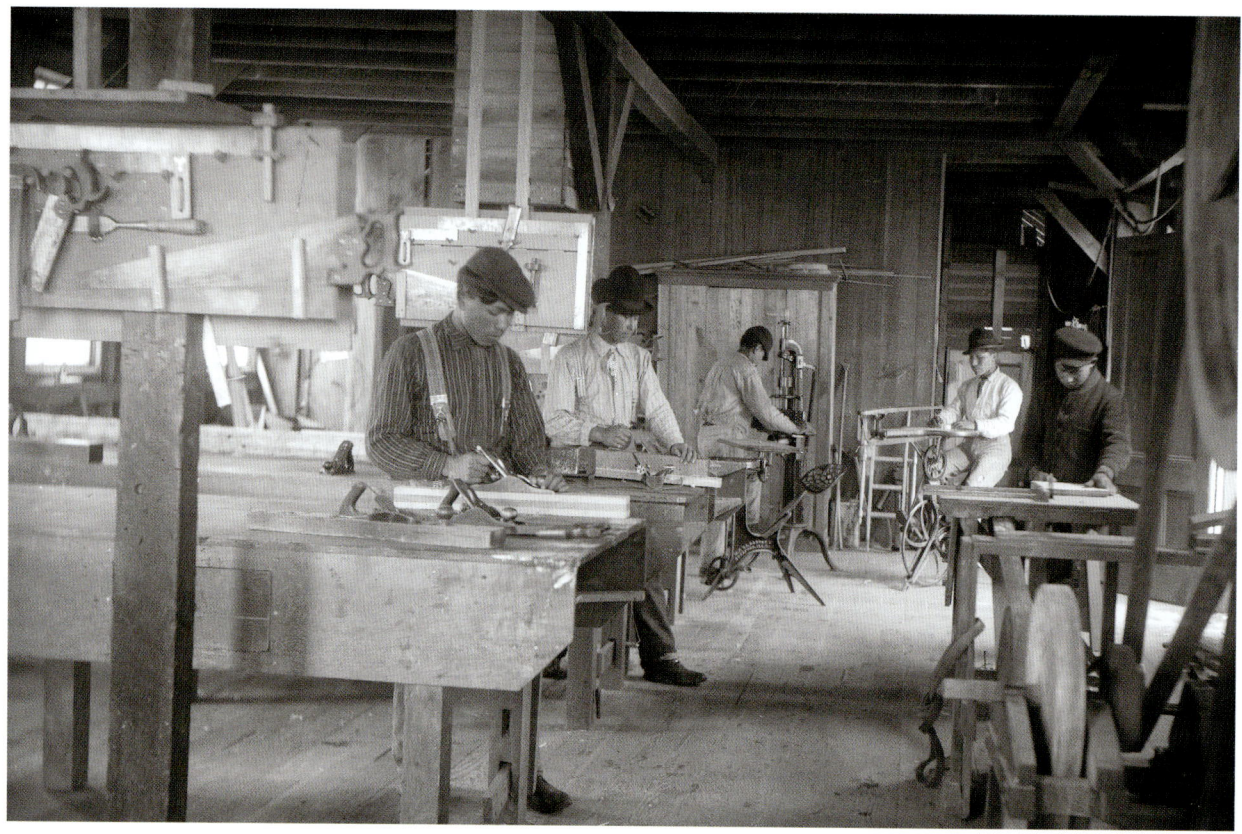

PLATE 94. Industrial School boys in the carpentry shop, date unknown.
Courtesy of the National Park Service, Sitka National Historical Park, 26121.

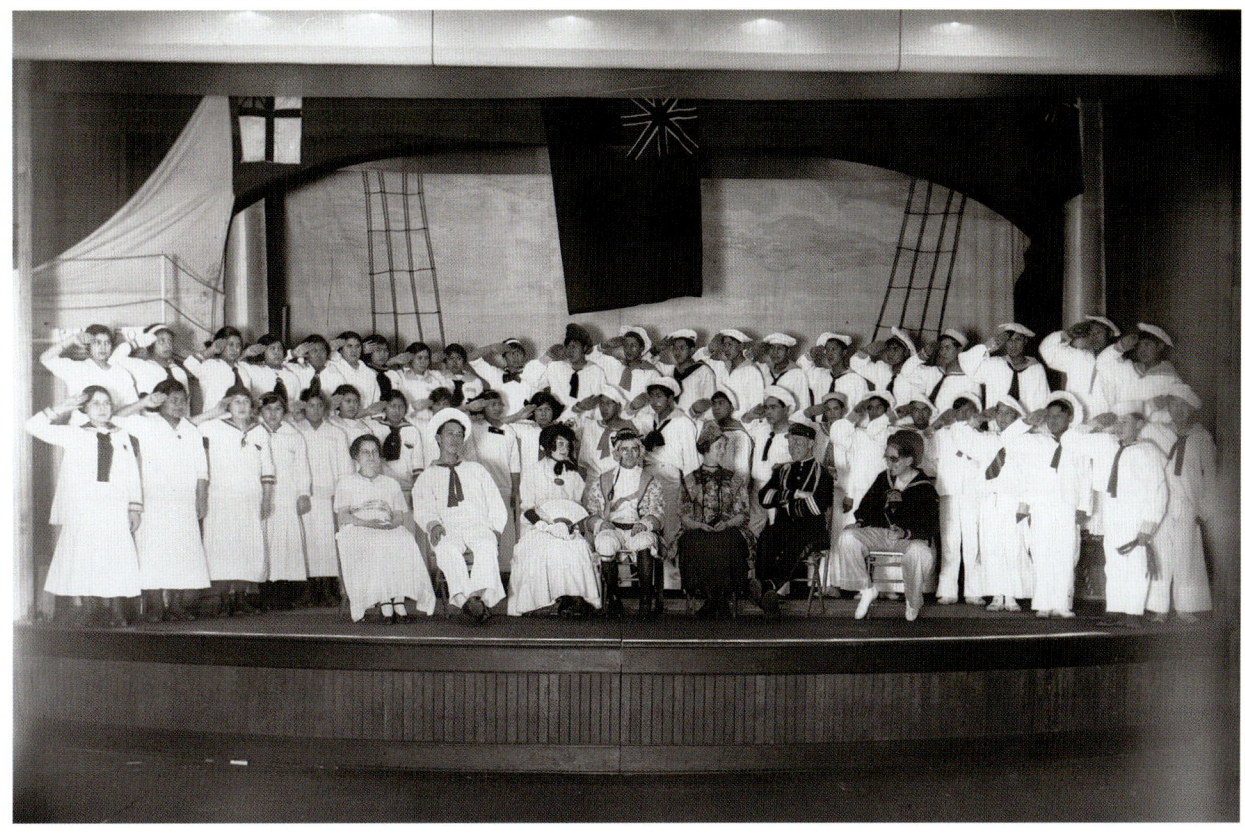

PLATE 95. Teachers and older students of the Sheldon Jackson School performing in the Gilbert and Sullivan comic opera *H.M.S. Pinafore*, ca. 1915–29. Courtesy of the National Park Service, Sitka National Historical Park, 3758.

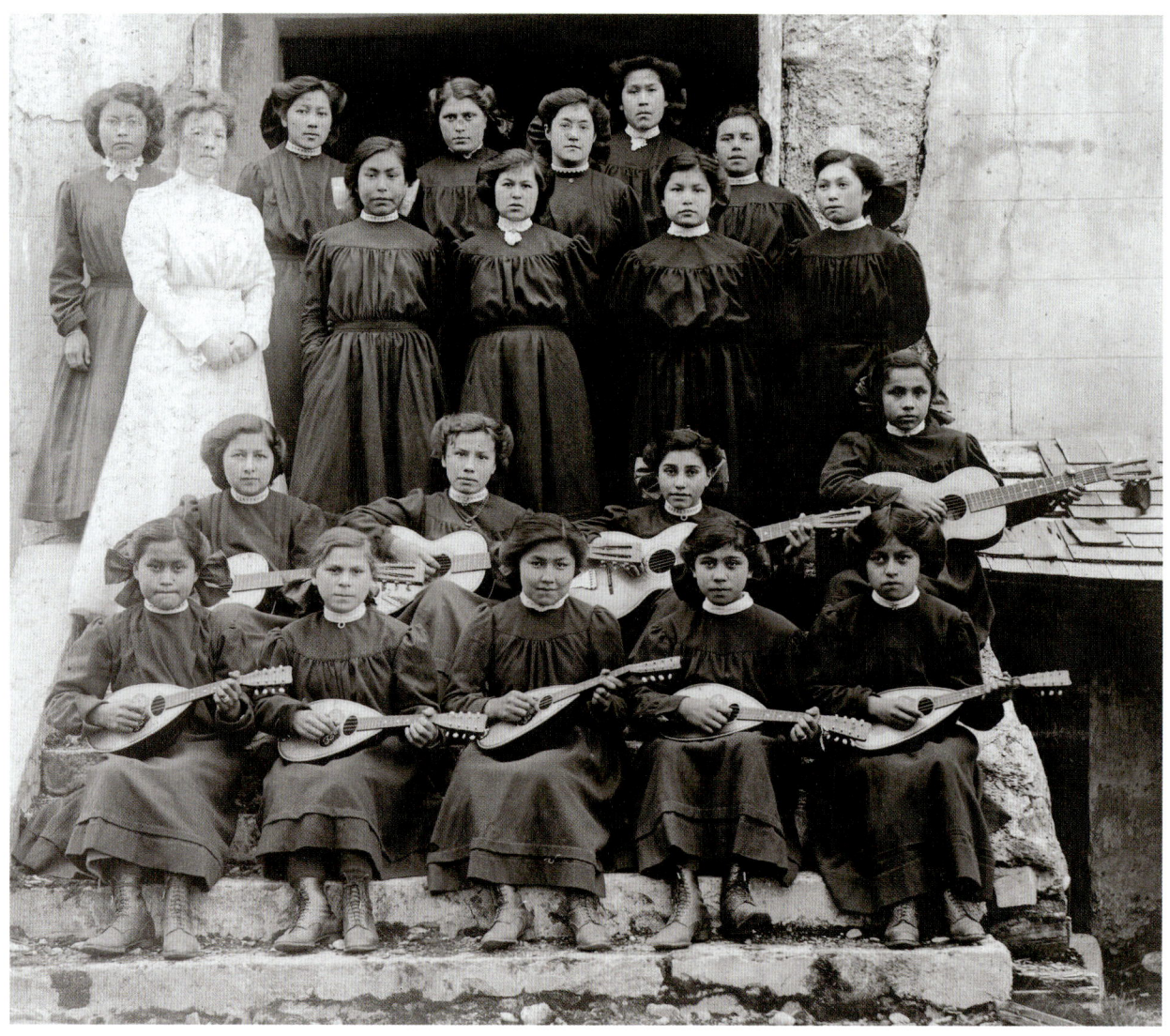

PLATE 96. A group of female students, some with musical instruments, at the Sitka Industrial and Training School with two teachers, ca. 1905–10. In the front row, first on the right, is Tillie (Howard) Hope (Aasdaak'aa) (1895–1975) Point House, Kiks.ádi clan. One of the teachers is Tlingit, one white. University of Washington Libraries, Special Collections, Elbridge Warren Collection. PH Coll 325.23.

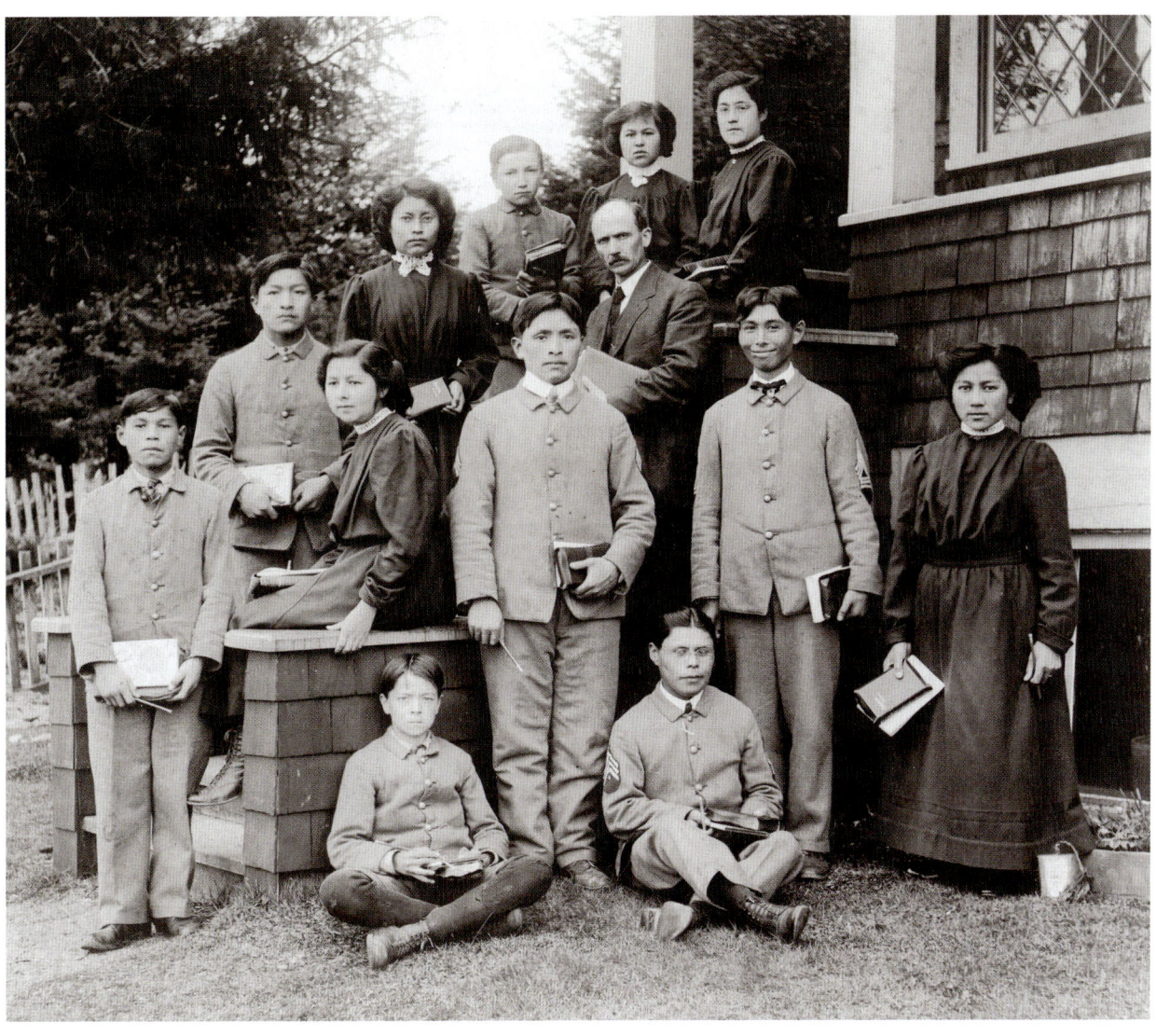

PLATE 97. A teacher with a group of older Sheldon Jackson School students in uniform, holding books, ca. 1910–15. University of Washington Libraries, Special Collections, Elbridge Warren Merrill Collection. PH Coll 325.27.

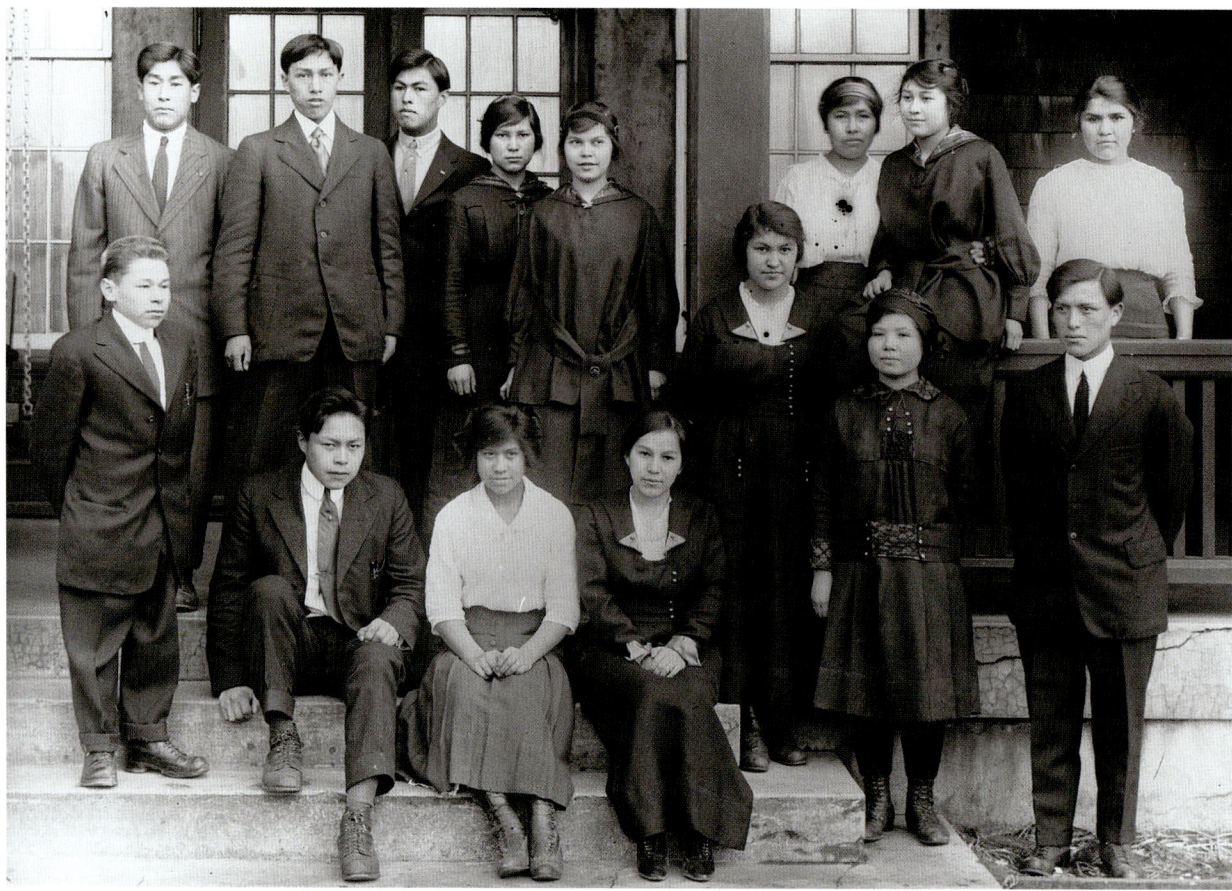

PLATE 98. Sheldon Jackson School. First graduating high school class, 1921.

Front row, left to right: Ned Luke Simeon (Semeon) (ca. 1897–1923) Russian-Tlingit descent, Kaagwaantaan clan, adopted son of Luke Simeon (Semeon) (Borbridge), Steel House (Shdeen Hít), Kiks.ádi clan. Seated: A. P. Johnson (Íxt'ik' Éesh) (1898–1986), Clay House (S'é Hít), Kiks.ádi clan; unidentified young woman; Dora Walton (1900–1976), (sitting) and Matilda Walton (b. 1901), daughters of Mary Walton (1881–1950), Kaagwaantaan clan, and stepdaughters of Rudolph Walton (Kawóotk', Aak'wtaatseen) (1867–1951), Kiks.ádi clan; Lucy Widmark (1902–57); Frank O. Williams (b. 1899), Chookaneidí clan.

Back row, left to right: George Fulton; unidentified young man; Andrew Davis(?) (Shooweeká), Wooshkeetaan clan of Angoon; unidentified young woman; Lenora Peters (1900–1998); three unidentified young women.

Identifications based on inscription on the back of the photograph. Courtesy of the National Park Service, Sitka National Historical Park, 03751.

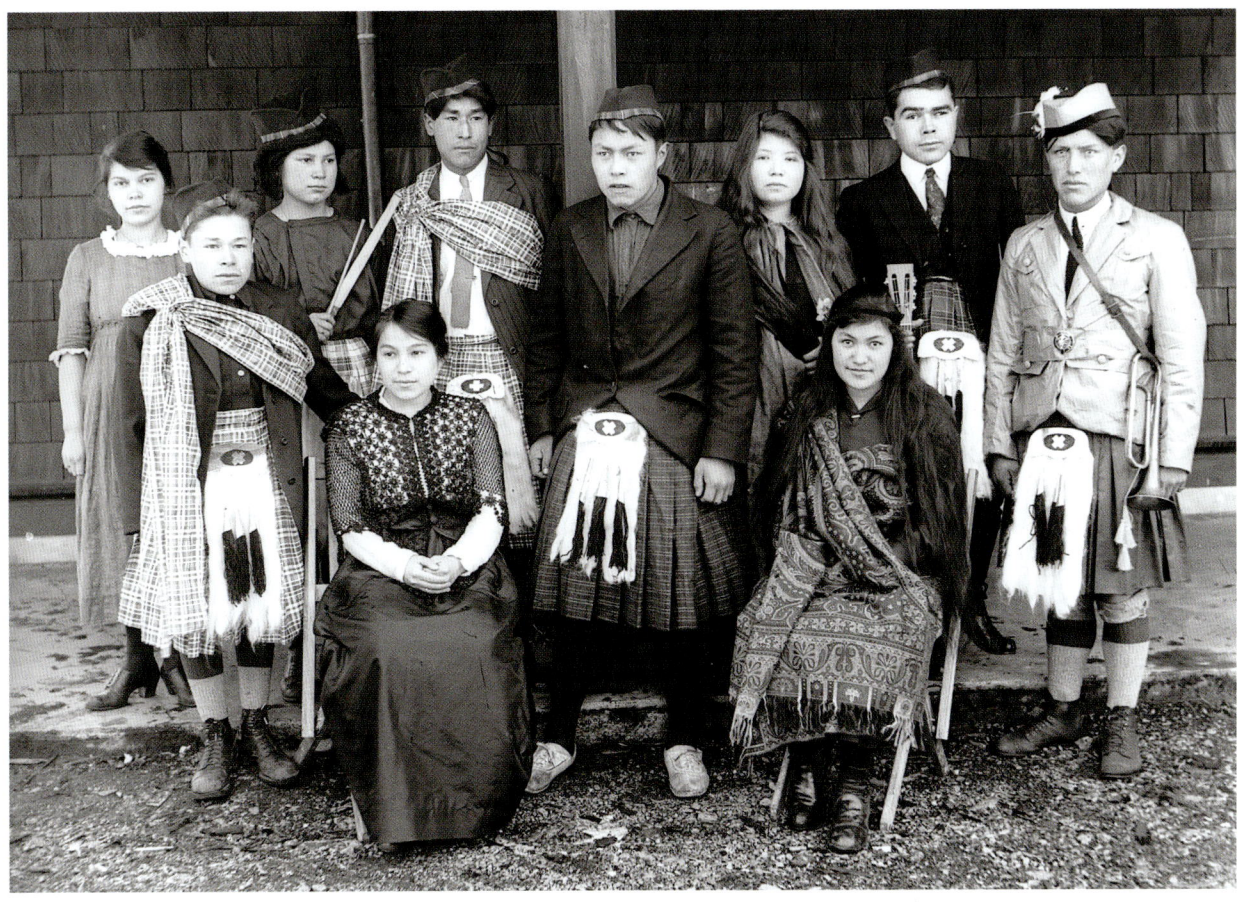

PLATE 99. Sheldon Jackson School students of the high school class of 1921 in front of the Allen Auditorium in costume for the play *Lady of the Lake* (with a Scottish theme). Front row, left to right: Matilda Walton (b. 1901) and Dora Walton (1900–1976), daughters of Mary Walton (1881–1950), Kaagwaantaan clan, and stepdaughters of Rudolph Walton (Kawóotk', Aak'wtaatseen) (1867–1951), Kiks.ádi clan. Next to Dora is Ned Luke Simeon (Semeon) (ca. 1897–1923), of Russian-Tlingit descent, Kaagwaantaan clan, adopted son of Luke Simeon (Semeon), Kiks.ádi clan.

Back row, right to left: Frank O. Williams Sr. (b. 1899), Chookaneidí clan; Steven Nicholas (b. 1893); Lucy Widmark (1902–57); A. P. Johnson (Íxt'ik' Éesh) (1898–1986), Kiks.ádi clan; George Fulton; Margaret Cox (b. 1902); Lenora Peters (1900–1998).

Identifications are based on an inscription on the back of the photograph. Courtesy of the National Park Service, Sitka National Historical Park, 03809.

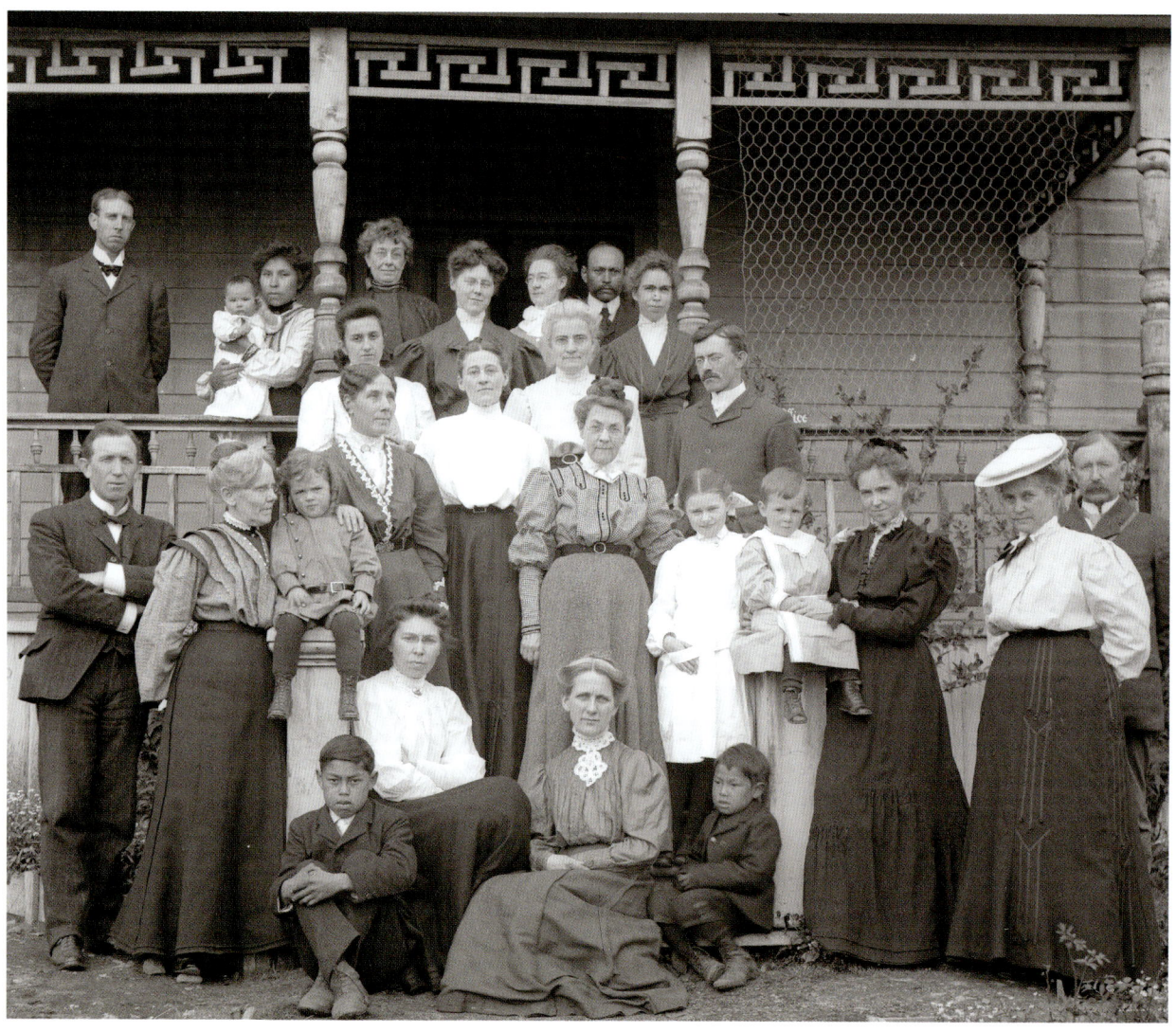

PLATE 100. A group of Sitka Industrial and Training School teachers and staff members with their spouses, 1900s. In the top row, holding a baby, is a Tlingit woman; in the bottom row are two Tlingit boys. The boy on the left might be David Howard Sr., Point House (X'aaká Hít), Kiks.ádi clan of Sitka. Courtesy of the National Park Service, Sitka National Historical Park, 25918.

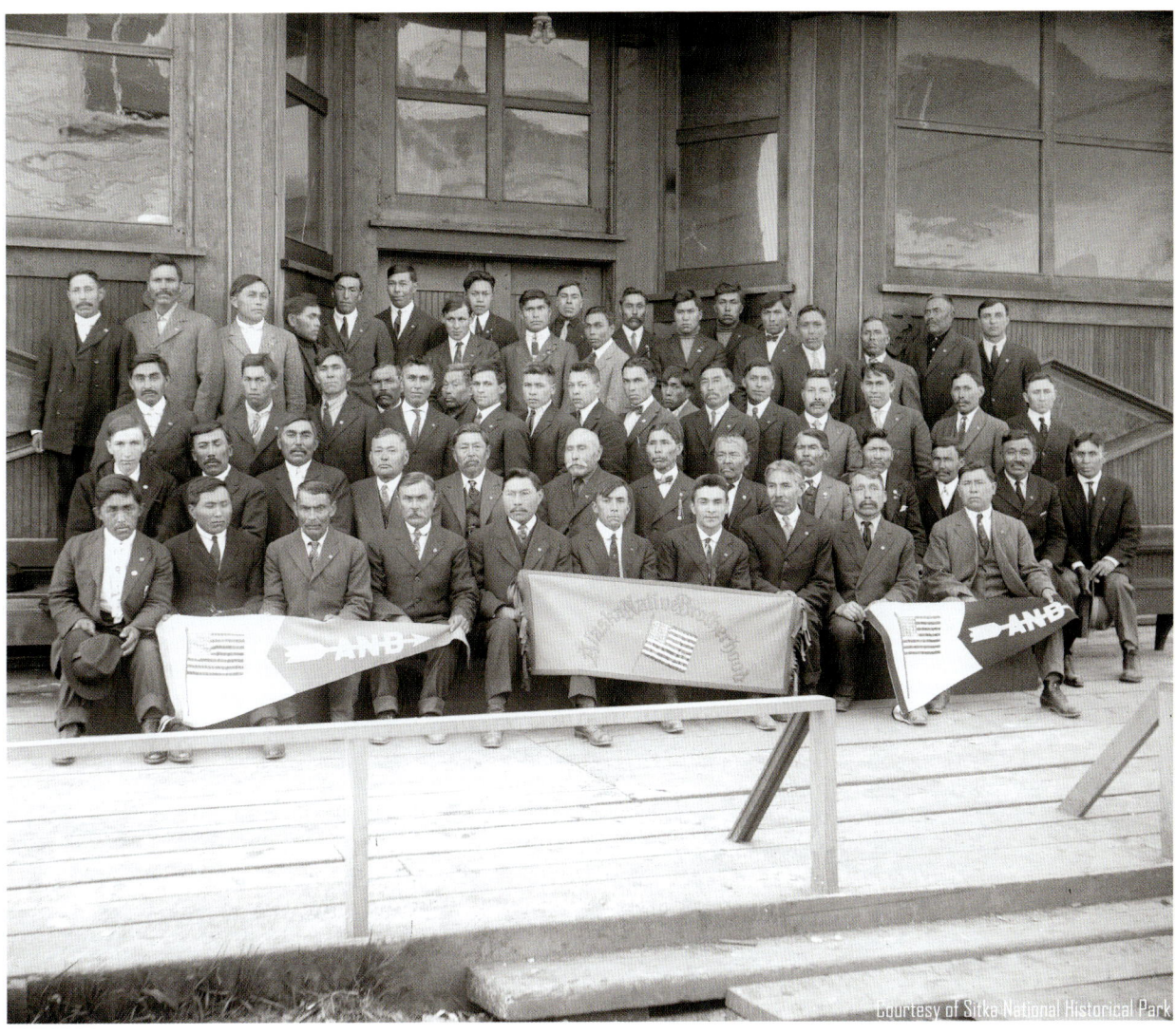

PLATE 101. Another ANB group in front of the ANB building, Sitka, ca. 1920. Front row, seventh from left, Andrew Percy Hope (Ḵaa.ooshtí) (1896–1968), Eagle's Nest House (Ch'áak' Ḵúdi Hít), Kaagwaantaan clan; ninth from left, Rudolph Walton (1867–1951). Second row, second from right, Peter Simpson Sr. (1871–1947), Tsimshian.

Third row: tenth from left, Innocent Sergius Williams (Nax'eidu) (1894–1986), Cow House (Xaas Hít) of the Ḵoosk'eidí clan, a subdivision of the Ĺuknax.ádi clan; at right, Ralph Young (1877–1956).

Fourth row, eighth from left: A. P. Johnson (Íx̲t'ik' Éesh) (1898–1986), Kiks.ádi clan; first on right: Frank Price (Saatan Éesh) (1886–1946), Eagle's Nest House (Ch'áak' Ḵúdi Hít), Kaagwaantaan clan of Sitka.

Courtesy of the National Park Service, Sitka National Historical Park, 25432.

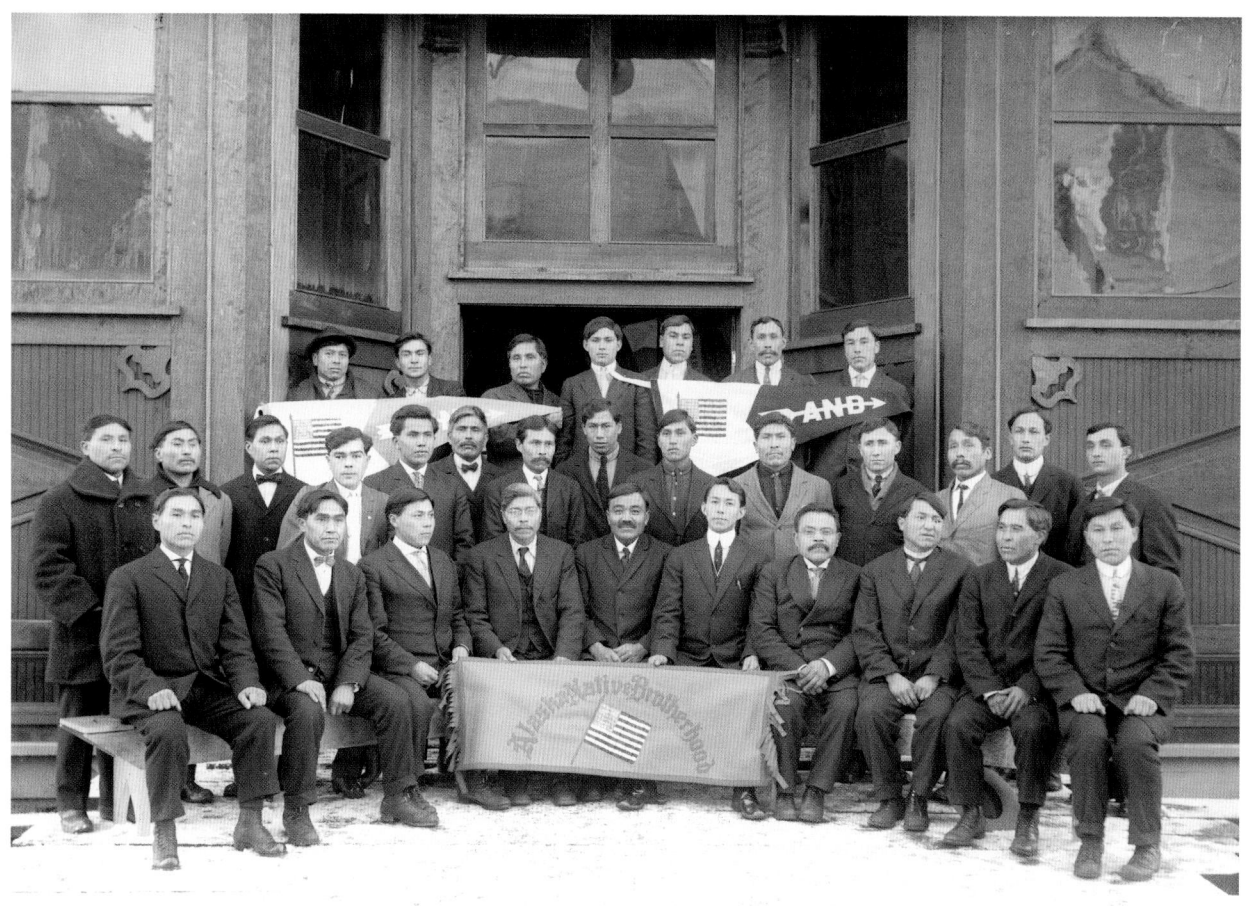

PLATE 102. Founders and early members of the Alaska Native Brotherhood (ANB) in front of the ANB building in Sitka, 1914.

Front row, left to right: James Watson (Lgeik'i Éesh) (1881–1926), Big Dipper House (Yaxte Hít), L'eeneidí clan of Juneau; Frank Mercer (Sgáaxk') (ca. 1876–1931), Killer Whale House (Kéet Hít), Dakl'aweidí clan of Klukwan; Herbert Murchison (b. ca. 1883), Canadian Tsimshian; Chester Worthington (Gunáak'w) (1868–1935), Killer Whale House (Kéet Hít), Naanya.aayí clan of Wrangell; Peter Simpson Sr. (1871–1947), Tsimshian, ANB grand president; Paul Liberty (Aanyáanáx) (1886–1920), Sun House (Gagaan Hít), Kiks.ádi clan; Edward Marsden, Tsimshian; Haines DeWitt (1884–1935); Peter K. Williams(?); Charlie Newton.

Middle row, left to right: John Willard (b. ca. 1890); John Johnson; Seward Kunz (Gageit) (1878–1934), Big Dipper House (Yaxte Hít) L'eeneidí clan of Auke Bay; Stephen Nichols (b. 1893); Donald Austin; George McKay; Cyrus Peck Sr. (X'anaxtáan) (1870–1922), Log Jam House, L'eeneidi clan of Auk Bay; James Morrison; Charlie Daniels (1891–1959); possi-

bly Don Cameron (1876–1938); Ralph Young (Looshkát) (1877–1956), Raven's Nest House (Yéil Kúdei Hít), T'akdeintaan clan; Rudolph Walton (Kawóotk', Aak'wtaatseen) (1867–1951), Kiks.ádi clan; William Jackson; Frank Price (1886–1946) (Saatan Éesh), Eagle's Nest House (Ch'áak' Kúdi Hít), Kaagwaantaan clan of Sitka.

Back row: James Gordon; Andrew Percy Hope (Kaa.ooshtí) (1896–1968), Eagle's Nest House (Ch'áak' Kúdi Hít), Kaagwaantaan clan of Sitka; George Bartlett (Naayiéesh) (1880–ca.1919); Thomas Williams; John Williams; George Lewis; Sergius Williams (1891–1963), Cow House (Xaas Hít), Koosk'eidí subdivision of the L'uknax.ádi clan.

Identifications are based on research by Richard Dauenhauer and Nora Dauenhauer (1994: 86–87). According to them, "This photograph has appeared in various publications, with considerable discrepancies in identification. The following is based on what we consider to be the most reliable published and oral sources." Courtesy of the National Park Service, Sitka National Historical Park, 25431.

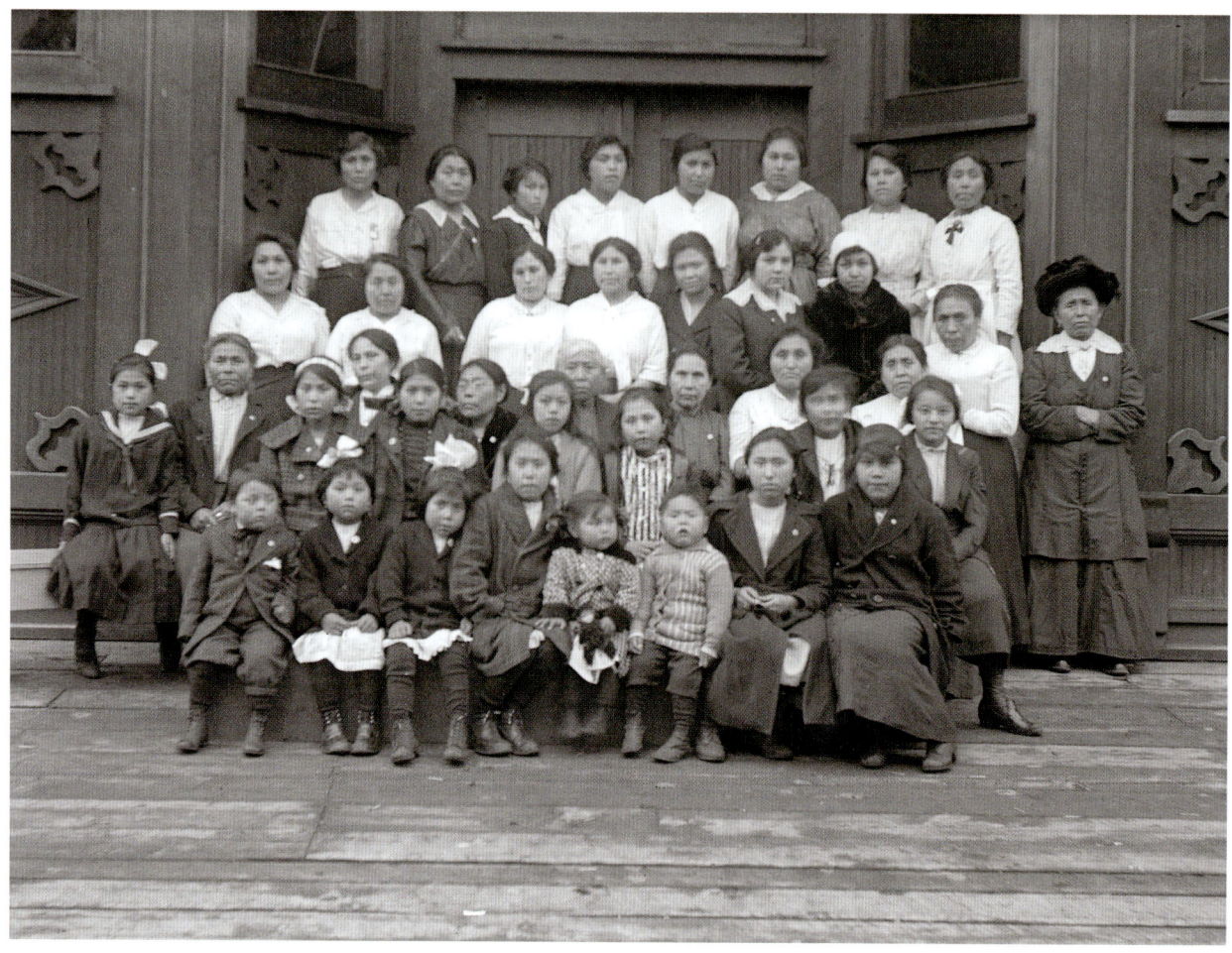

PLATE 103. Alaska Native Sisterhood members and their children in front of the Sitka ANB Hall, date unknown.
Courtesy of the National Park Service, Sitka National Historical Park, 25912.

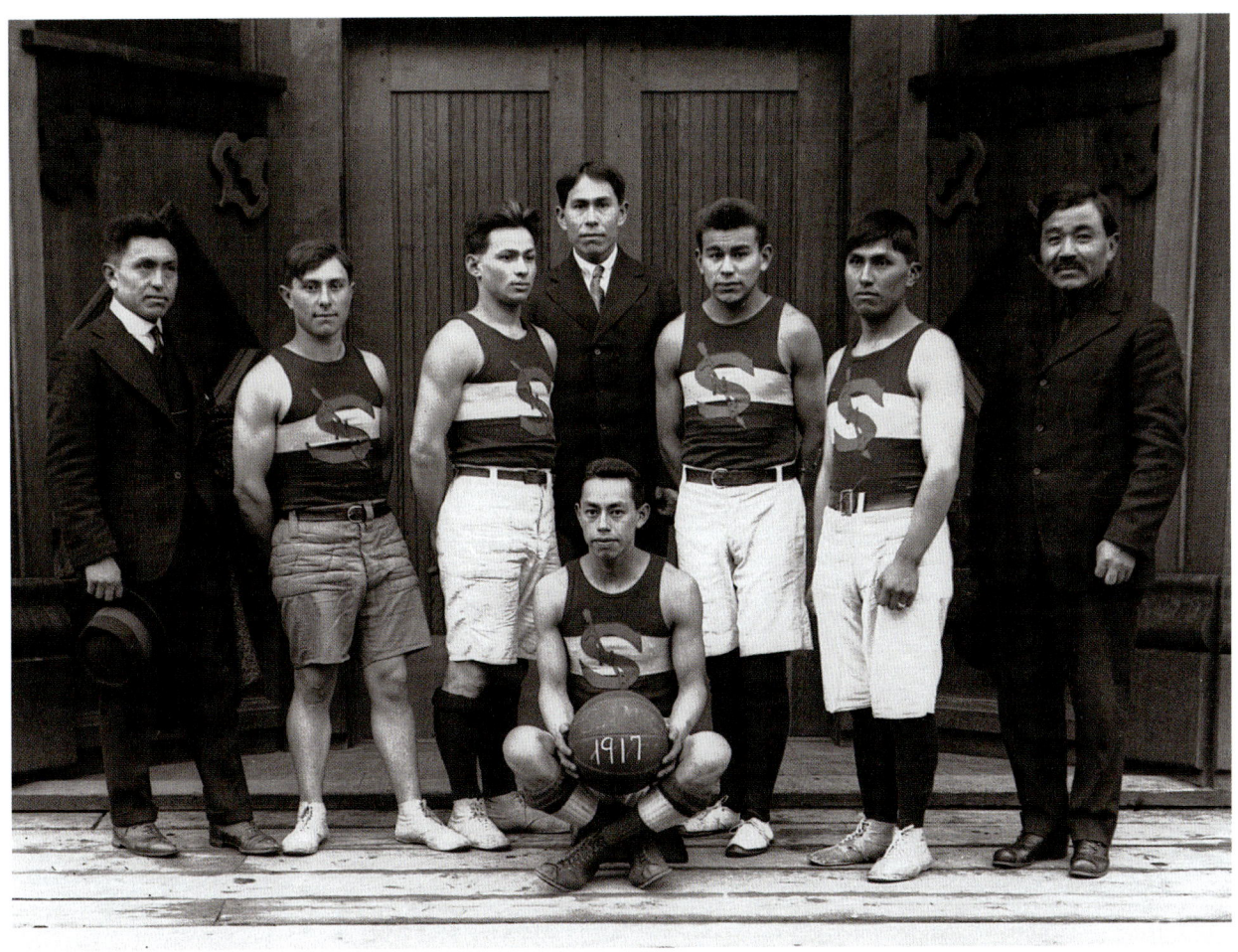

PLATE 104. ANB Basketball team, Sitka, 1917. Left to right: Tom Phillips; Howard Gray (1900–1983); Thomas Williams; Ray James (b. 1908); David Howard Sr. (Ltutéen) (1893–1974), Point House (X'aaká Hít), Kiks.ádi clan (seated, with the ball); Louis Simpson (Shḵ'awulyéil) (1896–1936), Point House (X'aaká Hít), Kiks.ádi clan; Charlie Daniels (1891–1959); and the coach, Peter Simpson (1871–1947), Tsimshian. (See Dauenhauer and Dauenhauer 1994: 87.) Courtesy of the National Park Service, Sitka National Historical Park, 03793.

TLINGIT AND CREOLE MEMBERS OF THE RUSSIAN ORTHODOX PARISH (ST. MICHAEL'S CATHEDRAL)

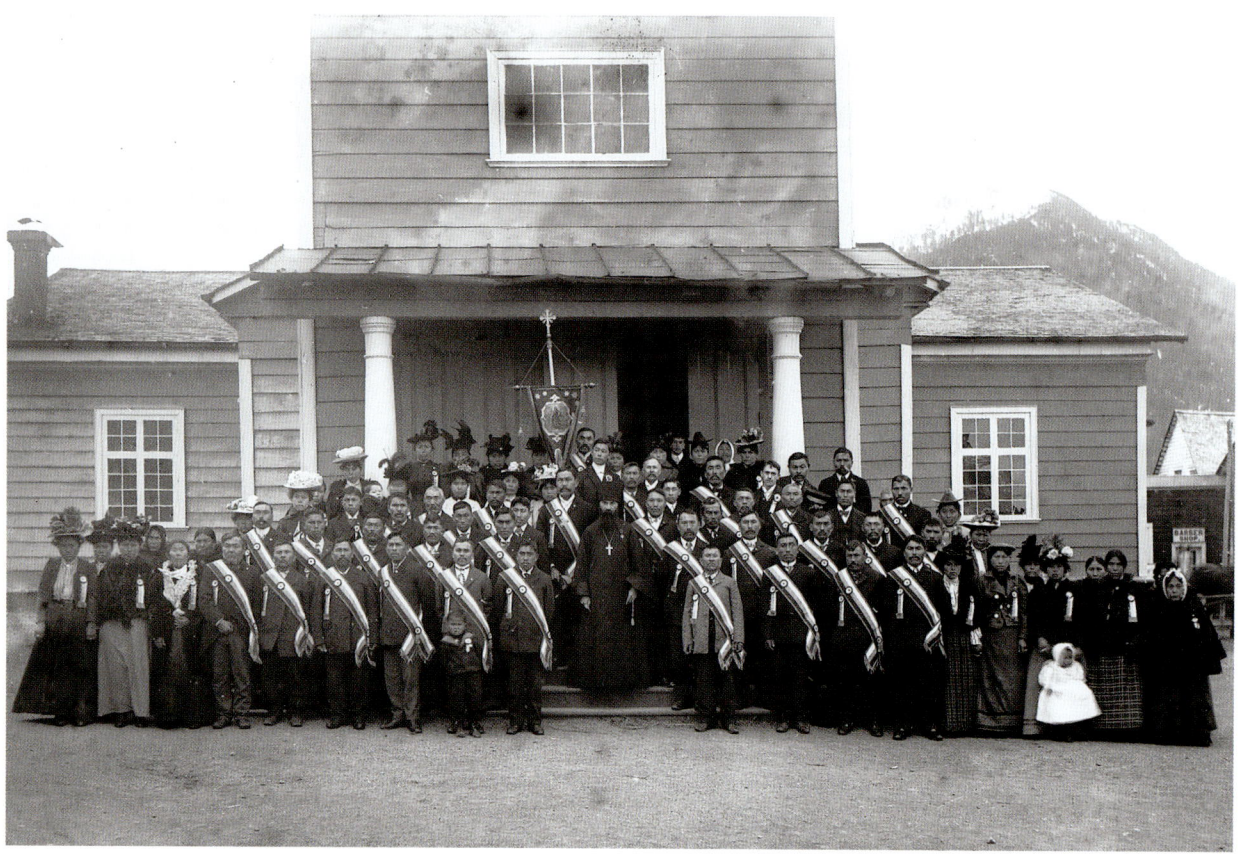

PLATE 105. Members of the St. Michael's Brotherhood on the steps of St. Michael's Cathedral, ca. 1900. The men are wearing the brotherhood sash, and the women are wearing a special ribbon. To the left of and slightly behind the Russian Orthodox priest at the center is Jacob (Iakov, Peter) Kanagood (ca. 1860–1908), president of the brotherhood. He was a high-ranking member of the Big Coho House (L'uk Hít Tlein) of the L'uknax.ádi clan of Sitka. The man in the third row, directly to the right of the priest, is Semeon (Simeon) Kakwaéesh (Luke Semeon, Luke Borbridge) (1869–1911), Steel House (Shdeen Hít) Kiks.ádi clan, the brotherhood secretary. Identifications by Mary Marks, Walter Soboleff, and Mark Jacobs Jr., 1980–1995. Courtesy of the National Park Service, Sitka National Historical Park, 03800.

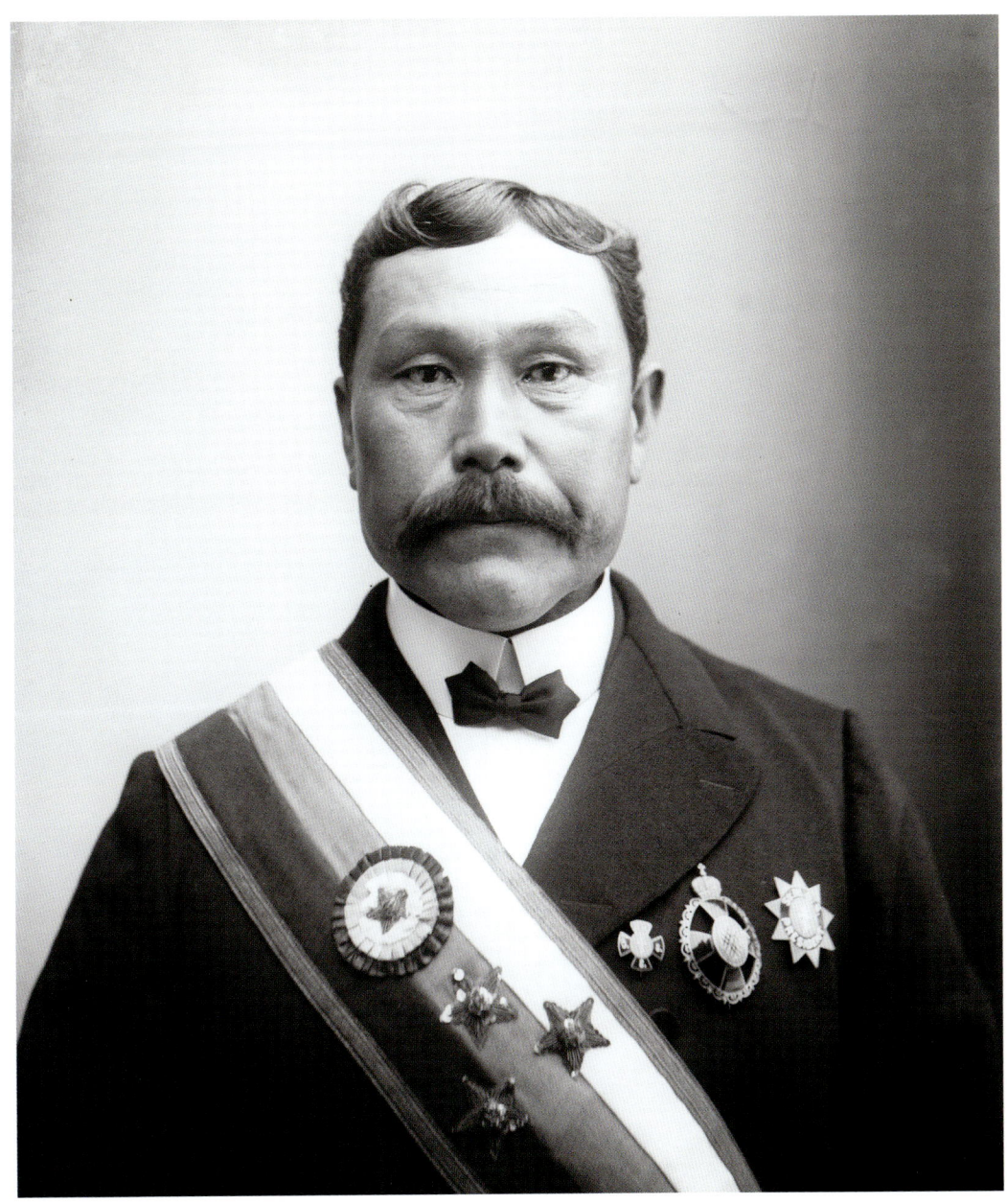

PLATE 106. Portrait of Jacob (Iakov, Peter) Kanagood (ca. 1860–1908), president of the St. Michael's Brotherhood, wearing the brotherhood sash and other insignia. Courtesy of the National Park Service, Sitka National Historical Park, 25419.

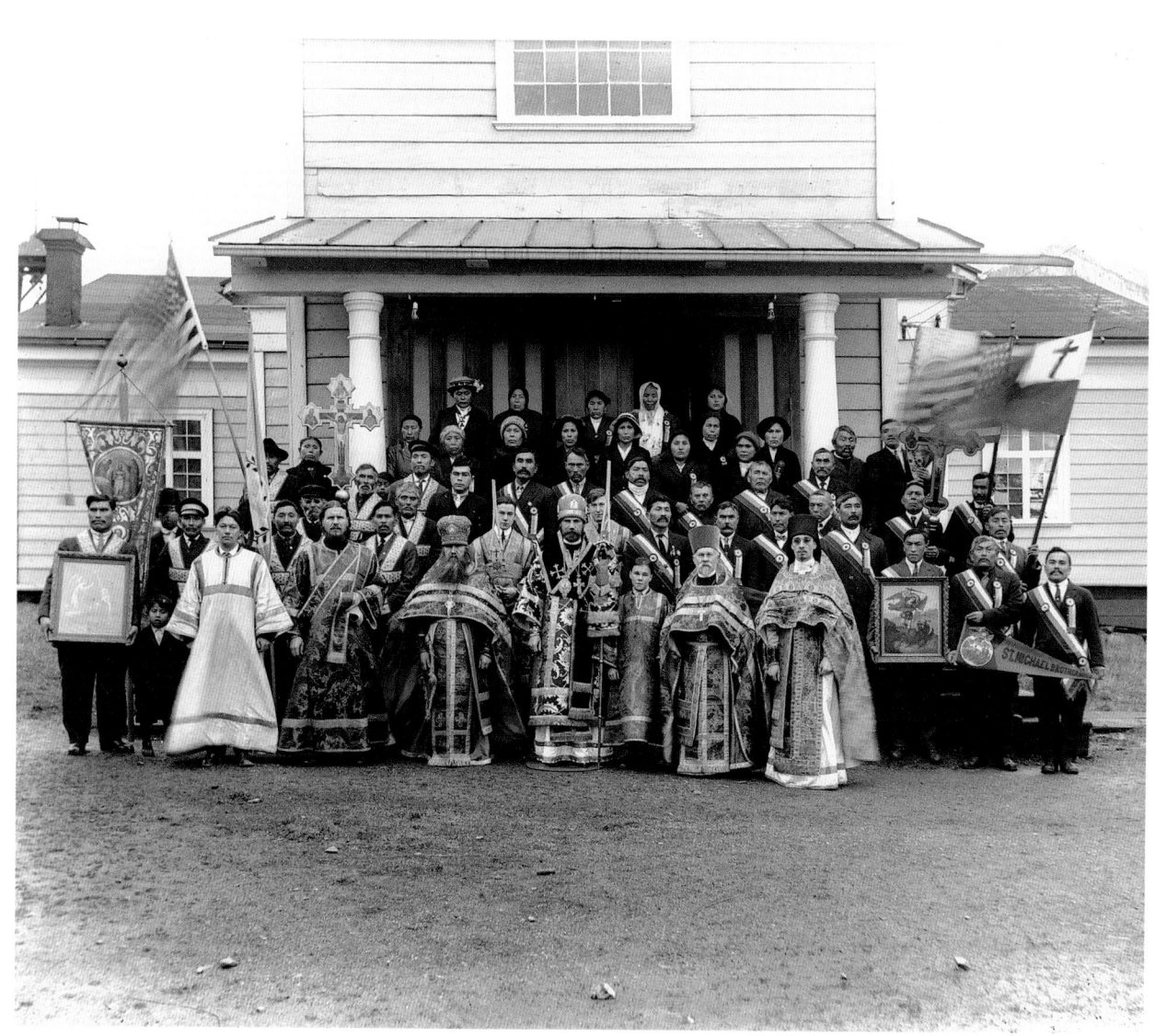

PLATE 107. Members of the St. Michael's Brotherhood and St. Gabriel's Brotherhood with Russian Orthodox clergy on the steps of St. Michael's Cathedral, 1916–17.

Front row, left to right: Scotty James (L'ashaa Éesh) (1886–1965), T'aḵdeintaan clan, holding the icon of Saint Gabriel; his son Peter James Sr. (T'aẖoo) (1912–82), Two Door House (Déiẖ X̱'awool Hít), Kaagwaantaan clan; Walter C. Decker (b. 1893) (Creole), psalm reader; Deacon Antonii (Anton); Archimandrite Amphilokhii Vakul'skii (1862–1933); Phillip Stavitskii (1884–1952), the bishop of Alaska; unidentified Creole altar boy; Father Andrei (Andrew) Kashevaroff (1863–1940) (Creole); unidentified priest; Charles Dick (Daanaẖ.ils'eix) (1893–1972), Platform House (Kayaashká Hít), L'uknaẖ.ádi clan, with the icon of St. Michael; unidentified man of the Ḵóok Hít; Frank Joseph (ca. 1875–1935), Box House (Ḵóok Hít), Ḵookhittaan subdivision of the Kaagwaantaan clan.

Second row, left to right: two unidentified men; Jim Kasakaan (Kasaẖaan) (b. ca. 1860), Kadak'w.ádi clan; Thomas Sanders Sr. (Aanilaaẖ) (ca. 1880–1954), Copper Shield House (Tinaa Hít), Kiks.ádi clan. Behind and to the left of Father Amphilokhii is Subdeacon Peter Kostrometinoff (1896–1941) (Creole); to the right and behind the bishop is Subdeacon Boris Kostrometinoff (1895–1931) (Creole); Harold (Peter) Bailey (Gooẖ Éesh) (1877–1941), Little Coho House (L'uk Hít Yádi), L'uknaẖ.ádi clan; Philip Jones (Sdayáat), Iceberg House (Xáatl Hít), Chookaneidí clan of Sitka; unidentified man; Thomas Dimitrii (Demetri) (Gaanduwei) (b. 1855), head of Iceberg House (Xáatl Hít), Chookaneidí clan.

Third row, left to right: Frank Kitka (Ganóosgu Éesh) (1889–1967), Outwards House (Daginaa Hít), L'uknaẖ.ádi clan (wearing a hat, partly obscured by a folded flag); Jim Andrews (Jeex'wán Éesh) (1854–1929), Chookaneidí clan (to the right of the cross); unidentified man; Stephen Nichols (1892–1910) (directly behind Father Amphilokhii); Billy Williams (X̱agoolhóosh) (1881–1943), Cow House (Xaas Hít), Ḵoosk'eidí subdivision of the L'uknaẖ.ádi clan; unidentified man; James Howard (Shtuwaa) (1876–1954), Little Coho House (L'ook Hít Yádi), L'uknaẖ.ádi clan (behind and to the right of Boris Kostrometinoff); unidentified man; Nicholas Kitka Sr. (Yéil.áẖji Éesh) (1847–1927), father of Frank Kitka (in front of pillar), Burnt Timbers House (Kaawagaani Hít), Kaagwaantaan clan; Charlie Joseph Sr. (Ḵalátk) (1894–1986), Box House (Ḵóok Hít), Ḵookhittaan subdivision of the Kaagwaantaan clan (far right, holding a banner, face partially obscured).

First row of women (under the porch), left to right: Naaẖ.oostí (right of pillar); two unidentified women; Mary Sanders (X̱aasteen) (b. 1885), Iceberg House (Xáatl Hít), Chookaneidí clan; unidentified woman; Mary Cheetiteex (Jeeditéx', Mamie Bean) (1898–1977), Kaagwaantaan clan, Charlie Dick's first wife (to the right and behind James Howard); Mrs. Thomas Dimitri (b, 1870) (slightly behind Mary Cheetiteex); Annie Jones (Mrs. Philip Jones) (b. 1891).

Identifications by Mary Marks, Walter Soboleff and Mark Jacobs Jr., 1980–95. See Kan 1999: 330–31. Courtesy of the National Park Service, Sitka National Historical Park, 03803.

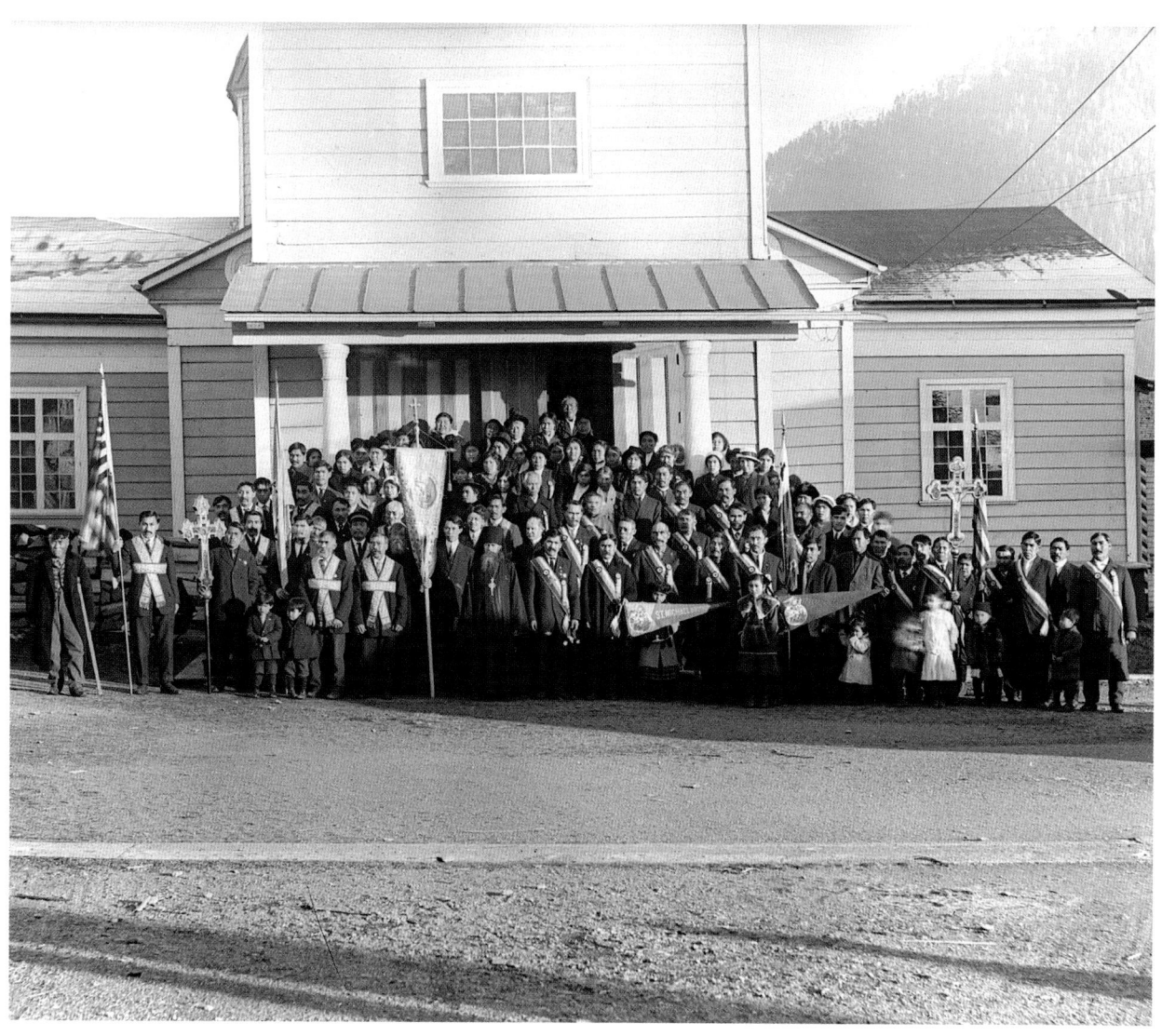

PLATE 108. Members of the St. Michael's and St. Gabriel's Brotherhoods in front of St. Michael's Cathedral, 1917–20.

Front row, left to right: unidentified man with a crutch; Alex Andrews (Ḵuxichx') (1886–1974), the head of Eagle's Nest House (Ch'áak' Kúdi Hít), Kaagwaantaan clan, holding a US flag; unidentified man; Peter James Sr. (T'aẍhoo) (1912–82), Two Door House (Déix X̱'awool Hít), Kaagwaantaan clan (small boy at left); one of Mary Marks's sons, Kiks.ádi clan (second small boy); Jim Andrews (Jeex'wán Éesh) (1854–1929), Iron House (Ḡayes' Hít), Chookaneidí clan, Mary Marks's father; a Kaagwaantaan man (Gishwaéesh?); Paul Liberty (Aanyáanáx̱, Pavel Baranov) (1886–1920), Sun House (Ḡagaan Hít), Kiks.ádi clan (to the right of the St. Gabriel's Brotherhood banner); unidentified priest; Harold (Peter) Bailey (Goox̱ Éesh) (1877–1941), Little Coho House (L'ook Hít Yádi), L'uknax̱.ádi clan; Philip Jones (Sdayáat), Iceberg House (X̱áatl Hít), Chookaneidí clan; Jacob Yarkon (Yakwaan, Stoowuḵáa, Xeitxut'ch), Wolf House (Ḡooch Hít), Kaagwaantaan clan, father of Cecilia Kunz and one of the main hosts of the 1904 Sitka potlatch; Cecilia Kunz (X̱intóow)

(1910–2004), Outwards House (Daginaa Hít), L'uknax̱.ádi clan (small girl in front of Yakwaan); unidentified man with a St. Michael's Brotherhood banner. The three men on the far right are, from left to right, Alex John (Saayi Latseen) (1897–1954), Big Box House (Ḵóok Hít Tlein), Kaagwaantaan clan; James Howard (Shtuwaa) (1876–1954), Little Coho House (L'ook Hít Yádi), L'uknax̱.ádi clan; Thomas Dimitri (Gaanduwei) (1850–1937), the head of Iceberg House (X̱áatl Hít), Chookaneidí clan.

At the far left of the third row, to the right of and behind the cross, is Jim Kasakaan (Kasax̱aan) (1860–1930), Kadak'w-.ádi clan. The older man to the right and slightly behind the unidentified priest is Peter I. Kostrometinoff (1859–1931), a lifelong Creole resident of Sitka and a prominent member of the St. Michael's parish.

Identifications by Mary Marks, Cecilia Kunz, and Mark Jacobs Jr., 1979–95. Additional identifications by Harold Jacobs, 2024. See Kan 1999: 338–39. Courtesy of the National Park Service, Sitka National Historical Park, 03798.

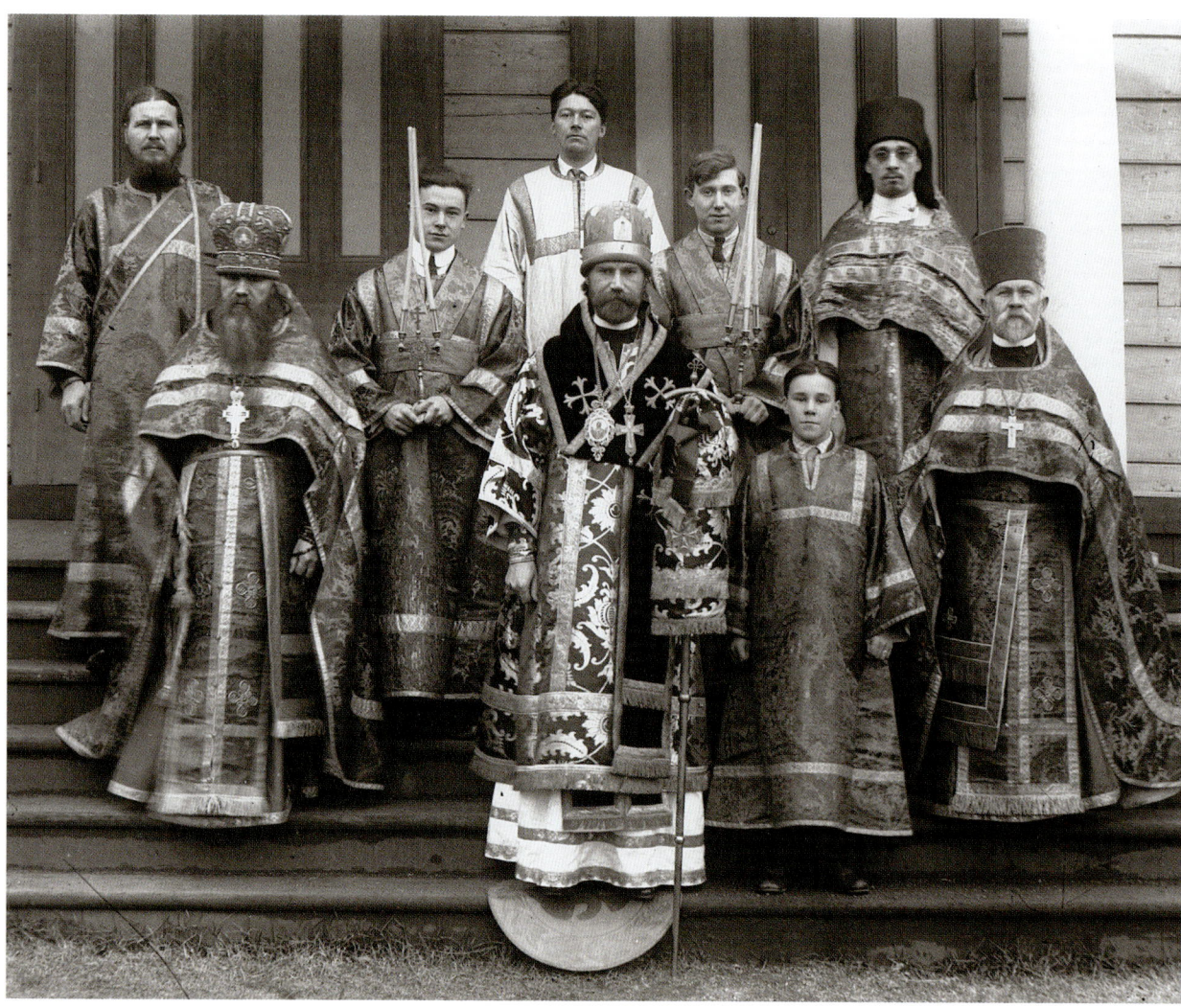

PLATE 109. Russian Orthodox clergy on the steps of St. Michael's Cathedral, 1916–17.

Front row, left to right: Archimandrite Amphilokhii Vakul'skii (1862–1933); Phillip Stavitskii, bishop of Alaska (1884–1952); unidentified altar boy; Father Andrew P. Kashevaroff (1863–1940) (Creole). Second row, left to right: Subdeacon Peter Kostrometinoff (1896–1941) (Creole); Subdeacon Boris Kostrometinoff (1895–1931); unidentified priest. Third row, left to right: Deacon Antonii (Anton); psalm reader Walter C. Decker (b. 1893) (Creole).

Courtesy of the National Park Service, Sitka National Historical Park, 03796.

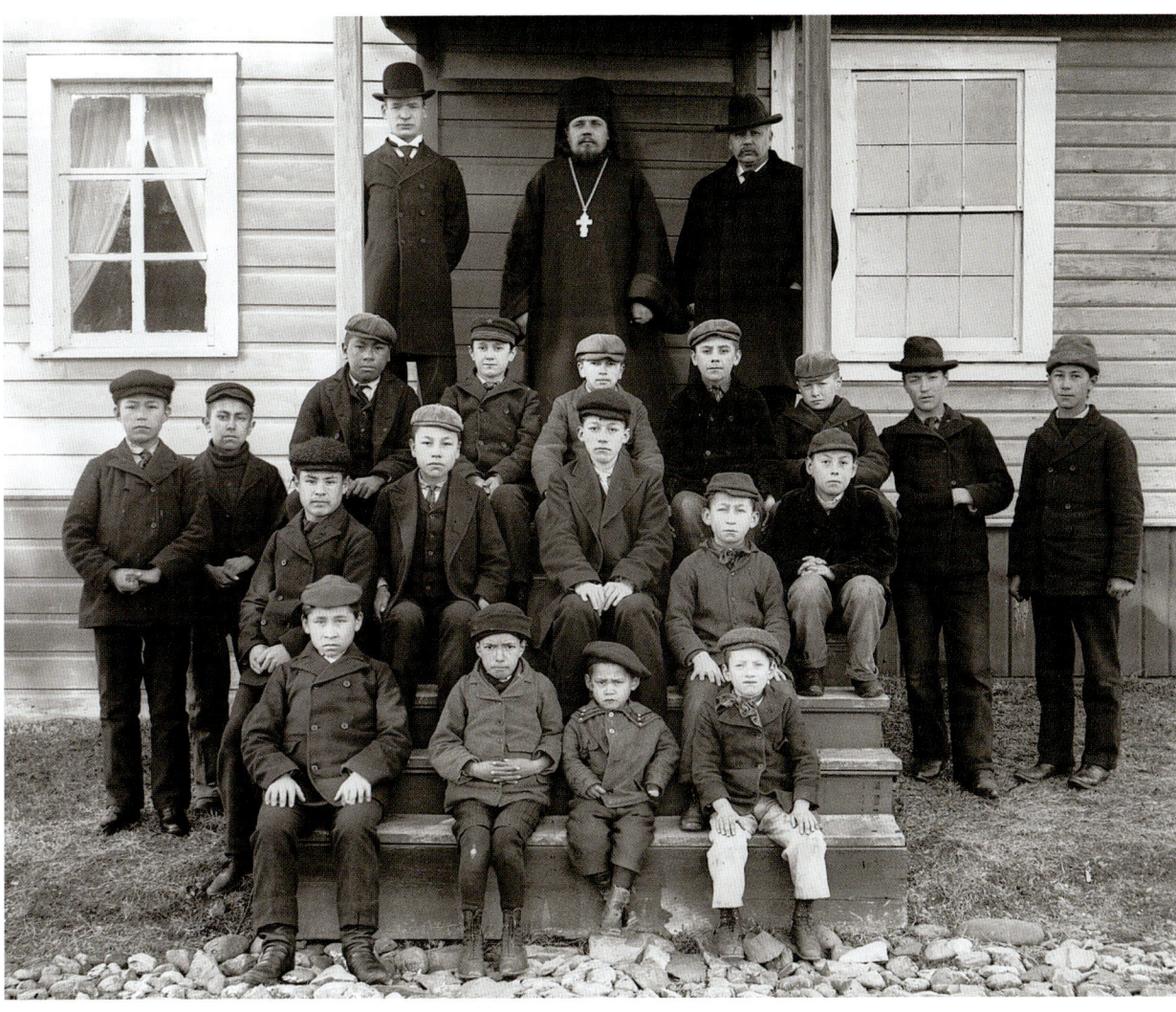

PLATE 110. Students of the Russian Orthodox seminary and orphanage (located in the Bishop's House) with a teacher and priest, Sitka, ca. 1905. Most of the boys are Creoles; several are Alaska Natives. At the right of the back row is George Kostrometinoff (Sergei Kostromitinov) (1854–1915), a Creole and a lifelong benefactor of the St. Michael's parish, ordained as a priest at the end of his life (see plate 115). Courtesy of the National Park Service, Sitka National Historical Park, 03805.

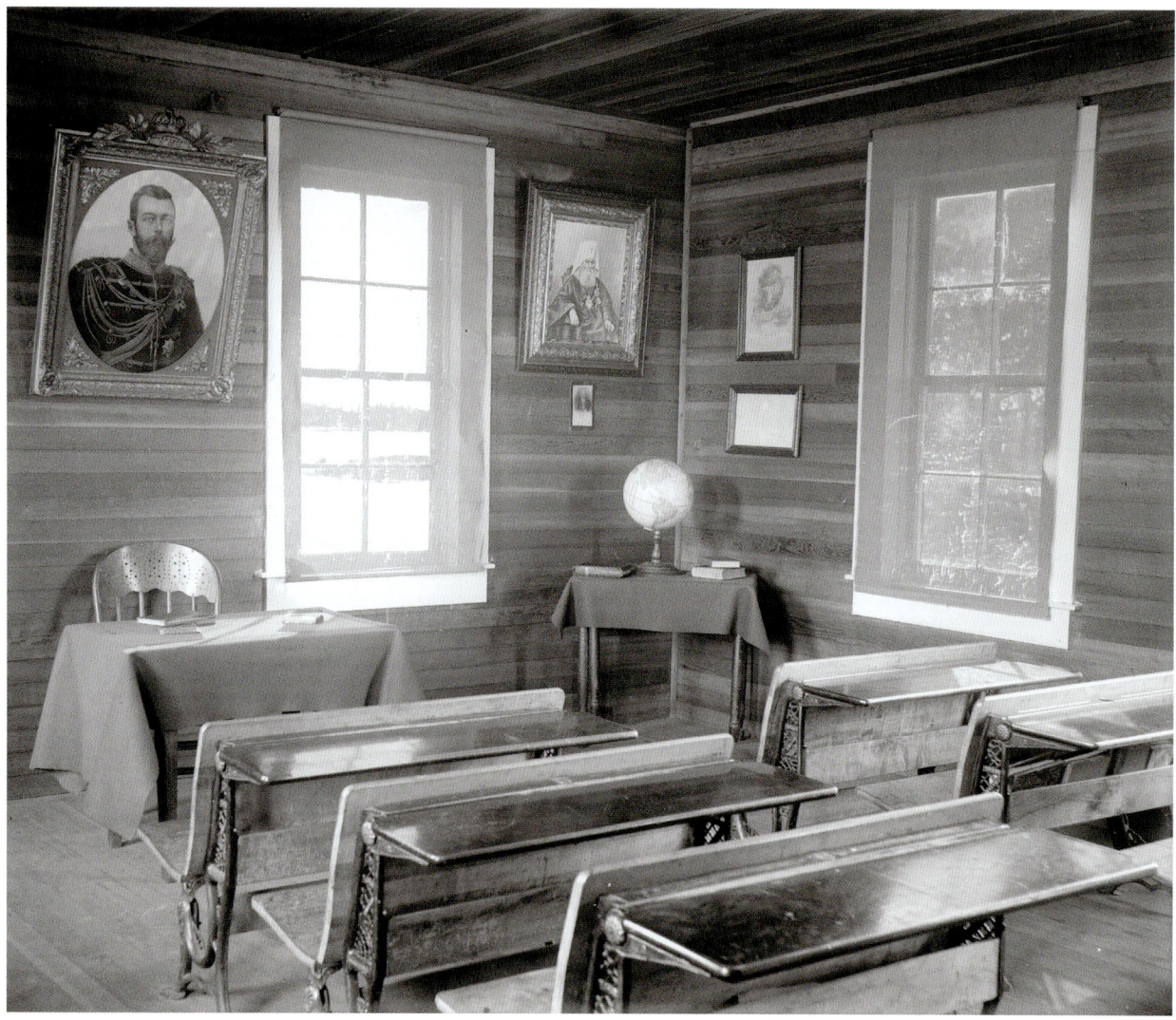

PLATE 111. A classroom in the Sitka Orthodox seminary and orphanage (Bishop's House) where many of the Creole and some of the Tlingit students studied, 1900–1917. To the left of the window is a portrait of Tsar Nicholas II; to the right of the window is a portrait of Bishop Innocent Veniaminov (Saint Innocent). Courtesy of the National Park Service, Sitka National Historical Park, 25409.

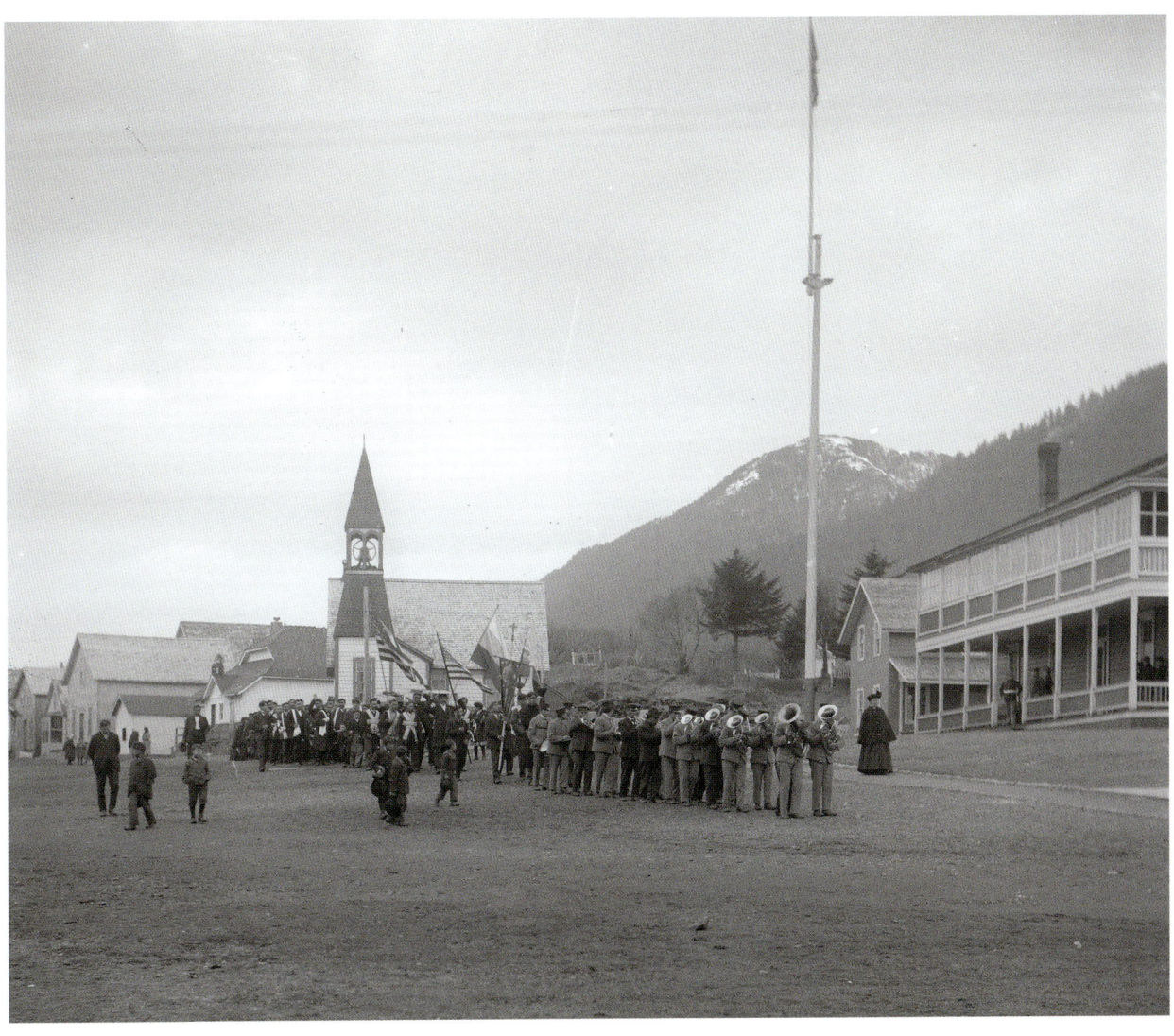

PLATE 112. St. Gabriel's Brotherhood funeral procession on the Sitka parade ground with Tlingit parishioners and Father Andrew Kashevaroff, ca. 1900–1917. Several Russian and US flags are on display. A Tlingit orchestra marches at the head of the procession. Courtesy of the National Park Service, Sitka National Historical Park, 25766.

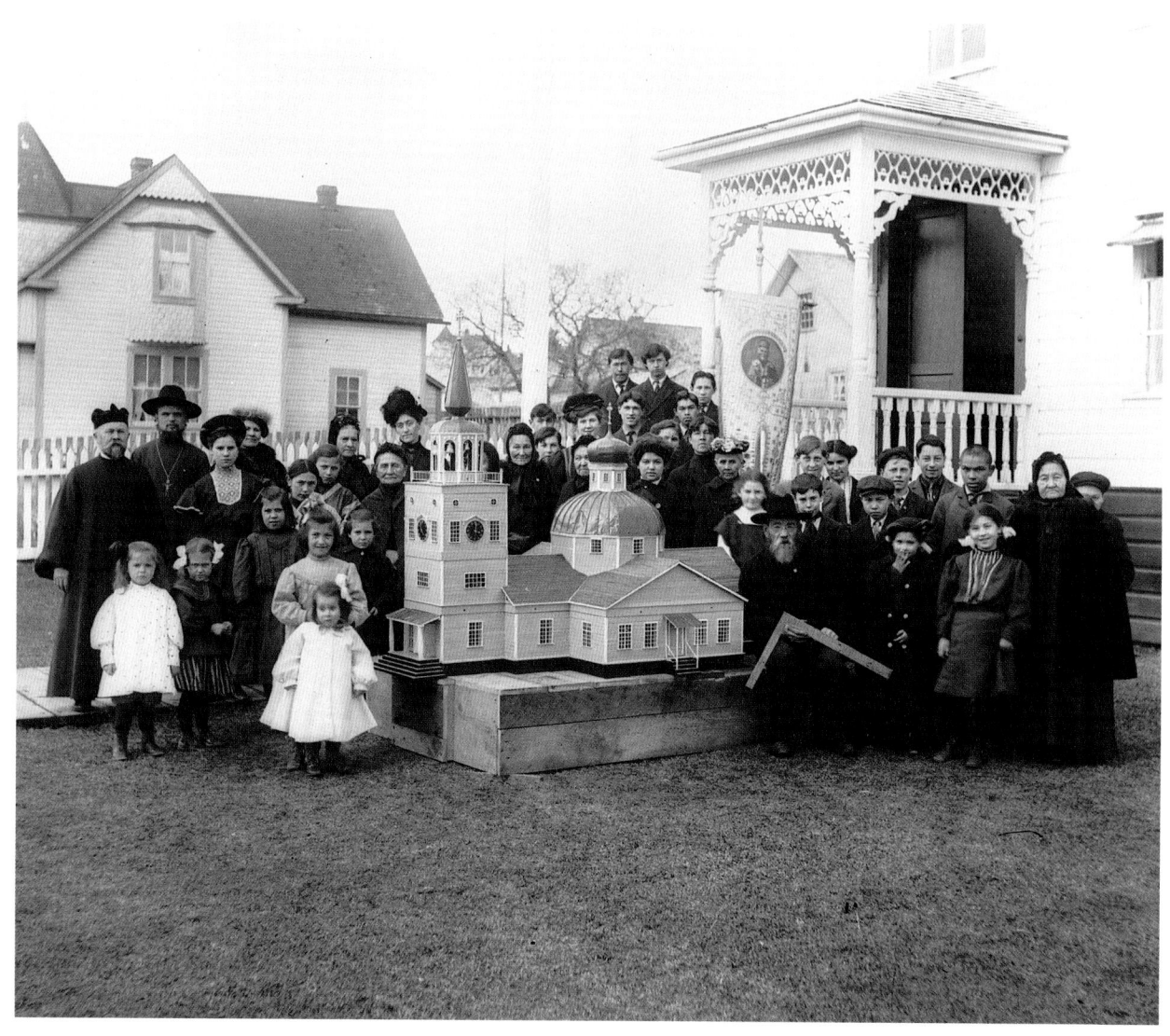

PLATE 113. Members of the Creole and Russian community, Russian Orthodox clergy, and several Tlingit boys with a model of St. Michael's Cathedral made by Vasilii Shergin, 1909. The priest on the far left is Father Andrew P. Kashevaroff (1863–1940). The man next to him might be Deacon Antonii (Anton). The little girl in front of Father Kashevaroff is Clara Triershield. To her right are Katy Panamarkoff, Anastasia (Noska) Triershield (1898–1977), and Nadja Kashevaroff (1902–72). The girl in a white dress in front of Nadja is Marie Louise Brightman (1906–87). The other girls pictured here are Xenia (Eugenia) Triershield (b. 1896), Pauline (Pelageia) Triershield (b. 1897), Zenia (Xenia) Hanlon (1903–59), and Legia (Lydia) Kashevaroff (b. ca. 1900). The woman to the right of Father Kashevaroff is Marie (Chubaroff) Brightman (1877–1960), mother of Louise Brightman. The old woman on the far right is "Babushka" Pelageia (Ris) Ponamareff (b. ca. 1835). The boy with very short hair to her left is Innocent Williams (Nax'eidu) (1894–1986), Cow House (Xaas Hít), Ḵoosk'eidí subdivision of the Ḷuknax̱.ádi clan; he was a Tlingit raised by a Russian woman. The boy next to him is John M. Illin (1895–1953), a Creole. Seated, with a ruler in his hand, is Vasilii Shergin (b. 1847). To his left may be Margaret (Hanlon) Osbakken (1900–1999). The older woman wearing a hat and standing two rows behind Shergin is Katherine (Tataouroff) Alberstone (b. 1858). The tall woman in the back and directly to the left of the cathedral model (wearing a hat) is Marfa (Bolshanin) Kashevaroff (1874–1931), the wife of Father Andrew Kashevaroff.

The middle-aged women standing next to the cathedral model include Luba (Shmakoff) Shergin (b. 1851), the wife of Vasilii Shergin; Mrs. Olympia Sipiagin (b. 1848); and Katrina Helstadt (b. 1830). The teenage boys and children include Nicholas Chernoff; Nick Belkoff (1890–1975), a Yup'ik Creole; Dora Williams; Mary Kashevaroff (1900–1971); Alec (Alexei) Oskolkoff (1893–1977), a Denaina Creole; Cyril Kashevaroff (1895–1948); Anton Shergin, the adopted son of Vasilii and Lubov Shergin; Fanny Panamarkoff (b. 1902); Anna Triershield (1892–1978); and Bessie Hanlon (1893–1968). The teenage boy on the right at the very back is Cyril Zuboff (Eech T'ei) (1892–1968), Killer Whale Chasing Seal House (Tsaa Yaa Ayanasnaḵ Ḵéet Hít), Daḵl'aweidí clan of Angoon. He was the son of Joseph Zuboff (1846–1911), a Russian merchant, and Mary Grant (Kaashdaa.át) (ca. 1870–1943), a Tlingit woman. Cyril Zuboff was a prominent leader of the ANB (see Kan 2013b: 26–28, 36–37; Kan 2021).

Identifications by Louise Brightman, 1979, and Harold Jacobs, 2024. Courtesy of the National Park Service, Sitka National Historical Park, 03802.

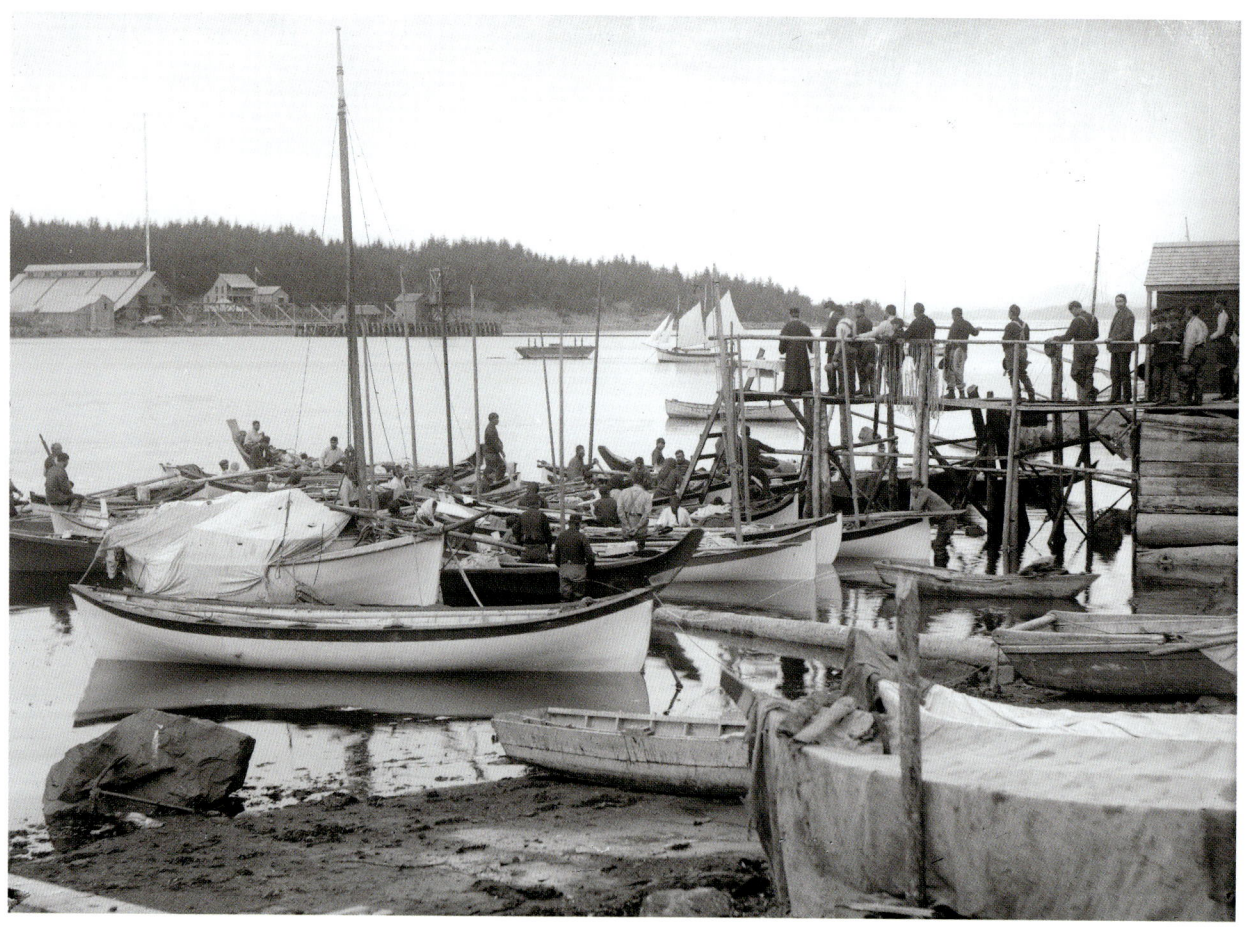

PLATE 114. An unidentified Russian Orthodox priest blessing the Tlingit fishing fleet at the start of the fishing season in the spring Sitka, date unknown. Courtesy of the National Park Service, Sitka National Historical Park, 26171.

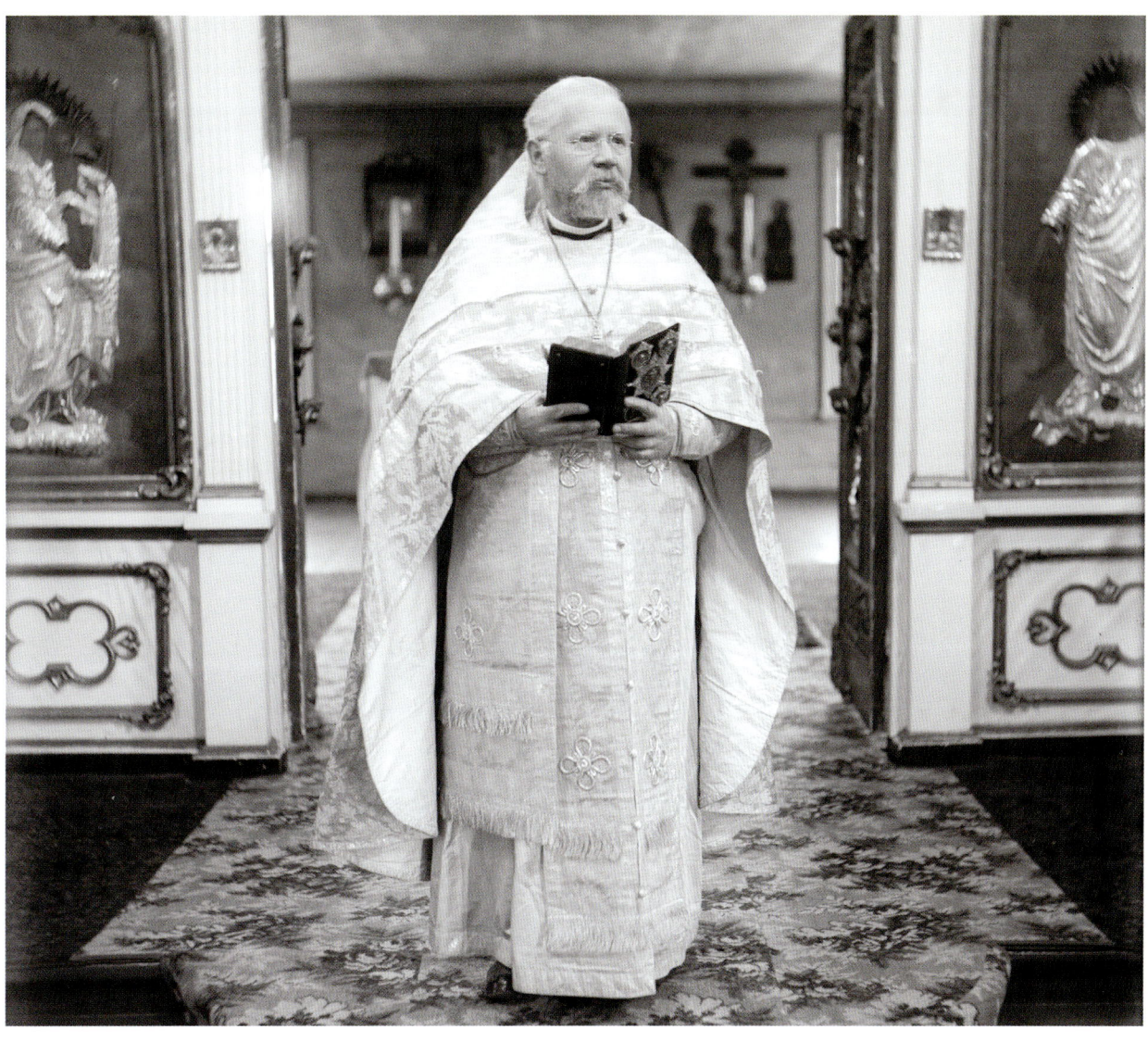

PLATE 115. Father George Kostrometinoff (Sergei Kostromitinov) (1854–1915) during services at St. Michael's Cathedral, 1910–15. Courtesy of the National Park Service, Sitka National Historical Park, 25402.

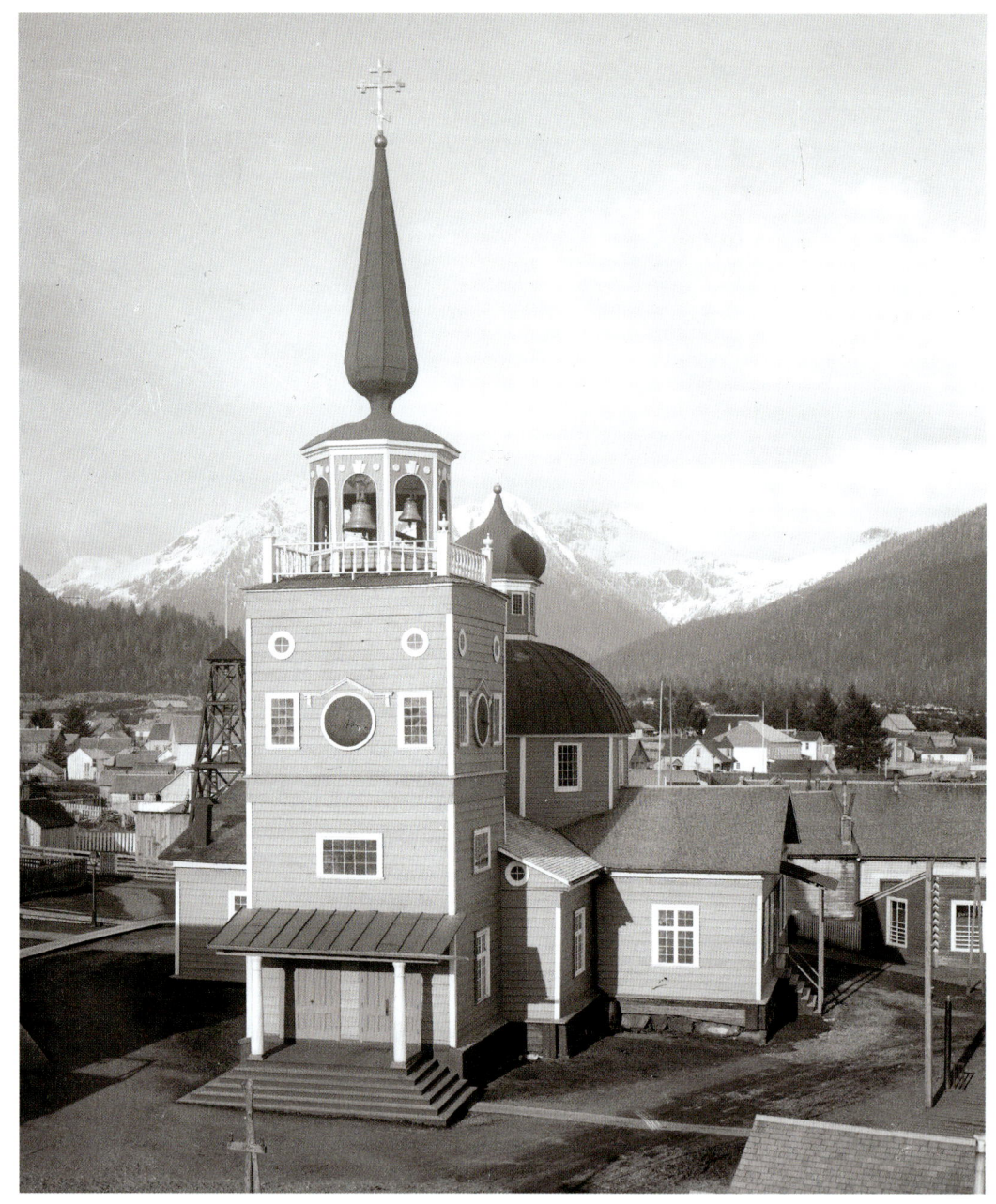

PLATE 116. St. Michael's Cathedral, date unknown. Courtesy of the National Park Service, Sitka National Historical Park, 25389.

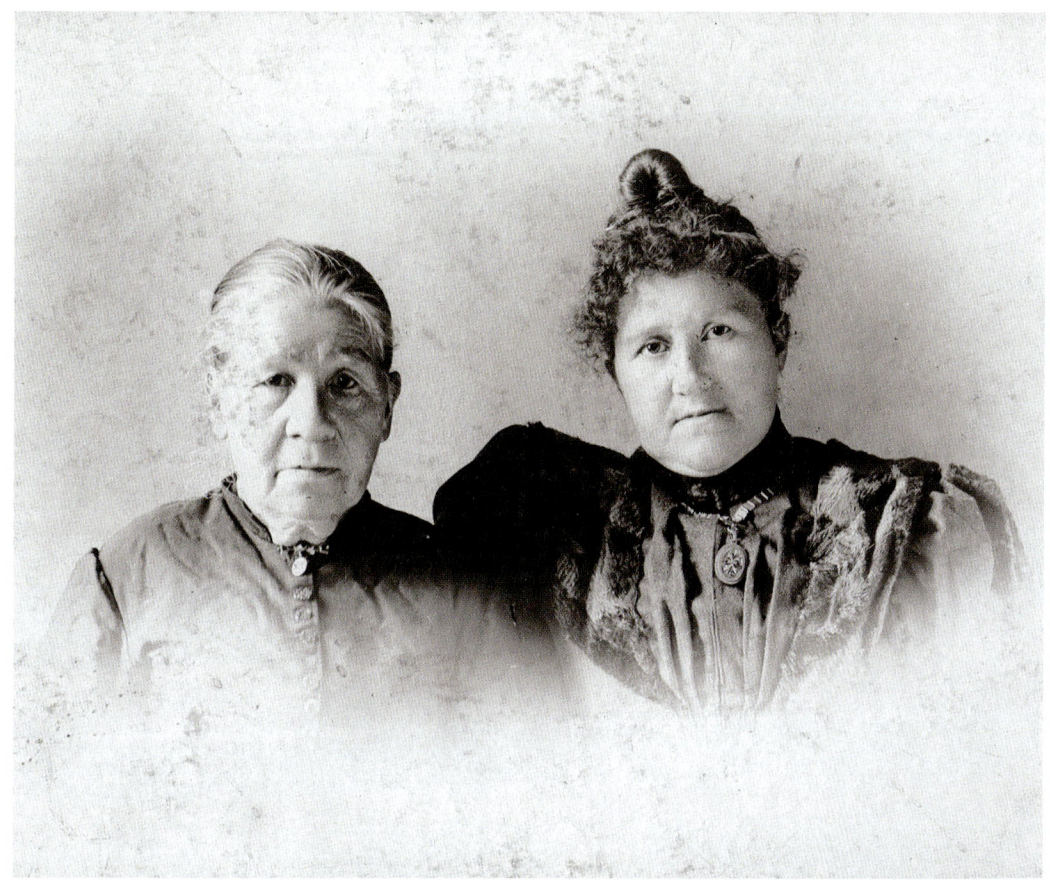

PLATE 117. Anastasia Shmakoff (b. ca. 1830) and her daughter Anna Shmakoff Hanlon (1861–1942), ca. 1900–1910. Photograph courtesy of Willis E. Osbakken, Anna's grandson. Copy in the author's possession.

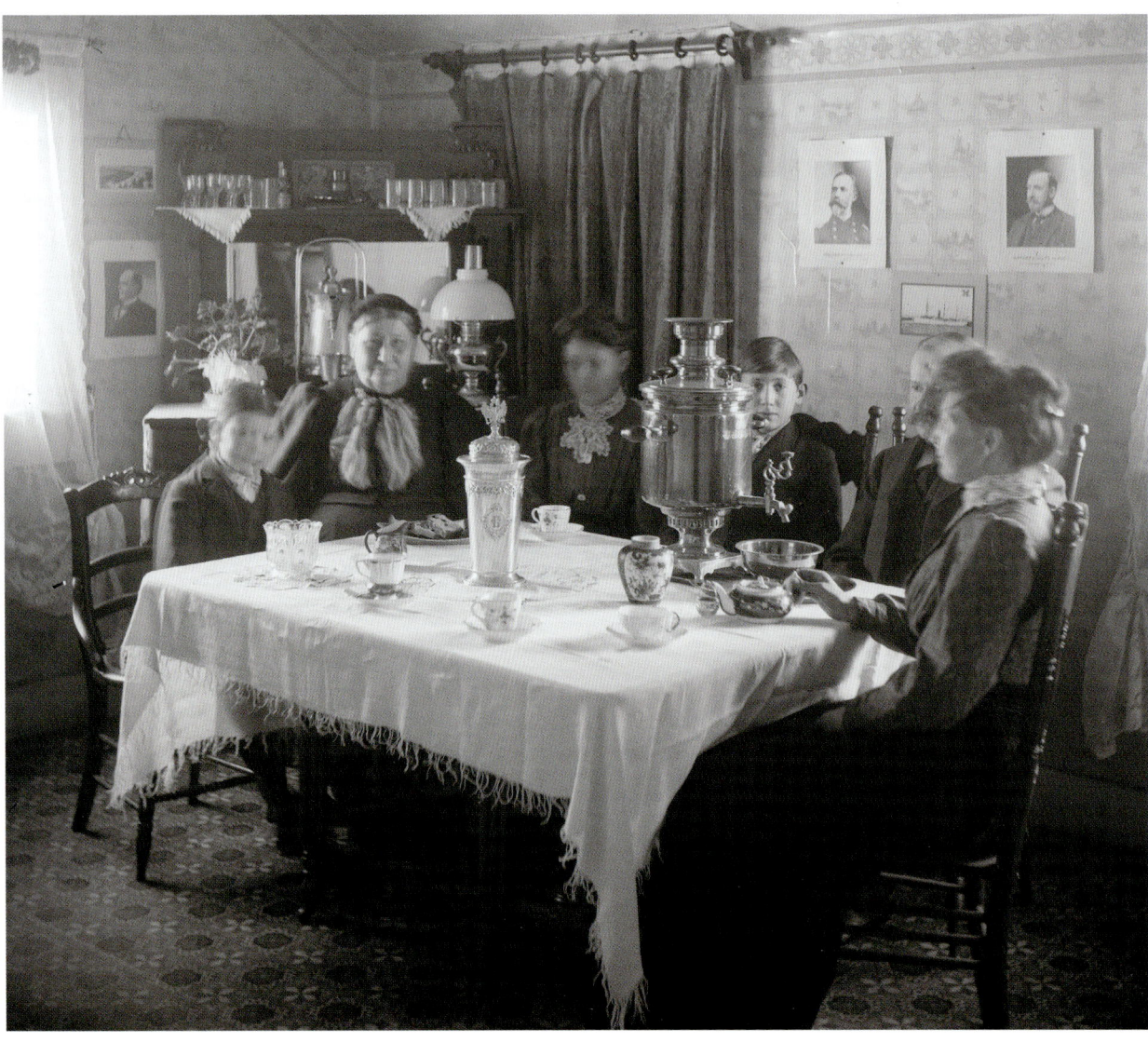

PLATE 118. Family of George Kostrometinoff (Sergei Kostromitinov) (1854–1915) at the dinner table, ca. 1906–10.

Left to right: an unidentified boy; George's mother, Anna (Milovidov) Kostrometinoff (1830–1907); George's daughter, Anna (1888–1948); George's son, Boris (1895–1931); George Kostrometinoff; George's wife, Natalia (Kashevaroff) Kostrometinoff (1866–1919). On the table are a samovar for making tea and a silver goblet presented to George by the Russian tsar in the early 1906 "in recognition of his faithful connection with the famous Russian cathedral in Sitka." See Kan 2013a.

Identifications on the back of the photograph. Courtesy of the National Park Service, Sitka National Historical Park, 26299.

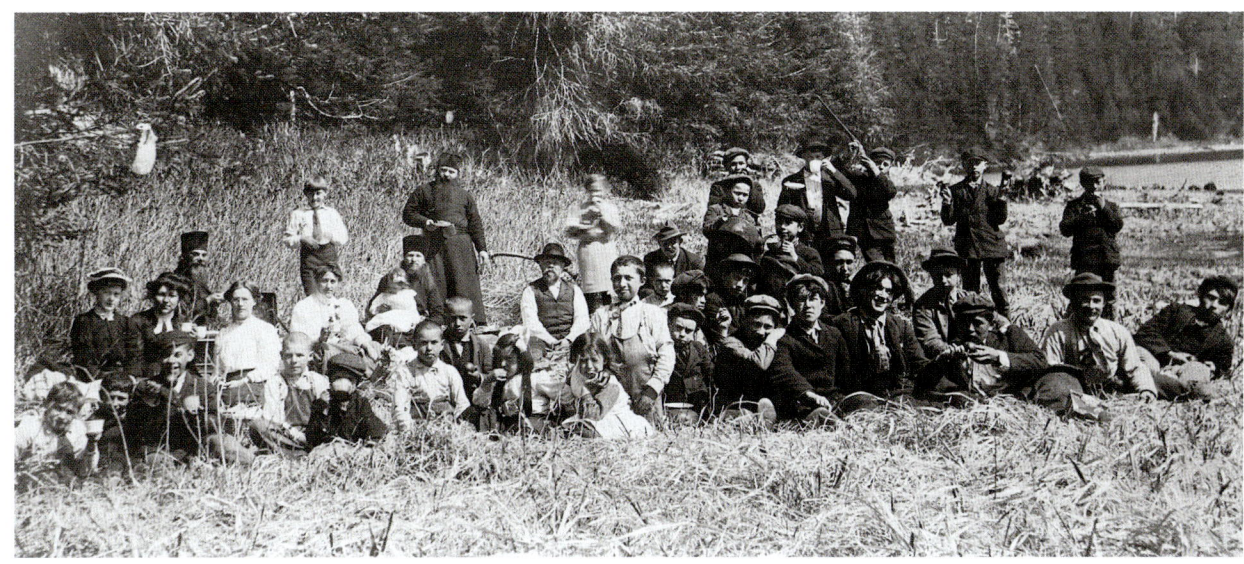

PLATE 119. Bishop Innokentii Pustynskii with a group of Russian Orthodox clergy and Creoles (including some adults and many students from the local Orthodox seminary) at a picnic near Sitka, ca. 1905. The bishop is standing with a plate in his hand. The seated man wearing a vest and hat is Father Andrew P. Kashevaroff (1863–1940). Among those pictured are the children of Father Kashevaroff as well as Elizabeth Hanlon Van Horn (1893–1968) (second row, first from the right); Anna Herman (b. 1889); Innocent Williams (Nax'eidu) (1894–1976); Nicholas Triershield; Anton Shergin (1897–1980); William S. Wanamaker (1889–1944); and Peter Chernoff. Identifications on the back of the photograph. Courtesy of the Sitka Historical Society, Sitka, Alaska. PH 5357.

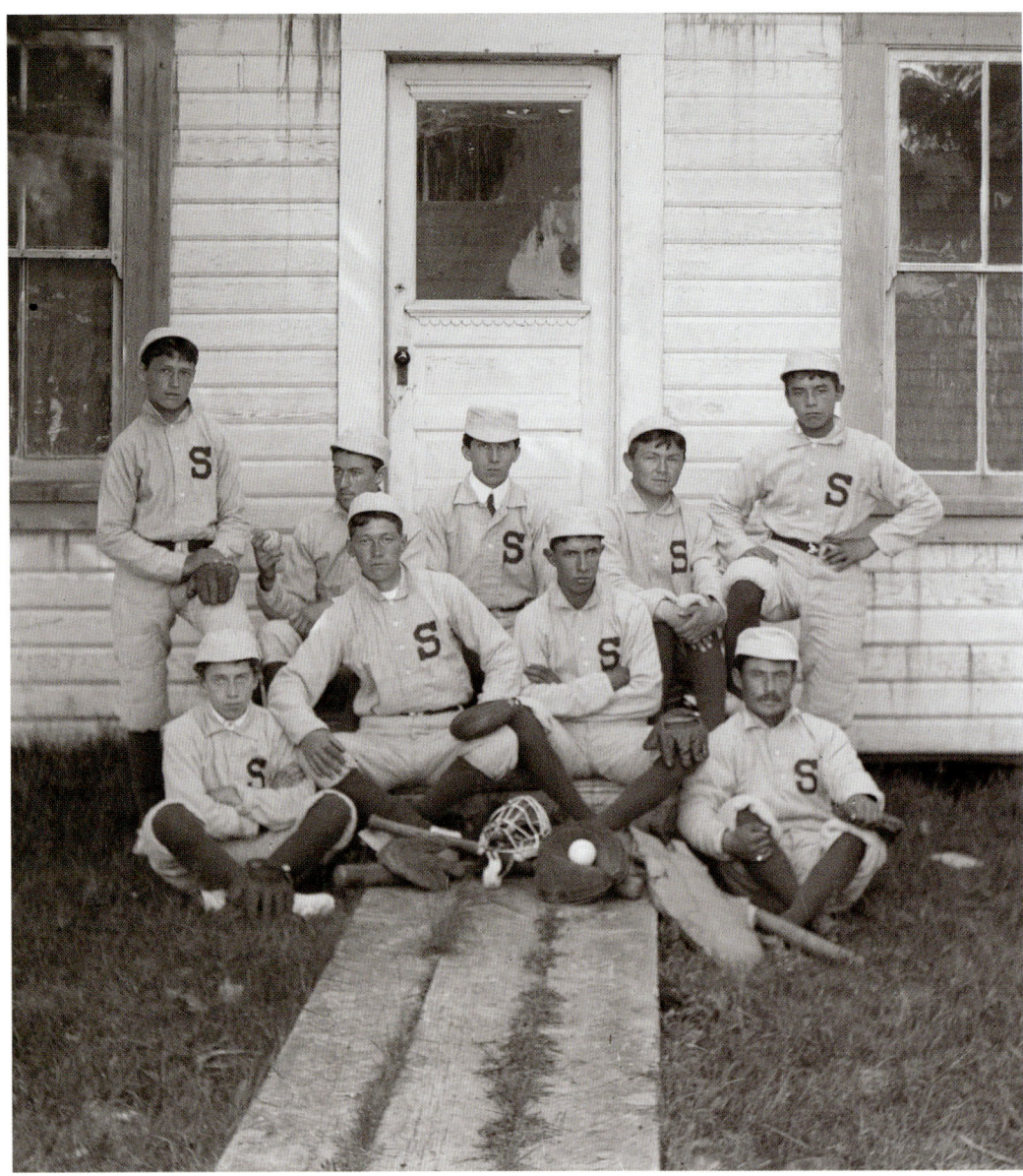

PLATE 120. A Euro-American baseball team, Sitka, date unknown.
Courtesy of the National Park Service, Sitka National Historical Park, 25790.

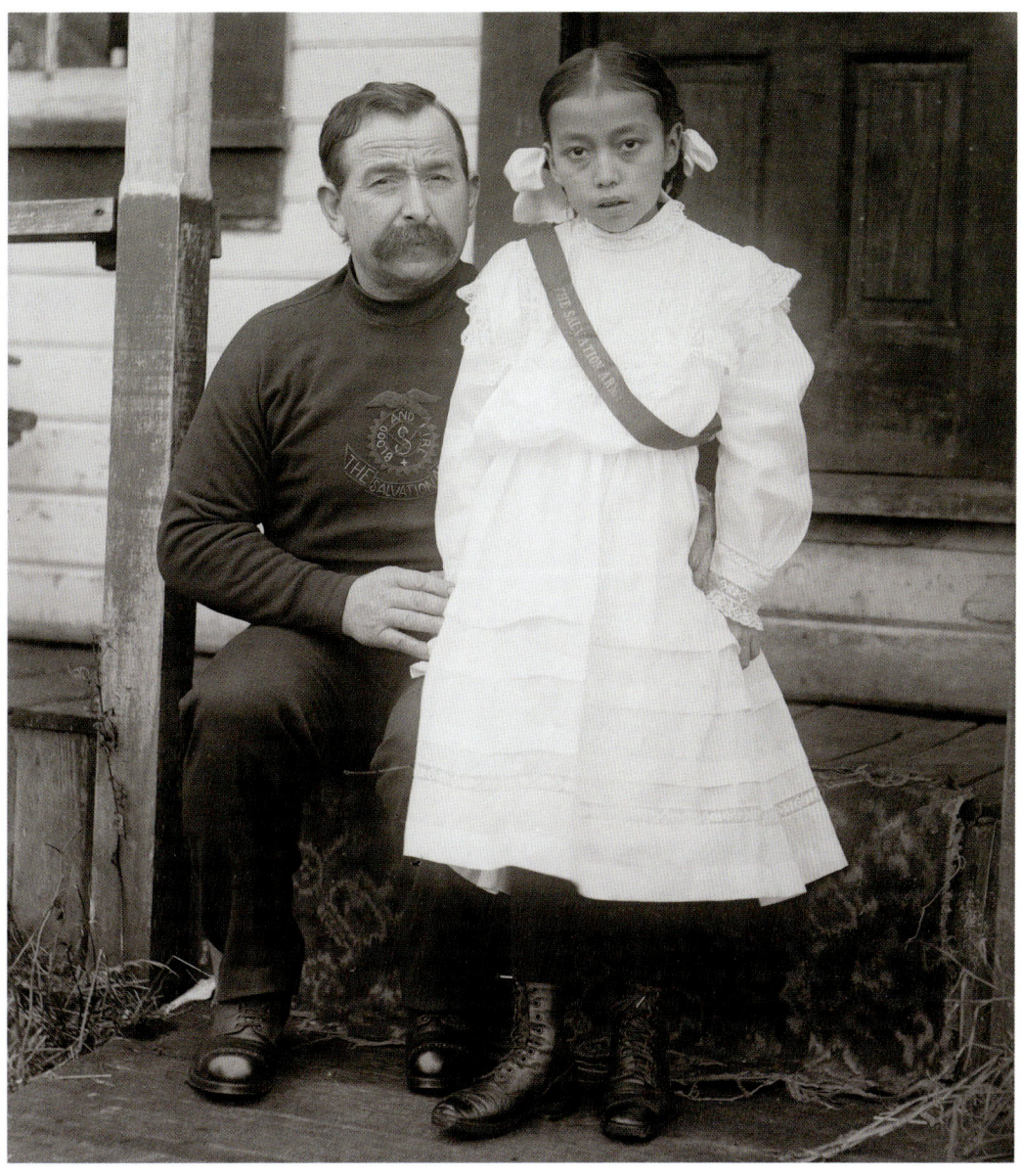

PLATE 121. Salvation Army Major Quick and his adopted Tlingit daughter, Sitka, date unknown. Courtesy of the National Park Service, Sitka National Historical Park, 26255.

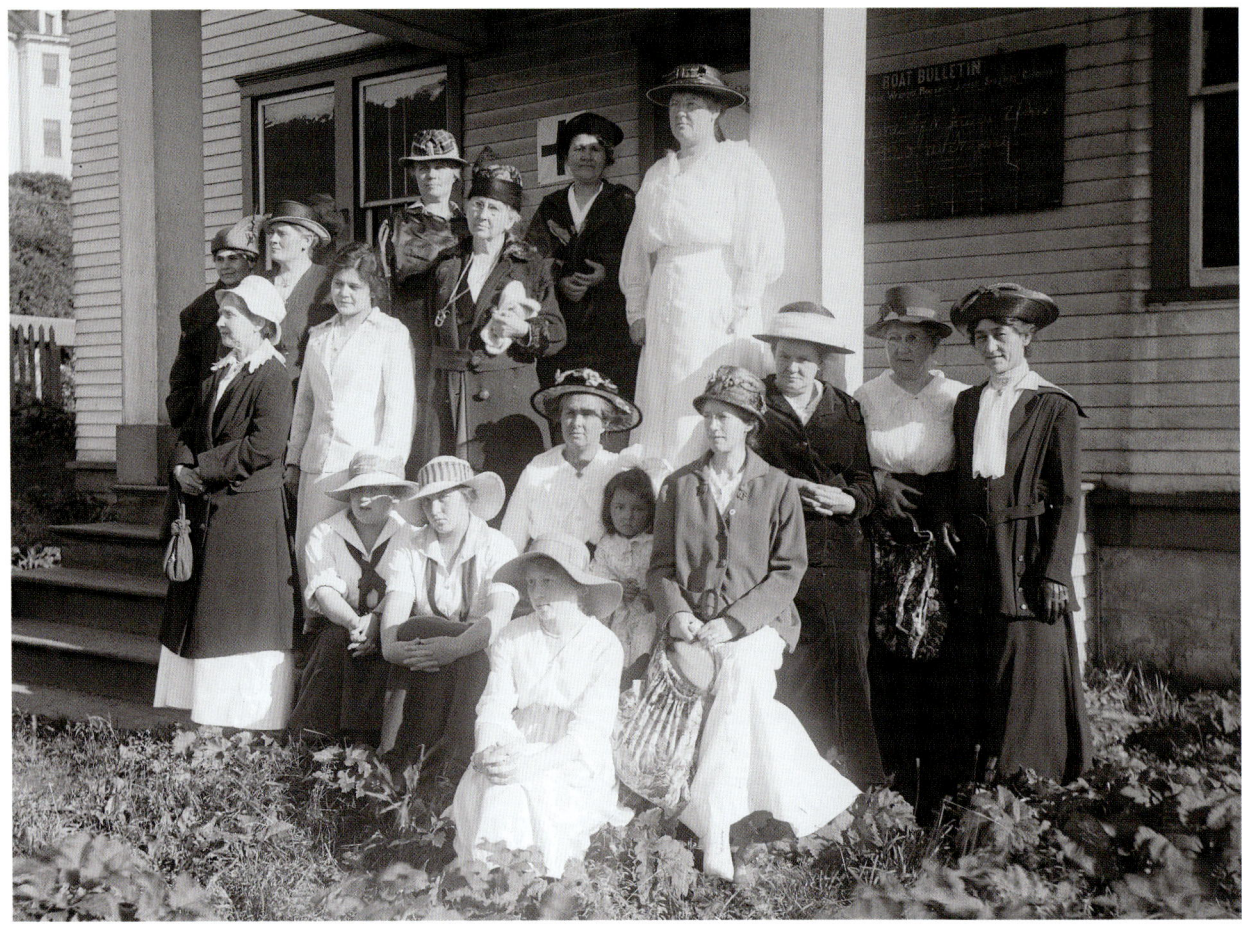

PLATE 122. Women of the Sitka Red Cross Auxiliary organization during World War I in front of the Red Cross building, Sitka, 1917–18. The Pioneer Home is in the background. Several of the women in the photo are Creoles.

The young woman sitting at the front of the group is unidentified. Front row, left to right: Mary Kashevaroff (1900–1971); Nadia Kashevaroff (1902–72); Mrs. Demidoff; Esther Demidoff (small child); Mrs. Robert DeArmond; Mrs. Ashball; Mrs. Goddard; Martha (Bolshanin) Kashevaroff (1874–1931), wife of Father Andrew Kashevaroff (both were Creoles). Back row, left to right (standing): Mrs. Peter Kostrometinoff (1866–1919); unidentified woman.

Identifications on the back of the photograph. Courtesy of the National Park Service, Sitka National Historical Park, 25544.

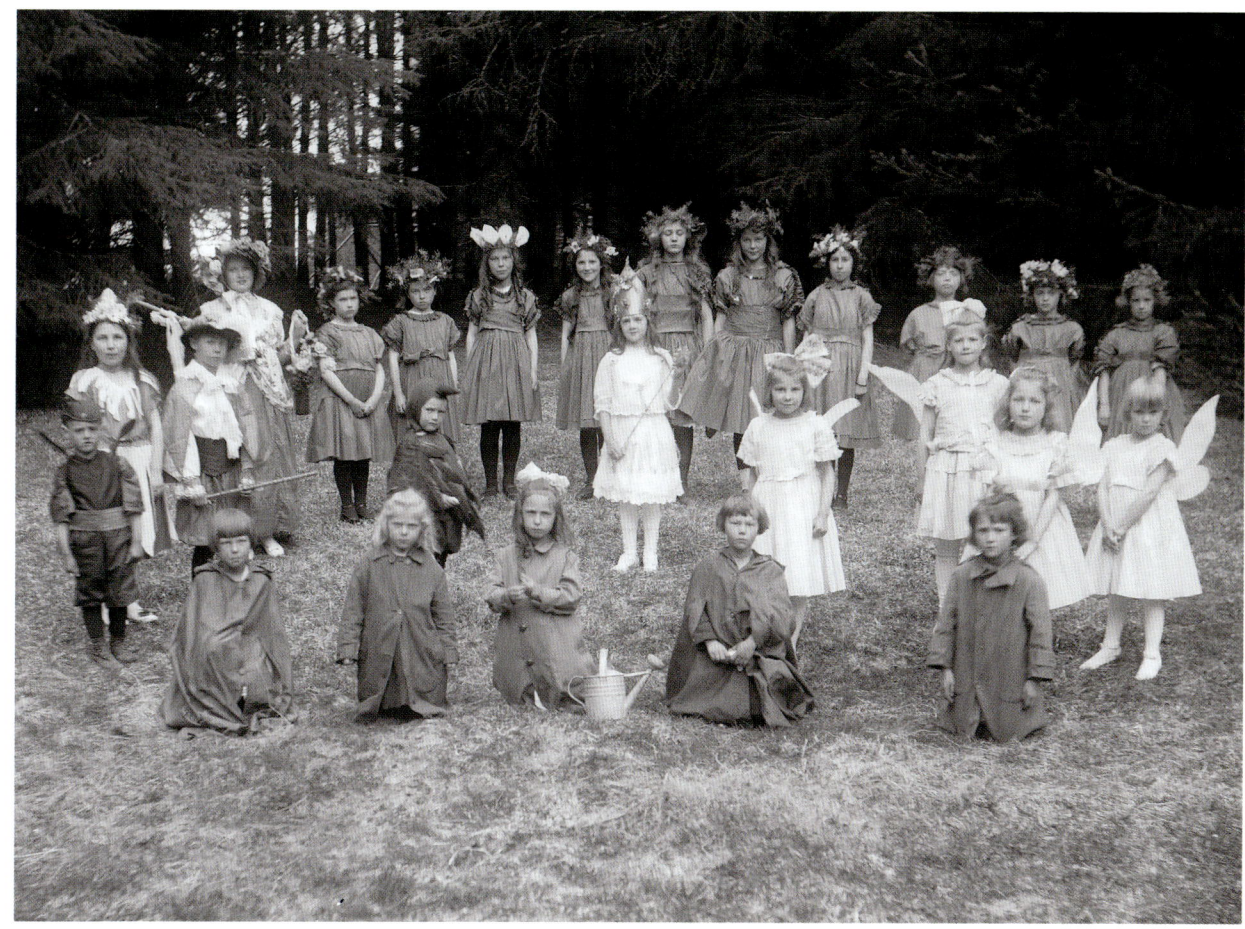

PLATE 123. May Day children's festivity, ca. 1921. Several of the children are Creoles. Front row, left to right: Evelyn Burke, Florence Peterson, Patty Mills, Nancy Burke, Hazel Hanlon. Behind them, four girls wearing angel wings, left to right: Kathleen Knudsen, Lena Tilson, unidentified girl, Martha Bredvick. Back row, left to right: Neil Bredvick, Mae Sarvella, Charlie Peterson, Frances Barron, Ruth DeArmond, Selma Gamble, Hilma Burke, Anna Hanlon, Martha Peterson, Christina Burke, Nadja Clements, Esther Gamble, Norma Beauchamp, Elva Bahrt.

Identifications by Eleanor Ludy (1911–2002) in 1980. Eleanor lived in Sitka in the 1920s. Courtesy of the National Park Service, Sitka National Historical Park, 25485.

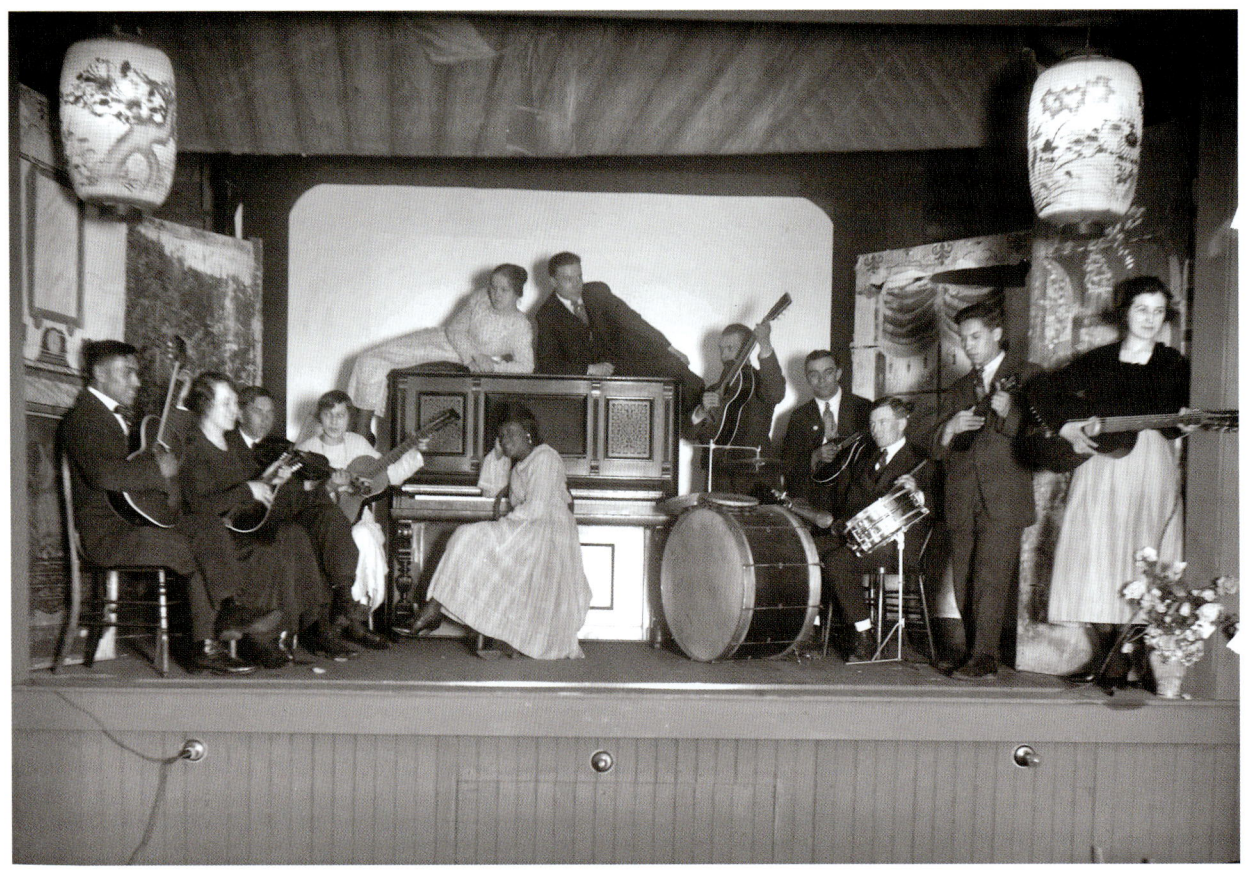

PLATE 124. An ethnically and racially integrated music group, Sitka, 1920s. Left to right: Innocent Williams (Nax'eidu) (1894–1976), Cow House (Xaas Hít), Ḵoosk'eidí subdivision of the L'uknax̱.ádi clan, a Tlingit raised by a Russian woman; Kitty Peterson; Nick Lindquist (Creole) (1900–1970); unidentified African American woman (at the piano); Dan Zeranoff (ca. 1900–1941) (Creole); Percy Hirst (1897–1926) (Creole); Don McGraw; George Allard (1901–77), son of a Creole man and a Tlingit woman; Zenia (Xenia) Hanlon (1903–59) (Creole). The couple on top of the piano are Peter Kostrometinoff Jr. (1896–1941) (Creole) and his wife, Helen L. (Peterson) Kostrometinoff (1900–1932). Identifications on the back of the photograph. Courtesy of the National Park Service, Sitka National Historical Park, 25477.

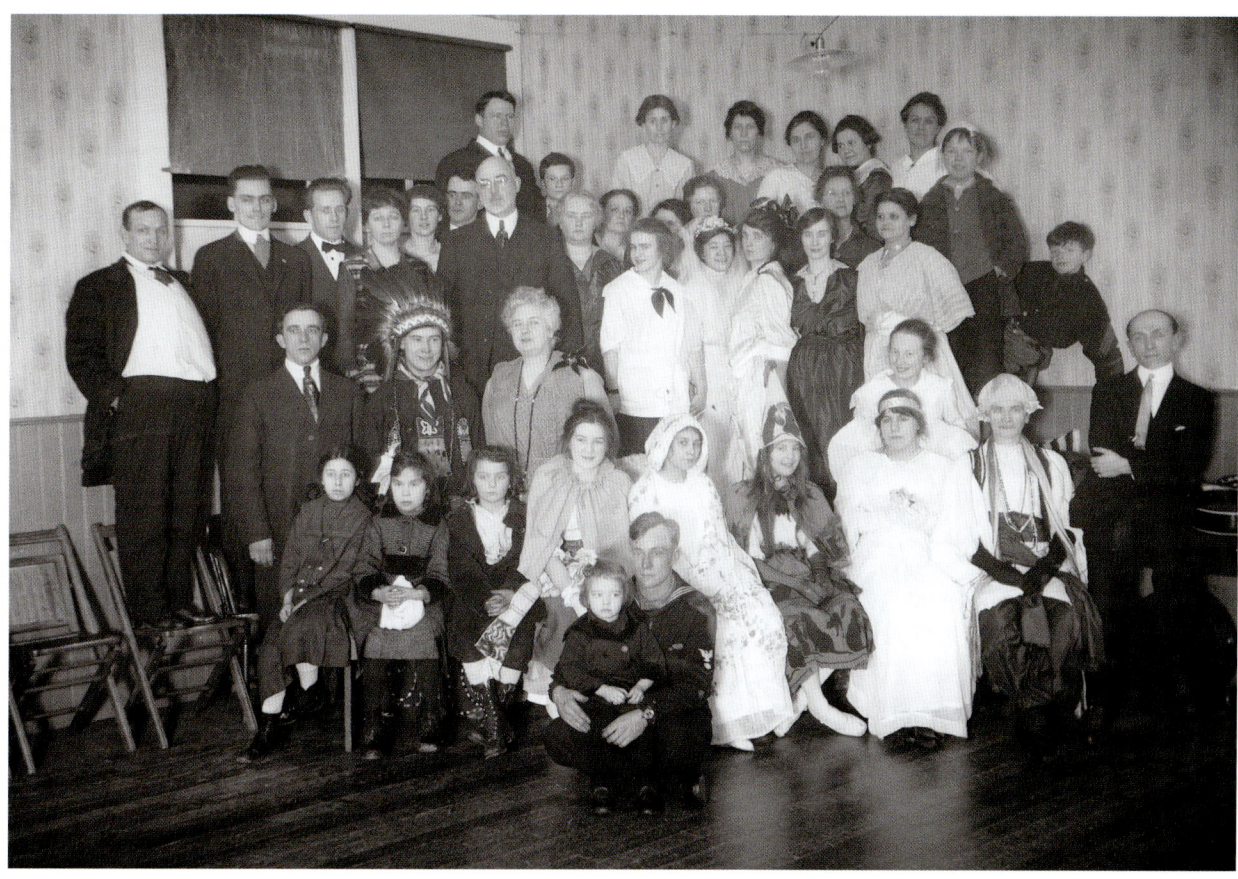

PLATE 125. Dance at Moose Hall, 1920. Several of the people are Creoles.

The inscription on the back of the photograph lists the names of some of the people pictured but does not specify their exact position. They include Martha June Demidoff (1923–2013) (Creole); Anna Kostrometinoff (1888–1948) (Creole); Mrs. John Triershield (Creole); Mrs. Iona Cook; William R. Hanlon Jr. (1906–80) (Creole); Bill Cook; Mr. Van Vard; Katie Van Vard; Elva Mary Lillian Bahrt (1911–89) (Creole); Anna Bang (b. 1901), a Chinese woman adopted by a local Euro-American couple; Helen L. (Peterson) Kostrometinoff (1900–1932); Mrs. Ashball; Mrs. McGrath.

Clearly identified persons are Mrs. Tilson front row, far right, wearing necklaces and head cover) Charlotte Burkhart, the little girl at the very front, held by an unidentified man dressed as a sailor; Mrs. Naja (Kaznakoff) Bahrt (1861–1938), Creole, wearing a white dress and silver necklace; Peter Kostrometinoff (1896–1941) (Creole), wearing an Indian bonnet; Chas. Mc-Grath, wearing glasses and a necktie).

Identifications by Louise Brightman (Creole), 1980. Courtesy of the National Park Service, Sitka National Historical Park, 25783.

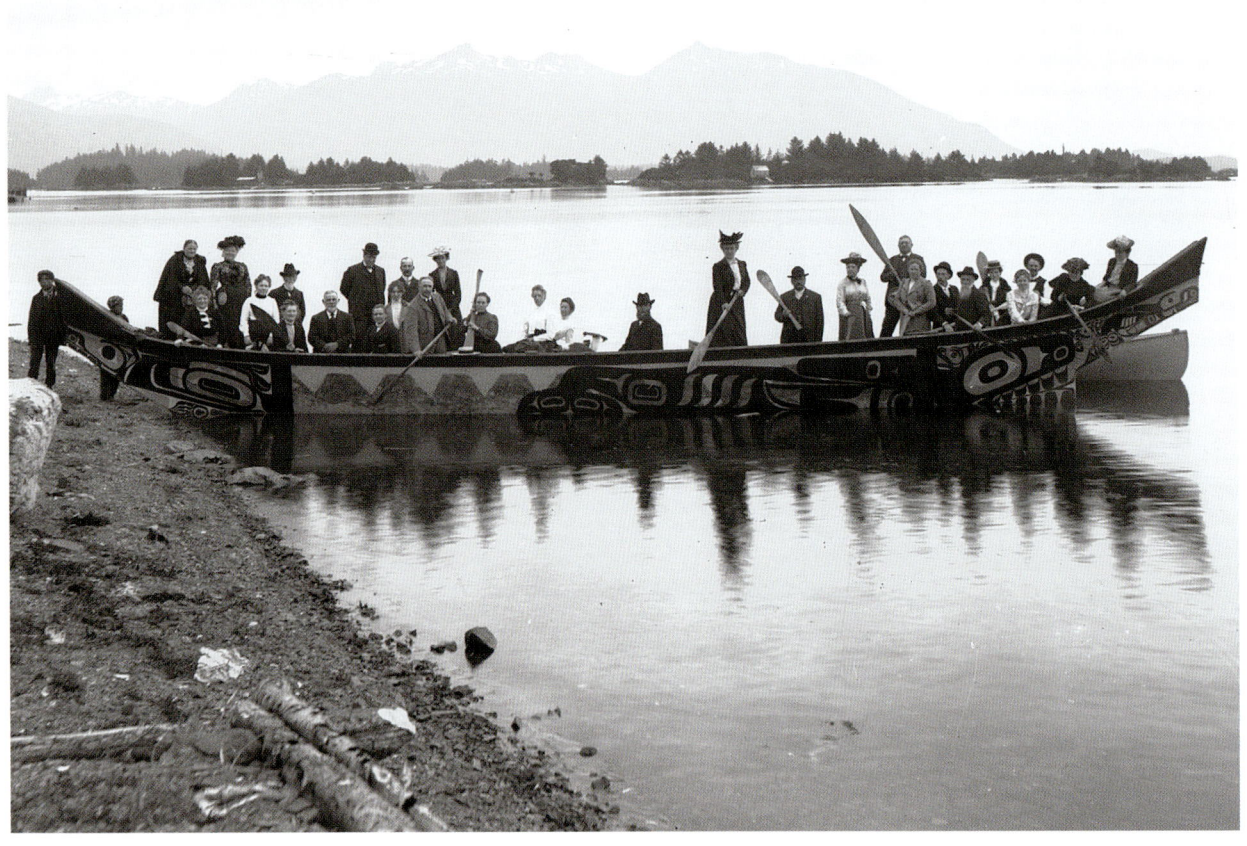

PLATE 126. The local Euro-American elite posing in a Native-style canoe in the Sitka Channel, ca. 1900.
Courtesy of the National Park Service, Sitka National Historical Park, 03812.

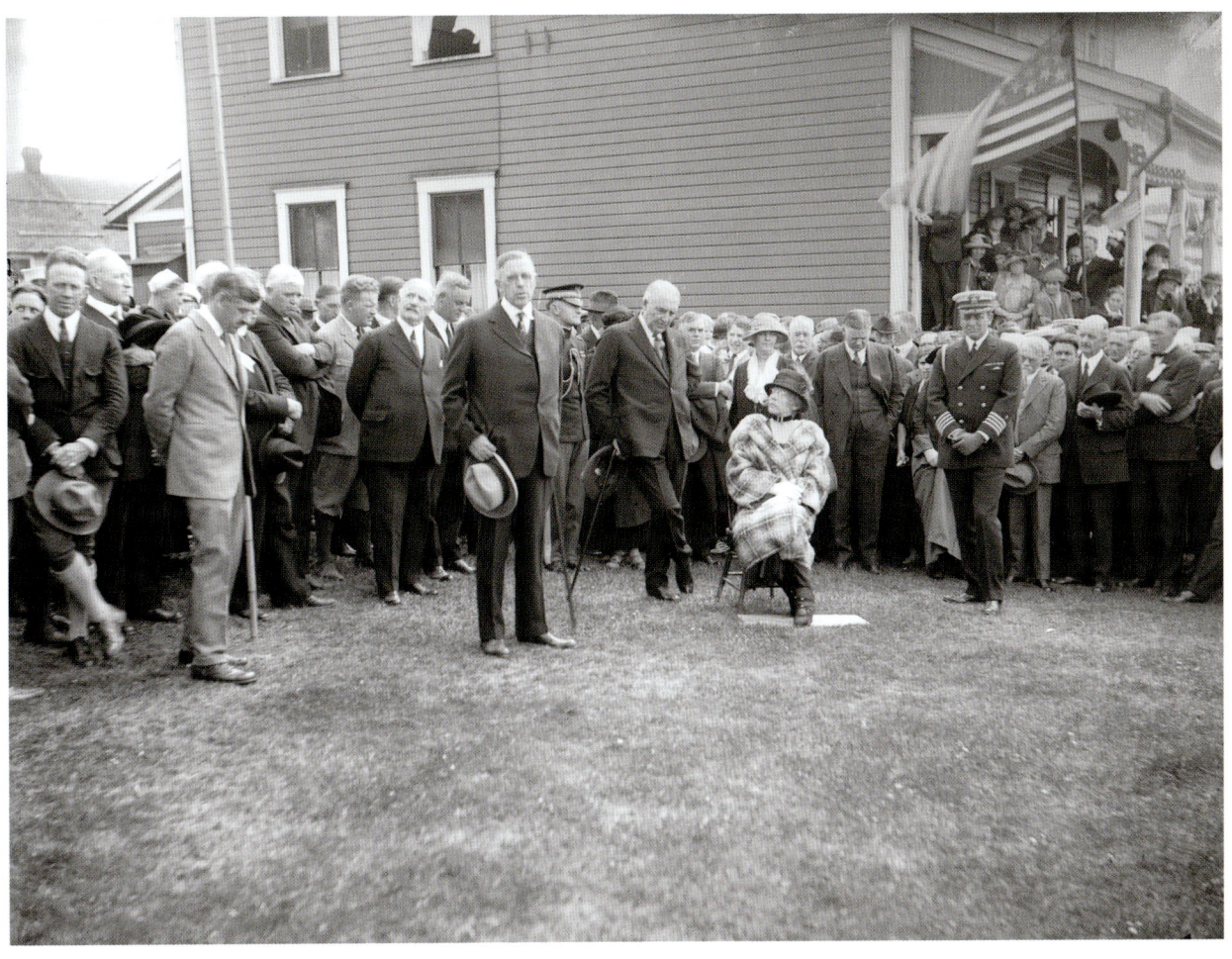

PLATE 127. President Warren G. Harding (1865–1923), First Lady Florence Harding (1860–1924), the Hardings' entourage, and local dignitaries in Sitka, June 1923. The man immediately to the right of the first lady is Herbert Hoover (1874–1964), who was then secretary of commerce. President Harding visited Alaska in June of 1923 and died two months later in San Francisco. Courtesy of the National Park Service, Sitka National Historical Park, 25760.

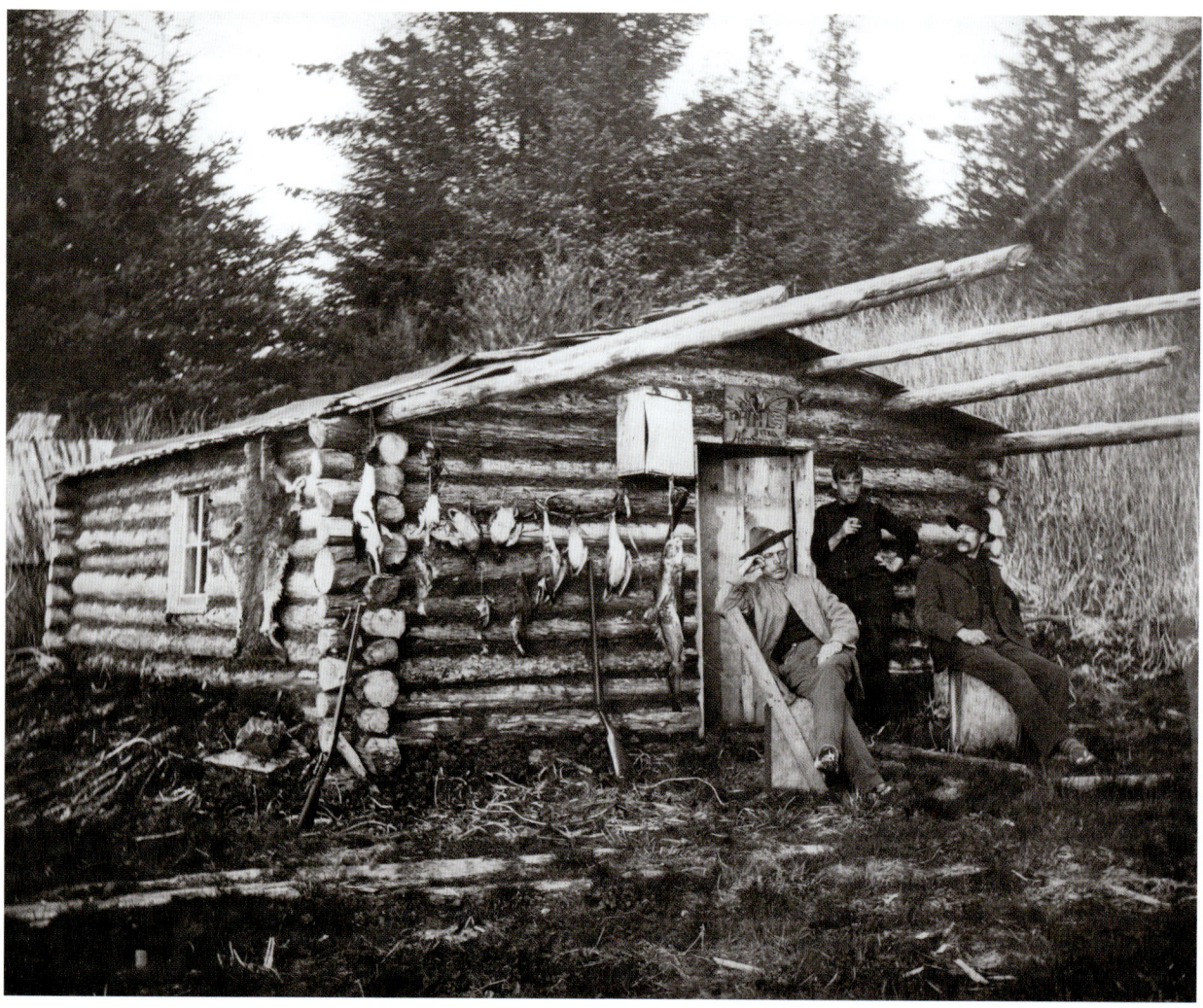

PLATE 128. Merrill with his catch and two companions at a cabin near Goddard Hot Springs, near Sitka, ca. 1900–1920. Photographer unknown. Alaska State Historical Library P57-239.

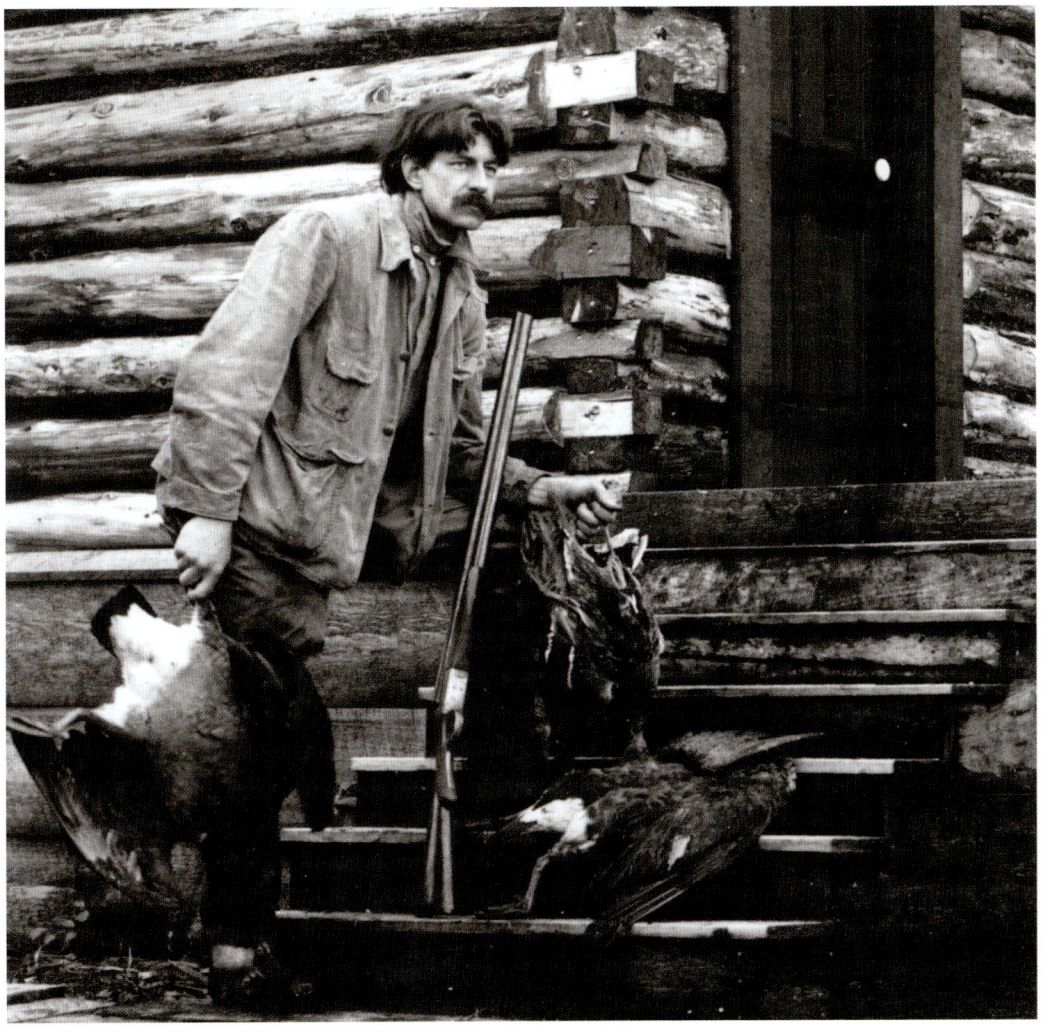

PLATE 129. A younger Merrill near his cabin, ca. 1900–1910. Photographer unknown. Alaska State Historical Library P57-238.

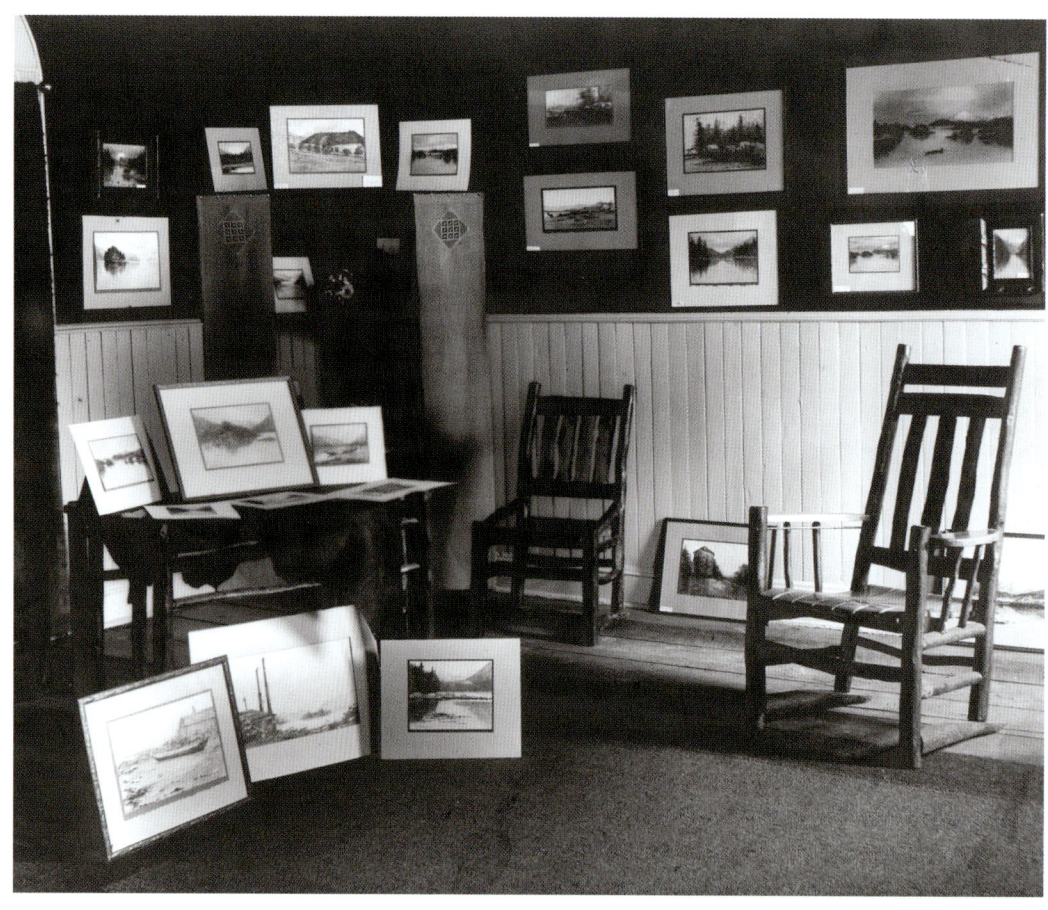

PLATE 130. Interior of Merrill's studio, date unknown. Alaska State Historical Library P57-249.

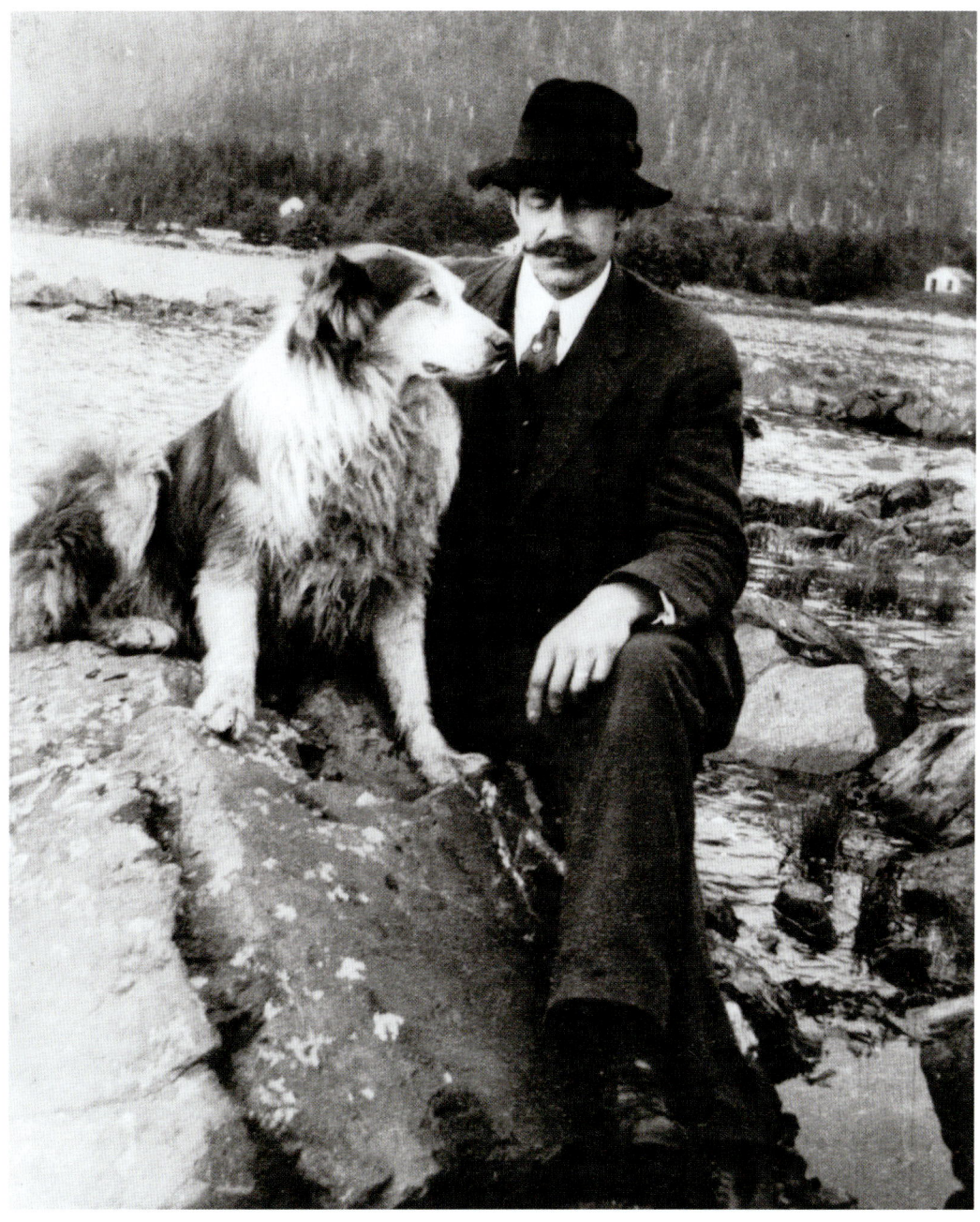

PLATE 131. Merrill and his dog on a Sitka beach, ca. 1910–20. Photographer unknown.
Alaska State Historical Library P57-236.

References

CHAMBERS, SCOTT

1977   Elbridge Warren Merrill.
Alaska Journal 7(15): 138–46.

COONTZ, ROBERT E.

1930   *From Mississippi to the Sea.*
Philadelphia: Dorrance.

DAUENHAUER, NORA

1995   Tlingit At.óow: Traditions and
Concepts. In *The Spirit Within*,
21–33. New York: Rizzoli.

DAUENHAUER, NORA,
AND DAUENHAUER, RICHARD

1994   *Haa Ḵusteeyí/Our Culture: Tlingit Life
Stories.* Seattle: University of
Washington Press. Juneau:
Sealaska Heritage Foundation.

DE LAGUNA, FREDERICA

1972   *Under Mount Saint Elias: The History and
Culture of the Yakutat Tlingit.* Washington,
DC: Smithsonian Institution Press.

GIDLEY, M.

2003   *Edward S. Curtis and the North American
Indian Project in the Field.* Lincoln:
University of Nebraska Press.

GMELCH, SHARON BOHN

1995   Elbridge Warren Merrill: The Tlingit
of Alaska, 1899–1929. *History of
Photography* 19(2): 159–72.

2008   *The Tlingit Encounter with Photography*. Philadelphia: University of Pennsylvania Museum of Archaeology and Anthropology.

KAN, SERGEI

1979–2021   Ethnographic fieldnotes from Southeastern Alaska, in the author's possession.

1999   *Memory Eternal: Tlingit Culture and Russian Orthodox Christianity through Two Centuries*. Seattle: University of Washington Press.

2013a   Sergei Ionovich Kostromitinov (1854–1916), or "Colonel George Kostrometinoff": From a Creole Teenager to the Number One Russian-American Citizen of Sitka. *Ethnohistory* 60(3): 385–401.

2013b   *A Russian American Photographer in Tlingit Country: Vincent Soboleff in Alaska*. Norman: University of Oklahoma Press.

2016   *Symbolic Immortality: The Tlingit Potlatch of the Nineteenth Century*. 2nd. ed. Seattle: University of Washington Press.

2020   "True Heirs of a Heroic Russian Past" or "Russians in Name Only": Sitka Creoles as Seen by the Late Nineteenth Century Russian Orthodox Clergy. *Journal of Frontier Studies* 4: 12–37.

2021   Orthodox Church Brotherhoods of the Sitka Creoles, 1870s–1910s. *Alaska History* 36(1): 53–71.

2022   What the "Last Tlingit Potlatch" of 1904 Was Really About. In *Up Close and From Far Away: New World Anthropology from Russian and American Perspectives*, edited by D. M. Bondarenko, R. J. Chacon, and R. N. Ignatiev, 9–28. Moscow: IEA RAS.

2023   Father Andrew P. Kashevaroff: A Russian Creole as a Cultural Intermediary and Translator in American Alaska. *Pacific Northwest Quarterly* 114(1): 3–21.

PREUCEL, ROBERT W., AND LUCY F. WILLIAMS

2005   The Centennial Potlatch. *Expedition* 47(2): 9–19.

SWANTON, JOHN R.

1908   Social Conditions, Beliefs, and Linguistic Relationship of the Tlingit Indians. *Twenty-Sixth Annual Report of the Bureau of American Ethnology*. Washington, DC: Government Printing Office.

TWITCHELL, X̲'UNEI LANCE, ED.

2020   *Tlingit Dictionary.* Juneau:
        University of Alaska
        Southeast and Goldbelt
        Heritage Foundation.

WILLETT, GEORGE

1914   Birds of Sitka and Vicinity,
        Southeastern Alaska. *Condor*
        16: 71–91.

WILLOUGHBY, BARRETT

1930   *Sitka Portal to Romance.* Boston:
        Houghton Mifflin.

WYATT, VICTORIA

1989   *Images from the Inside Passage:
        an Alaskan Portrait by Winter and
        Pond.* Seattle: University of
        Washington Press.

YAW, LESLIE W.

1985   *Sixty Years in Sitka.* Sitka, AK: Sheldon
        Jackson College Press.

ZOLLO, RICHARD P., RICHARD B. TRASK,
AND JOAN M. REEDY

1989   *As the Century Turned: Photographic
        Glimpses of Danvers, Massachusetts,
        1880–1910.* Norfolk, VA: Donning.

Index

Page numbers in *italics* refer to illustrations